D0065044

THE CAREER PSYCHOLOGY
OF WOMEN

THE CAREER PSYCHOLOGY
OF WOMEN

NANCY E. BETZ
Department of Psychology
The Ohio State University
Columbus, Ohio

LOUISE F. FITZGERALD
Graduate School of Education
University of California
Santa Barbara, California

1987

ACADEMIC PRESS, INC.

Harcourt Brace Jovanovich, Publishers
Orlando   San Diego   New York   Austin
Boston   London   Sydney   Tokyo   Toronto

ACADEMIC PRESS, INC.
Orlando, Florida 32887

United Kingdom Edition published by
ACADEMIC PRESS INC. (LONDON) LTD.
24–28 Oval Road, London NW1 7DX

Library of Congress Cataloging in Publication Data

The Career psychology of women.

    Bibliography: p.
    Includes index.
    1. Vocational guidance for women—United States.
2. Career development—United States.   I. Betz, Nancy E.
II. Fitzgerald, Louise F.
HF5382.65.C37   1987   331.7'02'088042   86-22284
ISBN 0—12—094405—7 (alk. paper)

PRINTED IN THE UNITED STATES OF AMERICA

87 88 89 90   9 8 7 6 5 4 3 2 1

To Ellen L. Betz, a fine psychologist, wonderful mother,
and, always, my best friend

N.E.B.

For John O. Crites and Samuel H. Osipow. . .
Models, mentors, and more. . .

Who taught me most of what I know,
and more importantly, what I don't.

L.F.F.

CONTENTS

IV. SUMMARY AND RECOMMENDATIONS

The field of vocational psychology and career development can be said to have begun in 1909 with the publication of Frank Parsons' landmark book *Choosing a Vocation,* which introduced the "matching men and jobs" approach to career choice. While vocational or career psychology as a field is, then, nearing 80 years old, interest in the vocational behavior of women is a much more recent phenomenon, dating only from the mid-1960s. Although a relatively new area, the study of the vocational psychology of women has grown impressively in the last 20 years. Scholars from a range of academic disciplines, including psychology, sociology, education, labor relations, management sciences, economics, and marriage and family relations have contributed theory and empirical research, as well as practical applications of the growing body of knowledge.

Our awareness of the need for this book arose when we agreed to write the chapter on the vocational psychology of women for the *Handbook of Vocational Psychology* (Walsh and Osipow, 1983). Although we were asked to prepare a 60-page chapter, our first draft of the chapter was 200 pages long and we hadn't yet finished our review of the literature. The sheer size and variety of the literature base was astonishing, given the relative recency of scholarly interest, and it became clear that 200 pages, not to mention 60, was inadequate to summarize and review the available body of knowledge. Although some edited volumes had appeared, there existed no comprehensive and detailed review of the processes and outcomes of women's career development covering the entire life span, from initial career decisions through occupational entry and the adjustment years. Accordingly, this book was written to provide such a review.

Because contributors to the field of the vocational psychology of women represent a broad range of academic disciplines, so too does the literature reviewed here. We have comprehensively reviewed the research on the vocational psychology of women as published in journals in psychology (e.g., *American Psychologist, Journal of Applied*

Psychology, Journal of Vocational Behavior, Journal of Counseling Psychology, Psychology of Women Quarterly, Sex Roles), sociology (*Journal of Marriage and the Family, American Sociological Review*), management (*Academy of Management Journal, Academy of Management Review*), education (*American Educational Research Journal, Harvard Educational Review, Journal of College Student Personnel*), counseling (*Journal of Counseling and Development, Vocational Guidance Quarterly*), and general science (*Science* and *Scientific American*), as well as journals appropriate to more specialized topics such as the study of mathematics. The books and articles reviewed span a similarly broad, interdisciplinary range. Although enriched by these perspectives, our own focus has remained a psychological one, as we have attempted to synthesize what is known about women's career behavior. To some degree, this has influenced what has been left in, as well as what has been left out.

Because of the breadth of literature reviewed herein, we view the book as useful to scholars, educators, and practitioners representing a range of academic fields. However, we see our work as especially pertinent to counseling and industrial psychologists, management scientists focusing on career development and/or women in management, and sociologists specializing in women and work. The book would be an excellent text for graduate level courses or seminars in these areas as well, and might be particularly useful in combination with a general vocational psychology or career development text such as Osipow's (1983) *Theories of Career Development*, the forthcoming revision of Crites' landmark (1969) work *Vocational Psychology*, or Hall's (1976) *Careers in Organizations*.

The book is divided into four sections. The first and last sections are small, each consisting of one chapter; not surprisingly, the first is an introductory chapter and the last consists of closing remarks. The large sections in the middle cover the two major stages of individual career development: career choice and career adjustment (Crites, 1969). Specifically, Part II, entitled "Women's Career Choices," reviews the individual and sociocultural factors that research has shown to influence the nature of women's educational and career choices and the extent of girls' and women's educational achievements and career orientation and motivation. The chapters in Part II cover Theories and Concepts of Women's Career Choices; Cultural, Subcultural, and Familial Influences; The Educational System; Counseling; Abilities and Achievement; Personality Variables; and Interests, Needs, and Motives. These encompass the range of variables examined in a traditional vocational psychological approach to the study of career choice and development. Part III covers the events that follow the women's initial choice of an occupation or career, that is, the processes of Career Adjustment. The five chapters in this section include A Model of Career Adjustment, Success and Satisfaction, The Interface of Home and Work, Dual-Career Couples, and Sexual Harassment, both at work and in the educational system. The book ends with a summary of the research and suggestions for further needs in the areas of theory and research, and for counseling, educational, and organizational interventions.

We are pleased to acknowledge the assistance and support we received in writing this book. We are grateful to the many individuals who provided assistance, including Judy Reuter at the Ohio State University, Bonnie Heaton at Kent State University, and Barbara Cogswell-Bailey, Robin Bronson, Barbara Hamill, Ruth Fassinger, and Matthew Hesson-McGinnis at the University of California at Santa Barbara. Special thanks to the excellent staff at Academic Press are also appropriate—we are very pleased to have had the opportunity to work with such a superb publisher. And, most significantly, we would like to thank those who have inspired us in the pursuit of vocational psychology and the career development of women—John O. Crites, Lenore W. Harmon, Samuel H. Osipow, and David J. Weiss have been crucially important as our models and mentors.

I

INTRODUCTION AND PLAN OF THE BOOK

INTRODUCTION TO
THE CAREER PSYCHOLOGY
OF WOMEN

The field of vocational or career psychology can be said to have begun with the work of Frank Parsons, who, in his 1909 book *Choosing a Vocation,* outlined the "matching men and jobs" approach to career decision-making. This approach, which specified that career choices should follow the three steps of (1) self-knowledge, (2) knowledge of occupational alternatives, and (3) a process of "true reasoning" to find a good fit or "match" between person and job, became a foundation of the field and a central basis for vocational counseling. Since 1909, major theorists such as Anne Roe, John Holland, Donald Super, the Ginzberg group, and John O. Crites have elaborated on the nature and process of career choice and development over the life span (see Osipow, 1983; Walsh & Osipow, 1983a,b, for extensive reviews of the field).

While the field of vocational psychology has had tremendous theoretical and applied utility, its focus has until recently been primarily on the career development of men (e.g., Osipow, 1975, 1983). In other areas of psychology as well as in various academic disciplines, women have been largely ignored by theorists and researchers. As Leona Tyler has said, "Much of what we know about the stages through which an individual passes as he [*sic*] prepares to find his [*sic*] place in the world of work might appropriately be labeled 'The Vocational Development of Middle Class Males' " (Tyler, 1977, p. 40). There are probably many reasons for the lack of attention to women, including assumptions that women didn't "work" since their "place" was in the home, and that if they *did* work, theories of career development generated with men in mind would be sufficient for the description of women's vocational behavior.

3

Although women were thus ignored and viewed as insignificant for psychology's first 50 or 60 years, the last 20 or so years have been characterized by an extensive and widespread growth of interest in women's career development. At the same time that women's labor force participation has been increasing dramatically, women's career development has been the subject of considerable theory development and research focused on understanding the processes involved, as well as the subject of practical efforts (e.g., counseling, education, and organizational interventions) designed to facilitate that development. Although the field is still a comparatively new one and much further work is needed, there is also a need for review and integration of what we know about women's career development after about 20 years of study. This book was designed with that purpose in mind, as well as with the objective of recommending areas in which more work is needed. This chapter will review the major myths and realities concerning women's career development and will proceed to a discussion of major issues in the area of women's career development, including ways in which it differs dramatically from that of men. Finally, the overall plan and contents of the book will be summarized.

TRENDS IN THE EXTENT OF WOMEN'S LABOR FORCE PARTICIPATION: 1900–1985

At the turn of the century, paid employment for women was the exception rather than the rule, and those women who did work outside the home did so only as preliminary to marriage and the bearing of children. The chief occupations held by women were domestic service, factory work, and teaching. By and large, the only women working throughout adulthood were those "unfortunate" enough to be without a husband—the unlucky spinsters and the widowed. Thus, when the family life cycle began, the work cycle ended (Perun & Bielby, 1981).

Although this pattern remained stable until about 1940, the World War II years were characterized by a dramatic influx of women into the labor force to fill jobs vacated by servicemen. Views of women as the delicate sex were temporarily suspended while women were needed in such dangerous or physically demanding jobs as explosives manufacturing and construction. In the post-War years, the percentages of women working both before and during marriage accelerated markedly. Overall, the percentage of women working has increased threefold since 1940, but, even more dramatically, the percentage of working mothers has increased *tenfold* since 1940! In the 1950s, one third of women were in the labor force (Russo & Denmark, 1984), while today almost two thirds of adult women are working outside the home.

Thus, a trend which began to accelerate after World War II has now firmly established women's "place" in the labor force and has led to the near-inevitability of work outside the home for American women. In 1984, 63% of all women aged 18 to 64 were working outside the home; by 1990 this figure should increase to 70–75%. Women workers are a significant proportion of the labor force, currently constituting 44% of all workers (United States Department of Labor, 1984). The odds that any woman will work outside the home at some time in her life are about 95 out of 100, and the average woman can expect to spend 29.3 years in the labor force, compared with 39.1 years for the average man. Over half of currently married women work; 61% of mothers with children under 18 are now working, as are 52% of mothers with preschool children (U.S. Department of Labor, 1984). Whereas about one third of working women are married and have husbands making adequate incomes, the other two thirds are women who are single, widowed, divorced, separated, or have husbands whose incomes were less than $15,000 in 1984 (U.S. Department of Labor, 1984).

In summary, women whose adult lives will *not* include work outside the home are increasingly becoming the exception rather than the rule. As was so well summarized by Hyde (1985), the fact that the majority of American women hold jobs outside the home is one of our country's best-kept secrets: "The working woman, then, is not a variation from the norm, she *is* the norm" (p. 169).

Paralleling the greatly increased labor force participation of women is dramatic change in the *aspirations* of young women, with most young women now expressing a preference to combine career and family roles in their adult lives. Since 1964, when Matthews and Tiedeman reported that 60–75% of women aged 11 to 26 planned to be married and not working 10 years from the time of the study, research has shown a consistent decrease in the number of women preferring marriage-only lifestyles. Rand and Miller (1972) described what they termed a new cultural imperative, "marriage and a career," in their finding that 95% of their sample of women of junior high through college age expected to both marry and work. Recent data support the trend described by Rand and Miller. For example, Komarovsky (1982) replicated, with a sample of women who were freshmen in 1979, a study she had originally done with college women in the 1940s. In 1943, 61% of the women preferred not to work after marriage, in contrast to only 5% in 1979. In 1943 only 12% of the women preferred a career without marriage or to combine a family and a career with minimal interruption of career pursuits for child-bearing, in contrast to 48% in 1979. A group first documented in 1979 were those who wished a career and marriage but no children—these represented 14% of the study sample. Zuckerman (1980), in a study of women in coeducational "seven sisters" colleges, found that 92% were planning to complete education beyond the Bachelor's degree. Harmon (1980), in a follow-up of women 6 years after college entry, found that 46% wanted to work most of their lives (versus 27% in 1968) and that only 2% wanted minimal employment (versus 16% in 1968).

Thus, trends over the past 20 years and recent data strongly suggest the importance of occupational pursuits in the plans and lives of women. It is clear that most women will work outside the home and that this work will play an increasingly important role in their lives. However, while the *extent* of women's labor force participation is approaching that of men, the *nature* of that participation continues to differ greatly from that of men, keeping working women economically disadvantaged, lower in status, and burdened with multiple role demands. The problems that have characterized women's occupational involvements and career development are summarized in the next sections.

PROBLEMS IN THE NATURE OF WOMEN'S LABOR FORCE PARTICIPATION

PROBLEM: THE WAGE GAP

Probably the most serious problem facing working women is the persistence of the large gap in earning power between men and women; despite decades of social, legislative, and demographic change, women's earnings continue to be only about 60% of those of men (Ferraro, 1984). Women's low earning power is more than unfair; it is a modern tragedy leading to the "feminization of poverty"—60% of working women earn less than $10,000 a year, and the majority of people with incomes below the poverty level are women. Unless a woman, working or not, has the support of an employed male, her chances of an adequate income, a "living wage" (aptly named), are nil (Ferraro, 1984; U.S. Department of Labor, 1984).

Two of the major reasons for the wage gap are sex-based wage discrimination and occupational sex segregation. Arguments that men are better prepared to make a decent living do not explain why the average male *high school dropout* earns more than the average female *college graduate* and why men who completed fewer than 8 years of elementary school earn more than do female high school graduates. Despite the existence of rampant race discrimination in this country, black men earn more than do women regardless of race (U.S. Department of Labor, 1984). Women's alleged lack of commitment to the work force does not explain "why a secretary with 18 years of experience, whose 'only' skills are typing, letter composition, office management, and the ability to deal with the public, is paid less than a parking lot attendant whose required education is the ability to drive an automobile" (Ferraro, 1984, pp. 1166–1167).

Fundamental to the problem of women's low earning power are sex-based wage discrimination and occupational sex segregation (Ferraro, 1984). Simply put, women get paid less than men for doing the same job, and the jobs in which women tend to be concentrated are by and large low status and low paying, with few, if any, opportunities for advancement. More specifically, even though women constitute 44% of the labor force, they continue to be concentrated in a small number of traditionally female jobs and professions. A majority of women workers are in "pink-collar" jobs (Howe, 1977), for example, clerical worker, retail salesperson, waitress, beautician, and housekeeping services (U.S. Department of Labor, 1984). In 1983, women represented 80% of all administrative support (including clerical) workers but only 8% of precision production, craft, and repair workers; women were 70% of retail and personal sales workers but only 32% of managers, administrators, and executives. Women were only about 6.8% of apprentices as of March 1984.

Women professionals are concentrated in professions of lower pay and status than the male-dominated professions; the vast majority of nurses, elementary school teachers, librarians, and social workers are female, whereas the majority of physicians, lawyers, scientists, and engineers are male (Prediger & Cole, 1975). Among the professions, women are particularly poorly represented in the sciences and engineering (Pfafflin, 1984). For example, although engineering is the largest professional field in this country, women are earning only about 10% of the Bachelor's degrees in this field (National Science Foundation, 1984) (it should be noted that the figure of 10% represents a marked increase from the 1% figure 10 years ago). Of the 2,500 engineering doctorates received in 1982, only 124 (or 0.05%) were earned by women (National Science Foundation, 1984).

Even within the same occupation or occupational field, women tend to be concentrated at lower levels while men predominate at the upper levels (Gottfredson, 1978). For example, within the teaching profession, the percentage of women decreases as the level of responsibility increases; women constitute 86% of elementary school teachers but only 26% of school administrators. Women constitute 51% of instructors in universities but only 5% of full professors (U.S. Department of Labor, 1977). Thus, not only are women found primarily in traditionally female occupations, but they are clearly overrepresented in lower-level, lower-status, and lower-paying occupations and positions.

Further, the career aspirations of young women and girls continue to focus on stereotypically female occupations. Almost all of the 95% of women planning both career and marriage in Rand and Miller's (1972) sample were planning to pursue traditionally female occupations. Occupations in the educational and social services, nursing, and clerical work were selected by 60% of the high school girls studied by Brito and Jusenius (1978) and Falk and Salter (1978), by 50% of those studied by Prediger, Roth, and Noeth (1974), and by the large majority of those studied by Fottler and Bain (1980). Harmon's (1980) study of women in their early 20s also supports the continued orientation toward traditionally female careers.

More recently, evidence suggests that, in comparison to men, women continue to select occupations from a more restricted range of options (Hesse-Biber, 1985), see fewer occupations as suitable (Poole & Clooney, 1985), and choose occupations less consistent with their vocational interests (Knapp, Knapp, & Knapp-Lee, 1985; Swaney & Prediger, 1985). While there does seem to be a small proportionate increase in the number of women pursuing nontraditional careers, for example, in medicine (AMA, 1977), dentistry, and engineering, the predominant pattern among women continues to suggest a limited and sex-stereotypic range of female occupational pursuits.

PROBLEM: UNDERUTILIZATION OF ABILITIES

Related to women's concentration in traditionally female and frequently low-level occupations is the finding that, in contrast to men in general, women's intellectual capacities and talents are not reflected in their educational and occupational achievements; women's career aspirations and choices are frequently far lower in level than are the aspirations of males with comparable levels of ability (Fitzgerald & Crites, 1980).

Probably the most dramatic illustration of the failure of intellectually gifted women to utilize their talents in career pursuits was provided by the Terman and Oden (1959) follow-up studies of a large sample of gifted California children. Terman's sample, originally obtained in 1921–1922, consisted of 1,528 children with measured IQs of at least 135. Of the sample, 671 were girls and 847 were boys. As mentioned earlier in the chapter, the oldest and most durable model of vocational choice, that is, the "matching" or trait–factor model (e.g., Parsons, 1909; Williamson, 1939) would yield the prediction that the intellectual capabilities of these children would lead to high educational and occupational achievement and productivity in adulthood.

The follow-up study of the gifted group at mid-life indicated that, as expected, the majority of men had achieved prominence in professional and managerial occupations. They had, by their mid-40s, been exceptionally productive scientists, made literary and artistic contributions, and become prominent lawyers, physicians, psychologists, and college professors. In contrast to the men, the women were primarily housewives or were employed in traditionally female occupations. About 50% of the women had been and continued to be full-time housewives. Of those who were working full-time, 21% were teachers in elementary or secondary schools, 8% were social workers, 20% were secretaries, and 8% were either librarians or nurses. Only 7% of those working were academicians; 5% were physicians, lawyers, or psychologists; 8% were executives; and 9% were writers, artists, or musicians. As children, these women had been as intellectually gifted as their male counterparts, but their achievements in adulthood were clearly in contrast to their early intellectual promise. Their sex was a better predictor of their occupational pursuits in adulthood than were their capabilities as individuals.

Bem and Bem (1976) described the phenomenon illustrated by the Terman study as indicative of the "homogenization of the American woman." In other words, women are socialized to pursue the same roles regardless of their individual capabilities and talents. A women's life roles and vocational choices are predictable not on the basis of her characteristics as an individual but on the basis of her sex. Such homogenization results in losses both to individuals and to society when women's talents are so poorly utilized. In terms of vocational theory, then, sex has been a far more powerful predictor of vocational choices in women than have the other individual factors postulated as important in theories focusing, either explicitly or implicitly, on men's career development.

PROBLEM: ROLE CHOICE OR OVERLOAD

A final set of major problems facing women in their career development has been due to the assumption that while the male adult role is primarily occupationally directed, the adult role for the female is primarily family directed. The assumption that, first of all, "women's place is in the home" has delayed or disrupted the kind of systematic career planning necessary for appropriate and satisfying educational and career outcomes. For example, as discussed by Kriger (1972), women's career decisions are delayed relative to those of men because the former involve two major decisions instead of one. That is, before women decide *what* occupation or career to pursue, they must decide whether or not and to what degree they wish to make outside employment a focus of their lives. Men, in contrast, are rarely allowed to consider the "whether" and begin instead with the "what," thus getting an earlier start in the process. Angrist (1974; Angrist & Almquist, 1975) has suggested that career planning is built into women's socialization as *contingency training*, which involves strategies to delay career decisions until the other "more important" decisions of marriage and parenthood have been made or until it becomes apparent that they may not occur. Thus, the establishment of a vocational role may be delayed until age 35 to 50 for women, versus the expected age of 20 to 35.

Once a woman has made career decisions, however, the assumption that she is still primarily responsible for maintenance of a home and family, as well as a career, creates obstacles in the form of role overload and role conflict. In other words, at the same time that women pursue careers, 90% still expect to have two or more children (Russo & Denmark, 1984). Whereas traditionally the family cycle, when it occurred, was to supersede the work cycle in women's lives, it now usually occurs concurrently. Most women in all marital and parental categories now work outside the home, thus seriously weakening the former strength of family variables in predicting women's work involvement (Perun & Bielby, 1981).

For women, the major practical implication of these changes is that they are now expected to successfully handle two full-time jobs, that is, one outside the home and the other that of homemaker and mother, the former paid and the latter unpaid. Although some studies suggest that men are sharing more of the family responsibilities (Weeks & Gage, 1984; Farmer, 1983), other studies suggest that men continue to view them as women's responsibility and are opposed to equal sharing of the family duties (Herzog, Bachman, & Johnston, 1983; Kassner, 1981; Russo & Denmark, 1984).

Thus, understanding the demands and processes of role overload and role conflict but, more generally, the ways in which vocational, marital, and parental roles are managed across the life span is of central importance in understanding women's career adjustment. Issues regarding the work–family interface and management of the "dual-career" lifestyle are the topics of chapters later in this book (see Chapters 12 and 13).

Also with respect to marital and childrearing responsibilities, there has been some tendency in the literature to suggest that work at home can, by itself, constitute a legitimate "career" option. Although we accept the legitimacy of this as a *lifestyle* choice, it is our premise that such work does *not* constitute a legitimate "career" in the sense used by vocational psychologists because (1) this work is unpaid and is also usually unaccompanied by such benefits as accumulation of retirement income; (2) has no opportunities for advancement; (3) has no training requirements or job security; and (4) would not be considered a legitimate career for a male (males who stay home are generally referred to as "unemployed"). Also casting doubt on the legitimacy of home/family work *alone* is the consistent finding that paid employment is associated with mental health in *both* sexes—the surplus of married women among the psychologically distressed is due primarily to those married women *not* employed outside the home, versus their healthier (albeit overworked), employed counterparts (Bernard, 1971).

SUMMARY AND PLAN OF THE BOOK

In summary, while women's rates of labor force participation are approaching those of men, women's restricted range of career options, their economically disadvantaged position in the labor market, underutilization of their capabilities, and the need for decisions concerning the role of career involvement in their lives are some of the major problems requiring a unique focus on women's career development versus that of men.

The following chapters will review what is presently known of women's career development. The chapters will be organized in terms of one of the most widely used distinctions in the study of vocational behavior, that is, that between vocational choice and vocational adjustment (e.g., Crites, 1969). Although the distinction is not totally clear-cut, career choice processes are generally thought to be those prior to actual choice of a career direction and would typically include the generation and exploration of alternatives, and decisions among and implementation of desired alternatives. The processes involved in women's vocational choices will be covered in Part II, beginning with theories and concepts used to describe and investigate those choices, moving to chapters on cultural, subcultural, and familial influences; education; counseling; and the relationships of individual variables (including abilities), personality variables (including self-concept, personality characteristics, and attitudes toward women's roles), and vocational interests to women's career choices. The section will end with a chapter providing several approaches to integrating research findings regarding factors related to women's career choices.

The processes of career adjustment are generally considered to be those which occur following initial occupational entry and are usually divided into the outcomes of *success* and *satisfaction*. The former refers to how well the employee meets the demands of the work environment, whereas the latter refers to the degree to which the job meets the employee's work-related needs and objectives. The processes underlying women's career adjustment to work, including variables of success and satisfaction, are covered in Part III. This section covers gender issues in vocational motivation and performance, as well as special topics such as discrimination, sexual harassment, dual-career issues, and the work–family interface.

Finally, Part IV assesses and summarizes the state of knowledge regarding both career choice and adjustment. The chapter provides recommendations for needed theory, research, and educational, counseling, and organizational interventions.

II

WOMEN'S CAREER CHOICES

WOMEN'S CAREER CHOICES:
THEORIES AND CONCEPTS

One of the major areas of interest to vocational psychologists over the years has been the explanation and prediction of patterns of vocational choice and development over the life span. Theories of and research investigating the individual and environmental factors related to an individual's vocational choice and adjustment have greatly contributed to both theoretical understanding and the practice of career counseling. Because research and theories have focused primarily on male career development, however, they have until recently neglected to consider the possible differential influence of major explanatory variables on the career choices of women versus those of men or the unique variables related to and dimensions descriptive of women's career development.

In addition to research focused on the applicability of existing theories of career development [e.g., Holland (1973) and Super (1957)] to women, there have been several conceptual advances related specifically to the description and explanation of women's career development. This chapter will review these concepts, beginning with variables used to differentially describe women's career development (i.e., dependent variables) and proceeding with a review of individual variables considered uniquely important to the understanding and prediction of that development.

CONCEPTS IN THE STUDY OF WOMEN'S CAREER
CHOICES: DEPENDENT VARIABLES

Because men were assumed to work and pursue careers, the study of the career development of men could focus on variables describing the nature of their career choices, for example, occupational field and level and congruence of occupational environment with vocational interests. Because women were *not* assumed to pursue careers, the study of their career development has necessitated the development of a number of additional variables describing the degree to which a woman intended to work at all and the importance, if any, of career pursuits in her life. The following section reviews the major dependent variables which have been used in the study of women's career choices.

HOMEMAKING VERSUS CAREER ORIENTATION

The earliest studies of women's career development focused on women's vocational or career orientation. In other words, studies investigating the kinds of vocational choices made by women were less important than were the issues of whether or not and *why* women pursued careers at all (e.g., Kriger, 1972). Thus, the earliest body of research attempted to differentiate and study the characteristics of homemaking- versus career-oriented women.

The first study attempting to differentiate and describe homemaking-oriented versus career-oriented women was that of Hoyt and Kennedy (1958). Homemaking- versus career-oriented women were first differentiated on the basis of their responses to a questionnaire concerning the relative importance of marital versus career roles. Using the Strong Vocational Interest Blank–Women [(SVIB–W) Strong, 1933] as a descriptive measure, career-oriented subjects were found to obtain higher scores on six scales, including artist, lawyer, psychologist, physician, and physical education teacher, while homemaking-oriented subjects scored higher on eight scales, including housewife, secretary, home economics teacher, and dietician.

The research paradigm developed by Hoyt and Kennedy (1958) was utilized in several subsequent studies, also using the SVIB–W as the independent variable of interest. In these later studies, Hoyt and Kennedy's findings that career-oriented women tended to obtain higher scores on occupations traditionally dominated by men while homemaking-oriented women obtained higher scores on the housewife scale and on nonprofessional or traditionally female occupational scales were essentially replicated (e.g., Munley, 1974; Vetter & Lewis, 1964; Wagman, 1966).

Based on the consistency with which the SVIB–W differentiated homemaking-oriented from career-oriented women, other studies used the SVIB–W to differentiate the groups and then examined background, ability, personality, and value differences between homemaking- and career-oriented women. Studies of group differences in family background characteristics (e.g., Gysbers, Johnston, & Gust, 1968), achievement motivation (Oliver, 1974; Rand, 1968; Tyler, 1964), personality characteristics (e.g., Rand, 1968), ability (Rand, 1968; Watley & Kaplan, 1971), and values (Goldsen, Rosenberg, Williams, & Suchman, 1960; Simpson & Simpson, 1961; Wagman, 1966), to be described in later sections, characterized early research on women's career development.

More recently, Tinsley and Faunce (1978, 1980) contacted a sample of women originally studied as college students 13 to 21 years earlier. Using a response of "Yes" to the question "Are you usually employed outside the home?" to indicate career orientation and a response of "No" to indicate home orientation, Tinsley and Faunce studied group differences in aptitude, vocational interests and needs, attitudes toward women's roles, and marital and family status. Although the variable of homemaker versus career orientation has occasionally been used in more recent research, its usefulness has decreased as more and more women have planned to pursue both career and family roles (e.g., Levitt, 1972; Oliver, 1974).

Assumptions that women must choose either home *or* career were replaced by aspirations of the majority of women to now combine family and career roles in their adult lives (Yogev, 1982). The question is no longer *"whether* to do both" but rather *"how* to do both" (Perun & Bielby, 1981; Richardson, 1974; Rooney, 1983). Thus, the dichotomous variable of career versus home orientation was replaced by concepts describing the nature and degree of career orientation.

VARIABLES DESCRIBING CAREER ORIENTATION

While studies done in the 1960s suggested that the majority of young women did not plan to work outside the home (e.g., Matthews and Tiedeman, 1964), studies in the early 1970s strongly suggested that the majority of young women planned to combine marriage and career (Rand & Miller, 1972; Watley & Kaplan, 1971). Rand and Miller (1972) suggested that a new cultural imperative to combine marriage and career had replaced the previous stress on the centrality of marital and motherhood roles in the lives of women. Because of the growing number of young women planning to combine career and marriage, the homemaking versus career orientation distinction decreased in usefulness as a dependent variable (Levitt, 1972; Oliver, 1974);

rather, it was necessary to describe the nature and degree of career orientation itself to understand women's career choice behavior.

The major approach to describing the *nature* of women's career choices involved the classification of preferences or choices according to the degree to which they were traditional versus nontraditional for women. Rossi (1965) was among the first to suggest the utility of differentiating career-oriented women into those pursuing traditionally female careers, that is, occupations in which women predominate, from those pursuing "pioneer" careers, that is, occupations in which men have predominated. Women pursuing nontraditional, or pioneer, occupations have also been defined as "role innovators" (Almquist, 1974; Tangri, 1972). Thus, the terms "pioneer," "innovator," and "nontraditional" have been used interchangeably to differentiate women pursuing male-dominated fields, which are assumed to require stronger and more consistent career commitment and involvement, from "traditionals," that is, those pursuing traditionally female occupations. Studies of characteristics differentiating pioneers from traditionals dominated research in the early 1970s and, as will be described in later sections, documented numerous important differences between the two types of women (e.g., Astin & Myint, 1971; Nagely, 1971; Standley & Soule, 1974; Tangri, 1972).

Related to the concept of traditionality versus nontraditionality for women are descriptions of the degree to which career choices exist in the sciences and mathematics. Since women are seriously underrepresented in careers in the sciences, mathematics, and engineering, much research has focused on these areas of study (Fox, Brody, & Tobin, 1980; Humphreys, 1982; National Science Foundation, 1984; Pfafflin, 1984). Math-relatedness and science-relatedness have been scaled and used to describe the content of women's choices.

For example, Table 2.1 shows the five levels of a science–nonscience continuum developed by Goldman and Hewitt (1976) to study sex differences in choices of college major. As shown in the table, disciplines illustrative of the greatest emphasis on science include physics and chemistry, whereas those representing the least emphasis on science include art and English. Similarly, Hollinger (1983) combined the ideas of traditionality and math- and science-relatedness in her study of mathematically talented adolescents. The six resulting categories were (1) nontraditional math careers (e.g., accountant, economist); (2) nontraditional science (e.g., chemist, physician); (3) neutral or traditional math–science (e.g., nurse, bookkeeper); (4) nontraditional non-math (e.g., lawyer); (5) neutral non-math (e.g., reporter); and (6) traditional non-math (e.g., librarian, social worker).

TABLE 2.1 Academic Disciplines Representative of Levels of Science–Non-Science Continuum

Level 1: Fine arts	Level 2: Humanities	Level 3: Social science	Level 4: Biological sciences	Level 5: Physical science
Art, studio	English	Agricultural economics and	Animal science	Applied mechanics and
Dance	French	business management	Bacteriology	engineering science
Design	History	Anthropology	Biochemistry	Applied physics and infor-
Drama	English and	Child development	Biological science	mational sciences
Music	American	Comparative cultures	Biology	Chemistry
Paint/sculpture	literature	Economics	Dietetics	Engineering, lower divi-
and graphic art	Spanish	Environmental planning	Food science	sion
Theater		and management	Kinesiology	Electrical engineering
		Home economics	Physiology	Information and computer
		Individual group	Plant science	science
		International relations	Prenursing	Mathematics
		Political science	Wildlife fisheries	Mathematics and computer
		Precriminology	biology	science
		Prepsychology	Zoology	Physics
		Psychology		Prepharmaceutics
		Social science		
		Sociology		

Note. Science–non-science continuum shown as suggested by Goldman and Hewitt (1976).

In addition to comparisons of women in traditional versus pioneer fields and science versus non-science fields, the concept of career orientation was extended and refined, beginning with the work of Eyde (1962). Rather than conceiving of career orientation as a single undifferentiated state defined in opposition to homemaker orientation, career orientation began to be conceptualized as a continuous variable reflecting the degree of preferred work involvement with or without concurrent involvement in the homemaker role. Eyde's (1962) Desire to Work Scale represented the first systematic attempt to assess career orientation as a continuous variable. Eyde's scale, which requested respondents to rate their desire to work under varying conditions of marital status, number and ages of children, and perceived adequacy of husband's income, defined stronger career orientations in terms of the extent to which a woman wished to work even if also married and a mother.

Almquist and Angrist (1970, 1971; Angrist, 1972) adapted Eyde's Desire to Work Scale for the assessment of "career salience," defined as "aspiration for work as a central feature of adult life, regardless of financial necessity and under conditions of free choice" (Almquist & Angrist, 1971, p. 263). Their Life Style Index contained items pertaining to motivation to work under various family conditions and items concerning adult role aspirations and preferences.

Other approaches to the definition and measurement of the concept of career salience were those of Masih (1967), Greenhaus (1971), and Marshall and Wijting (1980). Masih defined career salience as (1) the degree to which a person is career motivated, (2) the degree to which an occupation is an important source of satisfaction, and (3) the priority ascribed to career among other sources of satisfaction. Greenhaus (1971) developed a 27-item measure of career salience and a twenty-eighth item requesting subjects to rank six life areas, including career and family, in terms of their importance in the respondent's life. Marshall and Wijting (1980) defined "career-centeredness" as an orientation which prioritizes career activities, and "career commitment" as a commitment to steady pursuit of a career throughout one's life.

Similarly, Richardson (1974) distinguished "work motivation" from "career orientation." Richardson defined work motivation as the desire to pursue work outside the home, although not prioritizing work roles. Career orientation, on the other hand, was defined as the desire to pursue work as a primary life focus, with homemaking interests viewed as secondary. Maret-Havens (1977) developed a Labor Force Attachment Index based on participation and employment continuity, in which a score of 0 indicated no labor force attachment, whereas a score of 100 indicated continuous full-time employment. Finally, Perun and Bielby (1981) distinguished occupational behavior, shown by all women who work, from career development, shown by the minority of women, whose work follows an orderly sequence of successively higher-level stages within a specific profession or occupation. Thus, these definitions of career salience have in common the idea of prioritizing career, inconsistent with sex role expectations, versus simply working outside the home.

Most studies of women's career development have utilized either the home/career or traditional/nontraditional distinction or a measure of career orientation or salience as the dependent variable. However, the failure of a single distinction or variable to adequately describe women's career development has been noted (e.g., Osipow, 1983). For example, a woman pursuing a traditionally female occupation such as nurse or elementary school teacher could be as strongly career oriented as a woman pursuing a nontraditional occupation, such as medicine or law. Conversely, female role innovators (e.g., physicians) undoubtedly differ in the extent to which marital and family roles are salient to their life plans. Thus, Osipow (1983) has suggested the necessity of research designs which utilize the various possible combinations of such variables in describing women's career development.

CAREER PATTERNS

The third major approach to the description of women's career development utilizes the concept of career patterns, originally developed by Super (1957) and first used in the study of male career development.

In 1957, Super, noting both the centrality of homemaking in a woman's life and the trend for increased labor force participation among women, described seven career patterns of women: (1) the stable homemaking pattern, characterizing women who marry while in or shortly after leaving school and who have no significant work experience; (2) the conventional career pattern, characterizing women who work outside the home only until marriage; (3) the stable working pattern, describing women who work continuously over the life span and for whom work is their "career"; (4) the double-track career pattern, characterizing women who combine home and work roles continuously; (5) the interrupted career pattern, characterized by a return to work later in life; (6) the unstable career pattern, describing an irregular and repeated cycle of home versus work involvement; and

(7) the multiple-trial career pattern, which, similar to the same male pattern, consists of an unstable job history.

In a study of the frequency of occurrence of these patterns, Vetter (1973) found the following percentages in a national cross-sectional sample of women: stable homemaking, 22%; conventional, 27%; stable working, 3%; double-track, 14%; interrupted, 16%; and unstable, 18%. Multiple-trial was not used because of overlap with other categories.

Harmon (1967), in a 25-year follow-up study of University of Minnesota students, classified women's career patterns into five categories: (1) no job experience; (2) work experience only until marriage or the arrival of the first child; (3) combined work with marriage and children; (4) reentered the labor force when children were older; and (5) the single career woman.

While Super attempted to extend his theory's usefulness for women, a more heuristically useful model of women's career patterns was formulated by Zytowski (1969), who offered nine postulates designed to characterize female patterns of occupational participation. His central proposition was that the modal life role for women is that of homemaker, although he also stated that this role was not static and might ultimately bear no distinction from that of men. A second major postulate was that vocational and homemaker participation are largely mutually exclusive and that, consequently, vocational participation constitutes departure from the homemaker role. Zytowski further postulated that vocational participation patterns could be characterized based on three dimensions: age of entry, span (length in years) of participation, and degree of participation (i.e., the traditionality versus the non-traditionality of the occupation for women).

Based on these three dimensions, Zytowski described three resulting patterns: (1) the "mild" vocational pattern, characterized by early or late entry and brief and low-degree participation; (2) the "moderate" pattern, characterized by early entry and lengthy span but low-degree participation; and (3) the "unusual" career pattern, characterized by early entry, lengthy or uninterrupted span, and a high degree of participation.

A study by Wolfson (1976) was designed to investigate differences among groups of women characterized by Zytowski's patterns. Wolfson investigated the career outcomes of 306 women, then aged 43 to 54, who had received career counseling as college students in the 1930s. Instead of finding only three distinguishable career patterns, Wolfson found five: In addition to those formulated by Zytowski, Wolfson added a "never-worked" pattern and a "high-moderate" pattern, including women whose span of participation was 18 years or more. Wolfson found that college graduation, attendance in graduate school, and unmarried status were predictive of membership in the high-moderate or unusual groups. All women in the never-worked, mild, or moderate groups were or had been married, while half of those in the high-moderate and unusual groups were single. The largest percentage of subjects (49%) were classified into the mild category, while the fewest (0.05%) were characterized by the unusual pattern.

Thus, Zytowski's (1969) model attempted to combine a notion similar to that of career orientation (span of participation) with the traditional versus pioneer distinction (degree of participation). Although the model was a major contribution to the study of career patterns among women, it is inadequate in terms of many women who enter male-dominated occupations; unless she enters early and works continuously, a female scientist, for example, would be unclassifiable in this framework.

Ellen Betz (1984a) proposed that seven categories instead of three or five were necessary in order to encompass all possible combinations of the major variables, that is, high, medium, and low *span* of participation, as well as male-dominated and female-dominated *degree* of participation, in addition to the never-worked category. Betz also proposed that continuous, nontraditional employment is probably less "unusual" today than is full-time homemaking and proposed that the idea of high commitment to a pioneer occupation replace the term "unusual." Using her revised system of classification, Betz (1984a) conducted a large-scale follow-up study of recipients of the Bachelor's degree from the University of Minnesota in 1968. Betz' sample included one fourth of the graduates of the two largest colleges (i.e., education and liberal arts) and all graduates of the smaller colleges (such as home economics, business, and the sciences). Subjects were contacted 10 years after graduation—498 of 745 (or 67%) of those contacted returned the completed research materials.

In assigning women to career patterns, Betz defined commitment as low if the woman worked fewer than 4 of the 10 years following college graduation, moderate if she worked from 4 to 6.9 years, and high if she worked at least 7 of the 10 years since graduation. Percentages of women in each of the categories were as follows: (1) Never worked, 1.4%; (2) low-commitment in a traditional occupation (Zytowski's mild pattern), 12.4%; (3) low commitment in a pioneer occupation (a new category), 1.2%; (4) moderate commitment in a traditional occupation, 21.7%; (5) moderate commitment in a pioneer occupation (also a new category), 3.8%; (6) high commitment in a traditional occupation (Wolfson's high-moderate pattern), 35.9%; and (7) high commitment in a pioneer occupation, 23.5%.

Thus, Betz' results indicate a preponderance of subjects in the high (59.4%) and moderate (25.5%) commitment subgroups and only small percentages of women in the low-commitment or never-worked categories. Differentiating these groups was marital and parental status; the percentage of women who were married at the time of testing generally decreased with increases in span and degree of participation. The low-commitment pioneer and both high-commitment groups had the fewest children, in comparison to the low-commitment traditional and never-worked groups, who had the most children. Analyses of the occupational mobility of the women indicated the very interesting finding that women in pioneer occupations were likely to experience upward mobility, whereas those in traditional occupations tended to experience either horizontal or downward mobility. Traditional women were also significantly more likely to move from careers to homemaking over the 10-year span.

Thus, Betz' (1984a) study makes it clear that the pattern of high commitment to a pioneer occupation is no longer unusual, since it was followed by 23.5% of the sample. More unusual, rather, was the never-worked pattern, followed by only 1.4% of the sample. Betz' addition of the low-commitment–pioneer and moderate-commitment–pioneer categories proved useful, accounting for a 5% share of the sample, who would have been unclassifiable under previous schemes.

Finally, Betz pointed out the preponderance of married women in all career categories, ranging from 100% in the never-worked and low-commitment–pioneer categories to 58.1% in the high-commitment–pioneer category. Zytowski's (1969) hope that "altered social expectations and technological innovation will ultimately result in the obsolescence of this entire scheme" (p. 664) is not only supported by the subsequent work of Wolfson and Betz, but it illustrates the rapid and dramatic changes in the character of women's career involvement.

SUMMARY

The study of women's career choices, then, has involved the use of several dependent variables which attempt to take into account what is probably the major difference in the career development of women versus that of men, that is, the expectation that women's lives will usually include, if not revolve around, the roles of homemaking and childrearing. Since the assumption of competing roles was not previously considered relevant to the study of male career development, research on men could proceed directly toward examination of the content of career choice. Thus, the study of women's career development has been inherently more complex.

CONCEPTS IN THE STUDY OF WOMEN'S CAREER CHOICES: INDEPENDENT VARIABLES

While the independent variables utilized in the study of women's career choices have included those emphasized in the study of men, for example, abilities, interests, and socioeconomic and family background factors, the study of women's career development has utilized several additional independent variables and systems of classification emphasizing environmental as well as individual facilitators of and barriers to women's career development.

The variables of marital/familial status, sex role attitudes, and role conflict are the major independent variables considered uniquely pertinent to women's career choices and pursuits. The first attempt to include these variables was made by Sobol (1963), who proposed a classification of variables influencing the decisions of married women with children to work outside the home. This classification included (1) "enabling" conditions, that is, family characteristics including spouse's salary and satisfaction with the marriage; (2) facilitating conditions, for example, educational level and previous work experience; and (3) precipitating conditions, including individual characteristics such as self-concept and sex role attitudes. As would be true in subsequent work, Sobol's classification included both situational (e.g., marital) and individual (e.g., attitudinal) factors.

Psathas (1968) suggested several factors influencing women's occupational participation. Emphasizing cultural, situational, and chance elements of the environment, Psathas cited intentions to marry, time of marriage, the husband's economic situation and attitude toward his wife's working, and the woman's sex role preferences as influential determinants of women's decisions to work.

Other writers have focused specifically on barriers to women's career development. More than the approaches of, for example, Sobol (1963) and Psathas (1968), these approaches were based on a concern with women's lack of vocational achievements and failure to utilize their abilities and talents. Thus, these approaches sought to elucidate the barriers to women's vocational participation and achievement. Matthews and Tiedeman (1964) specified four conflicts unique to fe-

males: (1) the female's concern that career aspirations and achievements would necessitate the sacrifice of marriage; (2) sex-typed family
roles qualifying women for homemaker but not breadwinner roles; (3)
home–career conflict; and (4) the concurrence of desired age of marriage with the need to emphasize educational pursuits and goals necessary for career achievements.

Farmer (1976) suggested six internal or self-concept barriers to
women (including fear of success, sex role orientation, risk-taking behavior, home–career conflict, and low academic self-esteem) and
three environmental barriers (including discrimination, family socialization, and availability of resources such as child care). Similarly,
Harmon (1977) proposed that women's career development is affected
by both internal/psychological and external/sociological constraints.

Falk and Cosby (1978) detailed several problems both unique and
disruptive to the career development of women. These included the
female's socialization into the traditional role, the sex-typing of occupations, the perceived conflict between marital and occupational success, and the influence and pressure of significant others toward traditional role pursuits and away from nontraditional pursuits, for
example, educational and career achievements.

More recently, Perun and Bielby (1981) proposed that understanding the occupational behavior of women requires a life span perspective and acknowledgment of the effects of social-structural constraints
on women, which perpetuate occupational sex role stereotyping and
occupational sex segregation. They suggested that timing and extent
of synchrony of work and family cycles are important variables in the
career development of women.

Gottfredson (1981), in a model based on the concepts of circumscription and compromise, suggested that U.S. society functions to
limit individuals' *perceived* career options to a reduced range of appropriately sex-typed alternatives. Once this range is set—according
to Gottfredson, somewhere between the ages of 6 and 8—occupations
outside this range will not be considered except under unusual circumstances. Thus, Gottfredson's view suggests serious restrictive effects of societal sex role norms on women's aspirations. Astin's (1984)
view of the importance of the "structure of opportunity" in shaping
women's career decisions is similar to, although somewhat less explicitly formulated than, Gottfredson's (see also Farmer, 1984a; Fitzgerald
& Betz, 1984; Gilbert, 1984; and Harmon, 1984; among others, for
responses to Astin's proposals).

Finally, several theorists have attempted to provide first steps toward integrating the many variables developed in response to unique
aspects of women's career development with traditional variables in

the study of vocational behavior. For example, Senesh (1973), Osipow (1975), O'Neil, Meeker, and Borgers (1978), Farmer (1985), and Fassinger (1985) have presented comprehensive frameworks of factors influencing career development which they propose as useful for the study of women's career development.

More specifically, the frameworks proposed by Osipow and Senesh (Osipow, 1975; Senesh, 1973) include individual factors such as abilities, interests, and attitudes; social factors such as family, significant others, sex role and occupational stereotypes; and moderating factors including fear of success, role conflict, and discrimination (Osipow, 1975, p. 5). O'Neil et al. (1978) proposed that individual, familial, societal, psychosocial, socioeconomic, and situational factors are important influences on the extent and nature of women's sex role socialization and attitudes and, consequently, their career choice processes.

Farmer (1985) postulated that adolescents' career motivation developed through three sets of interacting influences, that is, background variables (e.g., gender, ethnicity), psychological variables (e.g., attitudes, beliefs, self-concept), and environmental variables (e.g., support from teachers and parents). Career motivation, in turn, could be subdivided into three aspects, including level of occupation chosen (aspiration), motivation to achieve a short range of challenging tasks (mastery), and degree of commitment to the long-range prospects of a career (career). Farmer's model has the advantage of being multidimensional at both the dependent and independent variable levels. Her research (e.g., Farmer, 1985) uses both multiple regression and path analyses to investigate the effects of the influencing factors on the dependent variables.

Finally, a multidimensional model incorporating a set of influencing factors similar to those of Farmer (1985) and O'Neil et al. (1978) is that of Fassinger (1985), elaborating on the model originally proposed by the present authors. This model, which will be discussed in greater detail in Chapter 9, incorporates background characteristics (e.g., previous work experience and academic success), environmental variables (e.g., role model influence and perceived encouragement), and psychological variables (e.g., self-concept and sex role attitudes) in a structural model designed to predict several aspects of women's career orientation and choice.

SUMMARY

While there is as yet no comprehensive theory of women's career development, the formulation of several new variables (both dependent and independent), the focus on unique barriers to women's career development, and the development of approaches to the classification of multiple influential factors in that development are important steps toward further understanding of women's career development and an enriched and more inclusive vocational psychology. The next six chapters will be organized around what have been referred to herein as the independent variables related to women's career development. Thus, these chapters will cover both environmental/sociocultural and individual variables, such as abilities, interests, and sex role-related characteristics shown to be related to women's career development.

In addition to reviewing research regarding a variety of individual and environmental variables, Chapters 3 through 8 will also include the full range of meanings and definitions associated with the term "career choice." Therefore, these chapters will include variables related to the *nature* of women's career choices and the extent of their success and satisfaction in *implementing* these choices, in particular, their educational decisions and achievements. Generally speaking, the topic of the second half of the book, vocational adjustment, can be differentiated from the topic of the first half, career choice, by the point of occupational entry. Thus, the educational pursuits necessary to implement decisional preferences and preceding the actual point of occupational entry will be viewed as crucial to the career choice process.

CULTURAL, SUBCULTURAL, AND FAMILIAL FACTORS IN WOMEN'S CAREER CHOICES

INTRODUCTION

The first set of important independent variables to be considered includes the stimulus variables of the environment and their effects on women's career choices and development. The discussion will begin at the most general level, exploring the effects on women of an American culture within which women's place has been viewed as in the home, not in the work world; the processes and effects of sex role stereotyping, occupational sex-typing, and insufficient role modeling will be explored. Second, the effects on women of certain kinds of subcultural statuses, such as socioeconomic, racial, ethnic, and religious, will be discussed. Third, the effects of a female's more immediate social environment, including family background factors, adult marital and parental status, and personal role models, on her career development and choices will be discussed.

STIMULUS VARIABLES: CULTURE

SOCIETAL SEX ROLE STEREOTYPES

Our society has traditionally specified different life roles, personality characteristics, and acceptable behaviors for males and females. Norms governing the approved masculine or feminine image are clearly defined and consensually endorsed (e.g., Broverman, Broverman, Clarkson, Rosenkrantz, & Vogel, 1970; Mischel, 1970; Steinmann & Fox, 1966) and become a powerful force in the socialization of children.

In terms of adult roles, men are expected to work and to be family providers. Women are expected to be nurturant wives and mothers who stay at home. In terms of personality characteristics, men are expected to develop those associated with competency, instrumentality, and achievement, while women are to develop those comprising a "warmth-expressiveness" cluster, including nurturance, sensitivity, warmth, and emotional expressiveness.

The psychological mechanisms by which children learn sex role stereotypes (i.e., normative expectations for the sexes) and develop sex-typed characteristics include reinforcement and punishment, modeling, and the adoption of rules, schemas, or generalizations based on observation of others or as they are taught by others (e.g., Hyde & Rosenberg, 1980; Williams, 1977). These mechanisms operate through the influence of parents, teachers, and the media, including literature and television (see Maccoby & Jacklin, 1974, and Williams, 1983, for more detailed reviews).

Parents often encourage the development of sex-typed interests and behaviors in their children, for example, by providing sex-typed toys (Maccoby & Jacklin, 1974) and are more likely to encourage achievement in their sons than in their daughters (e.g., Etaugh & Hall, 1980; Rubovitz, 1975). Teachers often encourage sex-typed activities (e.g., Fagot, 1981) and reinforce the development of sex-typed psychological characteristics. Several studies have suggested, for example, that teachers encourage different patterns of attribution of causation for success and failure experiences in boys and girls; Dweck, Davidson, Nelson, and Enna (1978) found that 4th- and 5th-grade boys were encouraged to attribute success to ability, and failure to lack of effort or external factors (e.g., bad luck), whereas the reverse pattern of attributions was encouraged in girls. Guttentag and Bray's (1976) review of research in this area led to the conclusion that teachers play a major role in inculcating and supporting children's sex role values. Guttentag and Bray (1976) reviewed research suggesting that teachers reinforce boys for achievement behavior and girls for being "nice." Fagot (1981) reported that *inexperienced* teachers of both sexes reinforced sex-typed behaviors in preschool boys and girls but that, interestingly, experienced teachers reinforced stereotypically feminine behaviors compatible with school performance in both boys and girls.

Stereotypes are also conveyed by children's textbooks and literature (e.g., Bergman, 1974; Key, 1975; Weitzman, Eitler, Hokada, & Ross,

1972) and in television content (Busby, 1975; Frueh & McGhee, 1975). Key (1975) summarized children's books as conveying the theme of "boys do; girls are," and Nilsen (1971) referred to the "cult of the apron" based on her finding that most adult female characters, including animals, are pictured wearing aprons. Even though women work outside the home, children's books have portrayed them almost exclusively in wife and/or mother roles (Key, 1975).

Thus, culturally based sex role socialization operates from early childhood to prepare young girls for the roles of wife and mother and to encourage in them the development of personality characteristics and behaviorial competencies that will facilitate the performance of those roles. Young girls are usually not socialized to prepare for career pursuits or to develop the characteristics and competencies necessary for such pursuits.

OCCUPATIONAL SEX STEREOTYPES

Related to sex role stereotypes are occupational stereotypes, or normative views of the appropriateness of various occupations for males and females. Although a number of studies have shown that occupational stereotypes are consistent and durable in adult populations (Albrecht, Bahr, & Chadwick, 1977; Panek, Rush, & Greenwalt, 1977), the study by Shinar (1975) is a classic in this area. Shinar asked college students to rate 129 occupations as masculine, feminine, or neutral, using a seven-point rating scale on which "Masculine" was a 1 and "Feminine" was a 7. The results indicated that both male and female students consistently stereotyped occupations as masculine or feminine. Mean ratings of masculinity/feminity ranged from the most masculine-stereotypic job of miner, which received a mean rating of 1.0 with *no variability,* to the occupations of receptionist (6.3), nurse (6.6), and manicurist (6.7). Other highly masculine stereotypic occupations were highway maintenance worker (1.2), heavy equipment operator (1.2), and U.S. Supreme Court justice (1.3). Among the professions, district attorney (1.6), engineer (1.9), federal judge (1.9), dentist (2.1), surgeon (2.2), physicist (2.3), veterinarian (2.7), and physician (2.7) were clearly masculine stereotypic, while nurse (6.6), head librarian (5.6), elementary school teacher (5.6), and dietician (5.3) were feminine typed.

Not only do adults stereotype occupations as appropriate for males or females, but children appear to learn these stereotypes very early. For example, Gettys and Cann (1981) found that children as young as

$2\frac{1}{2}$ were able to distinguish masculine and feminine occupations, while Tremaine and Schau (1979) found that preschoolers identified and agreed with adult job stereotypes. Occupational stereotypes are consistently found in elementary school children (Frost & Diamond, 1979; Gettys & Cann, 1981; Rosenthal & Chapman, 1982; Schlossberg & Goodman, 1972; Tremaine & Schau, 1979). Generally, findings suggest that stereotyping increases with the age of the child (Tremaine & Schau, 1979; Gettys & Cann, 1981).

One study illustrating the power of occupational stereotypes was that by Drabman, Robertson, Patterson, Jarvie, Hammer, and Cordua (1981). The study utilized a videotaped portrayal of a 7-year-old boy going to visit his doctor. The doctor was a woman (named "Mary Nancy" to double the sex-salience of the name), and she was assisted by a male nurse named "David Gregory." Immediately after viewing the tape, 1st-, 4th-, and 7th-grade children were given a multiple-choice quiz on which they were asked to recognize the names of the doctor and the nurse. In addition to the correct name, the distractors included a wrong same-sex name, the name of the opposite-sex character in the videotape, and a "wrong" opposite-sex name. In naming the doctor and the nurse, almost all 1st- and 4th-grade children assigned a gender-typed name, even if it was a name that had not appeared in the videotape. For example, no 1st graders chose a male name for the nurse—22% chose the wrong (never appearing) female name! Only 4% of the 4th graders chose a male name for the nurse. For the doctor, only 4% of both 1st and 4th graders chose a female name—41% of 1st graders chose the *wrong* male name rather than the correct female name. Among 7th graders, 53–79% chose the correct names for both nurse and doctor, and the ability to recall the correct gender name decreased after a 1-week interval. The authors conclude, distressingly, that children alter their perception or memory of a counterstereotyped videotaped presentation to fit previously learned occupational sex stereotypes and that stereotypic cognitive structures are capable of modifying long-term memory as well. Bem (1981) postulates the idea of "gender schema" to account for findings such as these.

According to Bem, the process of sex-typing leads to the learning of not only sex-appropriate attributes, behaviors, and roles, but of sex-based schema by which *new* information is processed. In essence, information consistent with sex role stereotypes would be processed more readily and retained longer than that which was inconsistent with stereotypes, for example, male nurses in the Drabman *et al.* study. Thus, the *effects* of sex stereotypes are extensive and continuing and serve to distort new information. (Further discussion of gender schema theory will occur in Chapter 7.)

Further, children's occupational preferences tend to be consistent with the occupational stereotypes they hold. Both boys and girls tend to choose sex-typed occupations (Frost & Diamond, 1979; Looft, 1971; MacKay & Miller, 1982; O'Bryant & Corder-Bolz, 1978; Tremaine & Schau, 1979), although girls are somewhat more likely to select stereotypically male occupations than are boys to select stereotypically female occupations (Gettys & Cann, 1981).

While children of both sexes select sex-stereotypic occupational choices, the smaller number and more limited range of traditionally female occupations (Bird, 1968) result in the limitation of girls' perceived options at very early ages. In Looft's (1971) sample of 1st and 2nd graders, Siegel's (1973) samples of 2nd graders, and Nelson's (1978) sample of 3rd graders, boys were found to indicate a wide variety of occupational preferences, almost all of them male-dominated. Girls, on the other hand, listed a smaller number of occupations, and their choices were dominated by two occupations—nurse and teacher. In Siegel's sample, for example, 70% of 2nd-grade girls selected either nurse or teacher, while the 32 boys chose 20 different occupations.

Finally, Kriedberg, Butcher, and White (1978) found that while some 2nd-grade girls expressed interest in male-dominated occupations, almost all 6th-grade girls were choosing traditionally female occupations. It is unfortunate indeed that occupational stereotypes have limited girls' perceived career options before they finish elementary school. In MacKay and Miller's (1982) study, 3rd- and 5th-grade boys most frequently chose the occupations of policemen, truck driver, pilot, and architect, while girls chose nurse, teacher, and stewardess. Umstot (1980) found that highly male-stereotyped activities among 3rd through 7th graders included being a soldier, TV service-person, and plumber, while highly female-stereotyped activities included knitting, sewing, selling perfume, and being a secretary. Hurwitz and White (1977) found that juniors in high school assigned female profiles to lower-paying, lower-status jobs than they did equivalent male profiles.

Findings of limited occupational preferences among children as young as 1st and 2nd grades are consistent with Gottfredson's (1981) theory of circumscription and compromise in career choice. Gottfredson proposes that individuals' occupational aspirations become circumscribed within a range of acceptable sex-typed alternatives, and that this acceptable range is normally set by ages 6 to 8. Further,

Gottfredson suggested that, once set, the range of acceptable alternatives is extremely difficult to modify. While the suggestion of such early constriction in choices is very difficult to accept, it does not seem to be inconsistent with available research data.

Not only do children of all ages hold occupational stereotypes, but these stereotypes are highly resistant to change. For example, in the study by Knell and Winer (1979), preschool-age children were read 12 stories portraying people in each of 12 different occupations. Six male and six female characters were used, and the design varied the extent to which occupations were portrayed with sex-appropriate versus -inappropriate characters. Occupational stereotypes were assessed before and after treatment. Although it was hypothesized that presenting nontraditional portrayals in videotapes would reduce stereotyping, no *effects* for the nontraditional treatments (either half or all 12 of the stories showing a sex-incongruent member of the occupation) were found. The only treatment effect was an *increase* in stereotyping among girls who had viewed the "traditional" tape (all 12 occupations portrayed by the "appropriate" gender). Boys' responses were highly stereotypic *regardless* of treatment. Yanico (1978), in a study varying the amount of sex bias in occupational information, also concluded that occupational stereotypes are amazingly resistant to change through treatment. Zuckerman and Sayre (1982), in a sample of middle-class children between ages 4 and 8, found that the children demonstrated less occupational stereotyping than expected but persisted in sex-stereotypic personal choices. Among the girls, 52% chose nurse, 16% chose teacher, 8% chose dancer, and 8% chose veterinarian. Among the boys, greater variability in choices was demonstrated, although 83% were sex stereotypic.

Although attempts have been made to justify the existence of occupational stereotypes on the grounds that certain kinds of job content are more congruent with the skills of males, while others are more congruent with female abilities, there is strong and consistent evidence that the proportion of men and women in an occupation is the best predictor of its job sex type (Krefting & Berger, 1979; Krefting, Berger, & Wallace, 1978). In two studies reported by Krefting *et al.* (1978), the actual percentage of men versus women in the job explained 48% and 70% of the variance in job sex types. As stated by Krefting *et al.*, the sex of the job holder is the basis of occupational stereotypes. A disturbing study (Heilman, 1979) reported that high school girls expressed more interest in male-dominated occupations when led to believe that the sex ratios would in the future be more balanced, but high school boys expressed less interest in those occupations when confronted with the prospect of sex balance. Thus, the lack of other women in an occupation serves to deter young women from selecting that occupation, and some males may prefer that the sex ratio in preferred occupations remains imbalanced. Finally, Arkin and Johnson (1980) found that while the *inverse* relationship between occupational value and desirability and the proportion of women expected to enter the occupation held for nonandrogynous subjects, androgynous subjects rated high-prestige occupations even more desirable when told that increases in the percentages of women were expected.

Not only do durable occupational stereotypes exist in both children and adults, but occupational informational materials designed for use at high school and adult levels have been documented to perpetuate occupational stereotypes in both text and illustrative material (Birk, Tanney, & Cooper, 1979; Lauver, Gastellum, & Sheehey, 1975; Yanico, 1978). Thus, materials that should serve to facilitate exploration of career options serve instead to reinforce the restrictions in women's options which result from occupational sex stereotypes in the culture.

LACK OF ROLE MODELS

Related to the existence of occupational sex types in limiting the options of women is the lack of female role models in nontraditional occupations. The importance of role models as vicarious learning is a major contention of child development and social learning theorists. As reviewed by Maccoby and Jacklin (1974), various major theorists and researchers of child development (e.g., Kagan, Mischel, Mussen, and Sees) stress the importance of imitation in the learning of sex-typed behavior. Social learning theorists, for example, Mischel, Bandura, Krumboltz, and Thoresen, suggest not only the importance of modeling but the greater effectiveness of same-sex models (e.g., Basow & Howe, 1980). Further, Bandura's (1977) self-efficacy theory postulates vicarious learning as one of four sources of experiential data contributing to the development of strong beliefs about one's behavioral capabilities.

Thus, if modeling is important to learning and if same-sex models are more attractive, the career development of women would be limited by the lack of adult women representing strong career orientation and varied career pursuits (Douvan, 1976). Indeed, the literature strongly suggests that a lack of role models hinders the development of women's educational and occupational potentials (O'Leary, 1974). Research has shown lack of role models to be a deterrent to women's pursuit of careers in science (McLure & Piel, 1978) and other pioneer fields (O'Donnell & Anderson, 1978).

SUMMARY

In summary, cultural attitudes and beliefs concerning women's roles and capabilities, through the mechanisms of sex role socialization and occupational stereotyping, operate to encourage the development of sex-typed psychological characteristics and to perpetuate sex-typed adult roles. Young women and girls learn not only that their appropriate adult roles are those of wife and mother but that if they do work there is a set of female-appropriate occupations from which they should choose. Thus, society influences girls and young women to limit their life roles and occupational options on the basis of gender alone, without regard for or interest in their unique individual capabilities and potentials for development. Bem and Bem (1976) have referred to this phenomenon as the "homogenization" of the American woman.

STIMULUS VARIABLES: SUBCULTURE

In addition to the overall culture in the development and experiences of females and males, the subculture in which she/he develops affects career development. Major variables describing that subculture include socioeconomic status, race, nationality, and religion.

SOCIOECONOMIC STATUS

The concept of socioeconomic status (SES) has been variously defined and measured; indices of SES have included the occupational or educational level of the primary breadwinner (usually the father) and family income. While occupational level is the most commonly used index, studies vary in the indices used and, unfortunately, often fail to specify how the index of SES was obtained. An additional problem for interpretive clarity is that indices of SES are not only highly correlated with each other but are strongly related to such variables as intelligence and race (Tyler, 1965). Thus, the effect of SES per se on occupational attainments may be difficult to disentangle from the effects of other variables covarying with SES.

In spite of definitional variation, socioeconomic status is one of the most consistent predictors of the occupational level achieved by males; higher family SES is related to higher achieved occupational levels in sons, whereas sons of lower-class backgrounds achieve lower occupational levels (Brown, 1970; Hollingshead, 1949; Sewell, Haller, & Strauss, 1957). As pointed out by Goodale and Hall (1976), sons are likely to "inherit" their fathers' occupational levels.

In contrast, data regarding the influence of parental SES on women's career development yield an inconsistent pattern of results. In some studies, higher SES was related to stronger career orientation and/or innovation in women (Astin, 1968; Astin & Myint, 1971; Burlin, 1976; Werts, 1965). Several studies have found that women pursuing male-dominated professions (e.g., medicine, academics) are significantly more likely than women in general to have fathers who are professionals (e.g., Cartwright, 1972; Freun, Rothman, & Steiner, 1974; Helson, 1971; Russo & O'Connell, 1980; Standley & Soule, 1974; Wertheim, Widom, & Wortzel, 1978).

Other studies, however, have reported negative relationships between career orientation and SES (Del Vento Bielby, 1978; Eyde, 1962; White, 1967), and still others have found no relationships between the two variables (Card, Steel, & Abeles, 1980; Crawford, 1978; Falk & Salter, 1978; Ridgeway, 1978). Marini (1978) suggested that while family SES is associated with higher educational aspirations in daughters, the relationship of family SES to girls' occupational aspirations is much weaker (if at all) than the relationship of SES to boys' aspirations. Similarly, Schiffler (1976) noted that the SES–aspirations relationship generally found is far less consistent in female samples.

While studies based on fathers' occupational levels provide a somewhat inconsistent pattern of findings, data regarding fathers' educational levels provide a more consistent pattern of findings and suggest that more highly educated fathers tend to have more career-oriented and innovative daughters. Higher parental education for women compared to men in the same occupations was noted by Astin (1969), L. R. Harmon (1978) in studies of Ph.D.'s, and by Constantini and Craik (1972), among others. Freun et al. (1974) reported that female medical school applicants had more highly educated parents than did male applicants. Women in pioneer career fields had more highly educated fathers than did women in traditional fields in studies by Burlin (1976), Greenfield, Greinder, and Wood (1980), Russo and O'Connell (1980), and Werts (1966), among others. Fathers' educational levels have been found to be positively related to daughters' educational aspirations (Falk & Salter, 1978) and career orientation (Gysbers et al., 1968; Patrick, 1973).

Thus, there is some evidence that women's career choices are influenced by the occupational level and, particularly, the educational level of their fathers. Having a highly-educated, professional father appears especially facilitative of a woman's pursuit of a male-dominated profession. The failure of SES variables to be as predictive of women's career choices as they are of men's may at least in part be explained by differential expectations of the sexes in this society. While high-SES families are very likely to encourage and facilitate achievement-related behaviors in their sons, the extent to which they do so in their daughters is probably a function of parental attitudes and beliefs with regard to women's roles in society and, possibly, the presence or absence of sons in the family. Thus, Goodale and Hall's (1976) suggestions that parental interest and support moderate the relationship of SES to career achievements seem essential to and, as will be discussed in a subsequent section, particularly valid for the understanding of women's vocational aspirations.

RACE

Most studies of race differences in American women's career choices have examined black versus white women; few studies have examined Hispanics, American Indians, or Asian Americans, for example (see Smith, 1983, for a review of this limited area of research). Thus, this review focuses on studies comparing black and white women.

Over the years, one of the most consistent findings regarding black women has been that, in comparison to their white counterparts, the majority have expected to work part or all of their adult lives (e.g., Gump & Rivers, 1975; Turner & McCaffrey, 1974; Smith, 1982). Although the actual labor force participation rate among white women is now catching up to that among black women (Almquist, 1979), the labor force participation rate among black women has traditionally been greater than that of white women (Gump & Rivers, 1975; Jeffries, 1976; U.S. Department of Labor, 1977).

Although the reasons for black women's greater labor force participation stem at least in part from the historical roles played by black women and men during the time of slavery, it has always been the case that black women are more likely than white women to be the sole support of themselves and/or their families. Black women are far more likely than white women to be heads of households (Clay, 1975; U.S. Department of Labor, 1977). The incidence of divorce is higher for blacks than whites at every level of education, occupation, and income (Norton & Glick, 1976), and the ratio of males to females is more disproportionate among blacks than whites. While the gender ratio among white adults is about 98 men to 100 women, the sex ratio among blacks has been dropping steadily since 1940. In 1977, the sex ratio among blacks aged 25 to 44 was about 80, i.e., there are only 80 black men in that age range for every 100 women. Translated into the individual level, there are *700,000* more black women than black men in this age range (Almquist, 1979). For highly educated black women there is an even greater disparity of equally well-educated black men. Along with the inherent shortage of men, high rates of marital disruption (Houseknecht & Spanier, 1980) help to explain why only 38% of black women aged 14 and over (versus 61% of white women) are married and living with their husbands. Black women learn that they cannot rely on marriage to produce a secure life and, rather, learn the necessity of self-support.

However, while black women's expected and actual labor force participation has exceeded that of white women, black women are even more disadvantaged than white women in the nature of that participation. Black women particularly and minority women in general are in a state of what has been referred to as "double jeopardy" (Beale, 1970) because they are both female and minority in a society which has traditionally valued neither group (Almquist, 1979). Thus, on many dimensions they are doubly disadvantaged. Black women are affected not only by sex discrimination but by race discrimination. As was so well stated by Almquist (1979), "In their push for freedom, dignity, and equality, black women confront the same barriers that white women do, plus the extra hardships imposed on them by racism" (p. 432). In terms of employment, the barriers of sexism are even more important than the barriers of racism.

Black women, first of all, earn less money than do women or men of any ethnic group and earn substantially less than do black men (Gump & Rivers, 1975; Smith, 1983; U.S. Department of Labor, 1980). Average annual salaries for full-time employed workers in 1979 ranged from about $16,000 for white men, $13,000 for black men, $9,500 for white women, and $9,000 for black women. Note that while black men are clearly disadvantaged relative to white men, males regardless of race are better off in terms of earning power than are females.

In terms of the nature of labor force participation, proportionately more black women than black men are in professional-level occupations, but proportionately fewer black women than white women are professionally employed (Gottfredson, 1978; U.S. Department of Labor, 1984). In 1977, 13% and 7% of black women and men, respectively, were in professional occupations, in comparison to 16% of white women and men. Even among black women professionals, the range of occupations is narrow; 54% of black women versus 39% of white women professionals are in teaching (Sorkin, 1972). Like white women, black women are concentrated in low-paying professions. In comparison to white women, black women are even more greatly concentrated in traditionally female occupations (Brito & Jusenius, 1978; Frost & Diamond, 1979; Murray & Mednick, 1977; Smith, 1982), particularly in domestic and service jobs (U.S. Department of Labor, 1977).

Almquist (1979), on the other hand, pointed out that the nature as well as the extent of black women's labor force participation is becoming increasingly similar to that of white women. In 1965, 24% of employed black women versus 62% of employed white women were in white-collar jobs—in 1977 the figures were 46% and 66% respectively. In 1965, 55% of black women were in service occupations—a whopping 30% were private household workers—but only 12% were secretaries or clerks. By 1977, the proportion of black women in service occupations had declined to 35%, including only 9% who remained private household workers, while the proportion in secretarial and clerical occupations had risen to 26%. Note that while the nature of black women's labor force participation is increasingly similar to that of white women, both groups of women have remained concentrated in low-level, low-paying, traditionally female occupations (Smith, 1982).

The fact that black women continue to be slightly more highly educated than black men yet continue to earn far less is, according to Almquist (1979), a result of sex segregation on the one hand (i.e., the concentration of women into a small number of low-paying professions and occupations) and of sex discrimination in pay on the other. Smith (1983) also pointed out that both blacks and women suffer from the phenomenon of "learning without earning" (Newman, Amidet, Carter, Day, Kruvant, & Russell, 1978), that is, the failure of educational attainments to translate into the higher occupational status and pay that is true of the educational attainments of white males.

Looking at labor force data from the 1950s to the present results in the conclusion that racial inequalities have declined over time, but that sexual inequalities have persisted or even increased (Almquist, 1979). Black women's status has improved, although not as quickly as has the status of black men, while the status of white women has not improved. Thus, black women have now nearly caught up with white women—together in a status that remains noticeably disadvantaged relative to that of males, whether black or white. In considering the improved status of black women, however, it is important to note that these improvements characterize the lives of younger rather than older black women. Older black women worked in an era in which there were few occupational roles for them other than in domestic work. In 1980, 50% of black women workers aged 65 or older were domestics, in contrast with one third of those aged 45 to 64, and "only" 10% of those aged 25 to 34 (Almquist, 1979).

Thus, black women differ from white women in that work is especially likely to play a major role in their lives and in the more frequent necessity of supporting themselves and their families. Black women, of course, are affected by racial as well as sexual discrimination. A review of differences between black and white women, however, should not obscure the greater salience of their similarities. Almquist (1979) pointed out that black and white women are far more similar to each other than is either group to males of their own race. In other words, although it is a disadvantage to be black, the disadvantages of being female are even greater. Black and white women are strikingly similar in their victimization by sex discrimination in employment and wages. As summarized by Almquist (1979), in the field of *employment*, sexual barriers to equality and achievement are stronger than racial barriers, but both affect the career development of black women.

In terms of educational and occupational aspirations, black females have higher aspirations than either black males or white females through high school, but, like white women, the aspirations of black women decline during college until they are *below* those of black males.

Further information about black women can be found in Smith's (1982) review of the educational and career development of black female adolescents, and Jones and Welch's (1980) discussion of the barriers to black professional women. A recent issue of the *Psychology of Women Quarterly* (Murray & Scott, 1982) was devoted to issues facing black women, including black adolescents, graduate students (Fleming, 1982), professionals (Gilkes, 1982; Burlew, 1982), and employed black mothers (Harrison & Minor, 1982).

NATIONALITY AND RELIGION

Although a comprehensive understanding of women's career development requires cross-cultural studies, a thorough review of knowledge and research concerning the career development of women in other countries is beyond the scope of this book. Certain generalizations may, however, be useful to keep in mind. First, the United States is one of the few countries, along with some other Western democracies, having a standard of living high enough to allow a significant proportion of the population to, in essence, work for "nothing" as a homemaker and mother. In most other countries of the world, women have traditionally worked, if not in factories and business, in agriculture. In many countries, women constitute significant proportions or even majorities in occupations which in this country we have considered "men's work"; for example, in the Soviet Union the majority of physicians are female. It may be noted that high-prestige professions in this country (e.g., physician) are of much lower prestige in countries in which women constitute the majority of workers, further supporting the suggestion that the substantial presence of females in an occupation reduces its prestige. These points support the importance of cultural factors in women's career development, as discussed earlier in this section.

In terms of the career development of women living *in this country,* several studies suggest that foreign-born women or women whose parents were foreign-born are more likely than other women in the United States to pursue nontraditional occupations. Astin's (1969) Ph.D.'s, Helson's (1971) mathematicians, Epstein's (1968) lawyers, and Epstein's (1973) black professional women were disproportionately foreign-born or were the children of at least one foreign-born parent. In Bernard's (1972) study, only 52% of Chinese female high school graduates, versus 67%, 74%, and 78% of white, black, and Puerto Rican samples, aspired to traditionally female occupations. However, few of Constantini and Craik's (1972) female politicians or Hennig's (1973) female executives were foreign-born.

While the data are too scarce to permit conclusive statements, it is possible that families new to this country perceive the system of public education as one of its primary benefits and, consequently, encourage daughters as well as sons to take advantage of the opportunities available. The fact that nontraditional occupations in which foreign-born women are found tend to be those requiring substantial education, for example, academician or mathematician, would tend to support this postulate.

In addition to the possibly greater appreciation of educational opportunities, there is ample evidence that other countries do not suppress the development of female mathematical and scientific talent with quite the vigor shown in this country. For example, Asian and Oriental women in this country do not show the disadvantaged position relative to men in mathematics participation and achievement, and the familiar stereotype of the lone Oriental woman in engineering and mathematics classes in which everyone else is male reflects a comfort with mathematics which has never characterized the average American female. As will be discussed in a subsequent chapter, mathematics is a "critical filter" for career development (Sells, 1982) in that having a math background is critical to a huge range of career options; the lack of a math background serves to dramatically and in "de facto" fashion limit career options.

Like research on the influence of nationality on women's career development, data regarding the effects of religion are also meager. The data that are available suggest that women of Jewish background are more strongly career oriented than are those of other religious backgrounds (Watley & Kaplan, 1971; Zuckerman, 1980). Religious background is, however, also related to the traditionality of sex role and lifestyle attitudes which, as discussed in Chapter 7, are also related to women's career development.

To summarize, research on the relationships of nationality of both birth and current citizenship and religious background and beliefs to women's career development is sorely needed and offers the potential of significant contribution to the understanding of women's career choices.

STIMULUS VARIABLES: THE IMMEDIATE ENVIRONMENT

Several aspects of the more immediate environment have been found to influence the career development of women. These include family background characteristics, variables related to marital and familial status as an adult, the availability of role models and supportive figures in the immediate environment, the educational system, and counseling services.

FAMILY BACKGROUND FACTORS

In addition to studies of the family's socioeconomic status, typically utilizing father's educational and/or occupational level as indices of that status, considerable research has investigated the impact of mother's educational level and occupational status on women's career development. A focus on the influence of mothers is found in studying women's career development, versus that of men, because of the assumed importance of the same-sex parent in influencing development.

The influence of maternal employment on women's career development has been extensively studied. Theoretically, working mothers are postulated to facilitate daughters' career achievements because they provide a female model of career pursuits (Douvan, 1976) and a model of the successful integration of family and work roles (DiSabatino, 1976; Hoffman & Nye, 1974). Generally, research has suggested that, in fact, working mothers are an important and positive influence on their daughters' career development.

Numerous studies have found that daughters of working mothers are more career oriented (versus home oriented) than are the daughters of homemakers (e.g., Almquist & Angrist, 1970, 1971; Altman & Grossman, 1977; Huth, 1978). Other studies have suggested that daughters of working mothers are more likely to pursue nontraditional occupations in comparison to daughters of homemakers (Almquist, 1974; Astin, 1967; Crawford, 1978; Epstein, 1968; Ginzberg, Berg, Brown, Herma, Yonalem, & Goralick, 1966; Haber, 1980; Tangri, 1972). Eyde (1962) found that the longer a mother worked after marriage, the greater the career involvement of her daughter. O'Leary (1974) reviewed research supporting the positive effect of a working mother (at least a relatively well-satisfied one) on women's career orientation. Kutner and Brogan (1980) found that 57% of female but only 43% of male medical students had working mothers. Stephan and Corder (1985) found that girls reared in two-career families were more likely to plan to combine family and work roles than were those reared in a traditional family.

While maternal employment may influence women's career development through its provision of a model of female employment and role integration, maternal employment is also related to other variables facilitative of women's career development. Studies have suggested that the daughters of working mothers develop generally more liberal sex role ideologies (Hoffman, 1974b; Hoffman & Nye, 1974), are less stereotypically feminine themselves (Altman & Grossman, 1977; Hansson, Chernovetz, & Jones, 1977; Vogel, Broverman, Broverman, Clarkson, & Rosenkrantz, 1970), and show greater self-esteem and more positive evaluations of female competence (Hoffman, 1974b) in comparison to the daughters of homemakers.

While maternal employment seems in general to facilitate women's career development, some research has suggested that daughters of homemakers who have positive attitudes toward career pursuits and/or who express dissatisfaction with the homemaker role are also more strongly career oriented (Altman & Grossman, 1977; Baruch, 1972; Parsons, Frieze, & Ruble, 1978). In contrast, daughters of working mothers who experience considerable difficulty and/or conflict in role integration may develop ambivalent attitudes toward their own future employment (see Baruch, 1972; Sorenson & Winters, 1975). Although studies of these latter relationships are few, it seems reasonable to conclude that maternal attitudes and role satisfaction, as well as maternal life roles, affect the kinds of career decisions made by daughters.

In addition to maternal employment, maternal level of education, like paternal level of education, appears to be positively related to women's career orientation and choice of nontraditional careers. Harmon (1978) reported that women receiving Ph.D.'s have more highly educated parents than do men receiving Ph.D.'s across academic fields, and Freun et al. (1974) reported that female medical school applicants have more highly educated parents than do male applicants. Mothers' levels of education were found to be related to greater career orientation in their daughters in several studies (Almquist & Angrist, 1971; Del Vento Bielby, 1978; Patrick, 1973). Highly educated mothers have been consistently overrepresented in samples of women preferring and pursuing nontraditional professions (Astin, 1969; Haber, 1980; Harmon, 1978; O'Donnell & Anderson, 1978; Hutchins, 1966; Russo & O'Connell, 1980; Wertheim et al., 1978).

In summary, the data generally suggest that women's career development is influenced by variables related to maternal employment and by the educational levels of both parents. As was previously suggested, however, aspects of the parent–child relationship may moderate the impact of these demographic variables on women's career development and/or may directly affect that development. Relationship variables investigated in the literature include identification with, perceived similarity to, and preference for one or both parents, emotional closeness versus distance in the parent–child relationship, and the extent of parental encouragement and support of daughter's achievement-related aspirations and behaviors.

Some studies suggest that career-oriented women tend to identify more with their fathers than with their mothers (Helson, 1971; Oliver, 1975; Sostek, 1963), while home-oriented women are more likely to identify with their mothers (Johnson, 1970; Oliver, 1975). Birnbaum (1975) found that nontraditionals said they had been closer to their fathers and resembled them intellectually. Since greater identification is postulated to increase the effectiveness of a role model, these findings are logical if parents model traditional sex role behaviors. Although a relationship between career orientation and father identification has been reported, Epstein's (1968) female lawyers reported feeling closer to their fathers than to their mothers, whereas Oliver's (1975) career-oriented women felt less accepted by their fathers than did the home-oriented women studied. Other studies have suggested that career-oriented women tend to more often come from homes characterized by parental permissiveness (Kriger, 1972) and greater psychological distance, facilitating the development of autonomy and self-sufficiency in parent–child relationships (Nageley, 1971; Tangri, 1972).

Although findings such as these are interesting and, in many cases, intuitively reasonable, the body of research concerning parental identification and psychological distance versus closeness is too small to permit conclusions. A larger and relatively consistent group of studies, however, support the important role of parental encouragement and support in daughters' career development.

Family encouragement was reported as a major facilitator by high school girls planning careers in science (McLure & Piel, 1978), by female medical students (Cartwright, 1972), and by samples of women pursuing male-dominated occupations (Haber, 1980; Houser & Garvey, 1985; Standley & Soule, 1974). For example, 72% of Standley and Soule's architects, lawyers, physicians, and psychologists reported being the child of whom their parents had been proudest, and 60% reported being their father's favorite child. The extent of encouragement from fathers has been found to differentiate pioneers from traditionals in several studies (Astin & Myint, 1971; Katz, 1969; Nagely, 1971; Turner & McCaffrey, 1974). Nontraditional women have also reported higher expectations from their parents in terms of educational attainments and occupational involvement (O'Donnell & Anderson, 1978; Patrick, 1973), while traditional women perceived their parents as less supportive of career pursuits than did pioneers in the study by Trigg and Perlman (1976). Farmer (1985) found that parent support was one of the strongest predictors of young women's career aspirations and motivation.

Possibly as important as parental encouragement of daughters' achievements is a concomitant lack of pressure toward the traditional female role. Parents who exert less pressure on their daughters to date, marry, and have children have been found to have more career-oriented daughters (Haber, 1980; Matthews & Tiedeman, 1964), as have parents who place less emphasis on the development of stereotypically feminine qualities (Turner & McCaffrey, 1974).

While parental variables, then, appear to be important in relation to women's career development, a major limitation of this research is the assumption that both parents are present while the girl is growing up.

Research on father-absent children has focused primarily on boys (e.g., see Bannon & Southern, 1980) and little is known about women raised in single-parent or adoptive homes or with relatives or non-family members. Dramatic increases in the number of single-parent homes (e.g., Hoffman, 1977; VanDusen & Sheldon, 1976) suggest that research based on nuclear family assumptions will be increasingly irrelevant to an understanding of the career development of many women and men.

A final family background variable is birth order. Numerous researchers have noted the predominance of first-borns (including "only" children) among high achievers (Eysenck & Cookson, 1970; Helmreich, Spence, Beane, Lucker, & Matthews, 1980; Schachter, 1963). Compared to the percentage of first-borns in the general population, first-borns were significantly overrepresented in Astin's (1969) and Helmreich *et al.*'s (1980) samples of female Ph.D.'s, in Standley and Soule's (1974) sample of female professionals, and in Patrick's (1973) sample of female graduates of highly competitive colleges. Nuttall, Nuttall, Polit, and Hunter (1976) found that even after controlling for IQ, first-born girls were higher in academic achievement than were later-borns. Other studies, however, have not found birth order to differentiate pioneers from traditionals (Crawford, 1978; Greenfield *et al.*, 1980), or to differentiate person-oriented from non-person-oriented individuals (Weller, Shlumi, & Zimont, 1976). The importance of this variable in women's career development is not yet firmly established.

THE INFLUENCE OF MARRIAGE AND CHILDREN

As stated by Osipow (1975), Matthews and Tiedeman (1964), and others, the major difficulty in women's career development is the certainty of marriage and motherhood in the future plans of most women. Indeed, the most consistent predictor of women's career orientation and innovation through the years is their adult marital/familial status or, among girls and young women, their plans for marriage and children. In considering the relationship of marital/familial status to women's career development, it should be noted that the relationship to labor force participation per se has been weakening as we have witnessed tremendous increases in participation among women in *all* marital and parental categories. However, the relationship of marital/parental status to career attainment, commitment, and innovation has remained strong.

Early studies found that career-oriented and/or employed women are less likely than home-oriented women to be married (e.g., Del Vento Bielby, 1978; Gysbers *et al.*, 1968; Harmon, 1970; Stake, 1979b; Tinsley & Faunce, 1980; Yuen, Tinsley, & Tinsley, 1980). Career-oriented women are more likely than home-oriented women to plan to defer marriage (Houseknecht, 1978; Parsons *et al.*, 1978; Tangri, 1972; Watley & Kaplan, 1971) and, when studied as adults, married at later ages than their home-oriented counterparts (Card *et al.*, 1980; Harmon, 1970). Stewart (1980) found negative relationships between marriage and children and career persistence and nature in women who were freshmen in 1960 and were followed-up in 1974.

In comparison to women who marry, women who remain single achieve higher levels of education (Gigy, 1980; Houseknecht & Spanier, 1980) and are substantially more likely to pursue male-dominated occupations (Astin & Myint, 1971; Card *et al.*, 1980; Del Vento Bielby, 1980; Gigy, 1980). Not only are professional women more often single than other women, they are more likely than *male* professionals to be single (e.g., Bailey & Burrell, 1981; Helmreich *et al.*, 1980). Among other things, the norm of hypergamy in this culture (the tendency for men to marry downward educationally) makes it easier for a professional man than a professional woman to find a mate.

In addition, Houseknecht and Spanier (1980) reported that women with 5 or more years of postsecondary education have one of the highest rates of marital disruption (i.e., divorce, widowhood, previous divorces among the currently married). Thus, it seems that highly educated, career-oriented women are more likely to remain single, to defer marriage, or to find their marriages disrupted. While the large majority of young women wish to combine career and marriage, for example, 95% in Rand and Miller's (1972) sample, and may not see marriage and children as a deterrent to a nontraditional career (Zuckerman, 1980), the data suggest that successful combination of marriage, children and high-level professional pursuits is not a simple matter. While marital status has little bearing on men's career development, it is an important variable influencing the career development of women.

Career-oriented women also tend to have and/or want fewer, if any, children (Card *et al.*, 1980; Greenfield *et al.*, 1980; Harmon, 1970; Tickamyer, 1979; Tinsley & Faunce, 1980), and the presence and number of children are negatively related to the pursuit of nontraditional occupations (Astin & Myint, 1971; Greenfield *et al.*, 1980). Just as female professionals are less likely than male professionals to be married, female professionals are less likely to have children and, if they do have children, tend to have fewer than do male professionals (e.g., Bailey & Burrell, 1981; Helmreich *et al.*, 1980). Studies of voluntary childlessness, which is increasing in frequency (Hoffman, 1977; Kearney, 1979), tend to corroborate the above pattern of findings in that voluntarily childless women are likely to be strongly career oriented, highly educated, and disproportionately employed (Houseknecht, 1978, 1979).

In early research on women's career development, the strong association between singleness and career orientation led to questions concerning the direction of causality—that is, did failure in or inadequacy with regard to heterosexual relationships lead to forced singlehood which, in turn, led to career orientation as compensation for lack of marital roles? Or did high achievement motivation and strong career orientation lead to reduced heterosexual affiliation and/or a decision that remaining single or deferring marriage would most facilitate career achievements? The former explanation, known as the deviance hypothesis (Almquist & Angrist, 1971) or the compensation model (Sedney & Turner, 1975), has not been supported by research. In contrast the latter explanation, known as the enrichment model (Almquist & Angrist, 1971; Sedney & Turner, 1975), has received considerable empirical support (Lemkau, 1979; Tangri, 1972).

That career-oriented women are not heterosexually deficient has been supported by Almquist's (1974) findings of equivalent frequencies of dating and extracurricular activities in girls planning nontraditional and traditional careers. Tangri's (1972) findings that role innovators did not differ from other women in their reported number of romantic relationships, and Colwill and Ross' (1978) finding that the scores of female medical students on the EPPS Heterosexuality Scale were higher than were those obtained in the normative group of female college students. On the basis of their research, Sedney and Turner (1975) concluded that career orientation develops in the context of normal heterosexual affiliation, and that dating frequency begins to decrease only in college, when serious pursuit of career goals increases in saliency. In a sample of male and female high school students, Lanier and Byre (1981) found a correlation of .79 between perceptions of a woman as professionally employed and perceptions of her attractiveness—clearly *not* a stereotype of an unattractive career woman!

While there is little support for a compensatory or deviance model (Helson, 1972), several studies suggest that high achievement motivation and career orientation follow from enriching experiences which lead young women to have broadened conceptions of the female role and of their own potential achievements (Helson, 1972). In addition to indicating that career-oriented and/or pioneer women are more likely to have well-educated parents and working mothers, research has also suggested that pioneer women had more work experience in high school and college (Almquist, 1974), had more role-broadening work experience in high school and college (O'Donnell & Anderson, 1978), and come from home environments fostering achievement, independence, and active exploration of the environment (Helson, 1972; Lemkau, 1979). Lemkau (1979) concluded that "it takes unusual but positive circumstances to foster the androgynous individuation which manifests itself in an atypical [innovative] career choice" (p. 237).

An important aspect of the environment is the attitude of significant men/males in that environment (or at least the women's perceptions of those attitudes). Hawley (1972) found that women pursuing traditionally female careers were more likely than those pursuing nontraditional careers to believe that men divided the world into women's roles/work versus men's roles/work and that they held traditional views of sex roles, whereas women in the sciences perceived men as more equalitarian. Edwards (1969) found that the values of marriage-oriented women were most closely related to the perceived values of their boyfriends. In contrast, the values of career-oriented women were unrelated to the perceived values of significant others and, rather, were self-determined.

Another issue of great concern has pertained to the effects of maternal employment on children. Generally, research suggests that *maternal employment does not* adversely affect a child's intellectual, social, or emotional development (see Etaugh, 1980; Hoffman & Nye, 1974).

Finally, Stewart (1980) suggested that marital/parental status sets broad limits on vocational behavior, and that within those limits, personality variables affect *specific* behaviors. Stewart (1980) found that a high degree of "self-definition" (related to instrumentality or independence) was related to professional status in relatively unconstrained women (single or, at a minimum, childless) and to freelance activity in the home in constrained women (married with children). Thus, marital and familial status served to moderate and clarify the study of the relationship of *personality* and career development.

INFLUENCE OF ROLE MODELS

The literature regarding the selection of occupational role models indicates that males almost always report other males (e.g., fathers, male professors) as their significant models and influences (e.g., Brown, Aldrich, & Hall, 1978; Weishaar, Green, & Craighead, 1981).

Females, on the other hand, are likely to report both male and female models (Andberg, Follett, & Hendel, 1979; Basow & Howe, 1978, 1980; Brown *et al.*, 1978; Kutner & Brogan, 1980; Weishaar *et al.*, 1981). Thus, while males follow a pattern of same-sex modeling, the lack of female occupational role models (Douvan, 1976; O'Connell & Russo, 1980) necessitates opposite-sex as well as same-sex modeling in the facilitation of females' career development (Douvan, 1976). As stated by Weishaar *et al.* (1981), in the absence of female models, women rely on male models. Phelan (1979) documented the critical importance of direct contact with faculty in the development of female scholarly orientation.

The literature suggests the importance of such models, male and female, in women's career development (O'Leary, 1974). Some studies have suggested that choice of a pioneer occupation is related to having a male model (Weishaar *et al.*, 1981; O'Donnell & Anderson, 1978). Handley and Hickson (1978) found that mathematically talented women who had chosen traditionally female math-related occupations (e.g., secondary school teaching) usually cited female models, while two thirds of those majoring in engineering, accounting, or mathematics cited male role models as most influential. Other research supports the importance of female role models. O'Connell (1978), in a review of barriers to women doing research in psychology, documented the importance of female role models for the pursuit of nontraditional occupational roles. For example, Andberg *et al.*'s (1979) study of female veterinary students suggested the important role of female veterinarians as occupational role models; Tidball (1980) found that colleges employing a greater proportion of female faculty members had proportionately higher-achieving female students. Support from teachers and professors was important in the selection of pioneer occupations in studies by Andberg *et al.* (1979), Angrist (1974), Kutner and Brogan (1980), McLure and Piel (1978), and Tangri (1972) and in the development of high career salience (Almquist & Angrist, 1970, 1971; Simpson & Simpson, 1961; Stake & Levitz, 1979). Farmer (1980) found that the support of teachers, parents, and peers was essential to the career motivation of 10th-grade girls.

While role models and encouragement and support from significant others appear to facilitate women's career development relative to that of other women, it should be noted that there has been a serious lack of female models of educational and occupational achievement for girls and young women to observe and emulate (Douvan, 1976), and that girls and women in general receive less support for achievement-related behavior than do men (Goodale & Hall, 1976; McLure & Piel, 1978). In a study of medical school students, Kutner and Brogan (1980) reported that the female students reported receiving more encouragement from male than female professors and physicians (not totally surprising, given the shortage of the latter) and that 50% had also been *discouraged* from their aspirations by parents and professors (versus only 14% of males). Thus, while the availability of environmental supports assists in the explanation of women's career orientation and innovation, the lack of such supports is a major barrier to the career development of most women.

SUMMARY

To summarize, a variety of variables in the cultural, subcultural, and social environments of females influence both the extent to which they develop strong levels of career orientation and achievement and the nature of their career choices. In a society which has not encouraged nor valued career orientation and career achievement in women, the development of those characteristics has to some extent depended on a more favorable immediate social environment, including familial encouragement and emphasis on educational attainment, positive role models (especially working mothers), and support for the postponement of marital and parental responsibilities while educational and career goals are being met.

But regardless of the favorable nature of the immediate environment, society has numerous ways of impressing upon women the advisability of conformance to the traditional female role. The educational system and counseling services have traditionally served to reinforce societal messages—these are the topics of the next two chapters.

WOMEN'S CAREER CHOICES:
THE INFLUENCE OF EDUCATION

INTRODUCTION

Two of the most important influences on women's career development are the educational system, discussed in this chapter, and the counseling profession, to be covered in Chapter 5. As will be discussed, the educational system and the counseling profession are extremely powerful influences, ranging from very negative if they serve to perpetuate traditional sex role stereotypes and sex biases to very positive when they are used in ways facilitative of sex fairness and the maximization of individual potential. Furthermore, these two institutions are among the most amenable to social change effort and, therefore, offer considerable promise for the facilitation of women's career development. This chapter provides a review of the relationship of the educational system to women's career development.

THE IMPORTANCE OF EDUCATION TO WOMEN'S CAREER DEVELOPMENT

It is probably difficult to overestimate the importance of education to career development and achievements. At a very basic level, early schooling serves as a major source of learning and socialization and conveys values regarding work and career that are influential throughout one's life. More specifically, the nature and level of obtained education are important in relation to subsequent career achievements and adult socioeconomic status and life-style. For example, an undergraduate degree is now a necessary minimum requirement for the pursuit of many occupations, and graduate or professional education is

53

the only route to careers in academe and most other professions. In general, appropriate educational preparation is a major "gate" for occupational entrance. Education creates options, while lack of education closes them, and without options, the concept of "choice" itself has no real meaning. Thus, the decisions the individual makes concerning her/his higher education, both the level and major areas of study, will be among the most *important career decisions* she/he ever makes. Further, success and survival in the educational programs chosen will be critical to the successful implementation of these career decisions.

While education is an important variable in the study of men's career development, the nature and level of obtained education are strongly related to *almost every major dependent variable* used in the description of women's career development. Along with marital status, education is considered to be the most important variable in women's career development (Gysbers *et al.*, 1968; Harmon, 1970; Watley & Kaplan, 1971; Wolfson, 1976). One of the most striking and consistent relationships is that the more education a woman receives, the more likely she is to be working outside the home as an adult, regardless of her marital or parental status (e.g., Blaska, 1978; Carnegie Commission on Higher Education, 1973; Houseknecht & Spanier, 1980; Huth, 1978; Vetter, 1980). For example, in 1977 62% of women with Bachelor's degrees and 85% of those with Master's degrees were in the labor force (Vetter, 1980). The effect of higher education was particularly striking for women with degrees in science and engineering—from 63 to 84% of Bachelor's degrees in science, from 78 to 88% of Master's degrees in science, and from 90 to 96% of women with science Ph.D.'s or professional degrees were employed. Also, close to half of Bachelor's and Master's degree recipients *not* in the labor force were working on advanced degrees!

Although an important reason for highly educated women to be out of the labor force is the presence of young children, this factor is usually superseded by advanced education in Vetter's (1980) sample of women scientists and engineers: labor force participation rates ranged from 51% of mothers whose highest education was the Bachelor's degree to 91% of mothers with a Ph.D. Overall, between 80 and 85% of women with degrees in science or engineering are in the labor force, with participation ranging from about 50% of women with Bachelor's degrees who have preschool children to more than 95% of women with doctorates or professional degrees. (Note that data such as these effectively counter arguments that education is wasted on women—clearly most highly educated women are indeed contributing in the labor force as well as in other ways.)

In addition to greater labor force participation, educational level is related to greater labor force participation among women, whether married or not (Blaska, 1978; Houseknecht & Spanier, 1980; Huth, 978), to stronger career orientation and career salience (Astin & Myint, 1971; Gysbers *et al.*, 1968; Harmon, 1970; Tinsley & Faunce, 1980; Watley & Kaplan, 1971; Wolfson, 1976), and to the choice of pioneer versus traditional occupations (Almquist, 1974; Astin, 1968; Greenfield *et al.*, 1980; Lemkau, 1979).

It should be noted parenthetically that even though education has a strongly facilitative effect on women's career achievements, the financial and status benefits of education for women have traditionally been far less than those for men. For example, U.S. Labor Department data indicate that while a woman with a college degree employed full-time earns more than a woman with less education, she earns no more than a *man* with an 8th-grade education (U.S. Department of Labor, 1984). A woman employed full-time who finished high school is no better off financially than men who failed to complete elementary school. Bailey and Burrell (1981) demonstrated how receipt of a graduate degree from Harvard is far more beneficial if the recipient is male than female. Substantial differences in favor of men in salary and in the rank and status of the position held were found in comparable samples of male and female graduate degree holders.

Given the importance, then, of educational attainments to women's career development, the factors influencing women's educational aspirations and achievements, and their experiences and satisfaction in the educational system, are of central interest to those interested in their career development. Yet, not unexpectedly, the educational system has practiced and perpetuated stereotypes and biases that have made educational progress and success in many ways more problematic for females than for males. Among other things, females have *lower* educational aspirations than do males of comparable ability (Sewell & Hauser, 1975) and the attrition rates are higher for females than males at every level of higher education. These findings hold even though females perform *better academically* in comparison to males at every level of education (Carnegie Commission on Higher Education, 1973; Tyler, 1965). Few would disagree that the education of women, like that of other minorities, has not been of either the quality or quantity of that received by white males (e.g., see Finn, Dulberg, & Reis, 1979) and that, therefore, a *potentially* facilitative influence on women's career development has been negated or at least reduced in effectiveness by stereotypes, biases, and barriers confronted by girls and women in the educational system. The next sections review the barriers to and biases about women in the educational system, beginning with elementary and secondary schools and continuing with higher education, including graduate and professional education. This chapter will continue the focus on environmental variables influencing women's career development by focusing primarily on external barriers in the educational system rather than on individual factors influencing educational achievement and attainment.

ELEMENTARY AND SECONDARY SCHOOL EDUCATION

Sex Bias in Education

The early schooling children receive is, of course, critical in terms of transmitting basic cognitive and social skills, but it is also a major source of sex role socialization, a source of messages concerning appropriate behaviors and roles for girls versus boys and women versus men. Unfortunately, schools have long been communicating to children the same sex biases which characterize society as a whole (see, for example, Kutner & Brogan, 1976; Lockheed & Ekstrom, 1977; National Project on Women in Education, 1978; Pottker & Fishel, 1977; and Westervelt, 1975, for comprehensive reviews of the literature on sex discrimination in education). Although both males and females are victims of sex discrimination in educational systems, females are assumed to be victims to a greater extent than males because the discrimination against females serves to limit and restrict their options and achievements (Kutner & Brogan, 1976).

Wirtenberg and Nakamura (1976) contended, for example, that education plays a dominant role in the ultimate sexual stratification of the labor force through its effects on females' aspirations, expectations, preparation, and occupational attitudes. As was mentioned in Chapter 3, occupational stereotypes are found consistently in elementary school children and influence their occupational preferences. Both boys and girls tend to choose sex-typed occupations (Frost & Diamond, 1979; Looft, 1971; Tremaine & Schau, 1979), although girls are somewhat more likely to select stereotypically male occupations than are boys to select stereotypically female occupations (Gettys & Cann,

1981). Although children of both sexes select sex-stereotypic occupational choices, the smaller number and more limited range of traditionally female occupations (Bird, 1968) result in the limitation of girls' perceived options at very early ages.

In Looft's (1971) sample of 1st and 2nd graders, Siegel's (1973) sample of 2nd graders, and Nelson's (1978) sample of 3rd graders, boys were found to indicate a wide variety of occupational preferences, almost all of them male dominated. Girls, on the other hand, listed a smaller number of occupations, and their choices were dominated by two occupations: nurse and teacher. In Siegel's sample, for example, 70% of 2nd-grade girls selected either nurse or teacher, while the 32 boys chose 20 different occupations. Finally, Kriedberg, Butcher, and White (1978) found that while some 2nd-grade girls expressed interest in male-dominated occupations, almost all 6th-grade girls chose traditionally female occupations. It is unfortunate indeed that occupational stereotypes have limited girls' perceived career options before they finish elementary school.

Although the educational system is certainly not the only source of sex bias and sex role stereotyping, it is a major one. Wirtenberg and Nakamura (1976) contended that research supports the existence of several educational practices contributing to the limitation of females' career options. These practices include use of textbooks and instructional materials containing sex role stereotyping, different curricula for males and females, and vocational counseling and testing (to be reviewed in the next chapter).

Pervasive sex role stereotyping in school readers and textbooks has been widely documented. For example, several major studies (Women on Words and Images, 1972; Howe, 1979; Key, 1975; Scott, 1981) have examined the portrayals of boys and girls and men and women in school readers and textbooks. The portrayals have consistently been stereotypic and, for those interested in equity for women, dismaying. At a very basic level, boys and men appear as story characters far more often than do girls and women, thus implying something about the relative importance and interest of the two sexes. Women portrayed in the readers have almost always been limited to the role of mother, and when they do work (generally as nurses, teachers, or secretaries), it is out of financial necessity rather than because of inherent interest or desire to use their talents and abilities. The predominant portrayal of women/females as mommies is well captured by Alleen Nilsen's (1971) term "cult of the apron," coined after she found that, of 58 children's books on display at a book fair, 21 had pictures of women wearing aprons. Even the female animals wore aprons! Men were portrayed as workers and fathers—the message conveyed has been that men work *and* have families but women do one *or* the other.

As dismaying as the differential role portrayals of adults are the portrayals of differential capabilities and personalities of boys and girls. One major difference may be summarized as "Boys do and girls watch." Boys are portrayed as active, resourceful, brave, and creative and as *problem-solvers*, whereas girls are portrayed as passive, helpless, and dull (Scott, 1981). Girls, through stupidity, get into rough spots from which boys rescue them. One children's book entitled "I'm glad I'm a boy! I'm glad I'm a girl!" taught such differences as "Boys invent things" and "Girls use what boys invent" (cf. Key, 1975, p. 56). Sexist views of women and men are being taught to children from the first school readers they use.

In addition to elementary school texts and readers, sex-biased content has been demonstrated to characterize texts in all substantive areas and from secondary school to higher education (e.g., see Key, 1975; Lockheed & Ekstrom, 1977; Martin, 1982; Pottker & Fishel, 1977). Women continue to be portrayed primarily in domestic situations. They were absent from history, philosophy, art, and music and were treated in biased and stereotyped ways (when not ignored completely) in psychology, medicine, anthropology, and education (Howe, 1979). The sexism and sex bias in teacher education texts (Sadker & Sadker, 1980) serves to ensure that teachers themselves will be taught biased ways of dealing with children.

In addition to the models of maleness and femaleness portrayed in their texts, the genders of school personnel have reinforced traditional stereotypes. Elementary school teachers are primarily female, but the principals (the "bosses") are primarily male (e.g., Lockheed & Ekstrom, 1977; Wasserman, 1974). High school teachers, while balanced by sex, teach in stereotypic subject matter areas—females predominate in the teaching of literature and the arts, and males predominate in the teaching of math and science (and, of course, the possible existence of a male high school home economics teacher or a female electronics teacher is difficult to imagine). Males also predominate in secondary as well as elementary school administration (cf. Lockheed & Ekstrom, 1977).

As reviewed by many researchers (Weitzman, 1979; Lockheed & Ekstrom, 1977; Maccoby & Jacklin, 1974; and Sadker & Sadker, 1985, among others), there is also evidence that teachers themselves respond differently to boys and girls. Although much more research is needed to understand teachers' reactions under different conditions, some preliminary generalizations are that boys receive more attention, both positive and negative, from teachers. While they may receive more disapproval, they also receive more positive attention, encouragement, and approval. Second, while there may not be differential encouragement of sex role-appropriate behaviors, sex role reversals are often punished, particularly if they occur in boys, and are almost never reinforced. What these findings suggest is that a boy, but not a girl, who behaves in stereotypically feminine ways will likely be punished. Given that stereotypic femininity is viewed as less socially desirable and "adultlike" than stereotypic masculinity, teachers are clearly treating the sexes inequitably. In contrast, a girl may be punished or, at a minimum, ignored and so not reinforced for the masculine-stereotypic behaviors traditionally considered socially desirable, adultlike, and mentally healthy (for example, an active and instrumental approach to her world and a mastery- and achievement-oriented spirit).

In addition to sex bias in materials and teacher behaviors are differential expectations for curriculum involvement and performance. As reviewed by Weitzman (1979) and Wirtenberg and Nakamura (1976), most schools have had a sex-stereotyped tracking system in which girls are channeled into "feminine" subjects such as English, social studies, typing, and bookkeeping, and boys are encouraged to "tackle" (note the athletic analogy) the hard sciences. Weitzman (1979) cited a 1970 listing of courses offered in the New York City public high schools in which 76 are designated "technical courses restricted to males" and the 36 courses in homemaking and office work subjects are designated for females. Saario, Jacklin, and Tittle (1973) reported results of a nationwide survey of sex-based vocational tracking: 93% of students in consumer and homemaking courses and 75% in office courses were female, while 92% of those in technical courses and 89% in trade and industrial courses were male. As reviewed by Wirtenberg and Nakamura (1976), girls are expected to excel in reading and language, while boys are to excel in math and science. Even though it may now be *possible* for girls to take industrial arts, such as shop courses in wood, electricity, and metal, and for boys to take home economics and secretarial courses, they are probably not encouraged to do so and may in fact be punished for crossing the boundaries of sex-stereotypic behavior. Joyce and Hall (1977) suggested the unique but insufficiently utilized role of guidance counselors in the encouragement of girls to take mechanical and electronic shop courses and math and science courses in high school. Although the important topic of sex bias in counseling will be covered in the next chapter, suffice it to say that without the interventions of counselors, teachers, and school administrators as well as of interested parents, the educational preparation of girls will continue to be different from and inferior to that of boys.

Thus, past educational practices have ensured that children learn early that gender is an appropriate basis from which to make educational and occupational decisions and that abilities, talents, and interests are less important, if important at all. Federal legislation and awareness of the existing biases has led to some attempts to design and implement nonsexist school curricula and to write nonsexist textbooks and readers. The report of the National Project on Women in Education, entitled "Taking Sexism out of Education," offered numerous guidelines for correcting sex biases in school curricula and changing teacher attitudes and behaviors and texts and other instructional materials. Guttentag and Bray (1976) provided a suggested nonsexist curriculum for early childhood through elementary school, while Kimmel, Dickenson, and Topping (1981) described a program for intervention in teacher education programs. (Kimmel *et al.* also noted the dismaying findings that students of both sexes enrolled in teacher training programs are the most traditional and conventional and, by implication, most biased of all college students.) While some efforts to change the educational system have been made, the situation in elementary and secondary school education continues to be characterized by biased and stereotypic treatment of the sexes (e.g., Scott, 1981). For girls and women, this treatment often serves to limit their view of their capabilities and options, and thereby adversely affects their career development.

WOMEN AND HIGHER EDUCATION

Because of the importance of higher education to so many occupations, particularly those in the professions, fulfillment of the promise of equal opportunity in this country has necessitated equal access to educational opportunities. Yet, as has been documented in considerable research and several major recent summaries of this topic (e.g., Carnegie Commission on Higher Education, 1973; Furniss & Graham, 1974; Howe, 1979; Randour, Strasburg, & Lipmen-Blumen, 1982; Rossi & Calderwood, 1973; Westervelt, 1975), women's opportunities in the educational system, particularly higher education, are nowhere near equal to those of men. Historically and even currently in some quarters, women have not been viewed as belonging in higher education, and their achievements have suffered accordingly. Although the literature on women in higher education is extensive enough to easily warrant several volumes, the following section will provide a brief overview of the status of and barriers to women in higher education, including graduate and professional school. The section will conclude with a summary of federal legislation designed to address inequities in the educational system.

WOMEN IN HIGHER EDUCATION: AN HISTORICAL OVERVIEW

As discussed by Merritt (1976) and Graham (1978), women have always had an uphill battle in American higher education. As recently as the 19th century, higher education was viewed as inappropriate for women. Although it was considered appropriate for women to be taught to play a musical instrument, embroider, or to speak a genteel language such as French, any serious "book learning" was viewed as potentially dangerous to women's fragile (i.e., "inferior") minds and, worse, to their reproductive capacities. An illustrative opinion of the purpose of educating women was "Chemistry enough to keep the pot boiling and geography enough to know the location of different rooms in her house is learning sufficient for a woman" (Merritt, 1976, p. 354).

At first, the few women who did receive higher education came from wealthy families who valued higher education; very often such women were both gifted and were the only children of encouraging fathers. However, in 1821, Emma Willard founded the first female college or "seminary" in New York with the idea that education should be more widely available to women. Although the curriculum at Willard's seminary was mostly stereotypically female (including the domestic arts; the "ornamental" studies of drawing, painting, and music; and religious and moral studies), there was also an opportunity to study the "natural philosophy" that men were also studying at the time.

The first coeducational college was Oberlin College, which opened in 1833. Women were first admitted in 1837, with the idea that this would provide ministers with educated and cultured wives. Although women were allowed to study the same subjects as men, they were at first limited to shortened versions of the men's courses. Further, women students were expected to perform domestic chores for the male students, such as washing their clothes and serving their meals, and were discouraged from speaking in public gatherings if men were present. Thus, although the founders of Oberlin were pioneers in advancing women's educational opportunities, they continued to devalue women's intellect and to insist on the maintenance of women's place as subservient to men.

Mount Holyoke College, founded in 1857, and Vassar College, opened in 1865, were the first women's colleges and the first to strongly emphasize academic rigor and achievement for women. Other "seven sisters" colleges such as Smith, Wellesley, and "Harvard Annex," later known as Radcliffe, followed shortly. In addition to women's colleges, the Morrill Act of 1862 assisted in the establishment of land-grant universities which, along with most other state university systems, were open to women.

Once colleges were open to them, women's enrollment began to increase. Although partly due to a shortage of male students because of the Civil War, women constituted 21% of college and university students by 1870. However, because of almost total employment discrimination against women, most educated women had few options other than elementary or secondary school teaching or marriage and homemaking.

By the end of the 19th century, women were also being admitted at least occasionally to graduate and professional schools, although progress was slow and painful. A short discussion of the case of medical school admissions is illustrative and not atypical. When Elizabeth Blackwell attempted to gain entrance to medical school in the 1840s, all of the nation's 42 medical schools were male-only institutions (Walsh, 1979). The Geneva Medical College put Blackwell's application to a vote of the *student body* and stipulated that *even one negative vote* was sufficient to reject her. To the consternation of everyone but Blackwell, the students thought that her application was a joke and voted unanimously to accept her. Although Blackwell was allowed to graduate, no other women, including Blackwell's sister Emily, were permitted to enroll. Emily was accepted at Rush Medical College in Chicago until the College rescinded her admission after being censured by the Illinois Medical Society. To fill the need for medical education for women, a few women's medical colleges were opened, and it was not until the 1870s that a few traditional, male-only medical schools agreed to admit women.

The increase in enrollment of women in higher education continued during the early part of this century, reaching a high point in the year 1930 but then showing a sharp decline that did not fully correct itself until the early 1970s. In 1900, women earned 20% of the Master's degrees and 6% of the doctorates, but by 1930 these percentages had increased to 40% and 15%, respectively. The decline that began then, probably as a result of the Depression and, later, World War II (after which women were sent home from the labor force in which they had actively participated) did not fully reverse until about 1970. Since 1970, women have made additional gains in higher educational enrollment.

One of the last bastions of male exclusivity within the higher educational systems has been the military service academies, for example, West Point and Annapolis. In 1975 President Gerald R. Ford signed into law a bill which authorized the admission of women to the United States Naval, Military, and Air Force Academies by June of 1976. Although the number of women in the service academies is still comparatively small (women were to be admitted on a "basis consistent with the needs of the services"), the existence of these schools as at least an *option* for women does represent an improvement over past denial of access.

Although women have, then, made progress in the educational system, they continue to be seriously disadvantaged relative to males. Women's current status in higher education is the subject of the next section.

THE CURRENT STATUS OF WOMEN IN HIGHER EDUCATION

Women have been and continue to be educationally disadvantaged in terms of both the level and nature of their obtained higher education. In terms of obtained *level* of education, "the higher, the fewer" has been and continues to be an accurate and succinct summary of the status of women in higher education. Women's enrollments exceed those of men only at the junior (2-year) college level and remain below those of men at every higher level, from 4-year colleges and universities to graduate and professional schools. (A professional degree is herein viewed as one requiring at least 2 years of college work for entrance and at least 6 academic years for completion. Professional degrees in medicine, dentistry, optometry, osteopathic medicine, pharmacy, podiatry, veterinary medicine, chiropractic, law, and theology are the main professional degrees as defined.) In every field, there is an *inverse* relationship between the level of the degree and the proportion of degree recipients who are women.

Although detailed data are available from several sources (Grant & Eiden, 1981; Pepin, 1980; Pepin, Knepper, Bales, Barttell, Shulman, & Williams, 1982; Randour et al., 1982), several overall conclusions regarding the enrollment of women in higher education may be stated. In terms of *growth* in enrollment, women's enrollments have increased at a faster rate than have those of men, particularly at the older age levels of 25 and over, the so-called "reentry" student. [Men's enrollments in 4-year colleges are actually declining, possibly because of the availability of other means to career entry (e.g., technical training, on-the-job training).] From 1963 to 1979 the percentage of women's enrollment in 2-year colleges had increased from 37 to 54%. From 1968 to 1979 women's enrollments in 4-year institutions increased from 41 to 48%. During the period from 1968 to 1979, the percentage of Bachelor's degrees earned by women increased from 38 to 48%.

Women's enrollment has also increased at the postgraduate level. During the period from 1960 to 1979, women's share of degrees increased from 32 to 49% at the Master's degree level, from 10 to 28% of doctorates, and from 3 to 24% of professional degrees. However, at the graduate and professional levels, women still constitute substantially fewer enrollees and degree recipients, and are more likely to be enrolled in less prestigious schools or in public versus private institutions, and to be enrolled part-time versus full-time, in comparison to male students.

Even though the percentage of women earning degrees has increased, their degrees are still predominantly in the female-dominated fields which provide lower pay and lower status (Peng & Jaffe, 1979; Randour et al., 1982; Thomas, 1980; Tremaine & Hartman, 1981). Table 4.1 shows the percentages of female degree recipients in 1979 as a function of degree level and academic field. It may be noted that at the Bachelor's degree level, women are still concentrated in the traditionally female fields of education, fine and applied arts, foreign languages, health professions, home economics, and library science. Note also that while in 1979 women earned 68% of the doctorates in home economics and 54% of the doctorates in foreign languages, they earned only 3% of the doctorates in engineering, 11% of those in physics, and 12% of those in business.

Although most women continue to earn degrees in traditionally female fields, there has been some movement into some of the male-dominated majors and professional schools. From 1970 to 1979 the percentage of women earning degrees in law increased from 5 to 28%, while the increase in medicine was from 8 to 23%. Women's share of Bachelor's degrees in business management grew from 9% in 1971 to 30% in 1979 and in engineering from <1% in 1971 to 8% in 1979.

To summarize at this point, the status of women in higher education is characterized by the juxtaposition of progress in enrollment and

TABLE 4.1 Percentages of Degrees Awarded to Women in Various Academic Fields

Academic field	Percentage awarded to women		
	Bachelor's	Master's	Doctorates
Agriculture	27	20	8
Architecture	26	29	23
Biological sciences	40	38	26
Business and management	31	19	12
Communication	50	49	28
Computer and information sciences	28	19	13
Education	73	69	42
Engineering	8	6	3
Fine and applied arts	63	54	35
Foreign languages	76	70	54
Health professions	82	71	37
Home economics	95	91	68
Law	40	16	15
Letters	58	61	41
Library science	95	80	51
Mathematics	42	35	17
Military sciences	3	0	—
Physical sciences	23	18	11
Psychology	61	54	40
Public affairs	53	51	30
Social sciences	42	35	29
Theology	26	32	5

Note. Data were obtained from the National Center for Education Statistics (1979, Note 1). Letters describes fields in the humanities, English, comparative literature, classics, linguistics, speech, creative writing, philosophy, and religious studies (excluding theological professions).

earned degree percentages and some movement into male-dominated fields and, in contrast, continued disadvantage relative to men as a group. Most women still earn their degrees in lower-paying, lower-status, female-intensive fields. There is also an inverse relationship between the *level* of the degree and the percentage of women earning the degree. At the graduate level, women are less often enrolled in the high-prestige universities and are more likely enrolled part-time versus full-time in comparison to men. Women predominate only in community colleges, which have less impact on ultimate economic and social mobility (e.g., Karabel, 1972; Wilms, 1980). The next sections summarize some of the barriers in higher education.

Overt Discrimination

The enrollment and progress of women in higher education has long been impeded by sex discrimination. In order to fully understand the effects of discrimination on women, it is necessary to distinguish overt or blatant discriminatory practices from those that are more subtle and, therefore, more pernicious and difficult to address.

The existence of overt sex discrimination in higher education has been amply documented (e.g., Furniss & Graham, 1974; Kutner & Brogan, 1976; Lockheed & Ekstrom, 1977; Merritt, 1976; Roby, 1975; Westervelt, 1975) and, because of recent federal legislation, is now illegal. Documented forms of sex discrimination in education have included those in admissions practices, financial aid practices, institutional regulations, and discriminatory faculty attitudes and treatment.

Examples of discriminatory admissions practices have included higher admissions requirements for female than male applicants, sex quotas for admission, and age restrictions on enrollment that constitute inadvertent discrimination against women. In terms of financial aid practices, men have traditionally received the bulk of financial aids and awards—obvious examples include athletic scholarships, the GI Bill, ROTC, and many prestigious fellowships reserved for male applicants (e.g., until recently the Rhodes Scholarship program), but the pattern has fit more general types of loans, fellowships, and graduate assistantships as well. Restriction of aid to full-time students has also served to discriminate against women.

Discriminatory institutional regulations have included, among other things, requirements that female students but not male students live in residence halls (thus adding an additional financial burden and decreasing the freedom of choice of the female student but not the male student) and the *exclusion* of married female students from university housing, *even* from married student housing unless the husband was a student (Westervelt, 1975). Traditional university housing practices have perpetuated a "women as property" assumption: until married, the female student must be protected by the university through its housing regulations, but once she is married she is someone else's (i.e., her husband's) problem.

Finally, overtly (as opposed to subtly) discriminatory faculty attitudes and practices include the sexual harassment of women students and differential criteria for the evaluation and recommendation of women students. Sexism in letters of recommendation is illustrative of the latter type of bias. Lunneborg and Lillie (1973), for example, found two major types of sexist comments in letters of recommendation for graduate work in psychology. One type, which theoretically could be used with male as well as female applicants, included description of an applicant's physical attractiveness (or lack thereof), implying that this was somehow relevant to admission to graduate school. The second type, used only with female applicants, included comments implying that although the applicant's record was good for a woman, she was being evaluated by lower standards than those applied to males; for example, "Although Sue's work on my research left something to be desired, her performance was actually quite good for a female student." Lunneborg and Lillie (1973) found sexist comments in the letters of only 1 of 85 male applicants to graduate school in psychology but in almost one third of the letters of female applicants.

Certainly the existence of such federal legislation as Title IX of the Education Amendments of 1972 and the Women's Educational Equity Act of the Education Amendments of 1974 has reduced the prevalence and amount of overtly discriminatory practices, but it has by no means eliminated them nor has it addressed the more subtle forms of bias and discrimination against women.

Subtle Forms of Discrimination

To understand subtle forms of discrimination against women, it is useful to define the *basis* of discrimination, which is *prejudice*. As originally defined by Gordon Allport in his 1954 book *The Nature of Prejudice*, prejudice is

> an antipathy based on a faulty and inflexible generalization. It may be felt or expressed. It may be directed toward a group as a whole, or toward an individual because he is a member of that group. . . . The net effect of prejudice, thus defined, is to place the object of prejudice at some disadvantage not merited by his own misconduct. (p. 9).

(Note that even in discussing prejudice and discrimination, women are excluded by use of the sexist "he" and "his.") Prejudice is, in essence, a negative *attitude* toward or sets of belief systems about a group of people. That negative attitude is built from the process of categorization and relies for its continuation on stereotypes constructed to describe the group and upon selective perception and denial of information contradictory to the prejudice, or stereotypes. Prejudices are tenacious mechanisms—they are highly resistant to change. *Discrimination* may be defined as behavior or treatment resulting from or caused by prejudice (e.g., see Frieze, Parsons, Johnson, Ruble, & Zellman, 1978); for example, resistance to admitting women to medical school, a discriminatory treatment, derived from a set of negative attitudes about women's capabilities and characteristics. The important point here is that legislation attempts to address discriminatory treatment but it does not address the prejudices underlying the treatment. The prejudices remain and, inevitably, exert themselves in ways outside the bounds of legislation. In other words, it is possible to legislate behavior change but far more difficult to bring about attitudinal change (Bernard, 1976).

In terms of the treatment of women in the educational system, the prejudices concerning or negative attitudes toward women exert themselves in subtle ways as well as the overt ways which have been the subject of equal opportunity legislation (see Nielsen, 1979; Bernard, 1976). Bernard (1976) has described at least two subtle yet effective means of discriminating against and discouraging women in higher education; these means are the "stag effect" and the "put down."

The stag effect, as defined by Bernard (1976), is a "complex of exclusionary customs, practices, attitudes, conventions, and other social forms which protect the male turf from the intrusion of women" (p. 23). At its most blatant, the stag effect took the form of male-only clubs and professional societies and activities, for example, male-only business and faculty clubs, the traditional golf game during which major decisions are reached. As related to students, the stag effect is usually reflected in various means of avoiding and failing to encourage and support women students. Epstein (1970a), Feldman (1974), and Schwartz and Lever (1973), among others, have documented females' lesser likelihood of being chosen as protégés and their consequent loss, both educationally and in terms of later job opportunities, of the benefits of close working relationships with professors. The failure of male professors to take female protégés may have been due to a failure to take women seriously as students, research collaborators, or future professional colleagues, a conviction that most women will leave the profession for home and family, or a focus on the woman student as a sexual being rather than on her roles as student and potential colleague. Regardless of its causes, avoidance results in feelings of loneliness and "invisibility" (Bernard, 1976) in women students.

One concept useful in understanding the basis of the stag effect and, in particular, its psychological effects on women is "status set typing" (Epstein, 1970a). Epstein has defined status set typing as a process in which "a class of persons who share a key status (e.g., lawyer) also share other matching statuses (e.g., white, male, Protestant) and it is considered *appropriate* that this be so" (Epstein, 1970b, p. 754). In other words, whether or not people admit it, certain predominant statuses or characteristics of people in a given setting (e.g., educational or occupational) become the *expected* (or even "correct") status characteristics, and those whose statuses do not conform to the expectations are viewed negatively because they, through no fault of their own, create discord relative to the expectations of the larger group. References to "lady doctor," "woman lawyer," "black engineer," or "male nurse," indicate discordant status sets. Not only do incongruent status characteristics make the dominant group uncomfortable, but the incongruent status becomes the most salient feature of the situation. In other words, a person's gender or race, if different from the dominant one in the situation, becomes more *salient* to interpersonal interactions than are situation-relevant characteristics, for example, one's role as student or colleague. When sex becomes the focus of evaluations and interactions within an educational or work setting, the person of the "wrong" sex usually suffers. For example, the dissimilarity of women on the status characteristic of sex may be part of male professors' avoidance of women students. For women pursuing male-dominated careers and in male-dominated educational environments (of which most in higher education are), the persistent feeling that one doesn't "fit" into the professional structure and environment cannot be facilitative of one's professional self-concept or satisfaction. Therefore, status as "different," or as a token, often has negative effects on both the formal, professional and informal, social environments created by faculty and peers and on one's self-image as a member of or apprentice in the profession.

As defined by Bernard, the "put down" involves the actual harassment of, versus simply ignoring, women students. Examples of the put down are demeaning comments about women, sexual jokes, and outright hazing. Accusations to a woman that she is "husband-hunting" rather than interested in real scholarship and outright comments by faculty that "education is wasted on women" are examples of the put down (Bernard, 1976). Examples of the put down in a medical school setting (see Walsh, 1979) are the use of textbooks such as Williams and Wilkins' *The Anatomical Basis of Medical Practice* (by now forced to withdraw from the market), which contained such insults as pictures of nude females in seductive poses with such captions as:

> We are sorry that we cannot make available the addresses of the young ladies who grace our pages. Our wives burned our little address books at our last barbeque get-together,

and

> If you think that once you have seen the backside of one female, you have
> seen them all, then you haven't sat in a sidewalk cafe in Italy where girl
> watching is a cultivated art. Your authors, whose zeal in this regard never
> flags, refer you to Figures 11–50 and 53 as proof that female backs can keep an
> interest in anatomy alive.

Another medical text available, entitled *Anesthesia for the Uninter-
ested* and in its 3rd printing, uses photographs of women in bikinis to
demonstrate the use of operating room equipment and, on the cover,
shows a male medical student groping a female colleague who is
wearing a miniskirt (Walsh, 1979). It would be hard for female medical students to avoid some feeling of devaluation and sexual objectifi-
cation when confronted by such texts.

Such subtle forms of discrimination, documented also by, among
others, Feldman (1974), the Carnegie Commission on Higher Education (1973), Holahan (1979), Merritt (1976), Rice (1977), Walsh (1977),
and Westervelt (1975), may have particularly pernicious effects on
women because they *are* so subtle, and because they ultimately dam-
age or destroy enthusiasm for and a sense of belonging in the field as
well as one's professional and even personal self-image (see Bernard,
1976). They may also be at least partly to blame for women's greater
attrition from higher education (see Carnegie Commission on Higher
Education, 1973; Feldman, 1974; Patterson & Sells, 1973).

Lack of Role Models

An additional barrier to women in education has been the lack of
female professional role models and mentors, most notably female
faculty within higher education (Douvan, 1976). The literature regarding the selection of occupational role models indicates that males
almost always report other males (e.g., fathers, male professors) as
significant role models and influences (e.g., Brown *et al.*, 1978;
Weishaar *et al.*, 1981). Females, on the other hand, are likely to report
both male and female models (Andberg *et al.*, 1979; Basow & Howe,
1978, 1980; Brown *et al.*, 1978; Weishaar *et al.*, 1981). Thus, while
males follow a pattern of same-sex modeling, the lack of female occupational role models (Douvan, 1976) necessitates opposite-sex as well
as same-sex modeling in the facilitation of females' career development; as concluded by Weishaar *et al.* (1980), in the absence of female
models women learn to rely on male models.

Even though male professors can serve essential role modeling and
mentoring functions for their female students, there is evidence that

the relative *lack* of female faculty is a deterrent to women's educational and career pursuits, *particularly* in science (McLure & Piel, 1978) and other pioneer fields (O'Donnell & Anderson, 1978). The facilitative effects of same-sex models and mentors were suggested by Goldstein's (1979) report that about 80% of the articles published by recent doctoral degree recipients were published by individuals whose faculty advisers were the same sex. Tidball (1980) also reported that as the proportion of women faculty relative to the number of women students increases, so does the proportion of women high achievers in professional life.

Higher Education for Women: The Null Environment

One of the most basic and most important concepts in understanding the difficulties faced by women in higher education is Jo Freeman's (1975) concept of the "null academic environment." Freeman studied the responses of male and female students at the University of Chicago to a questionnaire concerning the nature and amount of personal support they received for pursuit of their educational and career objectives. Freeman found that although male students perceived more support from the faculty (94% of which was male and 6% female) than did female students, a majority of students of both sexes perceived the faculty as generally unsupportive. Freeman termed this situation, in which neither sex felt encouraged, the "null academic environment." The problem for women students, however, was that they also felt little or no support from other people in their environments, as opposed to male students who reported significantly more support, from such sources as parents, siblings, other relatives, friends, and spouses or boyfriends/girlfriends. Along with the negative societal messages discussed in Chapter 3, it is fairly clear that the female student has come from and exists in an environment fundamentally lacking in support for her educational endeavors; the educational system, in doing nothing to create an environment of support for her, contributes by default to her ultimate failure. Freeman's (1975) "null environment hypothesis" is that "an academic environment that neither encourages nor discourages students of either sex is inherently discriminatory against women because it fails to take into account the differentiating external environments from which women and men students come" (p. 221). In other words, professors don't have to overtly discourage or discriminate against female students. Society has already placed countless negative marks on the female student's "ballot," so a passive approach, a "laissez-faire" attitude, will probably ensure her failure. Career-oriented female students, to survive, must do so without much support from their environments (Freeman, 1975; Holahan, 1979).

Thus, discrimination can result from errors of omission as well as of commission, and both have negative effects on females' progress and success in higher education. Freeman (1975) describes the different psychological environments confronted by the male versus the female student:

> The University is less of an intellectual seedbed than a psychological gaunt-let—and it is one that the male students run in full armor, while the women students trip through in their bare skins.
>
> Perhaps the best analogy for understanding the differentiating effect on men and women of the null environment is to be drawn from agriculture. If a farmer transplants into a field two groups of seedlings—one having been nourished thus far in rich fertilized loam and the other malnourished for having struggled in desert sand—and that farmer then tends all the seedlings with virtually equal lack of care, fertilizer, and water (perhaps favoring the loam-grown seedlings slightly because they look more promising), no one should be surprised if the lesser harvest is reaped from the desert-bred plants. Nor should we, with all the modern farm apparatus and information available, shrug complacently and lament that there is no way to make the desert bloom. (p. 207)

TOWARD EDUCATIONAL EQUITY FOR WOMEN

Although the educational system continues to be for most women a discriminatory or, at best, a null environment, the civil rights and women's movements led to some very positive changes in the educational system in the last 20 years. The most notable change has been federal legislation designed to ensure equal educational opportunity for women and minorities.

The Civil Rights Act of 1964 and supplementary laws prohibited sex and race discrimination in employment, including in the field of higher education, and Title IX of the 1972 Educational Amendments to the Higher Educational Act prohibited discrimination against women students in any institution receiving federal aid. The key provision in Title IX is as follows: "No person in the United States shall, on the basis of sex, be excluded from participation in, be denied the benefits of, or be subject to discrimination under any education program or activity receiving Federal financial assistance."

Title IX covers almost all aspects of student life, for example, admissions, counseling, financial aid, and access to courses and extracurricular activities, including athletics. Although the definition of discrimination was, not surprisingly, a major problem in the enforcement of Title IX, examples of previous practices that are now clearly illegal include requiring different courses for boys and girls, requiring higher grades for admission for women than for men, sponsoring summer "science camps" restricted to male students, and prohibiting women from using campus athletic facilities unless a male signs up for the facilities. Other important provisions specify that, in general, financial aid programs cannot be restricted to one sex and that institutions cannot treat male and female students differently in terms of actual or potential martial or parental status, nor can they ask marital status for admissions purposes. The extent of applicability, methods of enforcement, and actual impact of Title IX deserve an extended discussion beyond the scope of this book and for these the reader is referred to a variety of comprehensive reviews and analyses, for example, Fishel and Pottker (1977), and the 1979 (Vol. 49-4) special issue of the *Harvard Educational Review.*

Another major piece of federal legislation was the Women's Educational Equity Act of 1974, designed to provide grants for research and programs facilitating women's equity in the educational system. The act also provided funds for activities leading to improvements in the quality of counseling and testing services for women, and training for educational personnel (see Wirtenberg & Nakamura, 1976).

Other positive changes for women have included increased attention to the development of nonsexist educational curricula (e.g., National Project on Women in Education, 1978) and the rapid and extensive growth of the curricular area of Women's Studies. The academic field of women's studies, because it provides recognition for women's scholarly, artistic, and humanistic contributions to society, provides young women with models of female achievement in the educational realm.

SUMMARY

To summarize, education is on the one hand a major if not crucial route to women's career achievements and success and yet, ironically, the educational system has served as one of the major barriers to women's career development as well. Even though the educational system has been a barrier to women, it is a system wherein interventions designed to change it are possible and possess tremendous potential for widening the opportunities and improving the status of women.

In considering the material presented in this section, several additional points should be noted. First, in considering the influence of higher education on women's career development, its correlates should be noted. Higher education in women is related not only to career achievements but to a greater tendency to remain single, to higher rates of marital disruption (e.g., divorce), and to lower fertility rates (Houseknecht & Spanier, 1980). Higher education in women is also related to more liberal attitudes toward women's roles (e.g., Mason & Czajka, 1976) and to such characteristics as autonomy and the desire for direct versus vicarious achievement (e.g., Ginzberg et al., 1966). Thus, educational level is related to a number of other major variables positively related to women's career development. Since few studies have controlled some of these variables while varying others, it is difficult to make conclusions regarding the degree of directness and the relative strength of these variables in influencing women's career orientation and innovation. Further research from which directional inferences can be made is needed in order to clarify the effects of educational level and other related variables on women's career development.

A second major point is that the influence of educational level on career achievements and the pursuit of nontraditional occupations is even stronger for graduates of women's colleges (Astin, 1977; Brown et al., 1978; Douvan, 1976). Women's colleges have the advantage, first, of providing women with greater opportunities for academic and campus leadership than do coeducational colleges (Astin, 1977). In part, this is because in the absence of the men, to whom they have traditionally deferred, women must take leadership roles. In addition, many women are more willing to assume leadership and to behave in dominant, assertive ways when they are not worried about offending men or reducing their femininity in men's views (Brown et al., 1978). A second advantage of women's colleges is that they tend to encourage women to pursue unconventional areas of study and therefore encourage women's pursuits of traditionally male career fields (Tidball, 1980). Even though women's colleges, like coeducational colleges, have been dominated by male faculty, there are at least a few more females in faculty and administrative positions to provide models for female students.

On the other hand, Oates and Williamson (1978) have suggested that the superiority of women's colleges in producing highly achieving women is primarily due to the success of graduates of the highly selective "seven sisters" schools: Barnard, Bryn Mawr, Mount Holyoke, Radcliffe, Smith, Vassar, and Wellesley. It may be college selectivity, rather than its sex composition, that facilitates women's later achievements. Studies of the achievements of female graduates of the (now) coeducational Ivy League colleges, for example, Harvard, Yale, and Princeton, are needed because only these really provide an appropriate comparison to the seven sisters schools.

Finally, while the present chapter has focused on the general situation for women in higher education, specific topics deserve more attention than is possible, given the scope of this book. The performance and adjustment of female graduate and professional school students and the phenomenon of the "reentry" woman student are examples of such topics. In general, more research is needed on a variety of topics related to women in education. Because the educational system plays a crucial role in career options and decisions, research leading to greater understanding of its effects on girls' development and decisions is necessary. Randour *et al.* (1982) suggested that, given women's continued lack of equality in higher education, continued monitoring of the level and nature of women's involvement is essential. Further, they suggested the importance of research on the relationship of institutional factors (e.g., degree level, public versus private institutions, full- versus part-time study) to subsequent educational and occupational outcomes.

Continued attention to educational equity for women is particularly important, given that the 1980s began with a national administration somewhat hostile to affirmative action programs and resistant to the enforcement of antidiscrimination legislation. Psychologists, educators, and others committed to facilitating women's career development must ensure that research and positive change within the educational system continue to receive effort and attention.

THE INFLUENCE OF COUNSELING INTERVENTIONS ON WOMEN'S CAREER CHOICES

Career counseling is usually conceptualized as a process of facilitation, that is, the counselor assists the client in a process of self-exploration and clarification, information gathering, and decision making that results in a career direction or choice that is acceptable to the client and is realistic in terms of her or his interests and abilities. The entire process connotes an "opening up," adient, or exploratory quality that is presumably facilitative of personal growth and development. However, even a cursory review of the literature reveals much speculation that, rather than widening women's options, career counseling, with its traditional armamentarium of interest measures and occupational information, has often limited women's choices and reinforced traditional female vocational behavior.

The principal reason suggested for this occurrence is that many counselors appear to share the societal norm dictating that the biological roles of wife and mother are incompatible with, or at least take precedence over, the social role of worker. This chapter examines the literature on bias in career counseling, critiques it, and suggests directions for further research. In addition, we discuss the implications of recent theoretical developments (Astin, 1984; Gottfredson, 1981; Richardson, 1981) for the practice of vocational counseling with women.

DEFINITIONS AND EARLY RESEARCH

Schlossberg and Pietrofessa (1973) defined *counselor bias* as "an opinion, either unfavorable or favorable, which is formed without adequate reasons and is based upon what the bias holder assumes to be appropriate for the group in question. Bias is evident whenever it is assumed that someone can or cannot take a certain course of action because of her or his age, social class, sex or race" (1973, p. 44). This definition is similar to that of *stereotype*, which English and English (1958) define as "a relatively rigid and oversimplified or biased perception or conception of an aspect of reality, esp. of persons or social groups" (p. 523).

The first major study of sex role stereotyping in the mental health profession was that of Broverman and her colleagues (Broverman *et al.*, 1970). Although not directly related to career counseling or career counselors, their work has implications for both, and laid the groundwork for a decade of research into sex bias in the counseling profession. Briefly, the Brovermans asked a sample of clinicians to describe a healthy adult male, a healthy adult female, or a healthy adult (sex unspecified) on a questionnaire composed of 122 bipolar items, each pole characterized as highly masculine or feminine. The results indicated that the subjects rated the adult male and the adult of unspecified sex as being highly similar. However, the description of the healthy adult female differed in that she was seen as, among other things, less assertive, more passive and emotional, and less competent in science and math. One of the implications of the Broverman study that has escaped notice is that these are hardly characteristics that would be used to describe a competent professional person. The implications for any career counseling done by the clinicians in this sample (and, whatever they may call it, most clinicians do some career counseling at some point in most of their cases) is obvious.

Thomas and Stewart (1971) conducted the first direct investigation of sex bias among career counselors. They asked 62 high school guidance counselors to evaluate female high school students who were presented on audiotape as having either a conforming (home economics) or a deviate (engineering) career goal. Both male and female counselors rated the conforming goal as more appropriate than the deviate goal, and also rated the clients with deviate goals as being more in need of counseling than those with conforming goals. This study has been widely cited as demonstrating the biased reactions of guidance counselors to women who select nontraditional careers; however, careful review of the study suggests the existence of an alternative explanation of the results. It is possible that the subjects' evaluation of the client's choice and her need for counseling was realistic, based on the interest and ability information presented on the stimulus tape. This explanation cannot be ruled out, given the design of the study. A complete design would include a condition which presented a *male* client with background information and choices identical to those of the female client. If such a design resulted in differential ratings, alternative explanations would be ruled out; such data would constitute strong inference in support of the sex bias explanation.

Another widely cited investigation of counselor bias was that conducted by Pietrofessa and Schlossberg (1970). Utilizing an analogue paradigm, these researchers arranged interviews between counselor trainees and a coached female client in a counseling practicum. In the interview, the "client" revealed, among other information, that she was considering majoring in either engineering or education, and was unable to decide which to choose. Each interview was tape recorded and a content analysis was performed on the counselor responses. A response was considered biased against the female client when she expressed interest in the "masculine" field of engineering and the counselor rejected this in favor of the more "feminine" goal of education. Using this criterion, Pietrofessa and Schlossberg concluded that, of the statements which demonstrated bias, 81.3% were against women, while only 18.7% were biased for women (defined as counselor support or reinforcement for the engineering preference). They noted that the female counselor/subjects were as biased as their male colleagues, and that the biased statements most often took the form of emphasizing the "masculinity" of the engineering field.

It is difficult to evaluate the results of this study. On the one hand, the finding that 81% of counselor statements that indicated any preference were "anti-engineering" in nature seems to support the notion that these counselors-in-training were biased against such a nontraditional choice. Again, however, as with the Thomas and Stewart (1971) study, without information concerning the clients' interests and abilities, it is impossible to determine whether or not these responses show bias or appropriate reality testing. Similarly, examination of some of the actual statements that Pietrofessa and Schlossberg labeled as bias does not appear to support their interpretation, for example, "Engineering would take five years and elementary education would be four years. . . These are things you might want to consider" and "The coursework in engineering would be very difficult." These appear to be reasonable responses in the given situation. Only if the study had included a male client in a similar situation would it be possible to determine whether the counselors were exhibiting bias.

A third investigation in this "first wave" of research on career counselor bias was that conducted by Bingham and House (1973a,b). Utilizing a questionnaire methodology, these investigators asked guidance counselors what they knew and how they felt about women and work. More specifically, the counselors were asked to respond "Agree" or "Disagree" to 25 factual items (e.g., "On the average, women spend 25 years in the labor force") and 25 attitudinal items (e.g., "Something must be wrong with a woman who prefers to perform a traditionally male job"). Bingham and House (1973b) found that their subjects were misinformed on over 50% of the factual items presented to them. This was particularly true of the male counselors, who tended to believe that women are generally less able than men, that women currently have sufficient employment opportunities, and that women are not qualified to perform jobs traditionally held by men. Additionally, the subjects appeared somewhat naive concerning the existence of sex discrimination on the part of employers. Similarly, the companion investigation (Bingham & House, 1973a) demonstrated that the sample reported some very negative attitudes toward women and work. Again, this finding was stronger for the male counselors.

In reviewing these early investigations of bias in career counseling, it becomes apparent that it is not possible to draw firm conclusions, due to the studies' differing definitions and methodologies, as well as (with the exception of the Bingham & House investigations) the use of incomplete designs which allow for alternative interpretations of the data. A conservative conclusion would be that they are suggestive, but far from conclusive. However, pursuing a solely methodological perspective would sorely underestimate the impact these studies have had on the fields of counseling and vocational psychology. Their very citations have become a watchword for a generation of graduate students, stimulated a decade of research, and sensitized an entire profession to the position of women in the workplace. Without such early efforts, it is likely that a book such as this one would not have been written.

COUNSELOR BIAS IN THE 1970s: AN EXPLOSION OF RESEARCH

Following these three groundbreaking investigations, the mid-1970s yielded a large number of studies on the subject of career coun-

selor bias. In a study of school counselors, Ahrons (1976) found that
her subjects perceived career goals for women to be incompatible
with the social roles of wife and mother. Medvene and Collins (1976)
compared three groups of mental health professionals (high school
guidance counselors, psychotherapists, and advanced graduate students) by asking them to rate the appropriateness for women of 25
different occupations. They found that the male guidance counselors
displayed the most restrictive attitudes, as 90% of them rated less than
half of the occupations as appropriate for women.

Schwartz (1975) investigated bias among guidance counselors by
asking them to make occupational recommendations for intellectually
superior male and female students. Her subjects suggested low ability
level and female role occupations significantly more often for the
female students. Donahue and Costar (1977) reported that school
counselors chose lower-paying jobs, which required less education and more supervision, when case studies were described as female than when the identical case was designated male. This study
has been severely criticized by Smith (1979) on both logical and
methodological grounds; however, careful review of her argument,
the original study (Donahue, 1976; Donahue & Costar, 1977), and
Donahue's reply (Donahue, 1979) suggests that her position may not
be well taken.

Taking a different approach, Rohfeld (1977) investigated the recipients of career counseling. In her sample of high school women, 13%
reported that counselors had actively discouraged them from a nontraditional goal, while 25% said that their teachers and counselors implied that some jobs were for men and others were for women. In a
similar vein, Sauter, Seidl, and Karbon (1980) investigated the counseling experiences of a sample of freshman women with either a traditional or nontraditional career choice. They found a significant difference between the two groups in whether guidance counseling
influenced their career choices—the traditional group significantly
more often reported being influenced than the nontraditional group.
In fact, not a *single* nontraditional woman reported that guidance
counseling had an influence on her choice, while 25% of the traditional women reported being so influenced. Similarly, Houser and
Garvey (1983) note that, in their sample, women enrolled in a nontraditional vocational training program reported receiving more support
and encouragement than traditional women from every significant
group in their lives—except their guidance counselors!

ANALYSIS AND CONCLUSIONS

The literature on counselor bias has been criticized on several grounds (Lichtenberg & Heck, 1983; Smith, 1980; Whiteley, 1979). Buczek (1981) pointed out that a major methodological issue is the problem of the social desirability of the counselors' responses in the experimental situation (Abramowitz & Abramowitz, 1978; Abramowitz & Dokecki, 1977; Tanney & Birk, 1976). That is, counselors may believe that sexist responses are "socially undesirable" and therefore may feel pressure to respond in a nonsexist fashion, thus obscuring the true amount of variance. This could be particularly important as many current research procedures are quite transparent in nature, for example, presenting a female client in a highly nontraditional role (e.g., engineer) and then requesting the counselor to rate the appropriateness of her choice, her level of personal adjustment, and so forth.

The suggestion that counselors who participate in investigations of sex bias may attempt to present themselves in a favorable light, that is, as nonsexist, is an interesting possibility, but would only be true if the subjects believed that being nonsexist is socially desirable, something that has never been empirically demonstrated. Although it should be possible to compute correlations of responses on an instrument such as the Modified Questionnaire on the Occupational Status of Women (Bingham & Turner, 1981) with some standard measure of social desirability, such as the Marlowe–Crowne Scales, this has never been done. Until it is, suggestions that counselors bias their responses to appear sex-fair must be considered speculation.

A second issue that has been raised is the appropriateness of the dependent variables, both their sensitivity (Buczek, 1981) and their generalizability to actual counselor behavior (Smith, 1980). Despite the existence of a variety of process variables, researchers continue to rely on rating scales of adjustment, diagnosis, and so forth, doubtless because they are so easily available. Sound process research is painstaking, time-consuming, and costly, and is thus relatively rarely undertaken. Even analogue process studies are unusual, a notable exception being Buczek (1981), who used an incidental memory task to investigate counselor bias. Reasoning that an unanticipated memory task would not be reactive to socially desirable responding, Buczek required 89 advanced clinical psychology doctoral students to listen to an audiotape of a simulated initial interview with either a male or female client whose chief complaints were loss of energy, anxiety, and depression. During the interview, the client discussed both social and vocational concerns. After listening to the audiotape, the subjects completed several tasks, including writing down the facts they remembered from the interview, listing any questions they would want to ask the client, and evaluating different factors for their importance in treatment planning. Analysis of the data revealed that, overall, the subjects remembered significantly fewer concerns of the female client, and that the male counselors asked the female client significantly more questions related to social and family concerns. Buczek's methodology constitutes an extremely useful tool for further investigation, as her dependent variables (attention to client concerns and questions asked) are powerful ones in the counseling process.

A third problem with this body of literature lies with the subjects who have been investigated. Review of the research reveals that the studies that are cited as demonstrating bias in career counseling have utilized a wide variety of subjects, from research psychologists, social workers, teachers, and consultants (Kaley, 1971) to "mental health professionals" (Broverman, et al., 1970) to graduate students in clinical psychology (Buczek, 1981). A large body of work has been done with guidance counselors (Ahrons, 1976; Bingham & House, 1973a,b; Donahue & Costar, 1977; Friedersdorf, 1969; Medvene & Collins, 1976; Naffziger, 1972; Schwartz, 1975; Thomas & Stewart, 1971), while an equally large body of studies has investigated graduate students, or "counselors-in-training" (Fitzgerald & Cherpas, 1985; Hawley, 1972; Maslin & Davis, 1975; Medvene & Collins, 1976; Pietrofessa & Schlossberg, 1970; and others).

The strength of such heterogeneous sampling is that it may approximate the intent of Cook and Campbell's (1979) suggestion that the external validity of educational research may be increased by deliberately sampling for heterogeneity, thus allowing generalization across subgroups of populations. The weakness, of course, is that some of these samples are *not* subgroups of the population of vocational counselors, and their inclusion may serve to obscure or distort the phenomenon under study. Clinical psychologists, for example, although often confronted with vocational issues, are typically not trained to deal with them, whereas graduate students are, by definition, not yet fully trained, period. Orlinsky and Howard's (1976) data demonstrated that more experienced male therapists were more effective with female clients than inexperienced male therapists, a point which probably also applies to vocational counseling. The point is that we must become much more careful in defining our samples if we wish to become more definitive in drawing our conclusions.

A final point is possibly the most important. Despite nearly 15 years of research on the subject of bias in career counseling, we are still lacking a widely understood and accepted *definition* of such bias. For example, Price and Borgers (1977) had guidance counselors review the folders of 96 high school students and rate the appropriateness of the courses they planned to take in the following academic year. They found that females were rated as having more appropriate courses and concluded that this "contrasts with the literature, which indicates counselor bias against women" (Price & Borgers, 1977, p. 42). In contrast, Pietrofessa and Schlossberg (1973) reviewed statements made by counselors-in-training which suggested that engineering was more difficult than education, that it took more years of training, and that companies still managed to discriminate against women (all of which are true) and concluded that "counselor bias exists against women entering a masculine occupation" (p. 4). Finally, Buczek (1981) reported that counselors paid equal attention to the vocational concerns of male and female clients (and thus were not sex biased) but recalled fewer overall concerns of the female client (and therefore *were* sex biased).

A provisional attempt to unravel the threads of the research and come to some clear understanding of the phenomenon requires that we first define and distinguish between the concepts of *sex bias* and *sex role bias*. Sex bias can be defined as any set of attitudes and/or behaviors which favors one sex over the other. Thus, early work by Goldberg (1968), which reported that college students devalued articles purportedly written by women, can be said to demonstrate *sex bias*. It is important to note that the articles written by males were favored whether their content derived from a masculine field or a traditionally feminine field. In contrast, *sex role bias* can be defined as any set of attitudes or behaviors which favors sex role-congruent behavior and negatively evaluates sex role-incongruent behavior. For example, Fitzgerald (1980) reported that students rated nontraditional occupations (e.g., men as nurses, women as physicians) as less appropriate than traditional occupations (e.g., men as physicians, women as nurses). Such ratings constitute not sex bias, but sex role bias.

Most of the current literature on bias in career counseling is actually designed to assess sex role bias, although few studies employ the complete design (male and female client, traditional and nontraditional occupational choices) which would exclude competing explanations of the data. It should be noted that sex bias and sex role bias can operate simultaneously, much as a two-factor experiment can result in a main effect and an interaction. The literature on selection discrimination indicates that this is often the case, with men generally being favored over women, an effect that is sometimes moderated by high levels of ability, with sex appropriateness of occupation or position interacting with sex of candidate in the expected direction (Fitzgerald & Betz, 1983). Researchers investigating bias in career counseling should begin to design studies that can reliably sort out the variance attributable to sex from that resulting from role congruence.

Complicating the problem, and basic to an understanding of it, is what Lichtenberg and Heck (1983) have termed the "tendentious and adversarial" nature of the debate over the presence and effect of sex bias in counseling. Clearly, this is a political issue as much as it is a scientific one, and ideological considerations play no small role in the debate. Smith (1980) suggests that some researchers are motivated to seek and find bias, while Richardson and Johnson (1984) pointed out that "It is probably true as well that others are motivated to find an *absence* of bias (for example, Stricker's 1977 paper in which he criticized methodologies in studies that reported bias while defending studies with similar methodologies that reported an absence of bias)" (pp. 861–862). Ideological considerations become entangled with methodological ones and the analogue study is alternately praised as rigorous or damned as trivial, depending, at least to some degree, on the politics of the reviewer, and/or the outcome of the study. Similarly, naturalistic or field research is extolled for its external validity or dismissed for its lack of rigorous controls, and so the debate continues.

Thus, it is difficult to answer definitively the question "Is there bias in career counseling?" Informal observation, personal experience, and intuition all strongly say "Yes"—and yet, these data are not admissible as scientific evidence, but rather are the substratum of experience from which hypotheses are drawn. Richardson and Johnson (1984) pointed out that "the research on gender bias in counseling (has) not followed the principle that hypotheses are first generated in naturalistic studies, and then tested in controlled laboratory experiments" (p. 861), and it is this point which may well account for some of the muddle. Edwards and Cronbach (1952) discussed the normal progression of research, from *survey research* (in which variables of interest are identified, usually through naturalistic methods) to *technique research* (in which measurement and operationalization of concepts and variables are emphasized) to *laboratory research* (in which hypotheses are proposed and tested in controlled settings) and, finally, to *applied research*. This progression did not occur in the research on gender bias in counseling. Rather, as Richardson and Johnson (1984) pointed out, the appearance of the two classic studies (Broverman *et al.*, 1970; Chesler, 1972) stimulated, doubtless because of the dramatic nature of their findings, a large number of analogue and experimental studies before the nature and measurement of the pertinent variables were well thought out. It is possible that if this methodological "short-circuiting" had not occurred, the gender bias literature might demonstrate a more coherent appearance today.

Thus, we agree with Richardson and Johnson's conclusion concerning the importance of naturalistic methodology in this area. We suggest that an important focus of such research ought to be the identification and definition of relevant variables (such as the sex bias/sex role bias distinction made previously), possibly through the intensive examination of "extreme groups" in whom these variables, if they exist, are likely to appear. We realize the practical difficulties of locating even a small number of practitioners who are willing to publicly take a strong traditionalist position (and thus identify themselves as suitable subjects for such an investigation) but suspect that the yield will be worth the effort. Requesting former clients to retrospect about their counseling experience in a structured interview, possibly utilizing a critical incident methodology (Flanagan, 1954), is another method of "pointing up" important variables; clients are, surprisingly, an almost totally untapped source of systematically gathered data concerning the counseling experience. Finally, the examination of practicum and prepracticum training tapes, available for research in many training clinics, provides an extremely rich data base for such a purpose. If one accepts the hypothesis that (at least some) counselors-in-training are likely to demonstrate the general biases of the culture (which their graduate training hopefully removes, or at least, alleviates), then it should be possible to use such material to identify content and process variables that are useful to pursue in gender bias research. The research by Orlinsky and Howard (1980) provides support for the notion that counselors-in-training may well be more sex role biased than practitioners already in the field.

Until we carefully do our homework (e.g., define our terms, operationalize our variables, and carefully sample from appropriate, as opposed to available, populations), thus approaching even the moderate sophistication of psychotherapy outcome research (Orlinsky & Howard, 1980), most of our speculation concerning bias in vocational counseling remains just that.

RECENT THEORETICAL CONTRIBUTIONS

After several decades of theory building devoted mainly to predicting and explaining the vocational behavior of men, two major formulations have recently appeared that have made a conscious effort to describe the process of choice for both men and women (Astin, 1984; Gottfredson, 1981). Because these statements make a specific commitment to describing women's vocational behavior, it is important to examine them in terms of their implications for the practice of counseling. In addition, Richardson (1981) has recently published a major piece on the importance of the work–family interface that will be considered below.

GOTTFREDSON'S (1981) THEORY OF CIRCUMSCRIPTION AND COMPROMISE

Gottfredson has recently suggested that the occupational aspirations of women and men are determined to a large degree by self-concept (defined in terms of gender, social class, intelligence, and interests) and their perceptions of occupations (including sex stereotype, prestige level, and field). She posits that people develop perceptions of themselves as compatible or incompatible with occupations based on the degree of fit between their self-concepts and their occupational images. These perceptions, or preferences, as they are called, along with a person's notions of how accessible (i.e., realistic) is each of these occupations, define a *range of acceptable occupational alternatives* within which the person will make her or his choice. In other words, a person will not aspire to an occupation that is extremely discrepant in prestige level (in either direction) from that which would be expected in terms of social class and ability level; nor will an occupational alternative be acceptable that is extremely nontraditional in terms of its role stereotype.

Gottfredson further posits that, in the circumscribing and compromise process that results in a final choice, one is most able to tolerate a choice that is discrepant in terms of the interest–field match, and least able to tolerate a discrepancy in sex-typing—with the status–prestige match falling somewhere in between. She bases this assertion on developmental theory that suggests that gender identity is developed extremely early, followed by self-evaluations of ability and social class, whereas self-perceptions of interests and values, acquired later, are thus less fundamental to the self-concept and easier to relinquish. Gottfredson thus asserts that the majority of women are in lower-level, feminine-stereotyped positions because that is where they wish to be, and questions the practicality—and ethics—of counselors "tinkering" with a process so basic (Gottfredson, 1981).

The implications of such a position for vocational counseling with women are clear—and, to some, alarming. The ubiquity and intensity of the sex role socialization process should not be taken as reasons for accepting it. After all, it is only slightly over 100 years ago that the buying and selling of human beings in the institution of slavery were also ubiquitous in this country—and, interestingly enough, one of the primary social arguments rationalizing this institution was that blacks supposedly were "better off," and, in fact, would actually *choose* the institution over the vagaries and dangers of freedom if given the opportunity to do so. The point is that it is not possible to argue the primacy of free choice while postulating a deterministic model. As one of us has argued elsewhere, the difficulty of confronting the socialization process should not be given as a reason for cooperating with it (Fitzgerald & Crites, 1980). Gottfredson's variables are important and powerful in the counseling process; however, the model contains problems other than philosophical—e.g., how does one reconcile relinquishing aspirations for a high-level, investigative occupation (say, geologist) because it is nontraditional for women? The strong and negative relationship between prestige and pay, on the one hand, and the proportion of women employed in a given occupation, on the other, suggest that following the model closely would lead, indeed, to circumscription and compromise—and to conflict, particularly for high-ability women. Additionally, the fact that most women are in feminine occupations is open to other than a person-centered explanation; and, finally, Gottfredson's model does not account for the increasing number of women who are opting for the skilled trades, definitely in the masculine area.

Rather than accepting the socialization process, we suggest that counselors confront it (Fitzgerald, 1986; Fitzgerald & Crites, 1980), pointing out both the advantages and disadvantages of "bucking the system" (Haring-Hidore & Beyard-Tyler, 1984). In doing so, counselors can change, rather than tinker with, the system.

ASTIN'S (1984) SOCIOPSYCHOLOGICAL MODEL OF CAREER CHOICE AND WORK BEHAVIOR

In a major theoretical paper devoted explicitly to explaining women's career choice and work behavior, Astin (1984) posited that all humans are motivated to expend energy (i.e., to work) to satisfy what she labels needs for *survival, pleasure,* and *contribution.* Survival needs refer primarily to physiological survival, pleasure needs encompass the intrinsic satisfactions available from work, and contribution needs appear to include both the need to be useful to society and the need to be recognized for one's contributions. These three needs, though assumed to be the same for both men and women, can be satisfied in many different ways and their actual channels are determined, according to Astin, by the sex role socialization process, on the one hand, and the perceived structure of opportunity, on the other. It is these last two variables, both nonpsychological in nature, which are posited to explain gender differences in the occupational distribution of workers. We have presented a detailed analysis of Astin's model elsewhere (Fitzgerald & Betz, 1984; see also Farmer, 1984a; Gilbert, 1984; Hansen, 1984; Harmon, 1984; and others) and so will limit this commentary to an analysis of one central tenet of the model and the implications of that tenet for the practice of vocational counseling with women.

Astin explicitly stated that a woman can satisfy her needs through either paid employment or what she labels *family work*. Thus, "family work (i.e., being 'employed' as a homemaker) satisfies survival needs to the extent that the homemaker has a contract (e.g., marriage) or an implicit understanding with someone who acts as the breadwinner. Thus, the homemaker satisfies her survival needs indirectly" (p. 120). This focus on the value of family work, a focus that is appearing with some regularity in current literature, meets with mixed reaction. On the one hand, Kahn (1984) stated, "A major strength of Astin's model is the recognition that women can meet survival, pleasure, and contribution needs through work, whether it be paid or unpaid. . . legitimizing traditional 'women's' work as real may encourage men to do more unpaid work in the home" (p. 145). On the other hand, Nevill (1984) wrote, "When a word such as 'work' can be applied too broadly, it loses the value of clarity" (p. 131), while we have stated, "Despite the well-intentioned nature of attempts to establish the value of 'family work,' such attempts are detrimental to women and will continue to be so until such time as society decides that such work is truly valuable and rewards it in the same way that it rewards other activities that it values: with a substantial amount of money" (Fitzgerald & Betz, 1984, p. 138).

The increasing emphasis on what Astin labeled "family work" appears to be one manifestation of the recent recognition that work and family roles constitute interlocking, not separate, domains (Kanter, 1976; Pleck, 1978; Rapoport & Rapoport, 1965; Richardson, 1981). Thus, Pleck (1977) described how the male work role, the female work role, the female family role, and the male family role should be conceptually analyzed as components of an interlocking work–family role system. Similarly, Richardson (1981), in a thoughtful analysis, refuted the myth, long prevalent in the social sciences, that occupational and family roles "constitute two separate and nonoverlapping roles" (Kanter, 1977, p. 8). She presented a conceptual framework based on the following four assumptions:

1. Major social roles provide the basic structure of the adult life experience.
2. Occupational and familial roles are the major life roles for adults in our society.
3. Work and intimacy are processes that occur in both occupational and familial roles.
4. Gender, race, and class are critical variables that affect the nature and process of role interactions.

Richardson (1981) then demonstrated the usefulness of the framework for a reanalysis of various topics relevant to the vocational psychology of women, particularly role conflict.

This "legitimization" of the importance of work–family interaction for understanding the vocational behavior of women (and men) is an important development in the field of vocational psychology. It is, in fact, the premise of our book that the interface of home and work is the most salient characteristic of women's vocational behavior (see, in particular, Chapter 12). However, one implication of this line of thought appears to us to be unfortunate, that is, the trend toward defining "family work" as a career choice, not qualitatively different than the choice of, say, computer programmer or accountant. The equating of a nonstructured, noncompensated set of activities (i.e., housekeeping, which has no requirements for entry, no structured standards for performance, nor even necessarily any broad agreement on the nature and extent of the tasks involved) with the standard notion of occupation appears to render the terminology scientifically useless.

However, our objection is not only definitional; rather, we wonder whether such efforts, well intentioned though they may be, are not detrimental to women's attempts to achieve equity in the world of work and elsewhere. Analyses such as those of Pleck (1978) make it clear that while work roles and family roles *interact*, they are *not* the same. Similarly, Richardson's (1981) notion that work and intimacy are functions of the person, not the role, and can be satisfied in either the family or occupational arena, implies that there are, in fact, separate arenas. While it is clear that housekeeping is quite physically demanding, particularly when children are involved, and it is certainly true that society has woefully undervalued the contributions of women who are not "employed" in the traditional sense, neither of

these considerations present compelling arguments for eliminating
the housework–paid work distinction. The point is more than theoretical; there are considerable "real world" consequences. If not working (i.e., being a housewife) continues to be thought of as a legitimate
"career" for women, women will continue to be taken less than seriously in the world of work. Another consequence may be that girls
will continue not to prepare themselves appropriately for employment and so remain at risk of eventually joining the cadre of "dis-
placed homemakers" who slowly and painfully attempt, in their middle years, to rejoin the world of work. Wampler (1982), discussing the
counseling implications of the housewife role, concluded, "the
fulltime housewife role has negative effects on women, and these
effects appear predominantly in middle age" (p. 127). She noted that
the problems resulting from the housewife role, for example, low self-
esteem, stem principally from its low status, the dependence it fosters,
and the structure of the role. "This review suggests that the most
obvious intervention is for the housewife to get a job" (Wampler,
1982, p. 129). She then outlined other interventions for the client who
either does not wish paid employment or finds it impossible.

The persistence of the notion that nonemployment (i.e., being a
housewife) is a legitimate option for adult women is a direct result of
the traditional notion that a woman's place is in the home. We submit
that this position is a sexist one as it is applied exclusively to women
(for example, it is likely that few, if any, counselors would agree with a
male client that his decision to marry and stay home was a healthy
choice) and that it is detrimental to their well-being, as it deters
women from obtaining economic security over which they have firm
control. Counselors should consider their position on this issue very
carefully, as it is the central conflict that women bring to vocational
counseling.

SUMMARY AND CONCLUSIONS

The present chapter has reviewed the current status of theory and
research on career counseling with women. We conclude that widespread assumptions of bias in such counseling, while certainly plausible, have not been unequivocally demonstrated to be so. This most
likely results from lack of precision in the definition of variables, as
well as the use of samples which are sometimes more available than
appropriate. The chapter outlined some avenues of inquiry, including
theoretical and methodological suggestions, and concluded with a cri-

tique of recent theory focused on women's vocational development, particularly with reference to counseling.

Consistent with our focus on theory and research, we have offered no discussion of practical technique. Readers interested in the more direct application of these ideas are referred to standard textbooks in the field (e.g., Crites, 1981) for basic approaches and to specialized discussions of career counseling with women (e.g., Fitzgerald, 1986). However, it seems important to emphasize that the goal of such counseling is to expand women's options, success, and satisfaction in the occupational structure. One of the most crucial factors in achieving this goal is for the counselor to avoid being another barrier to the woman's career development.

ABILITIES, ACHIEVEMENT, AND WOMEN'S CAREER DEVELOPMENT

INTRODUCTION

As mentioned in Chapter 1, one of the most serious problems related to women's career development is the chronic underutilization of their abilities and talents in career pursuits (Fitzgerald & Crites, 1980). Using Terman and Oden's (1959) follow-up study of gifted children as an example, it was shown that women's intellectual gifts have by and large been wasted, with significant cost both to themselves and to society. In this chapter, several paradoxes concerning women's abilities and achievements will be discussed, as will the relationship of women's abilities to their educational and career achievements. Women's underutilization of their abilities, particularly those in mathematics, and the importance of math as a "critical filter" in women's career development will also be discussed. Prior to discussing relationships between women's abilities and their vocational behavior, however, the issue of sex differences and similarities in vocationally relevant aptitudes will be discussed.

SEX DIFFERENCES IN COGNITIVE AND PHYSICAL ABILITIES

The cultural belief of female intellectual inferiority has long been used to justify women's lesser record of educational and occupational attainment. Further, the supposition of female physical inferiority has been used to defend discriminatory practices with regard to women's pursuit of occupations requiring physical strength, exertion, and endurance. Thus, beliefs concerning women's intellectual and physical inferiority have served as powerful barriers to their career development and as justification for discrimination against women.

Although beliefs concerning female inferiority will undoubtedly persist, considerable research has investigated actual versus stereotypically believed sex differences. In the area of intellectual/cognitive functioning, research has focused on both general intellectual functioning and the more specific verbal, mathematical, and spatial abilities in particular. Major reviews of this research have been undertaken by Maccoby and Jacklin (1974) in their landmark book *The Psychology of Sex Differences* and by Janet Hyde (1981) in her metaanalysis of studies of sex differences in cognitive abilities.

With respect to general intellectual functioning, measured by such tests as the Stanford–Binet and the Wechsler scales (the WAIS, the WISC, and the WPPSI; see Walsh & Betz, 1985, for a complete description), there are no sex differences in normal populations (Maccoby & Jacklin, 1974). However, intellectual impairments that would adversely affect school performance occur more frequently in boys than in girls. For example, boys are born retarded more often than girls, are afflicted with dyslexia and other learning disabilities three to ten times more often than girls, and are three to four times more likely than girls to stutter (Maccoby & Jacklin, 1974; Williams, 1983). Because of the greater frequency of such disabilities among boys, boys are also significantly more likely than girls to be in programs for the educationally handicapped (Maccoby & Jacklin, 1974).

With respect to more specific abilities, Maccoby and Jacklin (1974) concluded that while the sexes do not differ in general intelligence, females generally obtain higher mean scores on tests of verbal ability, while males generally obtain higher mean scores on measures of mathematical reasoning and spatial visualization abilities. However, Maccoby and Jacklin offered several interpretive cautions in conjunction with this review. First, consistent sex differences in these abilities do not appear until adolescence, by which time children have had ample opportunity to learn sex role-appropriate characteristics and the cultural expectations for females versus males. Second, while the majority of studies have suggested this pattern of sex differences, many studies have failed to show these differences or have found differences in the opposite direction. For example, no sex-related cognitive differences were found in Sherman's (1979) sample of 9th and 10th graders. Sex differences in the mathematics performance of 9th graders have been shown to be negligible in several other studies (e.g., Chipman & Thomas, 1985; Chipman & Wilson, 1985; Wise, 1985).

Third, it is impossible to separate performance on "ability" tests from previous educational background and other experiences. In other words, the concepts of ability and achievement, while conceptually distinguishable, are very difficult to separate in actual practice, that is, on standardized tests (Green, 1974; Walsh & Betz, 1985). Tests such as the Scholastic Aptitude Test (SAT) may be viewed as measuring "developed abilities" (Anastasi, 1982; Schaefer & Gray, 1981), a concept which includes the idea of innate intellectual potential but does not ignore the influence of education, training, and sociocultural expectations. Thus, the term "ability" as used in this section refers to *test performance* or *developed ability* rather than to innate potential.

Finally, and most importantly, it is essential to note that an observed "sex difference" refers to a statistically significant difference in the mean score obtained by a *group* of males versus the mean score obtained by a *group* of females. However, as every student of statistics is taught, statistical significance does not necessarily imply practical significance; in the case of "mean" sex differences, their magnitude is relatively small, ranging from .1 to .5 standard deviation for verbal ability and from .2 to .66 for mathematical ability (Maccoby & Jacklin, 1974). Hyde's (1981) metaanalysis indicated that the average effect size was .24 SD for verbal ability, .43 for mathematical ability, and .45 for visual–spatial ability. Even more suggestive of the trivial nature of these differences is the fact that they account for only about 1% of the variance in the criterion measure for verbal and mathematical ability (Hyde, 1981; Eccles, 1983) and for at most 4% in visual–spatial ability (Hyde, 1981).

The relatively small, even trivial, size of these differences in combination with the large degree of within-sex variability leads to near total overlap of the male and female score distributions. In other words, a sex difference in favor of males does not preclude findings of a large number of females whose scores are higher than those of the average male. Similarly, many males score higher than the average female on traits when females have the higher group mean. Thus, an observed sex difference is of almost no *practical* utility in the prediction of the capabilities of an individual based on her/his sex, and, consequently, is also an inadequate explanation for females' lesser achievements in certain areas (Eccles, 1983; Hyde, 1981).

In spite of the almost complete lack of utility of sex differences for the prediction or explanation of either individual differences or female underachievement, the literature is replete with research attempting to discern the degree to which sex-related differences in abilities are biologically versus sociocultually based. Although the bases of such differences are of theoretical interest, they are most significant in their implications for social policy. Similar to controversy regarding the causes of race differences in test performance, findings of biological causation could be wrongly used to suggest the immutability of race or sex differences in performance, while environmental/sociocultural causation implies the means of positive change as well as facilitating understanding of the differences. Thus, research on the causes of sex differences is difficult to separate from its inevitable political implications, no matter how "objective" the researcher. Given this, some of the hypotheses regarding the bases of sex-related differences in cognitive ability will be briefly discussed below.

Research investigating biological causation has focused primarily on postulated sex differences in brain lateralization and cerebral dominance and on the postulate that visual–spatial ability is an X-linked recessive trait. With respect to cerebral dominance, it is generally agreed that the two hemispheres of the brain are somewhat specialized for different functions, that is, the left for verbal–linguistic and the right for spatial–perceptual functions (Levy-Agresti & Sperry, 1968; Sperry & Levy, 1970). At some point in development, one hemisphere, usually the left (at least in right-handed people), becomes dominant in its control of an individual's behavior.

One relatively consistent sex difference is that of *earlier* lateralization (i.e., specialization, differentiation of function) in females than in males, so researchers have attempted to link earlier female lateralization to superiority of the left ("verbal") hemisphere and to inferiority of the right ("spatial–perceptual") hemisphere. For example, Buffery and Gray (1972) postulated that earlier lateralization was related to greater lateralization, and that the latter in turn facilitated the development of verbal but the hindrance of spatial functions. In contrast, Levy-Agresti and Sperry (1968; Levy, 1969) proposed that earlier lateralization was related to *less* lateralization, which, in turn, facilitated verbal but hindered spatial functioning.

Not only are these two major theories contradictory, but each has led to some supportive research findings and some contrary findings (e.g., Maccoby & Jacklin, 1974; Sherman, 1979). Further, neither of these brain lateralization models is consistent with findings of a *lack* of sex differences in other hemispherically localized skills. Interestingly, the left hemisphere, in addition to being lauded for its verbal skills, has been called the "intellectual, analytic, and businesslike" hemisphere, while the right hemisphere has been characterized as "spontaneous, intuitive, and experiential" as well as specialized for perceptual–spatial functions (Levy-Agresti & Sperry, 1968). Thus, if the right hemisphere were truly dominant in males, we should refer to "men's intuition" rather than to women's, and if the "businesslike" left hemisphere were truly dominant in females, then women should be found most often in corporate boardrooms and making the important decisions in society. Hopefully, the reader has noted that when biological evidence *contradicts* our stereotypes, it is ignored. It is only when the biological evidence supports our "a priori" belief systems that it receives publicity and credence.

A second major biological hypothesis is that exceptional spatial ability is a recessive trait carried on the X chromosome (Bock & Kolakowski, 1973; Stafford, 1961). A boy receiving the trait from his mother's X chromosome would manifest it, since there is no dominant factor on the Y chromosome to mask the recessive X. Since girls have two X chromosomes, they would need to inherit the recessive gene from both parents in order to manifest the trait. Although some early studies provided support for this hypothesis, three recent studies using very large samples have found no evidence for the hypothesis (Bouchard, 1976; Defries, Ashton, Johnson, Kuse, McClearn, Mi, Rashad, Vanderberg, & Wilson, 1976; Williams, 1975). These data, along with the consistently low performance of Turner's syndrome (XO) females on spatial tasks, seem to discount the hypothesis of X linkage.

Other explanations for observed sex-related cognitive differences have focused on sociocultural factors, primarily those related to sex role socialization and stereotyped expectations of the performance capabilities of the two sexes. Sociocultural factors are implicated by such findings as the failure of sex differences to occur prior to adolescence or to occur consistently across schools or countries (e.g., Fennema & Sherman, 1977). Cross-culturally, for example, while math and science are viewed as male domains in this country, Asian and Oriental women are expected to be (and, lo and behold, *are*) just as competent in math and science as their male counterparts. A recent report of the Finnish Ministry of Education, summarized in the popular press, provides an interesting illustration. Concerned with the fact that 62% of the gymnasium (a college preparatory high school) students were girls, the Minister of Education stated that "Entrance is based on test scores, and boys tend to be afraid of languages and even of mathematics, while girls are not nervous about these subjects. The schools are just too demanding for the boys" (as reported in the *Columbus Dispatch*, February 8, 1981). It may be granted that this statement may not have been based on anything more than casual observation of a sex difference in enrollment, but its diametrical opposition to beliefs held in this country is interesting indeed.

Sociocultural explanations of sex differences in verbal ability relate to societal expectations that girls will talk more than boys and the consequent tendency of parents to talk more to female versus male babies (see Frieze *et al.*, 1978), facilitating further development of girls' abilities. Interestingly, views of reading as a feminine domain may hamper boys' performance—Williams (1983) summarized evidence suggesting that boys who view reading as a masculine domain read better than do boys who view it as feminine. Nash (1979) reported that in countries such as England and Germany, where reading is viewed as a male-appropriate activity and where there are more male elementary school teachers than is true in this country, boys have higher reading achievement scores than do girls.

Because of the crucial importance of math performance and achievement to educational and career decisions, factors influencing females' serious underutilization of their mathematical abilities will receive separate discussion. However, there is extensive evidence for sociocultural determinants of sex differences in math performance. As has been mentioned, differences do not occur until adolescence and they do not occur cross-culturally. In addition, in this country, societal stereotypes and attitudes convey the belief that math is a "male domain" (Osen, 1974), that girls do not need to study math (Fennema & Sherman, 1977), and that females are incompetent in math (Osen, 1974). In fact, Osen summarizes societal attitudes as perpetuating the notion that females cannot and should not succeed in math.

That girls and their parents and teachers internalize these beliefs is well documented. For example, girls may avoid high achievement in math because they fear social disapproval (Benbow & Stanley, 1980), and girls are less likely than boys to view math as useful to them (Fennema & Sherman, 1977; Hilton & Berglund, 1974). Girls are less confident of their math abilities than boys at ages prior to the appearance of sex differences in math achievement (Fennema & Sherman, 1977) and, as adolescents, are less confident *even when* their mathematics performance is equal to or superior to that of boys (Fennema & Sherman, 1977; Frieze, Fisher, Hanusa, McHugh, & Valle, 1981).

One major and critical manifestation of such beliefs is the role they play in females' premature cessation of coursework in math (Ernest, 1976; Fennema & Sherman, 1977). The crucial importance of math background to performance on math aptitude and achievement tests is well documented (Ernest, 1976; Green, 1974) and, in fact, most studies report that sex differences in math achievement are negligible or nonexistent when the amount of math background is equivalent between the sexes (Fennema & Sherman, 1977; Chipman & Thomas, 1985). Fennema and Sherman (1977) stated that "While it is possible to show differences in mathematics achievement or aptitude between groups of males and females *unequal* in mathematical background, reporting such findings as 'sex differences' in mathematical 'aptitude' erroneously implies that these differences are due to differences in inherent ability and can thus be attributed to sex per se" (p. 66). Thus, the failure of most studies of sex differences in mathematics achievement to control for math background renders their findings of limited utility at best and, at worst, subject to serious and damaging misinterpretation and misuse.

With regard to spatial ability, several investigators have argued that the childhood experiences of boys are more conducive to its development than are those of girls (Lunneborg & Lunneborg, 1986; McDaniel, Guay, Ball, & Kolloff, 1978; Sherman, 1967). Girls characterizing themselves as tomboys, allowed to explore and manipulate the outside environment like their male counterparts, do not show the spatial ability disadvantage found in girls as a group. Further, Fennema and Sherman (1977) found that when the number of spatially related high school courses (e.g., shop or drafting) was equivalent for males and females, sex differences in spatial ability disappeared.

Newcombe, Bandura, and Taylor (1983) developed a scale to measure spatial activities/experiences and reported that activities judged important to the development of visual–spatial abilities were more often masculine typed (e.g., archery, building model planes, or electronics circuitry) than neutral or feminine typed (e.g., sewing or figure skating). Although greater access to such activities would therefore seem to favor the development of greater spatial abilities in males, the correlation between amount of such experience and DAT-measured spatial ability was $r = .40$ in a sample of females, indicating the importance of such background experience. Similarly, Lunneborg and Lunneborg (1986) developed the Everyday Spatial Activities Test to examine the contribution of differential spatial experiences to educational and vocational behaviors. Not surprisingly, college women reported less spatial experience overall than did college men, and in both sexes, the amount of spatial experience was significantly related to measured spatial ability and mechanical reasoning scores.

To summarize, while biologically based explanations of sex differences in specific abilities cannot be ruled out and may explain some of the observed variance, sociocultural explanations remain important on both logical and empirical grounds. More importantly, observed sex differences, whatever their cause, are simply inadequate to explain the serious underrepresentation of women in high-level careers requiring superior academic aptitude. Even if, as suggested by Maccoby and Jacklin (1974), sex differences in mathematics and spatial abilities would lead to predictions of fewer female than male Nobel prize winners in science, the predictions of frequency of female winners would far exceed the actual number found. Observed sex differences do not explain the underutilization of the potential wealth of female intellect and talent.

Concerning sex differences in physical abilities, the larger size and greater strength and power of the average male in comparison to the average female is well documented (e.g., Harris, 1976; Williams, 1977). Few would dispute the suggestion that the best male tennis player or golfer could usually outperform the best female in the sport. While such differences may affect the nature of athletic competition, they have few, if any, implications for women's ability to successfully perform most or all jobs. For example, Wardle (1976) subjected female subjects to tests of physical strength, energy, and endurance simulating the requirements demanding jobs such as mining. On the basis of subjects' performance, Wardle concluded that women possess the capacities for most physically demanding jobs, including those of mining and deep sea fishing. Interestingly, job analyses revealed that nursing (a job thought "appropriate" for the "weaker" sex) requires as much expenditure of energy in a typical work shift as do mining and fishing, said by Wardle to be the most demanding male-dominated jobs. In addition, it should again be recalled that because of the tremendous within-sex variability, there are women stronger than most men and men who are weaker than the average female worker. Not all women, or men, wish to pursue work requiring considerable physical strength and exertion, but women as well as men deserve that choice.

WOMEN'S ABILITIES AND ACHIEVEMENTS: THE PARADOXES

It is both inherently logical and consistent with the matching model of career choice that individuals possessing higher levels of ability should also achieve higher educational and occupational levels. Higher levels of intellect, as measured by intelligence tests or tests of scholastic aptitude such as the SAT and Graduate Record Examination (GRE), facilitate both access to and completion of undergraduate,

graduate, and/or professional degree programs. These programs, in turn, are essential prerequisites to many well-paying and respectable careers.

Among men, the relationship of intellect to obtained educational and occupational levels is usually proportional. (Tyler, 1978). Among women, however, the relationship begins to break down in adolescence and by college age and beyond has broken down almost completely for the majority of women. Women fail to use their talents and abilities in educational and career pursuits, resulting in losses both to themselves and to a society which needs their talents.

Ironically, females start out as the higher achievers in comparison to males and, as children, are more likely to utilize their abilities in educational pursuits. Girls perform better academically than boys at all educational levels. Studies going back as far as 1929 have shown that girls obtain higher school grades than do boys, beginning in elementary school and continuing through college (Carnegie Commission on Higher Education, 1973; Hyde, 1985; Tyler, 1965). Among 1960 Project Talent seniors, 51% of the girls in comparison to 39% of the boys reported high school averages of mostly A's and B's (Carnegie Commission on Higher Education, 1973).

The school progress of girls is also superior to that of boys. Girls less frequently need to repeat a grade, and girls are more likely than boys to be accelerated and promoted (cf. Hyde, 1985). In college, women consistently receive higher grades than do men in major fields ranging from the humanities and social sciences to the sciences, engineering, and even mathematics. Women's grade point advantage ranges from one half to one full grade point, depending on the major field.

In addition to obtaining higher school and college grades, women receive higher grades in relation to their SAT scores *and* their high school grade point averages (GPAs) than do men. Thus, the predicted college GPA would be higher for a given female than for a male with an equivalent record of test scores and high school grades (Carnegie Commission on Higher Education, 1973).

Although women, then, earn significantly higher grades throughout school, their future career development is negatively affected by both the nature and the quality of the education they receive. Specifically, women begin to avoid coursework in math and science as soon as such coursework becomes elective rather than required (Ernest, 1976), usually in secondary school, and by college, are concentrated in a narrower and narrower range of traditionally female majors (Pfafflin, 1984; Randour *et al.*, 1982). Further, women are less often enrolled in high-prestige, research-oriented universities, both private and public.

In the first case, an important group of private, prestigious universities includes the formerly all-male Ivy League schools. Although these have now begun to admit women, the numbers are relatively small, especially at schools such as Princeton and Yale. In the case of public research-oriented universities, many of these were land-grant universities focusing on the fields of agriculture, engineering, and the natural sciences, fields in which women continue to be seriously underrepresented. On the other hand, women are overrepresented at colleges and universities emphasizing teacher training (Carnegie Commission on Higher Education, 1973).

Women's underutilization of their abilities is even more apparent in the occupational realm. Assuming few or no major gender differences in vocationally relevant abilities, we would assume an approximately equal tendency of women and men to achieve high occupational levels and to achieve eminence. Unfortunately, this has not been the case, with only negligible representation of women among the eminent throughout history. For example, fewer than 10% of the people who could be characterized as eminent based on having entries in standard biographical dictionaries have been women, and more than half of those women listed were so because they were sovereigns and were thus eminent by birth or, even worse, were the wives or mistresses of famous men (Anastasi, 1958). (It should also be noted that throughout much of recorded history, a woman could not get her work recognized unless she adopted a male pseudonym, for example, George Sand, or used only initials, for example, A. B. Smith as a hypothetical example. Thus, tallying the number of eminent women by counting female names in biographical dictionaries surely underestimates the contributions of eminent women who could not reveal their sex and still get their work recognized.)

An early attempt to study eminence in women (Castle, 1913) found only 868 eminent women across 42 nations, extending from the 7th century BC. The largest number of these had achieved eminence in literature, but the highest *level* of eminence (as indicated by the number of lines allocated in the biographical dictionary) was achieved by sovereigns, political leaders, and mothers or mistresses of eminent men. Other nonintellectual ways in which women achieved eminence (or at least the fame necessary to end up in a biographical dictionary) was through great beauty, a tragic fate, or being immortalized in literature (Castle, 1913).

Among the women who would have been likely to achieve eminence had they been born male are the gifted girls-grown-up in the longitudinal studies of gifted children by Lewis Terman, Maud Merrill, and Robert Oden, as described in Chapter 1. As was mentioned previously, while the gifted boys grew up to achieve great worldly eminence, the majority of the gifted girls became housewives. Of those who did work outside the home, most had pursued traditionally female occupations and "pink-collar" jobs, such as secretary. Two-thirds of the women with IQs of at least 170 (clearly genius level) were either housewives or office workers. Further, although the girls were judged the most artistically gifted as children, and the seven most talented writers were girls, as adults, *all* of the artists and writers were men (Terman & Oden, 1959)!

Thus, ability and talent in gifted girls had almost no relationship to their achievements as women. At least seven talented writers, as well as unknown numbers of artists, musicians, biologists, geneticists, and astronomers were lost to the world. As stated in the report of the Carnegie Commission on Higher Education (1973), "The supply of human intelligence is limited, and the demand for it in society is even greater. The largest unused supply is found among women" (p. 27).

More recently, Card *et al.* (1980) reported the results of a long-term, follow-up study of the 9th-grade cohort of the original Project Talent study. Project Talent, conducted by researchers at the University of Pittsburgh (Flanagan, 1971), was a large-scale, longitudinal study of 440,000 9th through 12th graders carefully sampled from 1,353 secondary schools across the country. Students were originally administered a battery of tests in 1960. Follow-up surveys measuring subjects' educational and occupational attainment 1, 5, and 11 years after subjects' expected high school graduation were also conducted.

Card *et al.* reported that while the female students had had higher high school grades and scored higher on a composite of academic ability tests, by 11 years after high school, men had obtained significantly more education and were earning significantly more money. Sex differences in realization of potential were found across all socioeconomic status levels, and differences widened from the 5-year to the 11-year follow-up. The widening of the achievement gap was most apparent for the most talented female students, those in the top quartile as 9th graders. In other words, by age 29, the brightest men are beginning to manifest their intellectual potential, while the bright women fall further and further short of their potential for educational and occupational achievement.

More generally, as was mentioned in Chapter 1, women are (on the average) just as intelligent and capable as are men (on the average), yet they are seriously disadvantaged in occupational status and level and in earning power. In addition, women are concentrated in traditionally female, primarily low-level, low-status occupations and are seriously underrepresented in the majority of high-level occupations. Most of the latter are in the male-dominated fields of science and engineering, business, medicine, dentistry, and law (National Science Foundation, 1984; Pfafflin, 1984; Prediger & Cole, 1975).

Even in female-dominated occupations, the top-ranking, most prestigious positions are held by men. For example, professional interior design and clothing design are dominated by men, and while most "cooks" are female (particularly those at home), most "chefs" are male. As was discussed in Chapter 1, women represent a large majority of kindergarten and elementary school teachers but only a minority of school administrators (U.S. Department of Labor, 1984). Although women constitute half of university instructors (a position usually lacking both tenurability and full benefits), the number of female full professors, department chairs, and deans is insignificant. Thus, within a given occupation, men predominate at the upper levels and women predominate at the lower levels (Gottfredson, 1978).

In summary, girls surpass boys in school achievement at all levels, but in terms of ultimate educational and occupational *level* achieved, females lag far behind males. Numerous barriers to women's career development, both internal and external, operate to reduce the extent to which women's abilities, and even their superior performance in school, are actualized in later achievements, not to mention actual eminence.

Thus, while women who have achieved educationally and occupationally are of higher ability than women in general, women's educational and occupational achievements have been significantly less than those of men with comparable ability. Generally, it may be said that women's use of their abilities and talents in educational and career pursuits is confused and thwarted by sociocultural expectations and pressures toward traditionally female roles and against high, career-oriented aspirations.

In spite of these barriers, higher levels of ability *do* have a strongly facilitative effect on women's career development. Higher aptitude and achievement test scores have been found to differentiate career-oriented from home-oriented women in several studies (Astin, 1968; Rand, 1968; Tinsley & Faunce, 1978; Watley & Kaplan, 1971). For example, Watley and Kaplan (1971) studied women who had been awarded National Merit Scholarships from 1956 to 1960. When followed up in 1965, a large majority (65%) of these gifted women planned to pursue a career at some point in their lives; this percentage was higher than the general percentages of women planning to work outside the home at that time (the late 1960s). Further, however, those planning immediate careers had higher SAT scores than did those planning to defer careers or those oriented toward homemaking only.

Tinsley and Faunce (1978), in a follow-up study of women who had taken the SVIB–W as college freshmen, reported that those who were career oriented 13 to 21 years later had had higher aptitude test scores and higher college GPAs than did those who were home oriented. Ware *et al.* (1984) followed the progress of 300 gifted university freshmen, 150 male and 150 female, having equivalently high ability (mean SAT math score = 660; mean SAT verbal score = 630 for the women and 610 for the men), equal numbers of high school math and science courses, and equal and high stated interest in science majors. Even so, by the end of the freshman year, only 50% of the women, versus 69% of the men, had declared a major in science. This was the case despite the fact that women's 1st-year science grades were slightly higher than those of the men. What did seem to predict women's choice to major in science was extremely high SAT math scores, while men of varying (and often lesser) abilities chose science majors.

While high ability in general appears to be associated with career orientation, ability and achievement in math and science appear to be a particularly important variables differentiating women who pursue male-dominated occupations from those who pursue traditionally female occupations (e.g., Astin & Myint, 1971; Peng & Jaffe, 1979). Mathematics as a "critical filter" in women's career development is the subject of the next section of the chapter.

MATHEMATICS: THE CRITICAL FILTER FOR WOMEN

The critical importance of mathematics background for entrance to many of the best career opportunities in our society, for example, engineering, scientific and medical careers, computer science, business, and the skilled trades, is now generally agreed upon (Armstrong, 1985; Chipman & Wilson, 1985; Sells, 1982; Sherman, 1982b), and lack of math background constitutes one of the major barriers to women's career development.

The classic study of the importance of math to career options was that by Sells (1973). In a study of freshmen at the University of California at Berkeley, Sells found that only 8% of the women, versus 57% of the men, had taken 4 years of high school math. Four years of high school math was prerequisite to entering the calculus or intermediate statistics courses required in three fourths of the possible major field areas, and the University did not provide remedial courses to allow a student to complete the prerequisites post hoc. Thus, 92% of the freshmen women at Berkeley were prevented by lack of math background from even *considering* 15 of the 20 major fields at Berkeley! The five remaining "options" were predictable—such traditionally female major areas as education, the humanities, the social sciences, librarianship, and social welfare. Thus, decisions to "choose" these majors may have in many cases been by default, through failure to qualify for any major requiring math background.

Goldman and Hewitt (1976) also illustrated the determining character of mathematics performance. Using the five-level science–nonscience continuum to describe college majors (as shown in Chapter 2), Goldman and Hewitt found that SAT mathematics scores were the predominant predictor of choice of a science versus non-science major among college men and women. SAT verbal scores served as a suppressor variable in that their removal from the prediction equation increased the predictive usefulness of the math section of the test. Goldman and Hewitt concluded that the association between sex and choice versus avoidance of science-related careers is mediated largely by the sex differences in mathematics achievement.

Sells (1982) further elaborated the vital importance of math preparation for both career options and future earnings. Four full years of high school math are vital to surviving the standard freshman calculus course, now required for most undergraduate majors in business administration, economics, agriculture, engineering, forestry, resource management and conservation, health sciences, nutrition, food and consumer sciences, and natural, physical, and computer sciences. Only the arts, humanities, physical education, and the social sciences do not require math background. Further, Sells (1982) showed a strong and direct relationship between college calculus background and both starting salaries and employers' willingness to interview a student for a given job. Mathematics is important even for non-college-degreed, technical occupations; the U.S. Department of Labor's *Occupational Outlook Handbook* shows that high school math and science are "strongly recommended" for technical and trade occupations. As was so well stated by Sells (1982), "Mastery of mathematics and science has become essential for full participation in the world of employment in an increasingly technological society" (p. 7).

Given the importance of math background to career *options* rather than to "choices" by default, females' tendency to avoid math coursework becomes one of the most serious barriers to their career development. Further, it is fairly clear now that it is a lack of math background, rather than lack of innate ability, which is to blame for females' poorer performance on quantitative aptitude and mathematics achievement tests (Chipman & Thomas, 1985; Chipman & Wilson, 1985; Pedro, Wolleat, Fennema, & Becker, 1981; Sherman, 1982a; Wise, 1985). Thus, the critical issue is females' avoidance of math. The reasons for such avoidance and, by implication, interventions capable of helping young women to be full participants in an increasingly technological society, may be the most crucial issues in the study of women's career choices.

Regarding the first point, females' avoidance of math has long been documented (Eccles, 1983; Ernest, 1976; Chipman & Thomas, 1985). Girls take fewer math courses than do boys beginning in high school and continuing through college (Ernest, 1976; Fennema & Sherman, 1977; Pedro et al., 1981). Even boys who fall into the lower half of the achievement distribution are more likely than their female counterparts to continue the study of math (Sherman & Fennema, 1978). Although there are signs that girls are beginning to take more math in high school (e.g., Chipman & Thomas, 1985), several studies have focused on the reasons for female avoidance of this critical subject matter area.

The breakdown of females' full participation in math begins in adolescence, in about the 9th or 10th grades. Prior to this point, sex differences in math achievement and participation are not generally found (Chipman & Wilson, 1985; Wise, 1985). Beginning during the secondary school years, however, girls stop taking math and, not surprisingly, their math achievement test scores begin to fall below those of boys. Evidence that it is math coursework that is vital to math achievement comes from the findings that sex differences do not occur until females stop taking math, and that girls who continue the study of math achieve math grades as good as those of the boys (Chipman & Wilson, 1985).

Unfortunately, the performance decrements which follow cessation of math coursework create a vicious cycle, since math achievement then becomes an excellent predictor of plans to take additional math (Boswell, 1985; Brush, 1985; Chipman & Wilson, 1985; Wise, 1985). For example, the correlation between 9th-grade math achievement test scores and later high school math participation in the Project Talent sample was .62 (Wise, 1985). Among the Project Talent 9th graders, there were *no sex differences* in math achievement test scores, yet by 12th grade there were significant sex differences in math participation. Thus, a girl with a given level of math ability was less likely than a boy of equivalent capability to continue in math. Thus, the key question is "Why do girls stop taking math?"

The major explanations for females' avoidance of math beginning in adolescence derive from differences in the way female socialization, versus male socialization, influences attitudes toward and self-confidence with respect to math learning and performance. As was mentioned in the section discussing the bases of sex differences in math performance, societal stereotypes and attitudes convey the beliefs that "math is a male domain" (Osen, 1974), that girls do not need to study math (Fennema & Sherman, 1977), and that females are incompetent in math (Osen, 1974).

Considerable research has explored the degree to which girls have internalized such societally conveyed beliefs. Studies of such variables as beliefs in the utility of math to one's future life and career, confidence in one's ability to learn and to perform math, and math anxiety have used instruments including the Fennema–Sherman Mathematics Attitudes Scales (Fennema & Sherman, 1976) and their adaptation for use with college students (Betz, 1978), the Mathematics Anxiety Rating Scale [(MARS) Richardson & Suinn, 1972] and a short form of the MARS (Plake & Parker, 1982), the Mathematics Confidence Scale (Dowling, 1978), and the Math Attitudes and Math Usefulness Scales (Boswell, 1985).

There is considerable consistency in research findings. Females have been found to have less confidence in their math ability in comparison to males even when their objectively measured abilities are equal (Chipman & Wilson, 1985). Fennema and Sherman (1977) reported that males had more confidence in their math ability than did high school females after the 8th grade. Overall, data indicate that girls have less confidence *independent* of objective performance (Chipman & Wilson, 1985). The conclusion by Armstrong (1985) and Chipman and Wilson (1985) that math confidence is a better predictor of further math participation than is actual math achievement clearly suggests the role of girls' lack of confidence as a factor contributing to math avoidance.

Related to the issue of self-confidence is the widespread belief that boys do better than girls in math. Ernest (1976) reported the belief of male superiority not only among high school boys and girls but in both male and female teachers. Thus, a self-fulfilling prophecy of male success and female failure in math may be unconsciously set up by teachers.

Another concept closely related to that of math confidence is "math anxiety" (Betz, 1978; Hendel & Davis, 1978; Tobias, 1978). Math anxiety, defined as "feelings of tension and anxiety that interfere with the manipulation of numbers and the solving of mathematical problems in a wide variety of ordinary life and academic situations" (Richardson & Suinn, 1972), is postulated to underlie both avoidance of and poor performance in math courses and math-related majors and careers.

Just as girls have less confidence in their math abilities, they are also found to be more math anxious in many (although not all) studies. Boswell (1985) reported greater math anxiety among girls in all school grades, while findings of greater math anxiety in female versus male college students were reported by Betz (1978), Dew, Galassi, and Galassi (1983), and Llabre and Suarez (1985). In the latter study, women were more math anxious even though there were no sex differences in SAT math scores. On the other hand, Resnick, Viehe, and Segal (1982) did not find sex differences in math anxiety.

Math anxiety, like math achievement, is closely related to amount of math background (Betz, 1978; Hackett, 1985; Hendel, 1980; Richardson & Woolfolk, 1980). Thus, the vicious cycle is further complicated, with various forces leading to the development of anxiety and the avoidance of math coursework sometime in adolescence, both of which hinder subsequent math achievement, thus exacerbating anxiety and solidifying patterns of math avoidance.

Finally, an idea which takes into account both confidence and anxiety is that of "mathematics self-efficacy expectations," that is, an individual's belief in her capability to successfully engage in various math-related tasks. Basing their research on Bandura's (1977) theory of self-efficacy expectations as a major mediator of behavior and behavior change (see also Chapter 7), Betz and Hackett (1983) developed a three-part measure of mathematics self-efficacy; the scales assess confidence in one's ability to (1) complete everyday math tasks (e.g., balancing a checkbook), (2) complete math-related college coursework, and (3) complete math word problems.

Using this three-part measure, Betz and Hackett (1983) studied the mathematics self-efficacy expectations of college males and females. As predicted, the math-related self-efficacy expectations of college males were significantly higher than those of college females on all subscales, and students' math-related self-efficacy expectations contributed significantly to the degree to which students selected science-based college majors. Interestingly, the only items toward which females felt just as efficacious as males were those involving "female" domains such as cooking, grocery shopping, and sewing. [This finding is also supportive of research findings suggesting that the male-oriented content of math tests favors male versus female test performance, and that changing test content to include an equal balance of female-oriented and male-oriented domains would be fairer to female test-takers than is represented by current practices (e.g., Frieze *et al.*, 1978).]

Another important factor explaining females' avoidance of mathematics may be the lesser perceived utility of math to female versus male students (Chipman & Wilson, 1985). There is considerable evidence both for a relationship of perceived usefulness of math to participation in math (Armstrong, 1985; Lantz, 1985; Pedro *et al.*, 1981; Sherman, 1982a; Sherman & Fennema, 1977) and for girls' tendency to perceive math as less useful to them (Fennema & Sherman, 1977; Hilton & Berglund, 1974). Boswell (1985) reported that both males and females perceived math as more useful for men than for women. Eccles, Adler, and Meece (1984) compared several different theoretical explanations for sex differences in math achievement: self-concept theories, attribution theory, learned helplessness versus mastery orientation, and expectancy value theory. Eccles *et al.* found that the strongest mediator of both academic achievement plans and sex differences in math achievement was subjective task value, that is, perceptions of the utility and importance of math, interest in math, and perceived worth of effort needed to do well in math. In contrast, there was some evidence for sex differences in ability attributions consistent with the expectancy/self-concept perspective, and little support for learned helplessness models.

The influence of traditional life role expectations for females probably also reduces females' likelihood of continuing in math. Evidence of "sex role strain" in relationship to math was reported by Sherman (1983), and she further reported that 29% of girls said they would "play dumb," downplaying their abilities, while 76% perceived other girls as playing dumb. Similarly, Benbow and Stanley (1980) suggested that girls avoid math because they fear social disapproval. Sherman (1983) concludes that "After several years of research, it is my opinion that it is neither anxiety nor lack of ability that keeps women from mathematics. It is a network of sex role influences which makes mathematics and the careers mathematics are needed in, appear incongruent with the female role, especially with motherhood. When girls see that motherhood and demanding careers can be combined, a major source of resistance to mathematics will disappear. Research and action to reduce the perceived and real conflict between demanding careers and motherhood is of crucial importance" (p. 342).

In summary, young women who have continued coursework in mathematics and science have a far broader range of career options than do the majority of young women who have avoided such work. An emphasis on changing societal expectations and the expectations of girls and women with regard to the appropriateness and necessity of mathematics for women is essential to the facilitation of women's career development. Some specific changes that should be made are to require 4 years of math for all students so that the insidious effects of female socialization and the consequent effects of a breakdown in confidence can be thwarted (Chipman & Wilson, 1985), along with overt support for girls as both capable of and needing math. Such support should be built into school systems so that teachers and parents are informed regarding the problems and are involved in their solutions.

Additional useful possibilities include special programs for math-talented girls (Fox, Brody, & Tobin, 1985), the applications of Bandura's self-efficacy model to the treatment of math anxiety and math avoidance, Blum and Givant's (1982) programs at Mills College in California, Cronkite and Perl's (1982) math–science conferences for junior high and senior high school girls, and Kreinberg's (1982) descriptions of programs at the University of California–Berkeley to improve educators' ability to facilitate girls' confidence, participation, and performance in math. Lantz (1985) describes a number of strategies designed to increase math enrollment among women. Finally, several programs are discussed in Humphreys' (1982) edited volume *Women and Minorities in Science: Strategies for Increasing Participation,* Chipman, Brush, and Wilson's (1985) *Women and Mathematics: Balancing the Equation,* and Steinkamp and Maehr's (1983) *Women in Science.*

SUMMARY

One final point pertinent to the understanding of aptitudes in women is that the personality correlates of high aptitude (or at least measured, developed high aptitude) differ between the sexes. While traits related to masculinity appear to be negatively related to aptitudes in males, such traits as independence, assertiveness, an internal locus of control, and high self-esteem are positively associated with intellectual abilities and interests in females (Doherty & Culver, 1976; Kagan & Moss, 1962; Maccoby & Jacklin, 1974; Starr, 1979). While feminine-typed girls may be as *inherently* bright as androgynous or masculine-typed girls, the *expression* of high intellect appears to be facilitated by failure to conform to traditionally female sex role characteristics.

Moreover, research has suggested that between the 7th and 12th grades, the measured IQs of boys increase, while those of girls decrease (Campbell, 1976). Further, the largest declines are found among the most stereotypically feminine girls, with smaller or negligible declines among more masculine-typed girls. Thus, enriched, broadened environments which not only allow but encourage girls to develop both the competencies and traits characteristic of traditional masculinity as well as the positive aspects of femininity are likely to be helpful to female achievements.

In summary, aptitudes are important variables in women's career development, but societal attitudes and stereotypes lead many women to fail to fully develop, not to mention utilize, their intellectual capabilities. Until girls are helped to overcome the societal and internal barriers to the development of their intellectual potentials, the relationship of aptitudes to female career development will remain complex.

PERSONALITY VARIABLES AND WOMEN'S CAREER DEVELOPMENT: SELF-CONCEPT AND SEX ROLE-RELATED CHARACTERISTICS

A variety of personality characteristics have been found to be associated with the career development of women. In general, characteristics positively associated with women's career development are those more often associated with males or masculinity, while those negatively related to women's career development are stereotypically feminine traits. In this chapter, important personality and attitudinal variables related to women's career development are reviewed; these variables include the self-concept, variables related to sex role orientation, and attitudes toward women's roles.

SELF-CONCEPT

The crucial importance of a positive self-concept to psychological health and optimal functioning has long been a fundamental assumption in psychology (e.g., Rogers, 1951). Further, the self-concept plays a central role in at least one theory of career choice and development. For example, in Donald Super's (1957, 1963) theory, career choices are postulated to involve a process of implementing the self-concept in vocational roles. Not surprisingly, then, variables related to the self-concept have been shown to be of considerable importance to women's career development. In the discussion to follow, a number of aspects of the self-concept will be reviewed and research investigating their importance to women's career development will be summarized.

In reviewing the literature related to self-concept and women's career development, one begins with literature characterized by a variety of poorly defined but related terms operationalized by an equally wide variety of measuring instruments. Some studies fail to define the terms used or to clarify how the measures used relate to the constructs of interest. In addition, there is by no means agreement among researchers on the definitions of self-concept, self-esteem, and related terms, whether they are global, unidimensional terms or multidimensional concepts, nor on how they should be measured. Given this state of confusion, the consistency of self-concept-related variables as predictive of women's career achievements across studies using different terms, different definitions, and different measures attests to their importance. In the following sections, a general framework for considering variables related to the self-concept will be presented, followed by research relating these variables to women's career development. For more detailed reviews of the self-concept literature, see works by Burns (1979), Rosenberg (1979), Wells and Maxwell (1976), and Wylie (1974, 1979).

A useful framework for organizing research related to the influence of the self-concept on women's career development is the hierarchical model of Shavelson, Hubner, and Stanton (1976). According to their model, general or global self-esteem is composed of two second-order "facets," academic self-concept and nonacademic self-concept. Academic self-concept can be further divided into subareas such as English, math, history, and science. Nonacademic self-concept is subdivided into social self-concept, emotional self-concept, and physical self-concept, each of which is further subdivided. Finally, the lowest level of specificity includes evaluation of self-concept in specific situations. This model is both necessary and useful because research relating the self-concept to women's career development has used definitions and measures spanning the hierarchy from global to specific. The discussion to follow will begin with studies of global self-esteem and will proceed to examine more specific areas of self-concept.

GLOBAL SELF-ESTEEM

One source of the measures of global self-esteem, or overall self-evaluation and self-acceptance, is the self-esteem, self-acceptance, and self-confidence scales from widely used personality inventories such as the California Psychological Inventory (Gough, 1957) and the

16PF (Cattell, 1949; Cattell, Eber, & Tatsuoka, 1970). Other specially constructed measures include the Rosenberg Self-Esteem Scale (Rosenberg, 1965), the Coopersmith (1967) Self-Esteem Scale, and the Self-Assurance Scale of the Ghiselli (1971) Self-Description Inventory (SDI). Eight different measures were studied by Demo (1985).

Although sex differences in global measures of self-esteem are not consistently found, studies using such measures consistently report more positive self-concepts and higher levels of self-esteem among career-oriented versus home-oriented women (e.g., Tinsley & Faunce, 1980). Greater self-confidence and self-esteem have been found to be associated with stronger career orientation among adolescent girls (Baruch, 1976; Ridgeway & Jacobsen, 1979). Self-esteem is strongly related to achievement motivation in both male and female college students, but the relationship appears to be stronger for female students (Steriker & Johnson, 1977).

High levels of self-esteem are particularly characteristic of women in male-dominated occupations, such as Bachtold's (1976) women scientists, artists, writers, and politicians, Bachtold and Werner's (1970) psychologists, and Lemkau's (1983) physicians, attorneys, and others. Greenhaus and Simon (1976) reported that female students higher in self-esteem, as measured by the Self-Assurance Scale of the Ghiselli SDI, showed greater correspondence between their real and ideal choices than did students lower in self-esteem.

ACADEMIC AND PERFORMANCE SELF-ESTEEM

Although global self-esteem is related to stronger career orientation and greater likelihood of pursuing nontraditional careers, probably even more important to women's career development is that dimension of self-concept variously called academic self-concept (Farmer, 1976; Shavelson et al., 1976), confidence in achievement situations (Lenney, 1977; Maccoby & Jacklin, 1974), intellectual self-concept (Rand, 1968; Tinsley & Faunce, 1980), and performance self-esteem (Stake, 1979a,b). Because academic self-concept has been consistently shown to influence type and level of academic performance (e.g., Eccles et al., 1984; Eccles, Adler, Futterman, Goff, Kaczala, Meece, & Midgley, 1983) and because females are less confident in this domain than are males of equal ability (Gold, Brush, & Sprotzer, 1980; Maccoby & Jacklin, 1974; Stake, 1979a), lower levels of academic self-esteem may be a serious barrier to women's career development. The previous chapter dealt with this problem in the area of mathematics, discussing the serious negative effects of women's lack of confidence in their mathematics abilities.

In addition to overall levels of academic self-esteem, research has utilized several related but more specific, behaviorally based concepts, that is, expectancies for success and self-efficacy expectations.

EXPECTANCIES FOR SUCCESS

One closely related and widely studied manifestation of women's lower academic self-esteem is their tendency to underestimate their abilities and their probable levels of future performance, a phenomenon studied in the literature as sex differences in expectancies (e.g., see Eccles *et al.*, 1983, 1984; Meece, Eccles-Parson, Kaczala, Goff, & Futterman, 1982). Research has shown that women tend to provide lower estimates of their abilities, performance, and expectancies for future success in many achievement situations, even when their performance is objectively better than that of males (Crandall, 1969; Meece *et al.*, 1982).

For example, if college students are asked to estimate their exam performance, most studies indicate that females will estimate that they will get fewer points versus males (Block, 1976). Lower expectancies for performance have been found in females as young as preschool (Crandall, 1978) and elementary school age (Crandall, 1969).

Additional findings suggest that females' significantly lower expectancies for success occur primarily on masculine-stereotyped tasks (Deaux, 1984; Gitelson, Petersen, & Tobin-Richards, 1982; McHugh & Frieze, 1982), on tasks lacking clear performance feedback, and on tasks including elements of social comparison, social evaluation, or competition. For example, McHugh and Frieze (1982) showed that women's performance expectancies were lower for intellectual tasks but were higher for social tasks in comparison to males, and Deaux and Farris (1977) reported that women's performance expectancies were lower than those of men when an anagrams task was labeled "masculine" but were equal to those of men when the *same task* was labeled feminine. Similarly, House (1974) reported that female subjects working alone on an anagram task had performance expectancies equal to those of male subjects, but that females doing the same task under instructions involving competition with another subject had significantly lower expectancies in comparison with males in general or with females working alone.

Thus, some conditions appear to be related to significantly lower expectancies for success among females and, unfortunately, these conditions are similar to the conditions under which career achievements must occur, that is, as involving a role pursuit which our society has traditionally defined as a masculine versus feminine domain of activity, as usually involving some sort of social comparison or competition, and as not generally characterized by clear and unambiguous feedback. Thus, females' tendency to underestimate themselves may negatively influence their career development.

SELF-CONCEPT IN SPECIFIC SITUATIONS: SELF-EFFICACY EXPECTATIONS

Closely related to the concept of expectancies for success and also at the most behaviorally specific level of the hierarchy of types of self-concept is the concept of self-efficacy expectations. Developed by Bandura (1977), the notion of self-efficacy expectations refers to one's expectation or belief that one can successfully perform a given task or behavior. Bandura postulated that both behavior and behavior change are mediated primarily by expectations of personal efficacy. Efficacy expectations influence the kinds of behaviors attempted and the persistence of behavior when dissuading or disconfirming experiences are confronted. For example, self-efficacy expectations with respect to mathematics would influence approach versus avoidance behavior with respect to mathematics and the extent of persistence when a negative experience, such as failing a math test, was confronted.

Although Bandura's theory was originally used in the investigation of clinical phobias, Hackett and Betz (1981) proposed its particular utility for the understanding of women's underrepresentation in traditionally male-dominated careers. Using the concept of career-related self-efficacy expectations, Hackett and Betz contended that low career-related self-efficacy expectations mediated the effects of traditional female sex role socialization on women's later career choices.

More specifically, Hackett and Betz suggested that female socialization provides less access to the sources of information important to the development of strong expectations of efficacy with respect to career-related behaviors; such sources of information include performance accomplishments, vicarious learning (modeling), and encouragement and support for achievement-related behaviors. Figure 7.1 illustrates the postulated effects of traditional female socialization experiences on the development of strong, career-related self-efficacy expectations.

Based on their model, the research of Betz and Hackett and their colleagues (Betz & Hackett, 1981, 1983; Hackett, 1985; Hackett & Campbell, 1984) has indicated that females report lower and weaker

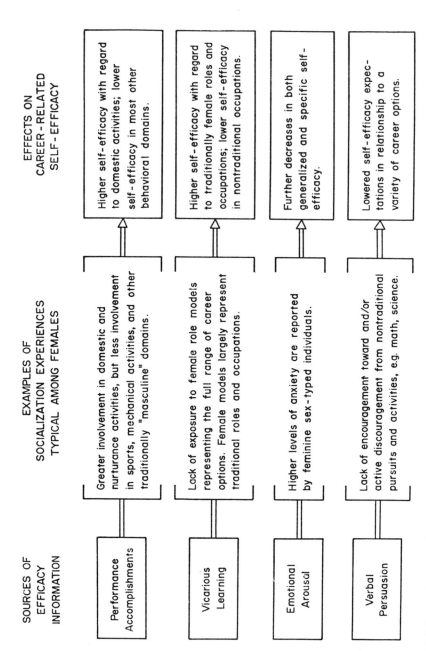

FIGURE 7.1 From Hackett & Betz (1981). Copyright © by Academic Press, Inc. Reproduced by permission of the publisher.

self-efficacy expectations with respect to their successful completion of male-dominated educational majors and careers and with respect to the study and performance of mathematics. Further, these lower expectations are related to major and occupational preferences and to the range of career options considered (Betz & Hackett, 1981; Hackett, 1985).

CAUSAL ATTRIBUTIONS FOR SUCCESS AND FAILURE

Related to females' devaluation of their performance capabilities and their low self-efficacy expectations is their greater tendency to attribute their successes to factors other than their own ability. Much research on causal attributions of success and failure has been based on a model developed by Weiner and his colleagues (1971), in which two dimensions of attributions, stable versus temporary and internal versus external, were postulated. Stable causes of events, such as ability, can be expected to remain unchanged in the future, while temporary or unstable causes, for example, luck, cannot be depended upon. Internal causes are part of the person (e.g., ability) while external causes are those from outside the individual (e.g., luck, task difficulty). The most commonly studied attributions are ability (internal and stable), effort (internal and either stable or unstable), luck (external and unstable), and task difficulty (external and either stable or unstable if the task changes) (Weiner, Frieze, Kukla, Reed, Rest, & Rosenbaum, 1971).

Attributions of the causes of successes and failures are theoretically related to both self-esteem and expectancies for future performance. Internal and stable attributions for success and external and unstable attributions for failure would seem to be most closely related to self-esteem—in other words, "taking credit" for successes and avoiding internalizing failures (*especially* when they were caused externally) allows maximal self-pride and minimal self-flagellation. Further, attributions of successes to stable causes would heighten expectations of future successes because the success-inducing conditions would not change.

Early research suggested that women tended to attribute successes to external factors such as luck, while men attributed it to their own abilities (Simon & Feather, 1973). These results were also found when people explained the behavior of another person (Deaux & Emswiller, 1974). When explaining failures, women were more likely than men to attribute failure to internal sources, especially to their own lack of abilities (e.g., McMahan, 1971, 1972).

Although interested readers should refer to Frieze, Whitley, Hanusa, and McHugh (1982) and Hansen and O'Leary (1985) for more comprehensive reviews of this literature, an interesting new perspective was recently proposed by Deaux (1984). Based on reviews of the studies of attribution patterns, Deaux (1984) proposed that differences in attributions are a function of differences in expectancies for success and failure which, in turn, are related to the sex linkage of the task. More specifically, Deaux (1984) summarized data indicating that when expectancies for success are low, failure is expected but success must be explained away; thus, failure can be attributed to internal and stable causes such as lack of ability while success is "explained away" with unstable causes such as luck or extreme effort. In contrast, when expectations for performance are high, success is expected and can be attributed to internal and stable causes such as ability. Failure is not expected and so is attributed to unstable causes or explained away using, for example, bad luck. The implication of Deaux's proposed explanation is that females' attributions for success and failure will become healthier only as females' performance expectancies increase but, unfortunately, maladaptive patterns of attributions do not facilitate such improvements when females do not take credit for their successes.

Summary

In summary, variables related to the self-concept are important in relation to women's educational and career development. In comparison to males, females generally seem to report less confidence in their academic and career-related capabilities and since beliefs are related to achievement behavior, females' lower self-concepts probably serve as a serious barrier to their educational and career achievements. This hypothesis is supported by other research findings indicating that stronger career orientation and innovation in women are related to higher levels of self-esteem. Although it is most likely true that women with greater self-esteem are better equipped to pursue their goals and to fulfill their capabilities in spite of societal barriers or lack of support, it is also possible that successful career pursuits lead to an increase or at least the absence of a decrement in self-esteem. Thus, higher self-esteem may "cause" career orientation, but career pursuits, particularly if they are successful, may "cause" higher self-esteem as well. Although the precise causes of the relationships are unknown, the importance of self-concept to women's career development is evident.

SEX ROLE-RELATED PERSONALITY CHARACTERISTICS:
INSTRUMENTALITY, EXPRESSIVENESS, AND ANDROGYNY

A major focus of research related to the psychology of women has been based on the concepts of psychological masculinity and femininity. Prior to the 1970s, masculinity and femininity were viewed as opposite points on a single bipolar continuum, such that greater degrees of masculinity implied lesser degrees of femininity and vice versa. So-called masculinity–femininity scales such as the MMPI Mf and the CPI Fe assessed position on this theoretically bipolar continuum. Essentially, this conceptualization of personality simply extended the idea of male and female as "opposite" biological sexes to include opposite personality characteristics as well.

This conceptualization, although widely utilized, presented a number of problems. First, it implied that failure to score in the direction consistent with one's biological sex was indicative of psychopathology, ranging from rejection of one's own "proper" sex role to homosexuality. Thus, within-gender individual differences were neither expected nor desired; rather, what was considered healthy was conformity to the appropriate gender role. When the conformity expectation was coupled with findings that the feminine role was viewed as less socially desirable (Rosenkrantz, Vogel, Bee, Broverman, & Broverman, 1968) and as less psychologically healthy than the masculine role (Broverman *et al.*, 1970), the bipolar conceptualization was seen to have highly detrimental consequences for women.

Beginning in the 1970s, a number of writers (e.g., Bem, 1974; Constantinople, 1973; Spence, Helmreich, & Stapp, 1974) suggested that masculinity and femininity were more appropriately conceptualized as separate, independent dimensions rather than as opposite ends of a single dimension. With this conceptualization, an individual of either sex could possess relatively high levels of both masculinity and femininity, relatively low levels of both, or a high level of one in combination with a low level of the other. In Bem's (1974) original formulation, a *balance* of masculine and feminine characteristics was postulated to be advantageous because balanced or "androgynous" individuals would have maximal behavioral flexibility and adaptability; such individuals would be freer of artificial sex role-related constraints on the extent of their behavioral and coping repertoires. For example, an androgynous individual would theoretically be able to display adaptive "masculine" behaviors (e.g., assertiveness, active problem-solving) *and* adaptive feminine behaviors (e.g., giving emotional support to others) as appropriate to situational demands.

In order to study the concepts of masculinity and femininity as separate dimensions, measures such as the Bem Sex Role Inventory [(BSRI) Bem, 1974] and the Personal Attributes Questionnaire [(PAQ) Spence *et al.*, 1974] were developed. These scales typically have consisted of separate scales measuring masculinity and femininity; item content consists of self-descriptive adjectives associated with traditionally perceived masculinity or femininity, respectively. For example, the BSRI includes the characteristics "Independent," "Assertive," "Self-sufficient," and "Acts like a leader" on the masculinity scale and the characteristics "Affectionate," "Compassionate," "Tender," and "Loyal" on the femininity scale. In addition to separate masculinity and femininity scores, the scales have provided means of combining the two to yield descriptions of degree of "sex-typing" versus balance or androgyny. For example, one commonly used scheme involves the classification of subjects as above or below the normative median on each scale; individuals above the median on both are classified as androgynous, those above the median on one and below on the other are "sex-typed" or "cross-sex-typed," and those below both medians are "undifferentiated" (Bem, 1977; Spence, Helmreich, & Stapp, 1975).

Although a large body of research literature has utilized these and other measures of sex role orientation (see the extensive review by Cook, 1985), there is an increasing tendency to avoid the terms "masculinity" and "femininity" in favor of terms which better summarize the actual behaviors and characteristics represented (Gilbert, 1985; Spence & Helmreich, 1980, 1981). The terms "masculinity" and "femininity" have been criticized because they perpetuate stereotypes and assumptions that behavior is gender based (Lott, 1985), because they imply false dichotomies which overemphasize between-gender and underemphasize within-gender differences (Lott, 1985; Wallston, 1981), and because they are not descriptive of behavior.

Rather, the term "instrumentality," referring to the capabilities of self-assertion and competence, has been suggested by Spence and Helmreich to descriptively summarize the key aspects of traditional stereotypes of masculinity. The term "expressiveness" best summarizes the central aspects of traditional femininity, that is, nurturance, interpersonal concern, and emotional expressiveness and sensitivity. Similarly, David Bakan's (1966) distinction between "agentic" (self-assertive, motivated to master) and "communal" (concerned with others, selfless) characteristics provides an alternative set of descriptive labels for what is measured by masculinity and femininity scales.

Regardless of the labels used to report the results of research in this area, this research has consistently and convincingly shown the importance of these constellations of characteristics, particularly instrumentality or masculinity, to women's career development. More specifically, instrumentality appears to be strongly related to both the extent and nature of women's career pursuits. Higher levels of instrumentality are related to stronger career orientation (Abrahams, Feldman, & Nash, 1978; Greenglass & Devins, 1982; Marshall & Wijting, 1980), to a greater extent of labor force participation following the birth of the first child (Gaddy, Glass, & Arnkoff, 1983), and to greater career achievement among working women (Wong, Kettlewell, & Sproule, 1985). Orlovsky and Stake (1981) reported that masculinity was related to stronger achievement motivation and to greater performance self-esteem and self-perceived capabilities among college women. Metzler-Brennan, Lewis, and Gerrard (1985) found that masculinity in both personality and childhood activities distinguished career-oriented from home-oriented women.

Most strongly related to instrumentality, however, is pursuit of careers in nontraditional fields for women. Among younger women, masculinity is related to stronger interests in and greater pursuit of math and science, more confidence in one's math abilities, and a greater likelihood of selecting a math-related college major (Hackett, 1985). The greater willingness to consider nontraditional college majors, or, alternatively stated, less susceptibility to the limiting influences of traditional female socialization, was the major explanation of Wolfe and Betz' (1981) finding that masculine-typed women were more likely than feminine-typed women to prefer careers that are congruent with their measured vocational interests. Thus, the trait–factor or "matching model" as a basis for career decision-making may be more common among women who have at least in some ways surmounted sex stereotyping.

Several other studies have shown that instrumentality and related characteristics are prevalent among women in male-dominated occupational fields (e.g., Bachtold, 1976; Bachtold & Werner, 1970, 1972, 1973; Helson, 1971; O'Leary & Braun, 1972). For example, Bachtold and Werner (1970) found that the personality characteristics of female psychologists were more similar to those of male psychologists than they were to women in general. Cartwright (1972) reported that female medical students were significantly more independent, individualistic, and autonomous and significantly less suggestible and submissive than women in general. Williams and McCullers (1983) reported that women in nontraditional fields scored higher on the BSRI masculinity scale than did women in traditional fields; the former group also reported more masculine play patterns and less coercion to fit the feminine stereotype.

Helmreich *et al.* (1980), in a study of male and female academic psychologists, found no sex differences on instrumentality characteristics which, in the general population, would be found more frequently among males. These findings, among others, have led to a general view that, at least in terms of personality, highly career-oriented women may be more similar in personality to career-oriented men than to women.

A final important point regarding instrumentality is its strong relationship to self-esteem and general psychological adjustment. Research has consistently shown moderate to strong positive correlations between masculinity and self-esteem and such indices of adjustment as lack of depressive symptomatology. Femininity, on the other hand, is only weakly or negligibly related to self-esteem and adjustment (Antill & Cunningham, 1979; O'Connor, Mann, & Bardwick, 1978; Orlovsky & Stake, 1981; Spence, Helmreich, & Stapp, 1975; Taylor & Hall, 1982; Whitley, 1984). Masculinity and self-esteem, then, both of which facilitate career development in women, are also related to each other.

Thus, the possession of characteristics associated with traditional masculinity appears to be importantly and positively related to career innovation and achievement in women. The extent to which the possession of traditionally feminine characteristics is related to career involvement is less clear. While some studies have suggested a relationship between expressiveness or femininity and home orientation (Abrahams *et al.*, 1978; Marshall & Wijting, 1980), other studies have suggested that career-oriented women score no differently on measures of femininity than do home-oriented women (Masih, 1967; Metzler-Brennan *et al.*, 1985; Rand, 1968; Yanico, Hardin, & McLaughlin, 1978). Farmer (1985) reported that highly career-motivated young women tended to be androgynous, possessing relatively high levels of both instrumentality and expressiveness. Thus, career-oriented women may more often fit Bem's (1974) ideal of androgyny, individuals whose behavioral repertoire includes both instrumental and expressive qualities.

The absence of a strong or consistent relationship between femininity and home orientation, coupled with the strong relationship of instrumentality to career orientation, led Spence and Helmreich (1980) to suggest that it may not only be the *presence* of instrumentality which leads some women to seek career achievements but the *absence* of instrumentality which leads home-oriented women to avoid such pursuits. In other words, home-oriented women may be motivated not so much by the desire to nurture but by doubts concerning their capabilities to cope and compete in the larger world. Thus, a "deficit model" of choice of homemaking as the central life pursuit would be suggested.

A final point concerning the relationship between masculinity and femininity and career orientation is that although instrumentality may facilitiate career pursuits, the performance of work versus home roles may influence one's own and other's perceptions of the presence versus the absence of such characteristics. For example, Eagly and Steffen (1984) postulated that stereotypes of the sexes derived not so much from gender per se but from the different social roles to which the two sexes have traditionally been assigned. Using the PAQ to measure perceptions of agency and communion, Eagly and Steffen found that college students perceived female and male homemakers as high in communion and low in agency and female and male employees as high in agency and low in communion. In other words, the salient variable in perceptions of others as "masculine" or "feminine" was not sex but social role.

To summarize, the constellation of personality characteristics summarized as instrumentality is important in relation to women's career development. Although a *lack* of instrumentality may be related to exclusive home orientation, the *presence* of instrumentality appears particularly important for the pursuit of careers in traditionally male-dominated fields. For an extensive review of theory and research concerning psychological androgyny, see Cook (1985).

ATTITUDES TOWARD WOMEN'S ROLES

A sex role-related *attitudinal* (versus personality) variable that has received considerable research attention is attitudes toward women's roles in society. Probably the first researchers to operationalize the notion of "attitudes toward women's roles" were Spence and Helmreich (1972), who developed the Attitudes Toward Women Scale (AWS), which contains 55 items (although there are short forms available). The items are categorized into six groups representing the following themes: (1) vocational, educational, and intellectual roles (e.g., "Women with children should not work outside the home if they don't have to" and "Women should be given equal opportunity with men for apprenticeships in the skilled trades"); (2) freedom and independence (e.g., "The modern girl is entitled to the same freedom from regulation and control that is given to the modern boy" and "Most women need and want the kind of protection and support that men have traditionally given them"); (3) dating, courtship, and etiquette (e.g., "The initiative in dating should come from the man" and "A woman should be as free as a man to propose marriage"); (4) drinking, swearing, and dirty jokes (e.g., "Intoxication among women is worse than intoxication among men"); (5) sexual behavior (e.g., "If both husband and wife agree that sexual fidelity isn't important, then there's no reason why both shouldn't have extramarital affairs if they want to"); and (6) marital relationships and obligations (e.g., "It is insulting to women to have the 'obey' clause remain in the marriage service," "It is childish for a woman to assert herself by retaining her maiden name after marriage," and "In general, the father should have greater authority than the mother in the bringing up of the children").

Although the AWS and its various short-form adaptations have been most commonly used in research in this area, another widely used measure of attitudes toward women's roles is Kalin and Tilby's (1978) Sex Role Ideology Scale. Developed to distinguish feminist from traditional sex role ideologies, the SRIS consists of 39 seven-point, bipolar items pertaining to work roles, parental responsibilities, personal relationships, special roles of women, abortion, and homosexuality. Beere, King, Beere, and King's (1984) Sex-Role Egalitarianism Scale assesses attitudes toward equality in marital roles, parental roles, employee roles, educational roles, and social–interpersonal–heterosexual roles. Dreyer, Woods, and James' (1981) 19-item Index of Sex Role Orientation measures the factors of home–career conflict, male–female division of household responsibilities, and attitudes toward women's work roles outside the home. Finally, other measures include Lyson and Brown's (1982) nine-item measure including scales for role appropriateness (e.g., attitudes toward working after children are born) and social/marital equality between the sexes; Tetenbaum, Lighter, and Travis' (1984) 32-item scale assessing attitudes toward working mothers; and Knaub and Eversoll's (1983) scale assessing attitudes toward the timing of parenthood.

In addition to multiitem scales such as the AWS and the SRIS, some studies have used single-item measures such as "Are you a feminist?" and "Do you use the term 'Ms.'?" (Fassinger, 1985; Smith & Self, 1981; Swatko, 1981). The assumption here, supported by the research of Smith and Self (1981), is that women who would use the labels "feminist" or "Ms." hold liberal, profeminist attitudes toward the roles of women in society. For a comprehensive review of measures of sex role attitudes and ideology, see Beere (1979).

Although sex role attitudes have been measured in a variety of ways, research to date has yielded a fairly consistent pattern of findings. First, studies have shown that women's attitudes toward women's roles are more liberal than those of men (Hare-Mustin, Bennett, & Broderick, 1983; Mezydlo & Betz, 1980; Spence & Helmreich, 1972; Zuckerman, 1981) and that younger women are more liberal than older women (Slevin & Wingrove, 1983; Stafford, 1984). Recent research also indicates that women are becoming more liberal in their role expectations and values in comparison to women in previous studies (Lyson & Brown, 1982; Mezydlo & Betz, 1980; Stafford, 1984; Thornton & Freedman, 1979; Zuckerman, 1981).

While women's attitudes may be changing slowly in the direction of greater liberality, the overall concept of attitudes toward women's roles has been found to be a *powerful* predictor of women's career involvement. More specifically, one of the most consistent (and, it should be noted, inherently logical) findings in the research literature concerns the greater tendency of career-oriented women to express liberal or feminist attitudes toward women's roles. More liberal sex role attitudes have been found to characterize career- versus home-oriented women (Smith, 1980; Stafford, 1984; Thornton & Camburn, 1979; Tinsley & Faunce, 1980) and pioneers versus traditionals (Bachtold, 1976; Bachtold & Werner, 1970; Gackenbach, 1978; Orcutt & Walsh, 1979). Stringer and Duncan (1985) found nontraditional sex role attitudes among women in the skilled crafts, labor, and technical fields.

In a large-scale study using structural equation modeling analysis of predictors of women's career development, Fassinger (1985) found that responses to the questions "I would label myself a 'feminist' in my beliefs and values" and "I prefer to use the title 'Ms.' when referring to myself" were among the strongest predictors of career orientation and the prestige and nontraditionality of career choices among college women. Parsons *et al.* (1978) found associations among the extent of identification with the women's movement and career aspirations, nontraditional values, and willingness to delay marriage. Dreyer-Arkin (1976) reported that feminists are more likely to value their own personal growth and achievement at least as highly as they do that of others (e.g., husbands), while traditional women tended to prioritize the needs of others versus their own.

Generally, more liberal sex role attitudes are related to greater labor force participation (Atkinson & Huston, 1984; Dreyer *et al.*, 1981; Stafford, 1984), to higher levels of educational aspiration (Dreyer *et al.*, 1981; Lyson & Brown, 1982; Zuckerman, 1981), and to stronger career motivation and higher career aspirations (Fannin, 1979; Fassinger, 1985; Illfelder, 1980; Komarovsky, 1982; Lyson & Brown, 1982; Parsons *et al.*, 1978; Stake, 1979b). Other related findings, however, primarily support the validity of the instruments used, for example, Tetenbaum *et al.*'s (1984) finding that working mothers have higher scores on the Attitudes Toward Working Mothers Scale.

In considering the strong relationships of liberal or feminist attitudes toward women's career development, it should be noted that feminist orientation and more liberal role attitudes are also strongly related to the tendency to be single or to be childless if married (Dreyer *et al.*, 1981), which, in turn, are also strongly related to career development. Further, more liberal sex role attitudes are related to perceived self-competence (Stake, 1979b) and to higher self-reported and objectively measured intelligence (cf. Williams, 1983) Thus, sex role attitudes are part of a facilitative constellation of characteristics which Lemkau (1977) postulated are due to an enriched background, allowing a girl to grow up with a broadened view of the female role and of her own capabilities and options.

In addition to suggesting the important facilitative effect of liberal or profeminist attitudes toward women's roles on women's career development, research investigating these attitudes has led to two additional findings having important implications for the success and satisfaction of working women. First of all, numerous studies have suggested that even traditional women's attitudes have changed in the realm of equal opportunity. For example, most women now would positively endorse the principle of equal pay for equal work (Smith & Self, 1981; Williams, 1983). However, traditional women tend to show an ideological duality, supporting equality in the labor market but *not* in interpersonal relationships with men (Smith & Self, 1981). Thus, it may be increasingly difficult to speak of attitudes toward women's roles as a unitary phenomenon, and it will be important to develop more specific and precise measures of attitudes in this realm. Further, given the very strong relationship of educational level to more liberated attitudes (e.g., in Dreyer *et al.*'s study, educational level explained 62% of the variance in sex role attitudes), generally higher levels of education in the U.S. population may lead to a more generally liberated as well as educated population.

The greater liberality of women's attitudes toward women's roles, in comparison to those of men, has also been suggested to have some potentially highly problematic implications for relationships between women and men. In terms of marital roles, most recent research (e.g., Fassinger, 1985) suggests that the majority of women, at least those who are or plan to be college educated, prefer egalitarian marriages, allowing them to pursue careers and share family responsibilities. In contrast, the majority of men continue to prefer traditional marriages, wherein if the wife does work after marriage, she stops working after the children arrive and never loses sight of the priority of her husband's versus her own career and of her responsibility for domestic and childrearing duties (Adams, 1984; Albrecht *et al.*, 1977; Kassner, 1981).

Given the likelihood that most women will marry, this discrepancy in preferences after marriage bodes ill for marital satisfaction, women's career development (since they will most likely do the bulk of the compromising), or both. Although available knowledge concerning dual-career marriages and the work–family interface is covered in later chapters, scholars and practitioners interested in women's career development and social change should be concerned with the nature, implications, and possible means of resolving such discrepancies in attitudes toward women's rights and roles in contemporary society.

SUMMARY

In summary, highly career-oriented women seem to be characterized by a constellation of personality and attitudinal characteristics emphasizing positive self-concepts, instrumentality and competence, androgyny, and liberated attitudes toward women's roles. The data clearly fit Almquist and Angrist's (1970) "enrichment" hypothesis, which may be summarized as explaining high achievement and role innovation in women as the result of an enriched background, above-average intellectual and personal assets, and an expanded view of what is possible for women.

VOCATIONAL INTERESTS, NEEDS, AND VALUES IN WOMEN'S CAREER DEVELOPMENT

This chapter will review the relationships of vocational interests and vocational needs, including achievement motivation, to women's career development.

VOCATIONAL INTERESTS

Early studies of women's vocational interests focused on factor-analytic studies and on comparisons of the interests of homemaking-versus career-oriented women. As early as 1939, Crissy and Daniel compared the factor structure of the Strong Vocational Interest Blank–Women (SVIB–W) and the Strong Vocational Interest Blank—Men (SVIB–M). Three of the four resulting factors corresponded to four factors in the men's scales—interest in people, interest in language, and interest in science. The fourth factor, on which the office worker, housewife, and stenographer–secretary scales loaded strongly, was labeled "interest in male association" and had no counterpart in the men's scales. Darley (1941) grouped these three scales under the factorial label of "nonprofessional interests," while Layton (1958) suggested that these three scales and the elementary school teacher scale were indicative of "premarital patterns of interest."

The first study using the SVIB–W to differentiate the interests of homemaking- versus career-oriented women was that of Hoyt and Kennedy (1958). In this study, homemaker and career groups were specified on the basis of responses to a questionnaire concerning the relative importance to subjects of marital versus career roles. Career-oriented subjects obtained higher scores on six SVIB–W scales, including artist, lawyer, psychologist, physician, and physical education teacher scales, while homemaking-oriented subjects scored higher on eight scales, including housewife, secretary, home economics teacher, and dietician.

Later studies utilizing the research paradigm developed by Hoyt and Kennedy essentially duplicated these results. For example, Wagman (1966) found that career-oriented girls scored higher on the lawyer, physician, and psychologist scales, while homemaking-oriented girls scored higher on the housewife, home economics teacher, and dietician scales. Subsequent studies (Parker, 1966; Vetter & Lewis, 1964; Wagman, 1966) revealed similar differential SVIB–W patterns for career-oriented and homemaking-oriented young women. Thus, a pattern of interest in culturally stereotyped "feminine" stopgap occupations was observed in marriage-oriented subjects (Levitt, 1972). Munley (1974), whose research used the revised SVIB–W (Form TW398), essentially duplicated the findings of previous studies. Munley summarized the trend for career-oriented women to obtain high interest-similarity ratings for occupations traditionally dominated by males and for homemaking-oriented women to obtain higher scores on occupations traditionally dominated by women, including several nonprofessional occupations. Interest in scientific and technical activities was also frequently found to differentiate career-oriented women from home-oriented women (Tyler, 1964; Tinsley & Faunce, 1978) and pioneers from traditionals (Rezler, 1967; Goldman, Kaplan, & Platt, 1973). Thus, interest in nontraditional occupations and activities appears to be related to career orientation in women.

While nontraditional interests do appear to be more characteristic of career-oriented than non-career-oriented women, the vocational interests of women in general have been strongly influenced by traditional sex role socialization. This influence, in turn, has led to a restriction in the range of women's expressed and measured interests and, consequently, has contributed to the limited range of career options both pursued by and suggested to women.

Historically, the vocational interests of the two sexes have been measured separately (Campbell, 1977). The construction of separate forms of the Strong Vocational Interest Blank for men (1927) and for women (in 1933) was based on the different item responses of men and women and on the marked differences between men and women in the extent and nature of their employment (Campbell, 1977). For decades, this system was generally accepted, although career-oriented women were frequently administered the SVIB–M rather than the SVIB–W because of the former's greater utility in suggesting pro-fessional-level careers (Campbell, 1977).

Although the more recent criticisms of sex bias and restrictiveness in interest inventories have largely eliminated the use of separate forms for males and females (see the expanded discussion below), males and females continue to respond differentially to many interest inventory items. Generally, women are more likely than men to indi-cate interest in social and artistic activities, while men are more likely than women to indicate interest in scientific, technical, and mechani-cal activities.

The existence of sex differences at the item level has resulted in different overall score patterns for the two sexes (Cole & Hanson, 1975; Prediger & Hanson, 1976). For example, on measures of the Holland themes using raw scores or combined-sex normative scores, females obtain higher mean scores on the Social, Artistic, and Con-ventional themes, while males obtain higher means on the Realistic, Investigative, and Enterprising themes (Gottfredson, Holland, & Got-tfredson, 1975; Holland, 1972; Prediger & Hanson, 1976). Similar find-ings have resulted using the Vocational Interest Inventory [(VII) Lun-neborg, 1977], a measure of Roe's eight fields of occupational interest. Findings of sex differences in basic dimensions of vocational interest are most evident and durable for Social and Realistic (Technical) in-terests. Social interests are far more predominant among females, while Realistic interests are found far more frequently among males (e.g., Lunneborg, 1979, 1980; Prediger, 1980).

One major implication of differential raw score patterns among males and females is that the resulting occupational suggestions tend to be correspondent with beliefs concerning traditionally female and traditionally male occupations. High scores on the Social and Conven-tional themes suggest traditionally female educational and social wel-fare and office and clerical occupations (e.g., Holland, 1973). In con-trast, females' lower scores on the Realistic, Investigative, and Enterprising themes result in infrequent suggestion of traditionally male professions (e.g., medicine, engineering, and science) and of occupations in management and the skilled trades (Holland, 1973). Thus, socialized patterns of interest lead to interest inventory results which perpetuate females' overrepresentation in traditionally female occupations and their underrepresentation in occupations tradition-ally dominated by males.

Such divergent and sex-stereotypic suggestions of occupational al-ternatives to males and females were the basis for the criticisms of sex bias and sex restrictiveness in interest inventories, extensively documented and discussed in a report funded by the National Institute of Education (Diamond, 1975). According to this and other discussions of sex bias, the use of separate forms for men and women, sexist language in occupational titles (e.g., policeman versus police officer), and raw scores or combined-sex normative scores, among other things, contributed to the failure of interest inventories to result in fairness in the suggestion of occupational alternatives to males and females. In other words, interest inventories served to maintain and perpetuate the limited range of occupations considered appropriate for and usually pursued by women.

In response to the criticisms of sex bias, many test developers have addressed these issues by combining the men's and women's forms, for example, the Strong–Campbell Interest Inventory, by eliminating sexist language, and by discussing issues of sex role socialization in interpretive materials (AMEG Commission on Sex Bias in Measurement, 1977). Other test developers have focused on reducing the sex restrictiveness of the resulting scores.

The two major approaches to reducing sex restrictiveness in the scores provided for basic dimensions of vocational interest are the use of same-sex normative scores and the use of sex-balanced items, that is, items endorsed approximately equally by males and females. The SCII, for example, provides same-sex normative scores for both the General Occupational (i.e., Holland) themes and the Basic Interest scales. The Unisex Edition of the ACT–IV [(UNIACT) Hanson, Prediger, & Schussel, 1977] and the revised version of the VII (Lunneborg, 1980) are based on the principle that if sex-balanced items are utilized, the sexes will obtain a more equivalent distribution of scores across the six Holland themes (UNIACT) or Roe's eight fields (VII). Thus, on the UNIACT, for example, the Realistic scale contains items pertaining to sewing and cooking, that is, *content* areas more familiar to females, in addition to items more reflective of males' socialization experiences, for example, the kinds of things learned in high school shop courses. The use of same-sex normative scores and sex-balanced interest inventories is intended to increase the probability that females who could potentially be interested in Realistic, Investigative, or Enterprising occupations will obtain interest inventory profiles suggesting those areas. Thus, such methods of constructing and scoring interest inventories are designed to facilitate females' exploration of the full range of occupational alternatives and to minimize the extent to which women continue to be directed toward traditionally female occupations.

While attempts to remove sex restrictiveness from interest inventories are important and useful, the more direct solution to the problem of sex-stereotypic vocational interests involves increasing the range of experiences relevant to the development of those interests. Until girls and women have the opportunity to engage in activities relevant to, for example, Realistic and Investigative as well as Social and Artistic interest areas, interest in nontraditional areas will not develop in the majority of women. Encouraging a wider variety of activities and experiences for young girls and, for women, encouraging involvement in jobs or job-related experiences beyond the limits of socialized interests and experiences is necessary; women's vocational interests and, consequently, their career choices, should derive from a rich background of experience and knowledge rather than from a background exposing them only to stereotypically female areas of activity and interest.

In conclusion, it appears that women who do develop scientific and technical interests often utilize these in the pursuit of nontraditional careers. However, the failure of many women to develop interests beyond the bounds of traditional female socialization continues to be a major barrier to their career development and seriously limits their vocational options.

VOCATIONAL NEEDS AND VALUES

Two major bodies of research have investigated vocationally relevant needs and values. The first major body of research is that in vocational and industrial/organizational psychology which has attempted to describe and measure the major dimensions of the needs of workers. Much of this research has been directed toward understanding of the job satisfaction of already employed individuals, and studies of women's job satisfaction are reviewed later in the book. However, the concept of work needs is another important individual difference variable that should be considered in the career choice process—choices correspondent with needs should increase the likelihood of subsequent satisfaction and tenure in the occupation (Dawis & Lofquist, 1984).

The second body of literature, more closely associated with personality theory, is that studying the concept of needs for achievement. The following sections summarize the contributions of each body of research to understanding the career choices of women.

In vocational theory and research, work needs may be defined as individual differences in preferences for the rewards, payoffs, or outcomes of a job or career. These rewards have generally been categorized as either "intrinsic" or "extrinsic." The concept of intrinsic work needs emphasizes that one's work should contribute to one's self-esteem, self-actualization, and enjoyment of life (e.g., Kanungo, 1979). Intrinsic work needs can also be thought of as those fulfilled by actually engaging in the work—activity, creativity, the opportunity to use one's abilities, and intellectual stimulation are examples of intrinsic work needs. Extrinsic needs are those for the rewards work brings *after* it is done, including the pay, fringe benefits, security, promotion, or for the external conditions of the work, for example, the surroundings, co-workers, and supervision. Work needs can be viewed in terms of both their absolute and relative importance to the individual; most career choices require one to compromise on some types of rewards in order to obtain others, and therefore the ability to set priorities is important.

Widely used measures of work needs include the Minnesota Importance Questionnaire [(MIQ) Weiss, Dawis, Lofquist, Gay, & Hendel, 1975; see also Weiss, 1973], Super's (1973) Work Values Inventory (WVI), and Manhardt's (1972) 25-item scale assessing the importance of 25 different work outcomes.

Research on women's work needs has focused on comparisons of the needs of homemaking- versus career-oriented women and on the work needs of women versus men. Early research comparing home-versus career-oriented women reported that career-oriented women obtained higher scores on measures of intrinsic work needs, for example, autonomy, achievement, management, and responsibility, while home-oriented women obtained higher scores on extrinsic or affiliative needs (Eyde, 1962; Hoyt & Kennedy, 1958; Rand, 1968; Oliver, 1975; Simpson & Simpson, 1961; Tinsley & Faunce, 1980). Yuen *et al.* (1980) reported that career-oriented women scored higher on the MIQ needs of Activity (the characteristic of being busy all of the time) and Responsibility, while home-oriented women scored higher on Security and Moral Values.

In an attempt to further explicate differences in the need structures of homemakers versus working women, Harmon (1977) suggested the possible applicability of Maslow's (1954) need theory to women's career development. Briefly, Maslow conceptualized five basic human needs arranged in a hierarchy from lowest to highest level needs. Lower-order needs included physiological and safety needs, followed by social needs. Higher-order needs were those for autonomy, esteem, and self-actualization. Maslow's concept of prepotency specified that higher-level needs could not be fully experienced until lower-order needs were satisfied; new needs were seen as emerging gradually as lower-order needs were met. Harmon noted that women have tradi-

tionally been taught to seek gratification of their needs through someone else, usually husbands or fathers. Homemakers, who therefore
may never learn to gratify their own lower-level needs, would be
unlikely to move beyond them to higher-order needs. Thus, Harmon
postulated that homemakers would be less likely than working
women to express higher-order needs such as esteem and self-actualization.

In two major studies of Harmon's (1977) postulates, Ellen Betz
(1982, 1984b) followed a large ($N = 504$) sample of women who had
received Bachelor's degrees from the University of Minnesota in
1968. Using Porter's Need Satisfaction Questionnaire (Porter, 1961),
scores for the importance to the individual of Maslow's five needs
were obtained. Discriminant analyses supported the existence of a
high degree of separation between high-level and low-level needs in
women. When women were divided into occupational groups, professional–managerial and clerical–sales women had the highest scores
on the higher-level needs, while homemakers were distinguished by
their higher scores on the lower-level needs of security/safety and
social.

In terms of Maslow's hierarchy, all three groups obtained their own
highest scores on self-actualization. The remaining ordering for professional–managerial and clerical–sales groups corresponded closely
to Maslow's theory; autonomy and esteem needs were next highest
after self-actualization, and social and security/safety were the weakest needs. Among homemakers, however, the order was reversed;
social was next in strength after self-actualization, and esteem was
weakest in strength.

Thus, the needs of working women were similar and yet differed in
major respects from those of homemakers. The hierarchies of working
women supported the ordering postulated by Maslow, but homemakers diverged considerably, with high-level needs at both the top
and bottom of their hierarchy and low-level needs falling in between.
In a subsequent study of perceived deficits in need satisfaction (Betz,
1982), homemakers reported greatest deficits in esteem needs and
employed women reported greatest deficits in meeting their needs for
autonomy.

In addition to findings that the needs of homemakers and career-
oriented women differ in important ways, research has investigated
the degree to which the work-related needs of women and men differ.
In evaluating studies of this type, it is vital to assess the comparability
of the samples of men and women in occupational level. That is, we
know that extrinsic work needs are more predominant at the lower

occupational levels at which most women are employed, while higher occupational levels, in which men predominate, facilitate the emergence of intrinsic work needs (Kaufman & Fetter, 1980). Thus, a general sample of employed individuals would be likely to show sex differences, but the differences would most likely be an artifact of differential occupational levels.

In studies controlling for occupational level, an overall pattern of gender similarity rather than difference is found. For example, women employed in high-level occupations seem to have needs similar to men employed in the same occupations, that is, strong needs for mastery, independence, and ability utilization, and weak needs to help others (Almquist, 1974; Wolkon, 1972). Kutner and Brogan (1980) found that the needs of female medical students were similar to those of male medical students; both sexes expressed strong desires to serve others, to be independent in their work, and to have the security and flexibility of a medical career. Males did rate income and prestige as more important than did females, while females saw medicine as offering potential for achievement and satisfaction beyond that available in traditionally female fields. Stake (1978) found that male and female college students had almost identical expectations from work, except that female students were more likely to expect intrinsic enjoyment in their work.

A number of studies have used Manhardt's (1972) job orientation scale to study the work needs of students, most often business students. Although these studies show large degrees of overlap in the interests of the two sexes, some fairly consistent differences also appear. Men place higher value on factors related to career advancement and recognition, including pay, promotion, and increasing job responsibilities, while women place higher value on characteristics of the work environment such as colleagues and work conditions (Bartol & Manhardt, 1979; Manhardt, 1972; Schuler, 1975). These studies also suggest that factors related to intrinsic job satisfaction, for example, intellectual challenge and the chance to be creative and to feel a sense of accomplishment, are at least as important to women as they are to men.

There is some evidence that women's values are becoming even more like men's over time, that is, increasing the value accorded to achievement and recognition and reducing the value of work conditions (Bartol & Manhardt, 1979). Beutell and Brenner (1986) reported several gender differences *counter* to stereotyped expectations; specifically, in a sample of 202 advanced business students, men reported significantly stronger needs for security and leisure time, while women reported stronger needs for accomplishment and development of their knowledge and skills.

Finally, in addition to the predominance of findings indicating increasing convergence in the vocational needs of males and females, it is also important to note that the major work needs are similar for the sexes, that is, both sexes value the opportunity to gain feelings of accomplishment, job security, income potential, and respect from others for their work (Beutell & Brenner, 1986).

ACHIEVEMENT MOTIVATION

The concept of achievement motivation was originated by Henry Murray, in his 1938 taxonomy of human needs. Building on Murray's theory, McClelland, Atkinson, Clark, and Lowell (1953) postulated an expectancy–value model of achievement motivation. In this model, achievement behavior was seen as determined by the interaction of the motive to achieve success, the motive to avoid failure, and extrinsic motivation. The tendency to achieve success was viewed as the product of the motive to achieve success, the probability of success, and the incentive value of success. Achievement motivation was assessed through responses to the Thematic Apperception Test, a projective test based on Murray's (1938) need theory.

The first research pertinent to the achievement needs of women utilized the chief experimental paradigm of McClelland, Atkinson, and their colleagues, that is, studies of the level of achievement motivation after instructions designed to arouse the motivation. When female subjects did not respond to the instructions designed to arouse their achievement motivation, it was suggested that they were less motivated than men (Veroff, Wilcox, & Atkinson, 1953). Interestingly, the researchers did not seem to think it important that under relaxed conditions females actually scored higher than males in the amount of achievement imagery in their TAT responses. Thus, this research provided a clear example of the way in which biases in expectations influence interpretations of data.

The fact that females gave ample achievement imagery under relaxed conditions is particularly noteworthy in a society which attempts to inhibit the achievement-related tendencies of women (Fitzgerald & Crites, 1980). Furthermore, there are now data suggesting that the achievement motives of women are often experimentally suppressed in groups, especially mixed-sex groups, but are enhanced when women are allowed to perform alone or are convinced that their achievements will not be noticed by nor offend men (Farmer & Bohn, 1970; Stake, 1976).

An additional concept expanding upon these ideas was that of Horner (1968, 1972), who postulated that women's achievement behavior is complicated by the pervasiveness of a motive to avoid success, in popular terms, the "fear of success." Horner introduced the concept of fear of success to explain the presence of negative imagery in college women's responses to the story cue, "After first term finals, Anne finds herself at the top of her class." Although this would appear to be a very positive position for Anne, 66% of Horner's original subjects (college women) wrote stories containing negative themes. Such themes included Anne's subsequent losses of femininity, eligibility as a dating or marriage partner, and chances for a happy, fulfilled life. The theme that Anne would become a lonely spinster devoting her life to her medical practice was illustrative. Other negative responses had Anne dropping out of medical school, for example, because she became pregnant, and actual denial of Anne's accomplishment, for example, Anne's grades were due to computer error or Anne was actually a fake student made up as a prank by the other medical students.

Although the concept of fear of success has generated hundreds of studies (Unger, 1979), its scientific merit is still debated. Unger pointed out that the presence of fear-of-success imagery varies with other variables such as sex role orientation, age, and experimental conditions. Spence and Helmreich (1983) summarized the problems with projective measures of fear of success, as well as other achievement motives. The lack of evidence for the reliability and validity of the measures utilized is alone sufficient to account for lack of consistency in the research findings. Sadd, Lenauer, Shaver, & Dunivant (1978) analyzed fear-of-success measures and derived two clear factors, one of which could be defined as general insecurity, doubt, and fear of assertiveness, and the other of which was concern about the negative consequences of success. In addition, Spence and Helmreich noted the problem of oversimplication resulting from unidimensional conceptions and measurement of complicated and probably multidimensional constructs. Thus, there is a need for additional work in the development and refinement of objective, multidimensional measures of achievement-related motives (Spence & Helmreich, 1983).

One promising, multidimensional conception of achievement motives is that of Helmreich and Spence (1978). Helmreich and Spence postulated the existence of three components of a broader achievement motive. The components were as follows: (1) mastery, or the preference for challenging tasks and for meeting internal standards of excellence; (2) work, or the desire to work hard; and (3) competitiveness, or the enjoyment of interpersonal competition. The three components were measured using the Work and Family Orientation Questionnaire [(WOFO) Helmreich & Spence, 1978].

Data obtained using the WOFO suggest that the structure of needs in men and women is similar, but that differences occur in the strength of various motivational components. In unselected groups, women score higher on work and men score somewhat higher on mastery and considerably higher on competitiveness. However, overall differences between subject groups are greater than gender differences within subject groups; for example, male and female college students and psychologists are less competitive than male and female varsity athletes and businesspersons.

In addition, instrumentality, as measured by the Personal Attributes Questionnaire (discussed in Chapter 7), is significantly correlated with all three components of achievement, but in particular, with competitiveness. When the degree of instrumentality is controlled, gender differences in work and mastery disappear, and differences are reduced on competitiveness. Thus, these components of achievement appear to be facilitated by processes similar to those of masculine sex role socialization; females who have had the benefit of experiences developing instrumentality and competence also have stronger achievement motivation in comparison to other women.

Interestingly, although work and mastery scores are significantly related to achievement both educationally and occupationally (in the case of psychologists and businesspersons), competitiveness is unrelated or even negatively related to such achievements (Spence & Helmreich, 1983). Thus, parental stress on competitiveness in sons may not be adaptive in terms of actual performance in major life domains. A final point made by Spence and Helmreich is that competitiveness is also strongly related to preferences for extrinsic rewards such as pay, promotion, and advancement. Spence and Helmreich postulated that an excess of extrinsic motivation, including the external locus of competitive behavior, may undermine the expression of intrinsic needs, which may in turn be related to the detrimental effects of competitiveness on performance.

A second multidimensional model of achievement motives having relevance to the understanding of women's career development is that of Lipmen-Blumen, Handley-Isaksen, and Leavitt (1983). They postulated three general "achieving styles": the direct, instrumental, and relational styles. The *direct* style involves achievement through one's own efforts and includes three substyles. An instrinsic substyle involves achievement of one's own standard of excellence. The competitive substyle involves competition with others, while the power substyle involves achievement through leadership and influence over others.

The *instrumental* style involves achievement through self or others as the means to goals. Individuals who use personal status, reputation, or personal or social assets to achieve their goals are using the personal substyle. Those who use social connections or networks are using the social style, while those who look to others for direction and help are using the reliant style. Finally, a *relational* style employs others in the service of achievement needs. A collaborative style involves group effort toward a goal, the individual being central to the achievements of the group. A contributory style also seeks to achieve through the accomplishments of a group, but the individual views himself/herself as playing a supportive rather than a major role. Finally, the vicarious substyle requires one to meet achievement needs through the achievements of others—the most obvious example here is the traditional woman who satisfies her achievement needs through vicarious pleasure over the achievements of her husband and children.

Lipmen-Blumen *et al.* developed the Achieving Styles Inventory to measure these concepts; each of the nine subscales is measured by five items, for a total of 45 items in the measure. Using 18 samples, a total of 3,294 subjects, Lipmen-Blumen *et al.* reported that the strongest style among both men and women was the intrinsic–direct style. However, among subjects under age 30, women scored significantly higher on the relational scales, particularly vicarious and contributory, and men scored higher on the personal and social–instrumental scales. Among over-30 subjects, the major discriminator of the sexes was the competitive–direct scale, on which men scored significantly higher.

In comparisons of homemakers and working women, homemakers were differentiated by high scores on the vicarious–relational and contributory–relational as well as intrinsic–direct scales. Employed women, in contrast, scored highest on intrinsic–direct, power–direct, and collaborative–relational scales. This latter pattern was similar to that obtained in groups of male managers, except that the direct styles were paired with instrumental styles in men, versus the collaborative style in women.

Although interested readers are referred to comprehensive reviews such as that of Sutherland and Veroff (1985) for additional information, the present discussion can be summarized as suggesting that males and females have equivalently strong intrinsic work motivation but that extrinsic motives differ somewhat between the sexes. Males appear to be more interested in competition and external symbols of accomplishment, and women appear to place greater value on collaborative work relationships and on the work environment itself. Thus, although there may be some differences in the manifestation of work-related motives, there do not appear to be important differences in the overall importance of achievement. Given the consistency with which women report strong needs to use their abilities and to experience feelings of accomplishment, further efforts to assist them in fully developing their potential through career pursuits appears to be warranted and necessary.

SUMMARY OF FACTORS INFLUENCING WOMEN'S CAREER CHOICES

The preceding chapters have reviewed issues in and factors influencing the career choices of women. Problematic aspects of the choices of women have included underutilization of their abilities, their overconcentration in a small number of traditionally female-dominated (and also generally low-paying) occupations and resulting underrepresentation in an extensive variety of traditionally male-dominated (and generally higher-paying) fields, and their avoidance of coursework in mathematics, resulting in externally based limitations in their career options.

Although the present authors would not wish to make general statements about the kinds of careers women *should* choose, we can state some objectives which, to the degree met, would represent improvement in the process by which women make career choices. First, most (if not all) women should pursue careers outside the home; the positive effects of working on mental health and the negative effects of *not* working have received consistent, widespread research documentation (Bart, 1971; Bernard, 1971, 1972; Radloff, 1975). Second, the career choices made should represent better matching of individual characteristics to the level and nature of the chosen field; in particular, the serious underutilization of abilities in women's career choices needs to be counteracted. Third, women's career choices should be made in the context of a broad range of perceived and real *options* rather than by default; thus, options should more often include careers in traditionally male-dominated fields, particularly those in mathematical, scientific, and technical areas. Women's career choices, then, should utilize rather than waste women's abilities and talents and

TABLE 9.1 Summary of Factors Facilitative of Women's Career Development

Individual variables	Background variables
High ability	Working mother
Liberated sex role values	Supportive father
Instrumentality	Highly educated parents
Androgynous personality	Female role models
High self-esteem	Work experience as adolescent
Strong academic self-concept	Androgynous upbringing

Educational variables	Adult lifestyle variables
Higher education	Late marriage or single
Continuation in mathematics	No or few children
Girls' schools and women's colleges	

should represent the full range of occupational possibilities rather than the restricted range of female-dominated professions and "pink-collar" jobs.

Given these goals, the research reviewed herein can be summarized as suggesting some facilitators of and barriers to women's career development. Table 9.1 summarizes those factors *generally* found to enhance the quality of women's career choices and the extent of their career achievements. In examining the table, it should be noted that the research findings describe groups of women and do not necessarily describe the factors which have influenced any particular woman. In other words, family background characteristics (or any other variables) found to characterize career-oriented women or women in male-dominated fields obviously do not characterize all such women.

Second, the manner in which these numerous factors interact to affect women's career development and the relative importance of their effects are poorly understood and in need of further investigation. This review has for practical reasons examined each factor separately but, in reality, the factors occur concurrently and in interaction with each other. As will be discussed further in Chapter 15, the study of the factors influencing women's career choices will be more informative as we use more inclusive research designs and sophisticated statistical analytic techniques capable of simultaneous examination of multiple potentially causal variables. For example, the development of theoretical models testable using covariance structure modeling (Bentler, 1980; Long, 1983), of which the more commonly known technique of path analysis is a specific application, has the potential to further advance our understanding of the factors influencing women's career choices.

Two such theoretical models currently being submitted to empirical examination using covariance structural modeling are shown in Figures 9.1 and 9.2, respectively. In diagramming a structural model, the circles represent latent variables or hypothetical constructs, which can only be inferred rather than directly observed. The arrows represent both the types and directions of postulated causal relationships between latent variables. In an expanded, testable model, each of the circles, or latent variables, would be associated with one or more "indicators" or measures of the constructs.

The model represented in Figure 9.1 is designed to examine individual differences in the realism of women's career choices. The realism of choice concept, based on the "matching model" (Parsons,

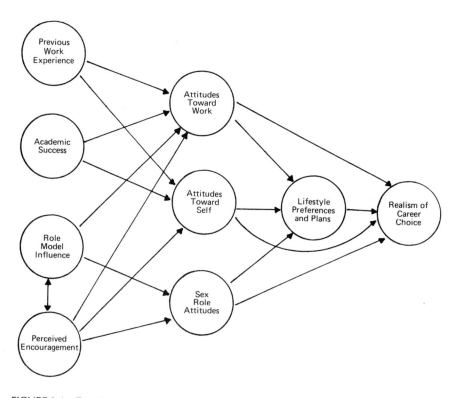

FIGURE 9.1   Betz/Fitzgerald model of career choice in college women. From Fassinger (1985). Copyright © 1985 by Academic Press, Inc. Reproduced by permission of the publisher.

1909), examines the congruence between an individual's abilities and chosen occupational level, and between that person's interests and chosen field of work. Although the commonly used dependent variable of traditionality/nontraditionality of women's occupational choice probably is related to realism (see Wolfe & Betz, 1981), the dependent variable used in the present model provides a direct, rather than indirect, representation of person–environment congruence.

The implicit assumption in the causal ordering of the model shown is that realism of career choice in college women is influenced by all of the other variables previously studied. The model contains four exogenous (independent) latent variables and five endogenous (de-

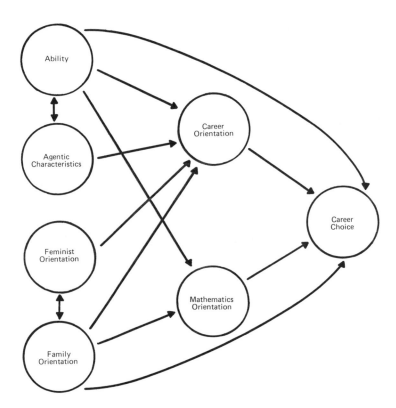

FIGURE 9.2 Alternative model of career choice in college women. From R. E. Fassinger, *The Testing of a Model of Career Choice in Two Populations of College Women* (Ph.D. Dissertation in progress, Department of Psychology, Ohio State University). Reproduced by permission of the author.

pendent) latent variables which appear significant based on the research reviewed. It is hypothesized in the model that the independent
variables Previous Work Experience, Academic Success, Role Model
Influence, and Perceived Encouragement directly affect the dependent variables Attitudes Toward Work, Attitudes Toward Self, and Sex
Role Attitudes. These dependent variables in turn affect the dependent variables Lifestyle Preferences and Plans and Realism of Career
Choice. In addition, it is hypothesized that there is a relationship
between the independent variables Role Model Influence and Perceived Encouragement.

An alternative model, shown in Figure 9.2, uses several characteristics of career choice as the dependent variable to be ultimately predicted—these characteristics are traditionality, prestige, and science-
relatedness (as defined in Chapter 2). The independent latent
variables Ability, Instrumentality, Feminist Orientation, and Family
Orientation are postulated to influence the dependent variables Career Orientation and Mathematics Orientation, which, in turn, influence career choice (along with further influences of ability and family
orientation on career choice).

Since both of these models are currently subject to empirical examination using the LISREL VI computer program (Joreskog & Sorbom,
1981) to examine the goodness-of-fit of the model to obtained sample
data (see Fassinger, 1985), they should be considered as illustrations
of some of the possible integrative, theoretical models which could be
developed and empirically tested. The particular advantage of the
method of covariance structure modeling is that it allows causal inferences from nonexperimental data. Further, it allows such causal inferences for multiple variables simultaneously, and it is thus far more
powerful than most traditional experimental designs. Research of this
kind, then, is now needed.

A final point regarding Table 9.1 is that the factors influencing wom-
en's career development will almost surely change as societal attitudes and norms change and as increasing numbers of women enter
the work force. If girls and women, like boys and men, begin to assume that career pursuits will be an integral part of their lives, we may
see changes in the nature of and influences on women's career
choices. As was so well stated by Osipow (1983), ". . . so much social
change is occurring in the area of sex and vocation that any theoretical
proposal made now is likely to be premature, as would be any generalization about women's career development" (p. 271). Thus, the study
of these choices will be a continuing and challenging endeavor.

The previous chapters have focused primarily on a review of research investigating the factors influencing women's career choices. Implications of this knowledge for counseling and educating women and further needs in research and theory development in the area will be summarized in Chapter 15. Finally, issues of career choice are only the first, albeit a vitally important, stage in women's career development. Once women make and begin to implement their choices, issues of vocational adjustment become salient. Part III of the book will cover women's vocational adjustment, including their career success and satisfaction.

III

WOMEN'S CAREER ADJUSTMENT

THE CAREER ADJUSTMENT OF WOMEN: AN ANALYSIS OF A PROCESS

The distinction between *content* and *process* models of vocational behavior, so prominent in the work on career choice, has also proven to be a useful way of thinking about career adjustment. Much as Holland (1973, 1985) and other trait and factor theorists focus on choice content, that is, *what* occupation a person will select, while process theorists attend more to choice process (i.e., *how* a person goes about selecting an occupation) so, too, do vocational adjustment models focus on person–job matching (or "fit") or, alternatively, on problem-solving, task mastery, developmental stages, and so forth. Thus, the most venerable model of work adjustment, the individual differences approach of the Work Adjustment Project (Lofquist & Dawis, 1969; Dawis & Lofquist, 1984), provides a simple but elegant schema for predicting success and satisfaction on the basis of the fit between worker traits and occupational requirements and reinforcers, while the process model proposed by Crites (1969, 1976) describes schematically the process a worker goes through in attempting to overcome frustrations and conflicts to reach occupational goals. The remainder of this chapter will review what is known about the process of women's career adjustment, as well as describe briefly some of the major barriers to this adjustment and the coping behaviors employed to overcome them.

THE MODEL

Based on early work in the psychology of adjustment (Shaffer and Shoben, 1956), Crites (1969, 1976) has proposed that workers are motivated to achieve certain goals in the work environment (generally, success and satisfaction, although more particular goals can also be postulated). According to this model, when

> a motivated worker encounters some thwarting condition, either frustration (external) or conflict (internal), [it] necessitates adjustive responses in order to fulfill needs or reduce drives. If the worker copes effectively with the adjustment problem, a tension or anxiety reducing response is made and career satisfaction and success are achieved. To the extent that the problem is not integratively resolved, the worker is less well career-adjusted. The dynamics of this process are the same at all points on the continuum of career development, but the content changes from one stage to another because workers mature and tasks change. (p. 109)

From Crites' (1976) discussion can be extrapolated, then, three major variables that can usefully be examined: *motivation* (e.g., work needs, values, job orientation, and so forth); *barriers*, which can be divided into *external frustrations* (e.g., overt discrimination in selection, pay, and the like) and *internal conflicts* (e.g., what has been termed home–career conflict); and *coping* (the responses that the worker makes to either eliminate the barrier and/or to reduce the feelings of tension and anxiety that arise from the frustration or conflict). The following sections will systematically examine each of these variables to review what is known about the process of women's career adjustment and to suggest directions for future research.

MOTIVATION

The first variable specified in the model of vocational adjustment is that of work *motivation*. Motivation can be defined as a stable predisposition to engage in certain behaviors when appropriately stimulated or aroused by the environment. Intellectually grounded in the seminal work of Henry Murray (1938) as well as in the influential expectancy–value theory of Atkinson (1958) and his colleagues (Atkinson & Feather, 1966; Atkinson & Raynor, 1974; McClelland *et al.*, 1953), the study of individual differences in work motivation has generated an enormous body of literature and has proven to be one of the most fruitful areas of research in the psychology of personality.

The variable most often studied in investigations of work motivation is that of need for achievement. Murray (1938) described the achievement motive as "the desire or tendency to do things as rapidly and/or as well as possible. . . to accomplish something difficult. To master, manipulate and organize physical objects, human beings, or ideas. . . . To overcome obstacles and attain a high standard. To excel one's self. To rival and surpass others" (1938, p. 164). Operationalizing this construct through the projective Thematic Apperception Test (TAT), Murray and others investigated differences in nAch under various manipulations of environmental conditions. It was from these early studies that the notion first arose that achievement motivation was somehow "different" for women than for men. As noted in Spence (1983), "the results from males generally conformed to prediction, . . . [but] the data from females were inconsistent and difficult to interpret" (p. 31). As a result, women were generally not studied in investigations of achievement motivation, and the theory developed almost exclusively from work with male subjects.

Investigations of other motivational variables (primarily the need for affiliation) also focused strongly on gender-linked differences in areas that were sex role salient. Thus, Hoffman (1974a) proposed that, while women were less likely than men to be motivated to achieve, they were correspondingly more likely to be motivated to affiliate, as well as to work for the approval of others. In this way, the groundwork was laid for a psychology of achievement motivation that reified empirical findings of motivational differences which paralleled sex role expectations concerning appropriate behavior for men and women. A relatively recent addition to the theory, the motive to avoid success, postulated by Horner (1968), reinforced the sex-stereotypic nature of this paradigm by hypothesizing that women are also likely to be characterized by a stable dispositional tendency to become anxious about achieving success, which tendency is thought to reduce achievement motivation and inhibit achievement-related behavior. Horner's concept, widely known as *fear of success*, commanded a great deal of attention during the 1970s, stimulating an outpouring of scholarly articles, as well as much discussion in the popular press.

Taken together, the combined effect of the research on achievement motivation in the Murray/Atkinson/McClelland tradition, as elaborated by Hoffman (1974a), Crandall (1969), Horner (1968), and others, was to provide scholarly underpinnings for the notion that women do not achieve in the world of work because *they themselves do not wish to achieve*, preferring to select occupations in which they can affiliate with others, and avoid situations in which occupational success might threaten their sex role success. This approach, which can be (not unfairly) labeled as "blaming the victim" held sway in motivational psychology for many years, and is only recently beginning to be challenged by new and innovative conceptions. The following section will briefly review recent work investigating achievement motivation in women, as well as other salient work motivational variables, with a specific focus on gender differences in these variables.

ACHIEVEMENT MOTIVATION

The most important challenge to classic achievement motivation theory has been posed by Spence and her colleagues (Spence, 1983; Helmreich & Spence, 1978; Helmreich, Beane, Lucker, & Spence, 1978; Helmreich et al., 1980). Although clearly tracing their work to the Murray/Atkinson/McClelland tradition, Spence and her coworkers questioned the classic conception of achievement motivation as a unidimensional construct. They posited, rather, that a multifaceted conceptualization would provide a more useful way of thinking about the concept. Operationalizing their construct with an objective, self-report instrument, the Work and Family Orientation Questionnaire (WOFO), their program of research provides dramatic support for their theory, as well as recasting previous work on sex differences in an entirely different light. According to Spence (1983), the WOFO consists of three relatively independent scales:

1. *Mastery:* The preference for challenging tasks and for meeting internal standards of performance
2. *Work:* The desire to work hard and do a good job
3. *Competitiveness:* The enjoyment of interpersonal competition and the desire to do better than others

Research with the WOFO has demonstrated consistent, moderate sex differences in unselected groups on the three scales, with men generally achieving higher scores on mastery and competitiveness, and women scoring significantly higher on the work scale. Investigations of selected high-achieving groups (e.g., varsity athletes, businesspersons, academic psychologists) show a similar pattern. The correlations of these scores with actual achievement reveal a highly interesting pattern: while both work and mastery are strongly positively correlated with success, competitiveness shows a consistent, *negative* correlation, particularly for those persons who also scored high on work and mastery. This pattern has been consistently demonstrated to occur whatever criterion of success has been used (GPA for college students, salary for MBA businesspersons, and, interestingly, citations for academic psychologists).

Clearly, this body of research goes beyond the question of gender differences and represents a basic reformulation of the theoretical framework of achievement motivation. However, the implications for discussions of women's achievement are both clear and dramatic. If *both* work and mastery strivings are strong predictors of success, then whatever sex differences do exist are not relevant explanations of different levels of actual achievement. (In this view, it should be pointed out that when scores on the instrumentality/masculinity and expressiveness/femininity scales of the PAQ are held constant, women and men do not differ on work and mastery. In other words, observed sex differences in these achievement styles can be accounted for by the personality characteristics of instrumentality and expressiveness, rather than by gender itself.) Further, if competitiveness is consistently negatively related to achievement and if men score consistently higher on competitiveness than do women (a difference, incidentally, that is *not* accounted for by PAQ scores), then we are left to wonder why it is that men, as a group, are consistently more highly rewarded in terms of salary, prestige, and so forth. Whatever the answer to that question, it apparently does *not* lie in the realm of achievement motivation. For purposes of the present discussion of the process model of vocational adjustment, it seems reasonable to suppose that there are no reliable sex differences in *level* of achievement motivation, and that differences in the *patterning* of motivational structure (i.e., work, mastery, and competitiveness) should, if anything, facilitate women's career development and vocational adjustment.

OTHER MOTIVATIONAL VARIABLES

In addition to the question of sex differences in achievement motivation, there has been a great deal of literature generated concerning the existence, nature, and extent of sex differences in other work motivational variables. Variously referred to as work values, needs, preferences, job orientation, and so forth, this class of variables is considered motivational in nature and individual (and group) differences are thought to be important for the prediction of vocational satisfaction, one of the twin criteria of vocational adjustment. For many years, the belief held sway that women, due largely to the demands of their sex role, worked for different reasons than did men. Men were thought to work for achievement, success, prestige, and the intrinsic value of the work itself; women, on the other hand, were thought to value the opportunity to interact with others, make friends, be socially useful, and enjoy pleasant surroundings. Another way of characterizing the issue was to suggest that men worked for *intrinsic* reasons, while women worked for *extrinsic* ones, a characterization that neatly evades the fact that success, prestige, and pay can hardly be considered intrinsic motives, while helping others and being socially useful are equally difficult to classify as extrinsic. Nevertheless, the dichotomization and polar opposition considered to be the essence of maleness and femaleness that pervaded every aspect of psychology until relatively recently also influenced work in this area, and research followed in the stereotypic mode.

The body of literature bearing on this issue is both conflicting and confusing, and support can be found for almost any position. For example, a sizable subset of studies exists that supports the traditional stereotypes (Wagman, 1966; Manhardt, 1972; Singer, 1974; Schuler, 1975; Bartol & Manhardt, 1979). In general, these investigations suggest that men value money, independence, and long-term career goals, while women care more about people and the work environment, as well as focusing more on short-term career goals.

On the other hand, a similarly sizable subset of investigations has failed to detect any meaningful gender differences (Saleh & Lalljee, 1969; Brief & Aldag, 1975; Brief & Oliver, 1976; Brief, Rose, & Aldag, 1977). In more recent work, Lacy, Bokemeier, and Shepard (1983) utilized survey data collected by the National Opinion Research Center over an 8-year period. They demonstrated that, in five separate samples, the sexes had very similar job attribute preferences, and both indicated that the meaningfulness of the work was the most important preference. Additionally, both education and age, as well as prestige, were better predictors than gender. Similarly, Graddick and Farr (1983), in a large-scale investigation of scientists and mathematicians, found that their female subjects were just as job involved and organizationally committed as were the male subjects, even though they (the women) indicated more feelings of family–work conflict and perceptions of poorer treatment on the job. Finally, Miner and Smith (1982), in a major investigation of managerial motivation over a 20-year period, found that sex differences in Form H of the Miner Sentence Completion Scale (which measures various components of managerial motivation such as competition, dominance, and assertiveness), originally strong, had disappeared over time. Their study is important, as they utilized several samples that differed dramatically geographically and collected their data at various points in time. The authors speculate that the changing sex ratio of the managerial occupation may be a factor in their findings.

Given these two strong and conflicting bodies of research, what can be said with confidence about the work motivation of women? It is most likely that no generalization is possible, as the question has yet to be properly framed. As we have stated before (Fitzgerald & Betz, 1983), women are not a homogeneous group, and generalizations about (unselected) group differences are not likely to be enlightening. It is clear that other variables, such as age, education, and social class, to name a few, are probably more powerful predictors than is gender itself. According to Pryor (1983), the level of analysis undertaken will itself obscure or reveal differences, depending on its sensitivity and sophistication. Another point, which can be illustrated by reference to Pryor's (1983) own work on job values in a large sample of Australian teenagers, is that it is most likely quite risky to generalize from one national group to another. The rate of sex role liberalization is not constant across cultures, and what is so for young women in New South Wales may or may not be so in the United States.

Thus, the answer to questions concerning possible sex differences in work motivation most likely parallels the famous answer to the question "Who is more intelligent, man or woman?", to which Dr. Samuel Johnson is reputed to have replied, "Which man? Which Woman?" In terms of the present discussion, it appears parsimonious to propose the null hypothesis, until it has been demonstrated to be rejected.

BARRIERS

The career adjustment process begins with the entry of the individual into the world of work. Thus, the first goal of the worker is to secure an initial position which is congruent with her or his interests, abilities, education, and training. This process, traditionally an anxiety-provoking experience, particularly in difficult economic periods, is exacerbated for women, who must deal with issues and problems unlikely to be faced by their male counterparts. Sex discrimination in selection, illegal since the passage of the Civil Rights Act of 1964, still operates as a barrier to women at this most fundamental level of vocational adjustment, the obtaining of suitable employment.

As noted in Fitzgerald and Betz (1983), discrimination can take any of three forms: *formal, informal,* or *inadvertent*. Formal discrimination exists whenever an occupation is formally closed to one sex or the other, even though biological sex is not a bona fide occupational qualification (BFQ) for successful job performance. Such formal discrimination, long a public and acceptable feature of the world of work, has, with the passage of the Civil Rights Act, passed into history. Although a few jobs still exist in which sex is considered a BFQ (e.g., only men are hired as guards in a male prison, and vice versa), they are rare enough to be noted in the popular press, a situation that is more or less the reverse of that which existed 20 years ago.

However, if formal discrimination has all but disappeared, informal discrimination remains widespread, not only in selection, but also in promotion and compensation, as well as in many other areas of occupational treatment which are difficult to examine and measure. Informal sex discrimination can be said to exist whenever members of one sex are accorded systematically differential treatment based on their membership in that gender group, rather than on work-related characteristics or performance. Such differential treatment, although often informally sanctioned by the organization, is not formal organizational policy. A great deal of research was conducted in this area during the 1970s, and the results were fairly consistent in their support for the hypothesis that women are often discriminated against in the selection process. The standard research paradigm, comparison of resumés identical except for sex, consistently yielded significantly higher ratings, and/or stronger hiring recommendations for male candidates than for female candidates (Dipboye, Arvey, & Terpstra, 1977; Dipboye, Fromkin, & Wiback, 1975; Haefner, 1977; and Zickmund, Hitt, & Pickens, 1978). Arvey (1979a) pointed out that although applicant sex accounts for only a small part of the variance when evaluators are allowed only one or two hiring choices, these choices are highly related to applicant sex. In other words, when there is only one position available, evaluators overwhelmingly select a male candidate.

In addition to documenting a simple main effect favoring men, the research on informal discrimination has also focused on other variables that might reasonably be expected to interact with gender to affect women in the selection process. Probably the most powerful of these is the sex-typing of the job under study, the hypothesis being that both women and men will be systematically underrated for jobs stereotypically assigned to the opposite sex. Arvey (1979b) has termed this the sex congruency notion, and relevant research appears to confirm it (Cash, Gillen, & Burns, 1977; Cohen & Bunker, 1975; Shaw, 1972). In a particularly creative field experiment, Levinson (1975) had pairs of male and female experimenters make telephone inquiries concerning 265 positions that had been selected from the classified advertisements of two metropolitan newspapers in a major southeastern city. The positions were classified as male or female on the basis of the relative distribution of men and women in each. In each case, one partner made a telephone inquiry for a sex-inappropriate job, followed a short time later by a matched call from the other partner, a sex-appropriate situation. Employer responses were carefully recorded, and 35% of the calls resulted in clear-cut discrimination (e.g., the caller of the "wrong" sex was told the job was filled, whereas the sex-appropriate caller was invited to fill out an application or come for an interview). In addition, 27% of the calls were classified as cases of "ambiguous" discrimination: for example, sex-inappropriate callers were discouraged from applying, and/or employers displayed surprise or dismay at the calls. Although plagued by the usual imprecision of field experimentation, this study provides powerful data in support of the sex congruency notion.

It is obvious that such discrimination "cuts both ways," as it were, and much has been made of the fact that men are systematically discouraged from entering the traditionally female-dominated occupations. Not only employers, but college students and counselors-in-training, have been shown to hold negative attitudes toward men attempting nontraditional career paths (Fitzgerald, 1980; Fitzgerald & Cherpas, 1985). However, it is important to point out that while sex congruency notions may pose a problem for individual men, the issue is of neither the same order nor the same magnitude as it is for women. After all, men are not attempting, in great numbers, to "breach the walls" of the traditionally low-status, low-paid feminine occupations, and commentary which attempts to be "fair" in this area appears to miss the point. In addition, it is not entirely certain that men in nontraditional occupations always, or even often, suffer from their token status. Fairhurst and Snavely (1983) hypothesized that male nurses should be more socially isolated than their numerically dominant female colleagues and thus more cut off from discussions of political information (e.g., ways of getting around formal rules, strategies for impressing superiors) and personal information that could affect performance. Their sociometrically based investigation failed to demonstrate any support for this hypothesis, and they concluded that the inherently higher status of the male gender was strong enough to overdetermine the usual detrimental effects of token status. Thus, while the sex congruency expectation is obviously a double-edged sword, it is also obvious that to equate the positions of the two sexes in this matter is spurious.

Another variable that has been hypothesized to interact with sex to influence the selection process is physical attractiveness. Physical attractiveness has long been assumed to be an advantage for the persons possessing it, particularly women. Because women have traditionally been defined by their biological/sexual functions of mating and motherhood, it follows that physical beauty, which presumably facilitates these functions, is a more salient feature in their lives than in the lives of men, who have other criteria on which they are evaluated (Bar-Tal & Saxe, 1976; Miller, 1970). Recent research in vocational psychology suggests that physical attractiveness may also be a powerful variable affecting women in the world of work. Early work in this area appeared to support the validity of a general "what is beautiful is good" hypothesis—that is, physically attractive persons are assumed to possess more socially desirable traits, as well as thought to be more successful than unattractive persons (Berscheid & Walster, 1974; Cash, Begley, McCown, & Weise, 1975; Cash, Kehr, Polyson, & Freeman, 1977; Dermer & Thiel, 1975; Dion, Berscheid, & Walster, 1972).

In addition to this attribution of "general goodness," Gillen (1975) has presented evidence that attractive persons are also assumed to possess "sex-typed goodness." In his research, attributions of masculinity on the Bem Sex-Role Inventory (Bem, 1974) increased with the attractiveness of the male stimulus persons. A similar phenomenon was observed for female stimulus persons on the feminine scales. Thus, attractive persons were seen as *more* sex role stereotyped than unattractive persons.

Dipboye *et al.* (1975) found that male college recruiters were more willing to hire a physically attractive candidate than an equally qualified unattractive candidate. Although male candidates were preferred to female candidates, attractive candidates were preferred to unattractive candidates, regardless of their sex. These findings were replicated by Dipboye *et al.* (1977). Cash *et al.* (1977) investigated the effect of candidates' sex and attractiveness on personnel consultants' judgments of qualifications, predictions of success, hiring recommendations, attributions of success and failure, and suggestions for occupational alternatives of candidates for masculine, feminine, and neutral jobs. Most of their major hypotheses were supported in that male candidates received more favorable personnel evaluations than females for masculine jobs, and females for feminine jobs. In particular, highly attractive male candidates for masculine jobs received the highest rating on all variables, followed by a "control" male of unknown attractiveness, and then an unattractive male. Interestingly enough, for the masculine job, the unattractive female candidate was more favorably evaluated on all variables than her attractive or "control" colleagues. This finding, which the authors do not directly address, is consistent with earlier results reported by Dipboye *et al.* (1977), indicating that whereas raters most often chose a highly qualified attractive male for a sex-neutral managerial position, the next most highly chosen candidate was the highly qualified *unattractive* female.

Reviewing these findings, Heilman and Saruwatari (1979) suggested that physical attractiveness may not always be an advantage in the work world, particularly for females. Drawing on the earlier work of Gillen (1975), which suggested that attractiveness exacerbates sex role stereotyping and noted that sex-typed feminine characteristics are not those judged appropriate or necessary for success in managerial occupations (Schein, 1973, 1975), these researchers hypothesized that women's attractiveness would prove advantageous only for a non-managerial lower-level position. For an upper-level managerial position, an attractive female candidate was hypothesized to be at a disadvantage. The data clearly supported the hypothesis for all dependent measures, including evaluation of qualifications, hiring recommendation, and suggested starting salary. For male candidates, on the other hand, attractiveness produced higher ratings regardless of the type and level of the position for which they were applying.

Other variables that have been suggested to interact with applicant sex have included sex of rater (Muchinsky & Harris, 1977; Rose & Andiappan, 1978), sex of subordinates in the job (Rose & Andiappan, 1978), level of applicant competence (Haefner, 1977; Heneman, 1977), and rater authoritarianism (Simas & McCarrey, 1979). This research has produced mixed results; however, whereas competent candidates are generally preferred to incompetent ones, highly competent males are preferred over highly competent females.

The final form of selection discrimination to be discussed may best be termed "inadvertent." By this, we are referring to the effect of certain selection devices on the selection ratio for women. The Uniform Guidelines on Employee Selection Procedures (Equal Employment Opportunity Commission, 1978) prohibit the use of any test or device that has an adverse impact on the selection rate of a protected group (i.e., women, blacks, etc.) and that cannot clearly be shown to be job related. The classic legal case in this area is Griggs versus Duke Power Company, in which the Supreme Court ruled that the use of a general intelligence test and a mechanical aptitude test and the requirement of possession of a high school diploma were illegal in the selection of common laborers, as they resulted in the selection of far fewer blacks than whites and were not job related.

Although paper-and-pencil tests most often result in adverse impact on blacks, performance tests, such as those required for selection into the police and fire services, more often affect female candidates adversely. Such tests often contain what amount to hidden requirements for height and strength that exceed established minimum qualifications (MQs), are not job related, and are illegal. Obviously, any test that uses height as a factor will have a negative effect on women. For example, in a now famous New York State Police case, the court found that a requirement that applicants be able to sight and fire over the roof of a police car had the effect of imposing an excessive height requirement. This requirement, rather than being job related, was actually contrary to established police procedure. A discussion of adverse impact and inadvertent discrimination involves highly complex legal and psychological issues that cannot be articulated at length here. However, the salient point is that selection devices of questionable validity may effectively close certain jobs to women even when employers are not consciously intending to discriminate against them. Combined with underevaluation by employers and other forms of informal discrimination, adverse impact is thus one more factor creating barriers to occupational entry for women.

Following entry into an occupation, and, specifically, an organization, a women faces the difficult process of organizational adjustment. Van Maanen (1976) has written perceptively of this process of "breaking in" or occupational socialization, and examination of his discussion suggests many ways in which the breaking-in period may frustrate women in their attempts to achieve vocational adjustment during this early part of the establishment stage.

Van Maanen (1976) suggested that breaking in involves three stages: anticipatory socialization, encounter, and metamorphosis, or change. Anticipatory socialization, as outlined by Merton (1957), actually occurs prior to occupational entry and is the process by which persons take on the values of the group to which they aspire. According to Merton (1957)

> For the individual who adopts the values of a group to which he aspires but does not belong, the orientation may serve the twin functions of aiding his rise into that group and of easing his adjustments after he has become a part of it. (p. 265) [generic masculine in the original]

Thus, to the degree that women have not been socialized to accept the salient values of an occupation or organization, they will experience both conflict (due to the internal value clash) and frustration (as their "inappropriate" values put them at variance with their male colleagues). Clearly, this is most salient for women attempting to adjust to more nontraditional occupations, as well as to the so-called "dog-eat-dog" business world. Harragan (1977) suggested that women have been excluded from many early socialization experiences that prepare men to cope effectively in the organizational world, particularly competitive sports and other activities that validate the appropriateness of competition, aggression, and "winning." On a more psychological level, Gilligan (1982) has recently suggested that women's early experiences may cause them to construct a moral and ethical structure that values relationships and responsibility to others over individuality, a focus that has long characterized the literature on masculine moral development. To the degree that Gilligan is correct, women will most likely have greater difficulty adjusting to organizational life and corporate cultures that emphasize competition, the profit motive (a motive not always congruent with responsibility toward others), and so forth. Thus, while generalizations are by definition just that, and unlikely to be predictive for any particular individual, it seems reasonable to suggest that women will not have engaged in the same anticipatory socialization process as their male counterparts, and that this may well present them with both internal and external barriers to their career adjustment during the breaking in process.

The second stage of organizational socialization, according to Van Maanen (1976), is what has been termed "the encounter." This phenomenon, similar in some ways to what Hughes (1958) has called "reality shock," largely encompasses structural variables of the organization, the degree of "shock" depending mostly upon the extent to which the person has correctly anticipated the various expectations of the organization. Initial adjustment difficulties during the encounter period are often exacerbated by organizational recruitment policies. As Shullman and Carder (1983) have noted

> Most organizations have traditionally treated recruitment as a process of selling the organization's image in a manner akin to individual attempts to put oneself in the "most favorable light." As the individual attempts to garner as many job offers as possible, organizations have attempted to attract the highest number of candidates possible. (p. 153)

Such practices may have a particularly unfortunate impact on women, as many companies, under affirmative action pressure to hire female candidates, may give an unrealistically "rosy" answer to the question "What is it like for women in your organization?" Having been assured that the organization is nonsexist, or even pro-women, in its practices and policies, a woman accepts the position, only to find herself faced with nonenthusiastic or rejecting colleagues, rigid schedules which do not interface well with the demands of home and children (Catalyst, 1981), sexual harassment, (Farley 1978; MacKinnon, 1978), and a salary that is, on the average, significantly less than that of her male counterpart (Fitzgerald & Betz, 1983). According to Van Maanen (1976) and others, such large discrepancies between expectations and reality can have a very negative impact on organizational socialization, leading to frustration, dissatisfaction, absenteeism, and eventual turnover.

Nor is this the only problem faced by a woman during the encounter period. Nieva and Gutek (1981) discussed the importance of informal networks for organizational success and the exclusion of women from many of these networks. They noted that such exclusion can come about as the result of overt ridicule and social rejection (Rossi, 1970), subtle intimidation through the telling of sexual jokes and "war stories" (Kanter, 1977), self-exclusion due to confusion concerning appropriate normative behavior (Bernard, 1972), and, probably most commonly, simple physical exclusion. This latter commonly involves the removal of certain activities "away from public settings to which everyone has access to more private ones from which they can be excluded—the bar, the men's room, the golf course, and private gatherings. When this happens, peer interaction is limited to the official occasions and meetings held at work, where only formally acceptable news and opinions are expressed for the public record" (p. 56).

In a similar fashion, women are not well integrated into the "mentor" or "coach" system so important for organizational success. Strauss (1968) has noted the importance of the "coach" as one who sees that the newcomer is properly groomed and instructed during the breaking-in period. As discussed by Van Maanen (1976), the coach's role is to "develop a new identity for the learner by guiding him [sic] along a series of successful organizational socialization" (Evan, 1963). Evan found that the level of recruit–peer group interaction was negatively related to the level of early turnover, and speculated that peer groups eased the person's passage into the organization, most likely by reducing strain and easing tension. Women are unlikely to be present in sufficient numbers to form a *significant* peer group, and it seems reasonable to speculate that they are also unlikely to be integrated into groups composed mostly of their male colleagues. Thus, their token status not only presents a barrier to their career adjustment, it also deprives them of what appears to be an effective coping mechanism.

The final process postulated by Van Maanen (1976) as part of the breaking-in phenomenon is metamorphosis, or change. This notion consists of solutions the newcomer has adopted to address the problems she or he has discovered during the first encounter with the organization. As such, they are properly classified within the Crites model as *coping mechanisms*. it is to these variables that we now turn.

COPING

Much of what has been written concerning the ways in which women cope has focused explicitly on the strategies used to manage the home—career interface, usually considered the principle barrier to women's career development. Thus, the literature is replete with both psychological and sociological investigations focusing on the various ways in which women attempt to negotiate this interface.

A more general approach to the issue of coping is to examine the degree to which women are mastering the tasks that are thought to be associated with each successive career stage. This approach, analogous to the concept of career maturity but applicable to the adult population, is theoretically grounded in the work of Super (1955) and methodologically tied to the Career Adjustment and Development Inventory (Career-ADI) (Crites, 1979), which is designed to measure mastery of various developmental tasks thought to be important for the negotiation of the establishment stage of career development. At the present time, only two investigations of this sort have been completed: the original validation study of the Career-ADI conducted by Crites (1979) and a study of some 300 college graduates conducted by Fitzgerald (1984). Briefly, the Career-ADI attempts to measure the mastery of six career development tasks:

1. Organizational adaptation
2. Position performance
3. Work habits and attitudes
4. Co-worker relationships
5. Advancement
6. Career choice and plans

Crites (1979) has determined that mastery of these tasks is significantly associated with vocational satisfaction, one of the two main criteria of career adjustment. In his original sample of 110 employed adults, he found no sex differences at either the item or the scale level, indicating that the women were demonstrating the same types and degree of career coping behavior as the men. A similar study, conducted by Fitzgerald (1984) on 328 college graduates ($N = 143$ men and 185 women) who were either 1, 3, or 5 years into the establishment stage again found no sex differences in scale means, sequence of task mastery, or relationship with the criterion variables of job satisfaction and self-perceptions of success. Thus, while it is clear that women face special barriers requiring coping behaviors not needed by men, it also appears that, on the more general tasks of career development and coping, women demonstrate the same type and level of career adjustment as do men.

Several writers have described roles which women adopt to cope with the specific problems arising from the perceived incongruity of their sex role with their work role. Thus, Bernard (1972) discussed the "stroking" function, that is, the expectation that women supply social and emotional support to those who achieve, rather than achieve directly themselves. In many ways, this is analogous to the "cheerleader" role, ubiquitous in American culture, both on the sports field and off. In both of these situations, the woman is seen as ancillary to the main business at hand, whether that be a corporate merger or a college football game. The traditional female occupations of nurse and secretary are the classic embodiment of the stroking function and the cheerleader role, while the occupation of teacher (particularly at the preschool and elementary school levels) is a clear extension of the mother role. Obviously, this "spillover," as Nieva and Gutek (1981) referred to it, of the female sex role into the work role operates to keep women on the periphery, a point also made by Epstein (1976) and many others. However, selecting an occupational role which is an extension of one's sex role is also one way of coping with the perceived conflict between the two, as well as of evading certain "nonfeminine" activities, such as competition, aggression, and so forth, for which women are often severely penalized. Thus, for those women who have the appropriate interests, ability level, and temperament, the "stroking" function, as embodied in the traditional female occupations, often represents an integrative solution. For other women, however—those with nontraditional interests, high levels of ability, and so forth—such a solution is maladaptive, generating as it often does a vocational lifetime of frustration and disappointment.

Nieva and Gutek (1981) discussed another sex role–work role combination often assigned to women, that of "prize" in the competition among men. As they somewhat dryly pointed out, while the role of prize does ensure a certain amount of organizational attention that might otherwise be denied, "the type of attention obtained in this role is not that which focuses on the woman's abilities or achievements" (p. 61). Needless to say, engaging in such a role does not represent a long-term solution to the problems of vocational adjustment, and most likely has deleterious effects in the short term as well.

Finally, Kanter (1977) discussed the role of the "pet," the helpless (but attractive) female who is protected by her male colleagues. Kanter (1977) has written perceptively of the various roles women may assume (or into which they are cast) to deal with the perceived incongruity of their status as women with their status as workers. She suggests that the *mother,* the *seductress,* the *pet,* and the *iron maiden* constitute four "role traps" that encapsulate women into categories that men can respond to and understand. The *mother* represents the organizational extension of the traditional nurturing role; the *seductress* is similar to the *prize,* described above; the *pet* is adopted by the male group as a cute little mascot, patronized and praised for exhibiting behaviors considered ordinary in a man; and, finally, the *iron maiden* is seen as the rough, nonemotional, nonsexual strong woman. Refusing to accept any of the other three clearly sex-linked roles, she is nonetheless sexually defined by this very refusal, and is often thought to be more militant and "tougher" than she really is.

It is important to point out that, while these roles are often adopted by women, possibly nonconsciously, for coping purposes, they are also likely to represent a "forced choice"—four options offered by the dominant male group to women who wish to participate seriously in organizational pursuits previously reserved to men. Interestingly enough, all four roles can be seen as methods for encapsulating women and allowing male coworkers to deal with them in terms of the usual, comfortable sexual and family roles: mother, sex partner, kid sister, and maiden aunt. As such, they are actually more mechanisms by which *men* cope with the conflict-arousing presence of women in previously all-male territory. This is an integrative response for men, as the female coworker can be "reconceptualized" in safe and familiar ways, and the threat and conflict are removed. For the woman, however, acceptance of these roles is at best adjustive. They may serve an anxiety-reducing function; however, they do nothing to actually change the situation and in the long run are probably detrimental.

SUMMARY

The present chapter has attempted to organize what is known about women's career adjustment and cast it in the framework of Crites' (1976) process model. With respect to *motivational variables,* women *as an unselected group* have not been shown to differ reliably from their male counterparts, and to continue to pursue such investigations is most likely to continue to ask the wrong question. The recent work of Spence and her colleagues concerning the multidimensionality of the achievement motive is a seminal example of the more sophisticated theoretical and empirical approaches that are required if we are to increase meaningful knowledge in this area.

With respect to *thwarting conditions* (i.e., barriers), it appears that women face not only the usual difficulties in vocational adjustment, but that these difficulties are often exacerbated by the presumed incompatibility of their sex role with their work role. Women share with other minority groups externally imposed barriers such as formal and informal discrimination that most white men are not required to face. Finally, there appear to be barriers and conflicts unique to women workers. Some of these have been briefly discussed above; however, others are complex and difficult enough to require more extensive treatment (e.g., sexual harassment, the home–work interface) and will be dealt with in separate chapters (see Chapters 12 through 14).

The last section of this chapter examined the theory and knowledge concerning what are commonly known as coping mechanisms. What little evidence there is suggests that women master general career developmental tasks in the same order and at the same rate as men. Such task mastery appears to be related to criterion variables of success and satisfaction in a similar manner for both sexes. In other ways, however, women require additional coping mechanisms to address the perceived sex role–work role conflict, and not all of these coping mechanisms are necessarily effective. Although quasi-theory and anecdotal material abounds on this topic, systematically collected data are notable by their absence.

In conclusion, we believe the present evidence concerning the process of women's career adjustment lends further support to the earlier statement that "the potential career development of women, although not fundamentally *different* than that of men, is a great deal more complex, due to that combination of attitudes, role expectations, behaviors, and sanctions known as the socialization process" (Fitzgerald & Crites, 1980, p. 45). The answer to the question of whether or not women and men have qualitatively similar vocational experiences is—as with so many similar issues—both yes. . . and no.

11

THE CRITERIA OF
CAREER ADJUSTMENT:
SUCCESS AND SATISFACTION

In contrast to process theories of vocational adjustment is the individual differences approach of Dawis and Lofquist (1983). According to these writers, vocational adjustment can be conceptualized in terms of the correspondence between the individual and the work environment. Individuals are thought to differ on various psychological and behavioral dimensions, the most salient of which (for vocational adjustment) are *abilities* and *values*. Similarly, occupations are believed to differ in the *requirements* they demand and the *reinforcers* they offer. Correspondence between the individuals' abilities and the occupational requirements should result in *satisfactoriness* (i.e., the worker is able to competently perform job tasks and is evaluated as competent or satisfactory. Informally, the individual is said to be successful.). In a similar fashion, if the reinforcers offered by a particular occupation match those valued by the job incumbent (e.g., salary, autonomy, advancement), then she/he is likely to be satisfied. The two criteria of vocational adjustment, success and satisfaction, should result in substantial *tenure*, that is, the individual remains on the job. Further predictions of the theory include conditions under which the worker will leave the job: abilities in excess of requirements should theoretically result in promotion or advancement of some sort, whereas workers possessing less ability than the job requires will likely be demoted or terminated. Finally, if the occupational reinforcers available do not match those valued by the individual, it is likely that she or he will voluntarily terminate employment in favor of a position that maximizes value–reinforcer congruence. Dawis and Lofquist (1983) have recently revised the theory to include personality style (process) variables, an addition that promises to greatly increase its predictive and explanatory power.

No discussion of women's vocational adjustment has yet appeared that directly compares the success and satisfaction of women with those of men, within the framework of Dawis and Lofquist (1983). It is the purpose of the present chapter to provide such a discussion and to examine the various issues, both methodological and conceptual, that bear on such a comparison. We shall see, in the following sections, that, although there are no data to support sex differences in general work-related abilities, women as a group experience less success than men. In terms of the Theory of Work Adjustment (Dawis & Lofquist, 1983), women in general should be as *satisfactory* workers as men. However, they obtain far lower levels of reward. We shall see further that the research on women's vocational satisfaction has been marred by extensive methodological flaws that prevent firm conclusions. Finally, we offer a discussion of the variables that must be taken into account if any clear understanding of women's vocational satisfaction is to be achieved.

SUCCESS

As Crites (1969) has noted, "the concept of vocational success is paradoxically both general and specific in its meanings. Workers from all walks of life know what you mean when you ask them what 'success' is. . . yet, each man [*sic*] defines success in his own way" (p. 409). Thus, success appears to mean both the same and different things to people, and it is from this paradox that much confusion arises concerning the nature of this concept, and, particularly, its relationship to other variables.

Probably the most commonly accepted definition of success in our culture is a monetary one, that of salary. Although economists may argue among themselves as to the exact nature of the appropriate criterion (i.e., salary, life earnings), the general notion of financial attainment is well established in the general culture as the predominant indicator of success. Distinct from this *nonpsychological* concept of vocational success is one of the cornerstones of personnel/industrial psychology—performance, or how well the worker performs her/his job. As early as 1926, Bingham and Freyd wrote

> From the management's point of view, the successful employee, in contrast to the unsuccessful, does more work, does it better, with less supervision, with less interruption through absence from the job. He offers a larger number of

good original suggestions looking toward improvement of conditions or of processes. He ordinarily learns more quickly, is promoted more rapidly, and stays with the company. (pp. 30–31) [generic masculine in the original]

Although few would disagree with this statement, which constitutes what Underwood (1957) would call a *literary definition*, considerable difficulty arises when one attempts to operationalize it within the context of formal performance appraisal (Crites, 1969; DeVries, Morrison, Shullman, & Gerlach, 1981). As we shall see when discussing perceptions of women's performance, the usual problems that plague performance appraisal are exacerbated for women, most usually through what Brogden and Taylor (1950) initially labeled *criterion contamination*, or the introduction of extraneous elements (in this case, sex role expectations) into the criterion.

Finally, of course, it is important to remember, as Super (1951) has pointed out, "One tends to forget that success is not only a *social* or *objective* matter, but also a *personal* or *subjective* matter" (p. 7). Thus, no matter how successful one is by objective standards, whether these be economic or organizational, in the final analysis, it is one's subjective self-evaluation that determines the psychological experience of success. Little is presently known about women's self-evaluations of success (or about men's, for that matter), as work is only beginning in this area (Frye, 1984); however, it promises to be a fascinating and fruitful area of inquiry. The remainder of this section will review what is known concerning women's vocational success, including *economic* or financial success, *organizational* or performance success, and, finally, *self-evaluations* of success.

ECONOMIC SUCCESS

Women earn less money than men. Despite active and sometimes heated debate concerning the cause of present wage disparities between the sexes, it is clear that when a monetary or economic criterion is applied, women are much less successful than men. Although it is widely popularly asserted that women have made enormous gains in the labor market and that wage disparity/discrimination is a thing of the past, Russo and Denmark (1984) have recently pointed out that this is simply not so. They stated, "In 1981, among year-round full-time workers, the average female worker earned only about 59% of her male counterpart. *Women workers with 4 or more years college education had about the same income as men with 1 to 3 years of high school. . . . Global statistics mask racial differences. Median salary* *figures by sex and race that year were: white men $21,160; black men, $15,119; white women, $12,287; and black women, $11,312"* (p. 1162; emphasis added). Ferraro made the point even more graphically: "In 1982, the majority of women working outside the home—60%— earned less than $10,000 a year" (Ferraro, 1984).

Not only do women as a group make much less money than men, due mostly to the fact that women workers are highly segregated into a few occupational categories that are then very poorly paid; but even within the same occupation, women make anywhere from 20 to 45% less than their male colleagues. For example, female computer specialists earn 80% of the median male income for full-time, year-round employment; however, among salaried managers in manufacturing industries, women earn only slightly more than half of the male median (U.S. Department of Labor, 1979).

Finally, it is clear that, at least in some cases, women are not only paid less than men, they are blatantly paid less than their services are objectively worth, even though the employer is clearly cognizant of the worth of the job. For example, in the landmark Supreme Court pay equity decision, *Gunther v. County of Washington* (1981), the court found that the county was paying its female jail matrons only 70% of the evaluated worth of their job, which had been established by a county-conducted job evaluation. The male prison guards, on the other hand, were paid 100% of the rate that had been established for their job. Thus, whether through the somewhat subtle operation of occupational segregation or the more straightforward operation of outright discrimination, women continue to be put at a tremendous financial disadvantage, not only when compared to unselected groups of men but also to male colleagues in the same occupation. In this sense, it is certainly possible to say that women are less vocationally adjusted than men.

Explanations for Women's Lesser Economic Success

There appear to be three main explanations for women's lack of economic success. The classic argument is that of *human capital theory*, which posits that individuals "invest" in themselves through education, training, and so forth. This investment, in turn, "pays off" in higher salaries, better jobs, etc., for those individuals who have accrued more human capital, that is, those who have the most to offer an employer. Similar in many respects to the sociological model of status attainment (Blau & Duncan, 1967; Sewell, Haller, & Ohlendorf, 1970;

TABLE 11.1   Mean Hourly Earnings on Most Recent Job by Sex, Race, and High School Curriculum

Sample	High school curriculum				
	Vocational	Business	College prep	General	All
NLS–LME sample					
White male	6.59	6.87	6.45	6.25	6.3
White female	3.17	4.14	4.05	3.75	3.9
Minority male	5.15	5.50	5.48	4.81	4.9
Minority female	2.99	3.86	4.03	3.41	3.5
Class of '72 sample					
White male	7.45	—	7.53	7.39	7.4
White female	5.49	—	6.27	5.36	5.8
Minority male	7.01	—	7.23	6.79	6.9
Minority female	5.29	—	6.04	5.23	5.5
Young Adult Worker sample					
White male	7.27 (+1.76)	—	9.80 (+3.46)	7.13 (+1.79)	—
White female	5.51 (+0.99)	—	5.99 (+1.38)	4.40 (−0.36)	—
Minority male	5.54 (−0.08)	—	7.98 (−0.67)	5.30 (−0.62)	—
Minority female	5.93 (+0.67)	—	4.48 (−1.26)	4.63 (0.22)	—

Note. Figures in parentheses are the absolute differences in wages between first job and most recent job: NLS–LME, The National Longitudinal Survey of Labor Market Experience; Class of '72, the National Longitudinal Study of the High School Class of 1972; Young Adult Worker Sample. From Fitzgerald (1985, p. 8). Originally adapted from Mertens and Gardner (1981, pp. 161, 163, 164).

Sewell, Haller, & Portes, 1969), human capital theory generates useful predictions when applied to white men, but does not fare so well when applied to women. We have already seen that women who have completed college educations do less well financially than men who are high school dropouts, although human capital theory would predict otherwise. Similarly, when young men and women with the same number of years of education and training (i.e., the same amount of human capital) are compared, in every instance, the men outearn the women. Consider, for example, Table 11.1. Table 11.1 contains simple cross-tabulations of earnings on the most recent job, by race, sex, and high school curriculum, for three national data sets: the National Longitudinal Survey of Labor Market Experience, the National Longitudinal Study of the High School Class of 1972, and the Young Adult Worker (YAW). All figures are presented for high school graduates with no postsecondary education (i.e., exactly 12 years of education). The YAW figures (Mertens & Gardner, 1981) also include, in parentheses, difference scores for the absolute change in earnings from the first job to the most recent job. A review of Table 11.1 reveals that white women in all categories consistently earn less than their male counterparts, whether black or white. Black women are even more dramatically disadvantaged, earning less than any other sex/race group, no matter what curriculum is being examined. While the earnings for white men increase fairly substantially from the first job to the most recent job, those of black and white women (as well as those of black men) increase more slowly, stay about the same, or actually *decrease* over time. This is consistent with the findings of Angle and Wissman (1983), who suggested that much of the gender gap in rate of economic return is attributable to the fact that men are paid more as they age and women are not. In sum, it seems reasonable to conclude (1) gender differences in pay and other forms of financial return cannot be adequately accounted for by differences in education and/or experience and (2) classical human capital theory, like so many other theories of human behavior, is of limited usefulness for predicting and explaining the experience of women.

Writing in a special series in the *American Psychologist* devoted to women and public policy, Ferraro (1984) suggested that more persuasive explanations for the persistent wage gap between men and women have to do with "the two pervasive, yet often subtle, forms of employment bias at work to depress women's wages: occupational segregation and sex-based wage discrimination" (p. 1166). With respect to occupational segregation, she went on to point out that "job segregation creates economic ghettos. Women are first channeled into certain sectors of the economy, then they are clustered into the lowest paying occupations within those sectors, and finally, they are confined to jobs, that, by virtue of being female-dominated, are undervalued and underpaid" (p. 1167).

It is certainly true that the overwhelming majority of women are clustered into a handful of occupational areas (see Fitzgerald & Betz, 1983, as well as Part II of this book). Dunton and Featherman (1983) discussed the importance of gender segregation in occupations for understanding women's lesser earnings and made several points. First, they underscored the fact that gender segregation in employment restricts the range of occupational activity for women, who remain concentrated in semiprofessional, lower white-collar occupations (Grimm & Stearn, 1974). It is important to note that "white-collar" (as well as "blue-collar") usually does not mean the same thing for men as it does for women, and this fact has caused some confusion in the literature. Sociologists are fond of pointing out that women as a group tend to be found in white-collar occupations, while men are more often found in blue-collar occupations, which supposedly have less status. However, Kahl (1983) noted that for men, white-collar employment means a professional, administrative, or scientific position, whereas for women, it usually means being a secretary. Similarly, the women who do enter the blue-collar sector tend to be over-concentrated in operative positions (74%, according to Ferraro, 1984), while men are more evenly distributed among various categories (e.g., craft, laborer, operative). Even within the operative areas, women are again concentrated into traditionally female (and low-paying) jobs such as textiles, laundry, and stitching, while men work in areas such as mining, welding, and precision machinery which, of course, pay more.

Dunton and Featherman (1983) discussed the two major explanations for occupational gender segregation: *employee tastes* (i.e., women enter a limited set of occupations because they find them attractive for their task content or working conditions; because they parallel the traditional female domestic tasks; or because they are structured in such a way as to allow coordination of family/work demands) and *employer tastes* i.e., women enter occupations that employers open to them; however, because of widespread perceptions of women's supposed lesser ability and career commitment, as well as sex role expectations, these occupations are quite limited). Dunton and Featherman (1983) noted that there has been no formal assessment or comparison of these alternative explanations of gender segregation in employment patterns; however, it seems likely that both exert influence and that this influence is interactive and thus self-perpetuating.

However, the mere fact that women perform (on the average) different work than men does not explain why it is that women's work is so poorly paid. After all, why is it that "a secretary with 18 years of experience, whose 'only' skills are typing, letter composition, office management and the ability to deal with the public, is paid less than a parking lot attendant whose required education is the ability to drive an automobile" (Ferraro, 1984, pp. 1166–1167). It is difficult to escape the conclusion that men are paid more for what they do quite simply because they are men. Consider, for example, Table 11.2, which contains the ten largest occupations for women and men in 1970, with 1970 median earnings. Note that almost all of these occupations are highly sex-stereotyped (e.g., teacher, nurse, and secretary) and that the median wages are, in most cases, far below those paid in the stereotypically masculine occupations (e.g., managers, truck drivers,

TABLE 11.2   The Ten Largest Occupations for Women and Men Ranked by Number in the 1970 Labor Force, with 1970 Median Earnings

Rank	Title	Number in experienced civilian labor force, 1970	1970 Median earnings
Women			
1.	Secretaries, except legal and medical	2,704,996	$ 4,803
2.	Sales workers	1,764,391	2,274
3.	Bookkeepers	1,307,251	4,477
4.	Elementary school teachers	1,214,743	6,856
5.	Waitresses	990,259	1,662
6.	Typists	961,857	4,042
7.	Sewers and stitchers	883,678	3,379
8.	Registered nurses	825,963	5,603
9.	Maids and servants, private household	680,420	1,093
10.	Clerical workers, unspecified	648,272	4,056
			$\bar{x} =$ $ 3,646
Men			
1.	Managers and administrators	3,114,276	$11,161
2.	Sales workers	2,369,269	8,121
3.	Foremen	1,468,320	10,018
4.	Truck drivers	1,442,046	7,246
5.	Farmers, owners and tenants	1,237,294	4,816
6.	Janitors and sextons	1,102,922	4,771
7.	Carpenters	916,005	7,025
8.	Automobile mechanics	821,822	6,862
9.	Miscellaneous machine operators, specified	770,656	7,116
10.	Farm laborers, wage workers	696,141	2,493
			$\bar{x} =$ $ 7,620

Note. From Sommers (1979, pp. 18, 19).

carpenters, and mechanics). It is clear from Table 11.2 that education and skill level are *not* the bases for compensation; in these data, male truck drivers are earning more than female nurses and teachers, who are required to complete far more education. In fact, male janitors are paid more than female bookkeepers! Table 11.3 displays the median weekly earnings of the same 20 occupations in 1982. Although some of the more glaring discrepancies have narrowed (for example, female bookkeepers now make $7.00 per week more than male janitors!), the general picture remains the same.

To complete the argument, it should be reemphasized that even when men and women are in the *same* job, the men are paid (often

TABLE 11.3   Median Usual Weekly Earnings in 1982

Occupation	Earnings
Women	
1. Secretaries, except legal and medical	241
2. Sales workers (retail)	167
3. Bookkeepers	240
4. Elementary school teachers	339
5. Waitresses	149
6. Typists	227
7. Sewers and stitchers	165
8. Registered nurses	366
9. Maids and servants, private household	111
10. Clerical workers, unspecified	236
Men	
1. Managers and administrators	518
2. Sales workers	239
3. Blue-collar worker supervisors	438
4. Truck drivers	331
5. Farmers, owners and tenants	—
6. Janitors and sextons	234
7. Carpenters	341
8. Automobile mechanics	308
9. Miscellaneous machine operators	322
10. Farm laborers, wage workers	185

Note. From Fitzgerald, (1985, p. 14). Adapted from Mellor (1984, pp. 20–23).

substantially) more. For example, Mellor (1984) wrote, "In each of the 10 lowest paying and the 10 highest paying occupations in which 50,000 or more of each sex were employed (in 1982), women were far less likely than men to earn $500 or more" [per week] (p. 23). In a similar analysis of the most highly paid occupations in 1981, Rytina (1982) wrote, "the earnings of women in these occupations do not approach the earnings of men. The $422 median usual weekly earnings of female operations and systems researchers and analysts, for example, would place just above the pay of electricians for men, an occupation which is well below the top 20 on the male ranking. The pay for women librarians is just above that of men working as precision machine operations, a classification which is in the bottom third of the male earnings ranking" (p. 30).

We submit that much of the observed discrepancy between the earned income of women and men is a result of the persistent misogyny of American society, with its continued overvaluing of whatever is male and the concomitant devaluation of whatever is female. It is this observation which is the core of current controversy concerning what has come to be called "comparable worth" or "equal pay for work of equal value" [The reader is referred to Blumrosen (1979) for a scholarly analysis of this concept. A short, nontechnical summary is available in Fitzgerald & Betz (1983) as well as Ferraro (1984).] Such devaluation, and the financial inequities which result, represent a serious barrier to women's vocational success, as well as being persistent and observable criteria of that lack of success.

ORGANIZATIONAL SUCCESS

Not only are women paid less than men, but they are also less likely to achieve organizational success, as exemplified by promotions, positions of power and autonomy, leadership roles, and so forth. According to Nieva and Gutek (1981), women tend to be concentrated at the bottom of most organizations. National statistics compiled by the Department of Labor (1979) support this statement at a general level, while studies of specific occupations demonstrate similar findings for business managers, high school principals, and academicians (Astin & Bayer, 1972; Miner, 1974; National Academy of Sciences, 1968; Ross, 1970; and others).

Several explanations have been proposed to account for women's relative lack of organizational success. Traditionally, of course, it was suggested that women did not achieve because they were not motivated to do so, because they lacked the requisite education and training, or because of their discontinuous labor market participation (i.e., they dropped out of the work force for extended periods of time to marry and raise children). Additionally, women were assumed to be not as committed to careers as their male peers, and thus did not value and work for the traditional organizational rewards, preferring to place a higher priority on their home and family life. However, it has become clear in recent years that this "person-centered" explanation is neither powerful nor convincing. In addition to the seminal work of Spence and her colleagues concerning achievement motivation (see Chapter 10), Malkiel and Malkiel (1973) have provided evidence that only half of the variance in job level can be accounted for by sex differences in education and experience. Similarly, although Nieva and Gutek (1981) reviewed some previous work that suggests the existence of sex differences in career commitment, recent research has found no such differences (Bruning & Snyder, 1983). A related study by Rynes and Rosen (1984) also found no sex differences in reaction to career opportunities. Contrary to prevailing stereotypes, the women in this study evaluated advancement opportunities much as men did, that is, the more factors that were changed (e.g., employer, location) the greater the pay raise that was required for compliance; however, the women were no less career mobile than the men.

Why, then, are women so much less organizationally successful than their male peers? One reasonable hypothesis is that, in many cases, women's performance is devalued on the basis of gender alone. The classic study in this area is that of Goldberg (1968), who demonstrated that professional articles supposedly written by a man were more highly evaluated than identical articles which were attributed to a woman author. Subsequent research has found the same pro-male evaluation bias operating in samples of businesspeople, academic department chairs (Fidell, 1970), and others. Similarly, Lao, Upchurch, Corwin, and Crossnickle (1975) found female scholarship applicants were rated as less intelligent and less likable than identical male applicants, while Deaux and Taynor (1973) reported similar findings for male and female applicants for a study-abroad program.

Much of the work on evaluation bias has been conducted within the context of managerial research. Like other "person-centered" paradigms, early work in this area appeared to be organized around the notion that women were underrepresented in the managerial ranks because they lacked the drive and aggressiveness necessary for success (Bond & Vinache, 1961; Maier, 1970). Thus, if women were found to be lacking in these characteristics (supposedly requisite for success), then negative attitudes toward women would be justified on the basis that women are actually less capable than men. An early illustrative study is that of Megargee (1969), who paired high-dominance subjects with low-dominance subjects in a laboratory investigation of leadership. He found that when the experimental pairs were of the same sex, high-dominance women were just as likely to assume leadership as were high-dominance men. Women, however, were much less likely to assume leadership when paired with a low-dominance male. Interestingly, these women often made the actual leadership decision, but managed to do it in such a way that it did not threaten implicit norms for appropriate sex role behavior. In a near-replication conducted recently, Carbonell (1984) found similar results on a masculine-typed leadership task.

Despite these results, however, most recent research suggests that women are actually quite similar to men in ways thought to be important to managerial success [e.g., leadership behavior (Day & Stogdill, 1972; Hansen, 1974)] and decision accuracy (Muldrow & Bayton, 1979). Thus, once again, the "person-centered" explanation for women's relative absence from middle and upper management does not appear to be well founded. Other evidence supporting this view is provided in an early study by Bowman, Worthy, and Greyser (1965), who found that even women who were acknowledged as capable were seen as undesirable for management. In this study of male executives (which was entitled "Are Women Executives People?"), the majority of the subjects believed that men are not comfortable with a female supervisor; many felt that placing women in managerial positions would have a negative effect on employee morale. Similar findings have been reported by Gilmer (1961) and Haavio-Mannila (1972).

Closely related to the notion that women lack the requisite managerial behavioral repertoire is the idea that they also lack appropriate personality characteristics. In a pair of studies reminiscent of the Broverman et al. (1970) investigations of stereotypes of mental health, Schein (1973) requested managerial personnel to rate the concepts "men in general," "women in general," and "successful middle managers." In a sample of 300 male middle managers, successful middle managers were described as possessing characteristics more commonly ascribed to men in general than women in general (1973). Schein (1975) later replicated these results with 167 female middle managers. More recently, Powell and Butterfield (1979) required 684 business students to describe the concept "good manager" using the Bem Sex Role Inventory (Bem, 1974). Contrary to their hypothesis that the good manager would be seen as androgynous, the authors found that their subjects of both sexes rated the concept as overwhelmingly masculine.

Whereas studies such as those of Schein (1973, 1975) and Powell and Butterfield (1979) assess sex role stereotypes and then postulate that such stereotypes will result in differential treatment of men and women, other studies investigate differential treatment and postulate sex role stereotypes as the causal factor. For example, Rosen and Jerdee (1973), postulating that stereotypes would lead to differential treatment of women on the job, found that bank supervisors were more willing to promote a male than a female candidate, were more likely to select a male employee to attend a conference, and were more willing to approve a male supervisor's request to terminate a problem employee. Interestingly enough, Rosen and Jerdee (1973) also reported the first empirical evidence that sex role discrimination operates to the disadvantage of men as well as women; they found that their subjects judged a request for a leave of absence to care for small children as significantly less appropriate when it came from a male employee than from a female employee. In a further study (Rosen & Jerdee, 1974), 235 male business majors rated a hypothetical female applicant as having less potential for the technical aspects of the job and for long service to the organization, and as less likely to fit in well in the organization.

Whereas studies such as those reported above provide indirect evidence for the effects of stereotyping on the evaluation and treatment of women and men in organizations, direct evidence is provided by studies assessing both stereotypes toward and evaluations of women in leadership positions. For example, Rice, Bender, and Villers (1980) reported that West Point cadets having traditional sex role attitudes reacted very negatively to a female leader. Terborg and Ilgen (1975) found that subjects with unfavorable views toward women would be more likely than those with favorable attitudes toward women to engage in discriminatory hiring practices but that attitudes toward women were unrelated to the likelihood of engaging in discriminatory treatment practices (e.g., promotion and salary decisions). Finally, Stevens and DeNisi (1980) administered the Women as Managers Scale (Peters, Terborg, & Taynor, 1974) to 143 male and 383 female subjects and found that subjects with positive attitudes toward women were more likely than those with negative attitudes to attribute a hypothetical female manager's success to ability and effort and her failure to bad luck and a difficult job. This effect was particularly strong for the male subjects.

Although the research results do, then, support the existence of stereotypic biases toward women and the relationship of these to discriminatory attitudes and/or behaviors, some writers have urged that they be interpreted with caution. Brown (1979), in his review of male and female leadership studies, noted that although "trait" studies consistently support the existence of the traditional attitude that women lack adequate leadership characteristics, there is a sharp division in the attitudes of managers and nonmanagers. That is, studies using students as subjects support the traditional female stereotype, whereas studies of practicing managers were not supportive. He suggested the possibility of a socialization process that modifies the attitudes of persons actually in the world of work. If this is so, the negative studies would be less damaging to women's career development than had been thought. Terborg and Ilgen (1975) supported this view when they suggested that

> At the time of hiring when little is known about the job applicant, it is relatively easy to categorize the female applicant as an undifferentiated member of the subgroup of women. However, once the female is actually placed on the job and more information is obtained concerning her performance, it becomes more difficult to stereotype her. Thus, these findings suggest that stereotypes influence sex discrimination most when little is known about the female's potential (e.g., hiring decision) and that the effect of sex role stereotypes diminishes as more information about the female worker is obtained. (p. 373)

Obviously, determination of the validity of this view will require longitudinal field research in which prior measurement of stereotypes is obtained. Bass, Krusell, and Alexander (1971) presented data that suggest that a "socialization" hypothesis may be overly optimistic; in their study of lower-, middle-, and upper-level male managers, they found that men who did not work with women had a higher regard for them than men who did.

Closely related to the literature on attitudes toward women is the body of research on women and leadership behavior, or leadership style. Even though this literature is much too voluminous to be adequately summarized in the space available, it is possible to identify significant themes that have emerged and to articulate questions for further research. The work on women and leadership has addressed itself to the following set of progressively more complex and sophisticated questions. The first question to be addressed was the simplistic one, "Are women as capable of leadership as men?" More sophisticated studies contemplated styles of leadership (e.g., "consideration" versus "initiating structure"). Noting that these styles bore a marked resemblance to approved sex role behaviors, these investigations raised the following question(s):

1. Are their sex differences in leadership style?
2. Is one style more effective for one sex than the other?
3. Is one style perceived as more appropriate for one sex than the other?

It is not clear from the literature that there are, indeed, clear-cut and reliable sex differences in leadership style. Chapman (1975) reported that, contrary to popular opinion, female leaders are not more task oriented or consideration oriented than male leaders. Similarly, Day and Stogdill (1972) found that male and female leaders who occupy parallel positions and perform similar functions exhibit similar patterns of leader behavior. However, Denmark and Diggory (1966) indicated that men use power much more often than women to maintain work group conformity, and Eskilson and Wiley (1976) found that male leaders in their role-playing task groups concentrated significantly more on recognizable leadership behavior. Maier (1970) noted that when information is absent, female leaders are less assertive than male leaders, but when tasks were more structured, no differences between male and female leaders were found.

In contrast to this body of research that reports no clear sex differences in leadership style is literature that assesses the reactions of observers (e.g., subordinates) to women leaders. Terborg (1977) wrote, "Some evidence suggests that behavior that is consistent with accepted sex-role behavior is evaluated more positively than where it is out of role; that is, women leaders are perceived better than men if they are high on consideration behaviors rather than initiating structure behaviors" (p. 658). Hagen and Kahn (1975) reported that, under conditions of competition (and out-of-role behavior), competent women were evaluated negatively; this effect did not appear under conditions of cooperation. Haccoun, Haccoun, and Sallay (1978) had 30 male and 30 female nonmanagement personnel rate the effectiveness of three different supervisory styles (directive, rational, or friendly) portrayed by male or female supervisors. The directive style was rated least favorably when it was displayed by female versus male supervisors, thus providing further support for the "out-of-role" hypothesis. Similarly, Rosen and Jerdee (1973) reported that male supervisors were evaluated more favorably than females when they utilized a reward style, whereas both males and females received higher evaluations when they employed a friendly–dependent style toward opposite-sex subordinates. The authors noted that "both males and females probably are expected to react more favorably to intimations of dependency coming from the opposite sex" (p. 46).

It appears, then, that although there are no clear-cut sex differences in management style, both superiors and subordinates may believe that there *should* be such differences. That is, female leaders who exhibit a "masculine" style (e.g., initiating structure, directive) may be negatively evaluated for employing out-of-role behaviors. These beliefs can be detrimental to women's career adjustment because they may affect both evaluations and effectiveness of women's leadership efforts. Indeed, subordinates' perceptions that a leader's behavior is inappropriate may, in fact, be all that is required to make it ineffective.

Although subordinates may in general react negatively to out-of-role behavior, other variables such as sex of subordinate (Haccoun *et al.*, 1978), the conservatism versus liberality of subordinates, and the particular occupation or work setting (Terborg, 1977) may influence these reactions. For example, female leaders in an engineering or aerospace firm may well be in a situation quite different than those in educational or social service settings in which there have traditionally been more women in leadership positions.

In summary, it is clear that women enjoy less organizational success than do men. It also appears that one of the major reasons for this is the operation of various types of attitudinal bias on the part of others in the organization, which serves to inhibit the achievements and advancement of women. Such attitudes, whether held by supervisors, peers, or subordinates, appear to be a major factor in preventing women from achieving the organizational success that would accrue to men of similar ability.

SELF-PERCEPTIONS OF SUCCESS

The final criterion of success to be considered here is that of women's perception of their own success. Unlike the nonpsychological criterion of salary or pay, or even the psychological one of promotion or perceived performance, self-perceptions of success are private and subjective as opposed to public and, at least theoretically, objective. Since, as Super (1957) has pointed out, success means very different things to different individuals, it seems reasonable to hypothesize that organizational (or nonpersonal) indicators of success, such as salary and promotion, will tell us little about the psychological career experience of women, except in those cases in which the individual woman values those indicators and incorporates them into her personal definitions of success. Thus, it would seem important for vocational psychologists and others interested in the career behavior of women to investigate this essentially phenomenological variable.

Despite the intuitive reasonableness of such an approach, it is only recently that work has begun in this area. Operating from both a phenomenological and developmental perspective, Frye (1984) has speculated that self-perceptions of success have to do with internalized evaluations of significant others (i.e., family, coworkers, peers) as well as evaluations of self in comparison to peers and in comparison to expected progress in terms of career developmental stage. In other words, subjective feelings of success are a combination of

1. The evaluations of significant others
2. Self-evaluations as compared to coworkers
3. Self-evaluations compared to age/career stage expectations

Frye (1984) has developed an inventory [the Career Perceptions Questionnaire (CPQ)] to measure this concept, which possesses acceptable reliability ($r > .85$ over a 2-week period) and demonstrates theoretically expected relationships with other variables. In a sample of 328 male and female college graduates who were in the early establishment stage, total scores on the CPQ were significantly positively related to career adjustment task mastery as measured by the Career-ADI as well as to global job satisfaction as measured by the Hoppock Job Satisfaction Blank. For purposes of the present discussion, it should be noted that there were no differences between the men and women in the sample on self-perceived success, despite the fact that the men earned substantially (and significantly) higher salaries. Put differently, although the men were *objectively* more successful (in terms of pay), the women reported equivalent *subjective* self-perceptions of success. In other words, they were as likely as the men to report that their families and supervisors thought they were successful, that they felt successful compared to their coworkers, and that their career was right about where it should be given their ages. Thus, these female professionals saw themselves as being as vocationally adjusted as their male cohorts. This line of research, though extremely promising, obviously needs more extensive investigation before conclusions can be drawn. In particular, the question can be raised as to whether this variable would operate similarly in a sample of blue-collar women, where salary might be expected to exert more influence.

SUMMARY AND CONCLUSIONS

In most objective senses, employed women as a group are less successful than employed men. They make considerably less money and are concentrated at the lower end of the organizational hierarchy. Often, they must cope with the attitudinal bias of coworkers, superiors, and subordinates, which creates barriers to their organizational achievement. Despite this situation, preliminary evidence suggests that, in at least one fairly representative sample, women perceive themselves as being no less successful in personal terms than their male cohorts. Although the significance of this finding is as yet unclear, Frye (1984) has presented data suggesting that self-perceptions of success are more highly related to satisfaction than is an objective criterion of success such as salary. It is to the discussion of women's vocational satisfaction that we now turn.

SATISFACTION

The literature on women's vocational satisfaction has remained in a state of impressive disarray for over 20 years. In 1964, Hulin and Smith remarked, "The relation of the sex of the worker to job satisfaction is. . . . [a] topic which has received a great deal of attention. The findings of the investigations on sex differences in job satisfaction, however, are somewhat contradictory and permit no neat cogent statement of the relationship between sex and job satisfaction" (p. 88). Similarly, in 1983, Varca, Shaffer, and McCauley concluded that "Although sex differences in job satisfaction have received attention in the recent literature, research findings are somewhat unclear" (p. 348). Thus, the situation remains essentially unchanged, despite nearly two decades of research activity. This section of the chapter reviews various themes in the literature on the vocational satisfaction of women, and attempts to identify variables that are important for understanding this affective component of their vocational adjustment.

THEORETICAL ISSUES

Mannheim (1983) pointed out that there are two competing hypotheses concerning possible gender differences in vocational satisfaction. One, the *situational* or *structural* view, suggests that any observed group differences in satisfaction are attributable not to gender *per se* but rather to other variables which consistently covary with gender, such as pay, job level, and promotion opportunities. This environmental hypothesis, then, would predict that when these factors are held constant, or statistically controlled, both sexes should demonstrate essentially equivalent levels of job satisfaction. A corollary which can be deduced from this proposition is that there should be more findings of sex differences in earlier research than in present work, as the occupational situations of men and women have become somewhat more similar over the years.

Early proponents of the structural view were Hulin and Smith (1964), who attempted to eliminate some of the methodological problems which had plagued previous work. They collected data from 295 male and 163 female industrial workers drawn from four different plants representing three different companies. All subjects were administered the Job Descriptive Index (JDI), which measures worker satisfaction with various aspects of the job: the work itself, pay, promotion opportunities, coworker relationships, and so forth. In a multivariate analysis, they determined that the women working in three of the four plants were indeed less satisfied with their jobs than were their male coworkers and they attributed their findings to gender correlates such as lesser pay and promotion opportunities. They concluded, "It is . . . likely that if these variables were held constant, or if their effects were partialled out, the differences in job satisfaction would have disappeared . . . [T]hough we can conclude now that women are generally less satisfied than men, additional precision concerning this conclusion could likely be gained by considering situational factors" (p. 91). A similar view was expressed by Quinn, Staines, and McCullough (1974), in their summary of job satisfaction trends in five American national surveys. They commented that, considering the large wage gap between men and women and the over-representation of women in lower status occupations, it is surprising that sex differences in overall job satisfaction have been only inconsistently observed. Several studies conducted in the 1970s also support this view, and attribute observed gender differences in job satisfaction to demographic or job characteristics (Crowley, Levitin, & Quinn, 1973) or to other structural conditions, such as differential access to organizational power (Kanter, 1976).

Two recent studies also tested the structural hypothesis and reported supportive results. Mannheim (1983) examined an Israeli sample of 91 male and 79 female industrial workers drawn from a representative group of manufacturing organizations. Although the gender groups were not formally matched, care was taken to sample only those plants that included at least 25% women in their manufacturing work force and in which the work groups consisted of both male and female workers. Global job satisfaction was measured by two Likert-type items taken from the Michigan Studies (Taylor & Bowers, 1972), and the researcher reported that there were no mean differences for the sexes on this variable. Unfortunately, since no data were reported on salary or other structural variables, Mannheim's results cannot be construed as providing firm support for the situational hypothesis.

Other recent studies examining this viewpoint were those by Golding, Resnick, and Crosby (1983) and Crosby, Golding, and Resnick (1983). Noting that many American researchers have either restricted their samples to professional women or lumped together women at various job levels, this research team examined 20 male attorneys, 17 female attorneys, and 20 legal secretaries on work satisfaction, work values, and the nature of their job-related gratifications and deprivations. They reported no significant differences on an item measuring global job satisfaction, although the female lawyers were significantly more likely than the secretaries to report that they got what they wanted from their job. Although there were minimal differences among the groups on any of the objective measures, the authors interpreted the responses to their open-ended questions concerning gratifications and deprivations as supporting status differences, but not gender differences.

The Golding *et al.* (1983) studies are somewhat difficult to evaluate, as much methodological information is missing from the report. In addition, they reported very substantial salary differences among the three groups (the women lawyers earned a salary about twice that of the secretaries, while the male lawyers earned twice again that much). In this regard, it should be noted that both the secretaries and the male attorneys reported being dissatisfied with their pay, but the female attorneys did not, a finding the authors interpreted in terms of relative deprivation theory (Stouffer, Suchman, DeVinney, Star, & Williams, 1949), an explanation also invoked by Varca *et al.* (1983). In short, these studies, though provocative, do not provide substantive support for a structural, or situational, view of vocational satisfaction.

In contrast to this structural view is what Mannheim (1983) termed the *socialization* hypothesis, an approach similar to the notion of "person-centered" explanations. This contrasting view suggests that observed gender differences represent true psychological differences in motivation for work that result from the differential socialization of men and women. Proponents of this view, most often sociologists, maintain that female sex role socialization stresses nonwork roles, which causes women to see the job as less central (Ritzer, 1972) and which would predict gender differences in job satisfaction, even when extrinsic factors are held constant. Although a hotly debated topic, the research findings on work centrality are nonconclusive. Saleh and Lalljee (1969) reported that men viewed their occupations as more central than did women, but Taveggia and Ziemba (1978) found in a later study that such differences were quite small. Rabinowitz (1975) also reported no differences in job involvement among white-collar workers, when situational factors were controlled.

Although the structural and socialization hypotheses generate clearly opposing predictions, it appears that no study has yet been conducted that directly tests the two approaches against one another. Although it is our view that the structural hypothesis is intuitively more reasonable, the crucial research has not really been done. The investigations that have been reported either do not employ complete designs or suffer from so many uncontrolled variables that they are not able to exclude competing explanations. The following section outlines variables that are likely to influence the findings on vocational satisfaction, and which must be taken into account if research is to shed further light on this issue.

VARIABLES IMPORTANT IN RESEARCH ON JOB SATISFACTION

In their seminal paper on gender differences in job satisfaction, Hulin and Smith (1964) observed that the then extant research was difficult to integrate because of the differing instrumentation employed by various investigators. Crites (1969) has noted that job satisfaction measures are of two types, each of which reflects differing theoretical views concerning the nature of the construct. Measures of *global* job satisfaction, best exemplified by the Hoppock Job Satisfaction Blank (JSB), elicit a general, undifferentiated reaction to the job as a whole, while *summative* measures, of which the JDI is perhaps the best example, request the worker to respond to items assessing job facets such as pay and promotion. Item scores are then summed to provide an overall measure of job satisfaction, although satisfaction with individual job facets can also be examined. It is our impression that studies utilizing global measures are less likely to demonstrate sex differences than are those that employ summative indices. In addition, it seems reasonable to assume that such summative measures will yield more theoretically interesting data for the study of women's career adjustment. Ultimately, of course, the question of which sort of measure best represents women's psychological experience can only be answered by longitudinal studies employing some ultimate criterion such as turnover, or, at least, an indicator of job withdrawal such as absenteeism.

A final note on the measurement of job satisfaction has to do with the, we believe, unfortunate practice of utilizing one-item "homemade" measures of unknown reliability and validity. A great deal of the research on women's job satisfaction rests on instrumentation of this type, a practice that is not justifiable, particularly given the availability of such widely researched measures as the JSB, the JDI, and the Minnesota Satisfaction Questionnaire (MSQ).

A second methodological issue that most likely contributes to some of the confusion in this section of the literature is that of the distinction among various types of satisfaction. Not only are the traditional distinctions between position and occupation (Crites, 1969) often ignored, but concepts such as career satisfaction and organizational satisfaction are also not properly distinguished. Attention to these definitional issues would likely contribute greatly to a better understanding of women's *vocational* satisfaction, a term we employ in its generic sense to encompass the affective reaction to various dimensions of the world of work.

Finally, we cannot avoid concluding that the widespread practice of ignoring individual differences in subject variables renders much of the literature on women's vocational satisfaction less than useful. As we note again and again, the curious practice of treating women as a homogeneous group, as if their mere *femaleness* were the only salient independent variable to examine, has resulted in a body of work that is contradictory and uninstructive. Researchers in this area must begin to take into account a wide range of individual differences variables before any conclusions can be drawn concerning women's work satisfaction. We suggest the following, as a beginning:

—Work needs/values, such as autonomy, recognition, status, and salary
—Demographic variables such as marital status, attitude of spouse, and presence and number of children
—Sex role-salient variables, such as desire to work, career salience, and career commitment
—Work variables such as kind, type, and level of job; status; fit with abilities/education; organizational climate; organizational policies toward women; and availability of childcare

Until such time as the necessary research is appropriately conducted, speculation concerning gender differences in job satisfaction will remain just that.

THE INTERFACE OF
HOME AND WORK

One of the most notable things about the research on women and work is that it has consistently demonstrated a certain oxymoronic quality. The questions (e.g., Why do women work? Do they work for the same reasons men work? What happens to their husbands and, especially, their children when they work? Is it injurious to their health, either physically or psychologically? Are they heterosexual failures?) manifest by their nature the implicit assumption that women who work are engaging in behavior that is, at the very least, out of the norm. These assumptions have permeated the research and theory concerning women's vocational behavior. For example, Super's (1957) pioneer paper on the career patterns of women characterizes these patterns in terms of the women's relationship (or lack thereof) to a husband and children. Much as the courtesy titles used for women (i.e., Miss or Mrs.) differentiated them by marital state, so, too, did vocational psychology assume that the important thing to know about women was their marital and maternal status and how these interfaced with their work behavior. Such assumptions are, even today, sometimes remarkably prominent. As recently as 1970, Veroff and Feld (1970) investigated work, marriage, and parenting as arenas in which men might satisfy several psychological motives; for women, they investigated only marriage and parenting. Similarly, Warr and Parry (1982) stated, "[We assume] the greater proportion of women with children at home are emotionally involved in the parenting role. . . and that in general this takes priority for them over paid employment. Overall, we expect this group to be of relatively low occupational involvement, especially when their children are young" (p. 502).

Feldberg and Glenn (1979) noted that researchers have used sex-differentiated models to study male and female work issues. They suggested that the *job model,* which treats the job as the primary independent variable, has been used to explain men's subjective work reactions, while the *gender model,* based on personal characteristics and family situations, has been used to predict women's career development, with little attention given to specific job circumstances. Similarly, Garbin and Stover (1980) acknowledged the increased interest in women and work, but remarked that "Scant attention has been given to the study of women as *workers*" (p. 160; emphasis added).

One outcome of this focus on the assumed priority of the biological over the vocational role has been a wealth of studies investigating the effects of women's working on their families, but little, if any, research concerning the effects of their families on women's work experiences, an effect that is very likely to be greater (Laws, 1979; Nieva & Gutek, 1981). The present chapter, while examining the research that investigates the effects of female employment on the women herself, her husband and marriage, and her children, will also attempt to look at the ways that family affects the women's career development. Finally, women's attempts to integrate these two areas (e.g., coping styles) will be examined.

THE EFFECT OF EMPLOYMENT ON WOMEN

The research on women and employment has examined the effect of work-for-pay on women's physical and psychological health and has used outcome measures ranging from suicide rate (Cumming, Lazer, & Chisholm, 1975), depression (Brown & Harris, 1978), and psychiatric diagnosis (Bebbington, Hurry, Tenant, Sturt, & Wing, 1981) to measures of satisfaction (Campbell, Converse, & Rodgers, 1976) and positive well-being. For example, Cumming *et al.* (1975) found that working women were significantly less likely than nonworking women to commit suicide, a finding supported by Shepherd and Barraclough (1980). War and Parry (1982) reviewed a wide variety of epidemiological studies of women and work and concluded that, in general, there is no support for the notion that employed women have "significantly lower psychological well being than do those without a job" (p. 507). Bernard (1971, 1972) interpreted the evidence more positively, noting that studies of working women show them to have fewer symptoms of psychological distress than do housewives. Sociologists (Safilios-Rothschild & Dijkers, 1978; Blood, 1965) point to the positive effects for the woman of the power provided by an independent financial base, while Hall and Hall (1980) have similarly identified economic gains for women as a major factor allowing them to extricate themselves from bad marriages. This emphasis on the positive effects of the power accruing from women's vocational involvement is a theme that runs through much of the current literature on women and work (Bird, 1979; Scanzoni, 1978).

Nye (1974) reviewed the literature on the psychological and physical adjustment of working mothers and came to the following conclusions.

1. Employed mothers, as a group, are physically healthier than housewives.
2. Employed mothers have a more positive self-image than do housewives.
3. Employed mothers report as much (or more) anxiety and guilt concerning their children as do housewives, but they report fewer of the physical symptoms such anxiety usually produces.
4. Employed mothers participate somewhat less actively in community organizations and in some forms of recreation than do their unemployed counterparts; however, there is no evidence that they perceive this pattern negatively.

Nieva and Gutek (1981), in their review of women and work, summarized the literature on power and concluded that working women enjoy increased power in the marital relationship, a conclusion reached earlier by Bahr (1974). Bahr pointed out the value of examining various dimensions of power (usually conceptualized as decision-making authority) rather than considering it to be a global construct. He noted that married women who work consistently demonstrate more power in financial decision making (Blood, 1963; Lamouse, 1969; Weller, 1968; and others) and have greater influence in fertility decisions and subsequent decisions concerning childrearing. However, they may lose power in the day-to-day arena of housekeeping, food purchasing, etc., as husbands of working wives share more responsibility in these areas than do husbands of housewives. It is, however, unclear that working women experience this latter situation as a diminution of power.

It should be pointed out that most scholars in this area note the extensive methodological weaknesses in the current literature. Thus, Bahr (1974) remarked, "Perhaps the greatest weakness of many existing studies is that adequate controls have not been employed. The wife's employment may be related to variables such as the husband's occupational status, family size, and age of children, among others" (p. 177). To this list could be added such psychological variables as ability, interests, career salience, and sex role attitudes. Similarly, Nieva and Gutek (1981) pointed out that the literature on women and work contains contributions from two distinct sources: developmental psychologists and family sociologists on the one hand, and industrial and organizational psychologists on the other, remarking that there has been little professional collaboration between these two groups; thus, each discipline brings its own theoretical and methodological strengths and weaknesses to an area requiring the perspectives of both. For example, "A weak feature of the family-oriented studies is that the work component is insufficiently defined. Women are divided into gross categories, that is, employed or not, employed part time versus employed full time. More recently, psychological variables such as whether the mother wants to work or not, whether she feels she has adequate child care or not, and the like have been included as potentially important variables. There has been little interest in the type of job [she] has, for example, how physically demanding it is, whether she is a supervisor or a subordinate, whether she has adequate resources on the job, whether her changes for promotion are excellent or nil" (Nieva & Gutek, 1981, pp. 39–40).

Noting such difficulties, Warr and Parry (1982) suggested a theoretical framework to guide research in this area. This conceptual frame encompasses three main constructs: the women's occupational involvement (e.g., desire to work, career salience), the quality of her nonoccupational involvement (i.e., her nonwork life), and the quality of her employment relationship (e.g., congruence, challenge, reward). They predicted that paid employment will be most beneficial where the three factors combine univalently: "Occupational involvement is high, the nonoccupational environment is adverse, and a women's paid employment is attractive to her" (p. 501).

Although their model is a promising one, their attempt to map it onto extant research is less so. In particular, their use of marital and parental statuses (i.e., whether the woman is single, married, or a mother) to estimate occupational involvement has the effect of assuming the relationship they set out to test. Also, their "lumping together" of various cultural samples (e.g., American, British, Indian, Welsh, and Pakistani women) without consideration of culturally influenced sex role expectations most likely obscures meaningful differences. However, the model does present a beginning paradigm to guide research and theory building in this area.

THE EFFECT OF WIVES' EMPLOYMENT ON HUSBANDS AND THE MARRIAGE

Because of the societal presumptions concerning "women's place," it has long been assumed that female employment not only produces conflict for the woman but produces destructive effects on her marriage and husband as well. Such assumptions have roots in two intellectual traditions: psychoanalytic psychology, which views women's nature as intrinsically passive, nurturant, and unaggressive, and the Parsonian sociology of functionalism, which suggests that female employment generates marital conflict and also confuses the family's status lines.

According to classical psychoanalysis, women's psychology and the physiology on which it is based suited them for the roles of childbearing and -rearing and the supportive, nurturing functions of wifehood. Employment was to some degree dangerous to women's psychological functioning, as it encouraged the nonfeminine aspects of personality and the development of the "masculine protest" (Deutsch, 1944, 1945; Lundberg & Farnham, 1947). It also presented a problem for husbands, who were assumed to be threatened when faced with the need to share power, and thus generated marital conflict.

Similarly, Parsons (1943) argued that the traditional family arrangement, in which the husband and wife operated in totally different spheres, worked well because it reduced the possibility of competition and conflict that might otherwise disrupt marital solidarity. Additionally, since family status was assumed to derive from the husband's occupation, a women's occupational involvement was liable to lead to status uncertainties and confusion, particularly if her occupation were more prestigious than that of her husband. According to Parsons, "There is much evidence that this relatively definiteness of status is an important factor in psychological security" (1943, p. 35). (Ironically, it can be pointed out that both Parsonian sociology and Freudian psychology serve a functionalist purpose themselves. That is, they both operate to perpetuate the status quo, one by appealing to a "natural order" philosophy, and the other by arguing that what is should be; otherwise, it would not have survived in the social order.)

Early research on this topic tended to find small but consistent differences in marital satisfaction in favor of families in which wives were not employed (Axelson, 1963; Feld, 1963; Gianopolous & Mitchell, 1975; Gover, 1963; Nye, 1963; Powell, 1963). These studies, mostly sociological in nature, investigated various samples with differing degrees of attention paid to factors such as social class, education, presence or absence of children, and so forth. Despite the lack of sophistication of some of these efforts, it seems reasonable to suggest that small differences did indeed exist, and that this was particularly true in the lower-class families. Thus, Nye (1974) pointed out that, up to this point, "the research is not completely consistent, but provides predominant support for the thesis that differences favoring the housewife occur mostly in the lower social classes" (p. 204). It is likely that, as Nye suggested, as more women moved into the labor market, the "working wife" became a more normative phenomenon. Thus, any negative reactions associated with a once-deviant pattern probably alleviated as the pattern became more widespread. However, the more traditional sex role ideology often found in working class families may have perpetuated dissatisfaction on the part of husbands who believed that they should be the sole breadwinners.

Burke and Weir (1976) directly tested the hypothesis that husbands of working wives would report more stress and less satisfaction than husbands of housewives in a sample of 189 middle-class Canadian couples. They compared mean scores on ratings of job pressures and life pressures; marital, job, and life satisfaction; importance attached to communication; and actual communication. They also reported differences favoring husbands of housewives on all variables except life pressures and actual communication. They interpreted their data to mean that "men whose wives work are subject to greater stress than men whose wives are not working, and they appear to be having more difficulty coping effectively with this pattern of daily living" (p. 285). However, it should be pointed out that the Burke and Weir data are badly flawed; not only did they perform numerous independent *t*-tests on what are undoubtedly highly correlated variables (e.g., well-being and satisfaction), but they reported elsewhere that the husbands of the working wives earned significantly less than did those of the nonworking wives, a powerful competing explanation of their results. Finally, the actual mean differences themselves, although statistically significant due to the power generated by the sample size, are extremely small (sometimes no more than one or two points on a scale running from 0 to 100) and appear to be of little practical importance. The most parsimonious interpretation would appear to be that the two groups were remarkably similar.

Noting the difficulties in the Burke and Weir (1976) research, Booth (1977) replicated their work on a stratified probability sample of Toronto families and reported no differences between husbands of working and nonworking wives. They noted that, if anything, the husbands of employed women appear to be minimally better off. It should be pointed out, however, that this study to some degree "stacked the deck" in favor of a finding of no differences, as the primary criterion variable was the presence of a stress-related illness, such as hypertension, angina pectoris, or acute myocardial infarction. It does not seem likely that even the most traditional of husbands would (literally) have a heart attack because his wife decided to work outside the home!

More recently, Locksley (1980), in a sophisticated analysis of a national sample, reported no evidence for any effect of wives' employment on marital adjustment or companionship, as evaluated by either the husbands or the wives. Rather, she found a strong main effect for sex. The wives in this sample, whether employed or not, reported considerably more dissatisfaction with their marriages than did their husbands. Locksley (1980) noted that her data supported Bernard's (1972) observations concerning the "more conflictual aspects of marriage for women than for men" (p. 345).

J. G. Richardson (1979) examined the related hypothesis that greater marital unhappiness would exist for both husbands and wives when the wives attained greater occupational status (i.e., worked at jobs that were more prestigious than those of their husbands). Using data from the National Opinion Research Center on 1,533 respondents, he assigned occupational prestige scores of low, medium, and high, yielding 304 cases in which wives ranked higher in occupational prestige (19.8%), 795 cases in which the couples ranked equal (51.8%), and 434 cases in which the wives ranked lower (28.3%). Using a simple dichotomy to code marital happiness, he found no support for his hypothesis.

What, then, can be said concerning the effect of wives working on marital satisfaction, particularly that of the husband? Probably, at this point, very little. Richardson (1979) pointed out the fallacy of deriving presumed psychological consequences from what is essentially a structural arrangement. It is unlikely that the sheer fact of the woman's employment will have a deleterious effect on the husband, particularly given all the data that suggest that working women perform almost as much housework and other support services as do housewives (Fitzgerald & Betz, 1983). Similarly, the notion that husbands of employed women are more likely to suffer high blood pressure, heart disease, and so forth seems somewhat bizarre from the vantage point of the mid-1980s. Finally, speculation concerning the effect of status differentials is made difficult by the differing meanings and values placed by individuals on occupational status, as well as by the confounding effects of income which, sadly, often trails prestige in the semiprofessional "pink-collar" occupations (Howe, 1977).

We are not arguing that the influx of women into paid employment has not to some degree altered the balance of power in American marriages. It seems very clear that it has. This change most assuredly has also had some effect on the psychological environment of the marriage. Rather, we submit that such psychological effects are not likely to be detected by broad-band studies that ignore not only individual differences in demographic variables (e.g., age, education, income, presence and number of children) but, particularly, the more salient psychological variables, such as sex role traditionality, career salience, marital expectations, and so forth. Until the appropriate research is conducted, all discussion lies in the realm of speculation.

THE EFFECT OF MATERNAL EMPLOYMENT ON CHILDREN

> The woman who begrudges her own children a few years of her undivided attention, perhaps cannot be suppressed, but she need not be admired. Her example is pernicious, her ethics immoral, her selfishness destructive to the nation. (Martin, no date, quoted in Hughes, 1925)

Hughes (1925) remarked over half a century ago, "It appears to be quite generally assumed that wage earning by mothers is detrimental to the race. The proof of this assumption is, however, not yet established" (p. 3). Over 60 years later, this situation remains essentially unchanged.

Perhaps the most cogent statement concerning beliefs about motherhood and the effects of those beliefs on women has been made by Russo (1976, 1979). She argued that the mother role exists on a qualitatively different level than other roles in our society, and that beliefs concerning motherhood approach a societal mandate that requires that a woman have children (preferably several) and raise them "well." In practice, raising them well has meant being physically present to serve the child's every need. Smith (1981) pointed out that researchers have, perhaps unwittingly, reinforced this point of view. "By choosing whom to study (mothers rather than fathers) and what to study (maternal rather than paternal employment) researchers have placed the responsibility for infant attachment on the shoulders of women and endorsed, indirectly though it may be, the motherhood mandate" (p. 196).

One of the most obvious results of the motherhood mandate is the widespread belief that maternal employment has detrimental effects on children. Many scholarly reviews have investigated the topic (Etaugh, 1974, 1980; Hoffman, 1974b, 1979; Hoffman & Nye, 1974; Siegal & Haas, 1963; Smith, 1981; Stolz, 1960; Yudkin & Holme, 1963), while the popular view was probably best expressed by one of Rapoport and Rapoport's (1969) subjects: "Oh, well, I guess you won't mind when your baby doesn't recognize you as its mother" (p. 14). Despite the widespread nature of such beliefs, there exist no concrete data supporting the notion that maternal employment per se is damaging to children, while much evidence suggests that the question is being improperly framed and inadequately investigated. This section of the chapter will review the relevant body of research and suggest guidelines for future investigations.

THE PRESCHOOL YEARS

Societal alarm concerning what are usually framed as the "consequences" of maternal employment has been greatest when the children in question are preschoolers. Based on psychoanalytic theory and improper generalizations from studies of institutionalized infants (Bowlby, 1982; Spitz, 1945), the belief has been widespread that women who work have deleterious effects on their children's intellectual and psychological development and on the quality of the mother–child relationship. Most reviews of the literature (Hoffman, 1979; Yudkin & Holme, 1963) emphasize that what research evidence there is is mixed, while Smith (1981) remarked that most of the work has been so poorly done that it is not possible to draw sound conclusions. As Stolz (1960) has remarked, "One can say almost anything one desires about children of employed mothers and support the statement by some research study" (p. 772).

Scholars do appear to agree that it is with regard to the preschool child that the research is least sanguine. Concern arises from several points of view: first, the importance of infant attachment to the mother; second, the importance of stability and continuity of caretakers; and third, the assumed critical importance of the first 5 years of life. Data can be cited in support of the notion that maternal employment may interfere with optimal attachment (Fleener, 1973; Farran & Ramey, 1977; Ricciuti, 1974) or, alternatively, that children of employed and unemployed mothers show similar patterns of attachment (Brookhart & Hock, 1966; Doyle, 1975; and others). Similarly, stimulating day care has been related to an increase in intellectual development in lower-class children (Honig, Caldwell, & Tannebaum, 1970; Ramey & Smith, 1977; Robinson & Robinson, 1971); however, Cohen (1978) found that, in their 2nd year, children of nonworking mothers developed an intellectual and social "edge" over their peers whose mothers were employed.

As Unger (1979) has pointed out, "When a variety of studies support a variety of conclusions, it is usually because the conceptualization of either the independent or dependent variable is not clear" (p. 331). We explore this position at some length below, and offer some suggestions for clarification. For the present, it seems most parsimonious to agree with Smith's (1981) conclusion that "For the vast majority of infant and preschool children. . . we simply do not know what the effects of maternal employment are" (p. 197).

MIDDLE CHILDHOOD

Although the research on middle childhood is also plagued with methodological difficulties, it yields somewhat clearer results than does that on infancy. The needs of the school-age child for self-esteem and a feeling of competence may be better met in families in which maternal employment dictates that children have more household responsibilities and that there be structured rules governing behaviors (Hoffman, 1974b, 1979).

Both Hoffman (1974b, 1979) and Smith (1981) noted that working mothers may be particularly appropriate for daughters. Daughters appear to profit in terms of less rigid sex role socialization (Almquist & Angrist, 1970; Eyde, 1970) and in the development of higher-level and more nontraditional, vocational aspirations (Baruch, 1972; Conway & Niple, 1966; Tangri, 1972), both of which are presumably due, at least partially, to the existence of a nontraditional role model. Hoffman (1979) also pointed out that daughters of working mothers are more likely to admire their mothers and to hold the female role in high esteem.

The data for sons, on the other hand, are somewhat more complex. Although sons of working mothers are also less stereotyped and more androgynous and sometimes display better personalty and social adjustment, as well as occasionally higher academic scores (Gold & Andres, 1978; Hoffman, 1974b, 1979), the data appear to differ by social class. Several studies of lower-class boys with working mothers indicated that these boys are less admiring of their fathers, presumably because working-class sex role ideology dictates that the father be the sole breadwinner.

Although this strain in the father–son relationship does not appear in middle-class samples (which are presumably more liberal in nature), there are some subtle suggestions that middle-class sons of employed mothers score lower on intellectual indices. Hoffman (1979) noted that the findings are not consistent but have occurred often enough to warrant further investigation. Reasons for the differential findings are not intuitively obvious and will likely require great care to untangle.

ADOLESCENCE

It is in samples of adolescents that maternal employment is most clearly related to positive characteristics. Hoffman (1979) pointed out that the needs of the adolescent for establishing independence and a certain "distancing" from the family of origin may not be well met by nonworking mothers, who observe their central life role coming more or less abruptly to an end. The adolescent's need to "launch" him- or herself (Okun, 1983) may be particularly threatening to a mother who is experiencing her own developmental crises—aging, loss of parent role, etc. It appears that maternal employment at this period fits well with the needs of both the mother and child. Hoffman (1979) noted that the employed mother may be psychologically freer to encourage the adolescent's independence strivings, as she has an alternative role in which she can invest her energies.

The positive relationship between maternal employment and favorable adolescent development, although particularly clear for daughters, appears to hold for both sexes. Gold and Andres (1978) demonstrated that both sons and daughters of working mothers achieved better personality adjustment on a variety of indicators than did adolescent children of nonworking mothers. Hoffman (1979) stated unequivocally, "the overall picture suggests that maternal employment is better suited to the needs of adolescents than is full-time mothering" (p. 864).

CONCLUSIONS

The most obvious observation that can be made with respect to the research on working mothers concerns the ubiquity of Western patriarchal values in such research. Even scholars who set out to discuss or investigate the "motherhood mandate" have found themselves linguistically enmeshed in its tenets. Thus, Smith (1981) referred to "substitute care," while Hoffman noted the effects of "surrogate caretakers," each phrase unmistakably implying the normalcy and primary of full-time physical care of the child by its biological mother. Other caretakers are, by definition, "substitute" or "surrogate"—by implication, less desirable and legitimate.

The ubiquity of the motherhood mandate in our language, and thus our thought, can be clearly seen when it is pointed out that the research discussed above is not actually concerned with maternal employment per se, although that is the way the independent variable is labeled and measured. Rather, what is actually being investigated is the "lack of full-time care by the mother," or more probably, the "effect of poor care" on the psychological and intellectual development of the child (see Scarr and Weinberg, 1986).

Such research has less to do with whether or not the mother is working (or going to school, or doing volunteer service) than it does with the nature of the experience to which the child is exposed. Smith (1981) makes this point clearly, albeit inadvertently, when she remarks, "Moreover, many of the studies cited to support maternal employment have been situations involving optimal day care, oftentimes arranged through a university or high-quality demonstration project" (p. 197).

This leads to a second observation, which is complementary to the first. Not only does current research assume that the primary care of the child is the natural province of the mother, but it also appears to assume that such care is uniformly of high quality, and thus preferable to any other care. That this is not so is apparent even from informal observation, not to mention the body of research on neglected and abused children (Starr, 1979). Although it is apparently widely ignored, women appear to display the same range of individual differences in abilities, interests, and personality characteristics as do men, and are most likely differentially suited to the mothering role, particularly as it is traditionally conceived.

The observations discussed above combine to suggest that if research is to be done on the factors related to the welfare of young children (presumably what the maternal employment literature is all about), an effort needs to be made to reformulate this research in more thoughtful ways. Such an effort would most assuredly require a multivariate approach, possibly based in the emergent methodology of structural equation modeling, to begin to disentangle the effects of the multiple variables that are currently "lumped together" under the rubric of maternal employment. Variables that should most likely be represented in such a model include

—Sex, race, and age of child
—Financial, ethnic, and socioeconomic status of family
—Presence/absence of father, sex role of father, father's occupation, father's parental involvement
—Present/nature of maternal employment, mother's sex role, maternal satisfaction, career salience, vocational satisfaction
—Quality of child's daily experience (affection, stability/continuity of care, intellectual stimulation, presence of siblings and peers, appropriate role models)

This is, admittedly, a formidable list of variables. However, it seems clear that to continue to study the supposed "consequences" of maternal employment without a thoughtful effort to accurately represent the basic variables is to perpetuate a disservice to mothers and children alike.

THE EFFECT OF MARRIAGE AND MOTHERHOOD ON WOMEN'S CAREER DEVELOPMENT

Although it is rarely talked about in these terms, it seems quite likely that the most unambiguous negative relationship in the work–home interface is not the effect of working women on their husbands or marriages, or even of maternal employment on children; rather, the clearest relationship is the negative one between marriage and motherhood, on the one hand, and the women's own career development, on the other. Thus, Frieze *et al.* (1978) noted that single, professional women tend to be more productive and successful than married, professional women (Astin, 1970) and went on to state, "Clearly, children interfere with career advancement for the prime caregiver, *usually the mother*" (p. 368; emphasis added).

It is clear that having children decreases a woman's chances of being successful in her career, and professional women especially report that parenthood is likely to interfere with their career development. On the other hand, children do not appear to be a salient factor in the vocational development of men, who, in fact, are likely to benefit from their married status "probably because the professional man's wife traditionally supports and aids him in his career in a way few men desire or are able to do for their wives" (Frieze *et al.*, 1978, p. 371). This section of the chapter will examine the evidence concerning marriage, maternity, and women's career development in an attempt to provide a feminist corrective to previous work on the "consequences" of maternal employment.

It has become commonplace in the literature of vocational psychology to assert that the major difficulty in women's career development is the uncertainty of marriage plans, and the difficulty of participating simultaneously in two activity systems whose claims are, both practically and philosophically, incompatible (Coser & Rokoff, 1971; Matthews & Tiedeman, 1964; Osipow, 1975, 1983). The literature supporting this assertion has been reviewed elsewhere (Fitzgerald & Betz, 1983) as well as in Section II of the present volume. That the perceived philosophical incompatibility of the biological role of wife/mother with the social role of worker is the most salient factor in women's career development is one of the major assumptions of this book. O'Leary (1977) referred to this type of conflict as *interrole conflict*, that is, conflict that occurs due to the incompatibility of the demands associated with two or more roles, and that is conceptualized as being primarily psychological in nature. Referring to this kind of conflict, Coser and Rokoff (1971) remarked, "The conflict derives from the fact that the values underlying these demands are contradictory; professional women are expected to be committed to their work 'just like men' at the same time as they are normatively required to give priority to their family. The conflict is one of allegiance, and it does not stem from the mere fact of involvement in more than one social system. It is a conflict of normative priorities" (p. 535). Although it is certainly plausible to argue that interrole conflict most likely exerts a deleterious effect on women's career development, the focus here is on the data documenting the more practical aspects of this incompatibility—what O'Leary (1977) referred to as *role overload*. As we have stated elsewhere, "Married career women are faced every day with the regrettable fact that Parkinson's Law does not have an inverse; time does *not* expand to encompass the work available! This 'corollary' has more impact for women than for men, for, typically, when women opt for careers, they are adding to their lives a new set of roles and role demands without a commensurate decrease in the old ones" (Fitzgerald & Betz, 1983, p. 137).

Despite the commonly accepted distinction between homemakers and careerwomen, it is clear that there is really no such thing as a "nonworking wife." Oakley's (1974) intensive interview study of London housewives revealed their average work week to be 77 hours, almost twice as long as that of wage-earning men employed outside the home. Although the research is somewhat unclear as to exactly how much time married women spend in homemaking activities, two facts appear to be well established: (1) careerwomen appear to spend somewhat less time on household responsibilities than their nonworking counterparts and (2) they still spend considerably more time on these tasks than do men. Despite egalitarian attitudes, the actual division of labor within the family consistently relegates the bulk of the responsibility for housework and child care to the woman (Blaxall & Reagan, 1976; Bryson, Bryson, & Licht, 1978; Epstein, 1970b; Walston, Foster, & Berger, 1978; and others). The research is clear that wives, even those with full-time careers, still perform the overwhelming majority of domestic tasks (Bird, 1979; Hall & Hall, 1980; Rapoport & Rapoport, 1969, 1971, 1976; Weingarten, 1978; St. John-Parsons, 1978; Rice, 1979; Scanzoni, 1972, 1978). For example, Berk and Berk (1979) found in their sample of urban families that two thirds of the husbands of working wives made no more contribution to after-dinner household tasks than did husbands of full-time housewives. In particular, the working mother retains almost sole responsibility for the care and well-being of children. Weingarten (1978) found that, although household chores were divided somewhat more equitably among couples in which the wife had an employment history comparable to her husband's, the child care responsibilities were still relegated almost totally to the wife.

Several writers have speculated concerning possible reasons for this phenomenon. Weingarten (1978) noted that, "at some level, most mothers feel guilty about the time they spend away from their children. The time working women devote to child care can be viewed as a function of what they want to do and what they feel they ought to do. . . wives consciously or unconsciously take on the child-care tasks as a means of 'compensation' for their hours away from home" (p. 51). Bird (1979) also discussed this phenomenon in terms of maternal guilt, which is presumed to be widespread. Walum (1977) proposed a different explanation: "Persons with greater power can enforce their decisions more readily than those who are relatively powerless. The structure of sexual inequality is such that males as a group have more power than females. Consequently, they are in the position to both make and enforce decisions. One of these decisions has been to assign child rearing to women" (p. 181). Or, as Polatnick (1973) has remarked, "Men as a group don't rear children because they don't *want* to rear them. . . it is to men's advantage that women are assigned child-rearing responsibility, and it is in men's interest to keep things that way" (p. 60).

Whatever the explanation of this pattern, its consequences are clear. The amount of time devoted to housework and, particularly, child care seriously limit one's ability to pursue a professional career. It is this societally sanctioned assignment of homemaking and child care to women that, more than any other factor, limits their career development and attainment.

THE INTEGRATION OF HOME AND WORK: COPING MECHANISMS

Role overload appears to be inescapable for any woman who attempts both marriage and a career. The problem is particularly acute for women with children. Noting the situation, social scientists have turned their attention to the strategies women have evolved to deal with it. Writing from the perspective of a sociologist, Epstein (1970) identified nine mechanisms that women might employ to meet the conflicting demands of their multiple roles. These mechanisms appear to represent what Merton (1957) has labeled as the "strain toward consistency."

1. *The elimination of social relationships.* When using this strategy, the woman becomes more selective in her choice of relationships, eliminating contact with those persons whose expectations cause her strain, for example, other women who do not work outside the home and who hold negative attitudes toward women who do. Rather, the woman chooses to associate with those who are more similar to herself, for example, other working mothers.

2. *Reduction of the total amount of contacts involved in the total set of relationships.* Women who use this strategy typically limit the size of their families, as well as their circle of friends.

3. *Reducing or controlling the number of statuses in the status set.* Since the engagement in multiple roles can present a very real problem in terms of time demands, the woman may choose to limit the number of obligations she takes on. Also, when the obligations associated with one particular role or status increase (e.g., the birth of a child), the woman may have to balance this by reducing the demands of another role (e.g., refusing a transfer or promotion, or possibly turning down an elective office in a professional association).

4. *The mechanism of redefinition.* This strategy, which Osipow and Spokane (1983) would label a rational–cognitive coping mechanism, involves the woman redefining and relabeling her occupational role as adjunctive to her family roles. For example, women who work with or for their husbands in a family business may define their work as "helping" the husband, thus reducing guilt about career involvement.

5. *Intermittent activation of statuses.* This strategy is most available to women whose professional status allows them flexibility with respect to time. For example, freelance writers, or psychotherapists in private practice, can manipulate their schedules to emphasize the role that is most salient at the time (particularly mother versus professional).

6. *Compartmentalization by scheduling.* This particular strategy involves careful scheduling to reduce or eliminate the spillover of work into family life. For example, avoiding evening or weekend work activities, or refusing to bring work home from the office, are common examples of this kind of strategy.

7. *Delegation of tasks and roles.* This strategy essentially involves the use of outside domestic help to perform many of the household chores that are part of the wife role. Of course, theoretically, this strategy could also involve delegating some of these tasks to the husband; however, as we have seen, this does not appear to be very successful.

8. *Increasing the observability of role demands.* Becoming well

known and visible in the community through organizational involvement (e.g., church activities, PTA) may result in the careerwoman being excused from many responsibilities (including family) because people know "how busy she is."

9. *Reliance on rules (or appeals to "third parties") for legitimization of role behavior.* The appeal of outside demands, such as publishers' deadlines and organizational schedules, may to some degree legitimize the women's noninvolvement or participation in certain family or social activities. Elsewhere, we have categorized this as the *"deus ex machina"* principle (Fitzgerald & Betz, 1983).

A number of studies have appeared indicating that women do actually adopt these coping mechanisms identified by Epstein (1970). For example, Johnson and Johnson (1977) reported that many of their subjects lowered their career aspirations while their children were young, and associated mainly with individuals possessing similar attitudes toward careers, marriage, and child rearing. Rapoport and Rapoport (1972) found three characteristic patterns of coping: (1) consciously setting aside leisure time for themselves, (2) delegating as many chores as possible to others, and (3) modifying their work involvement to fit in with their partner's career. These last two coping patterns appear to correspond with Epstein's mechanisms of *delegation* and *redefinition*. Van Dusen and Sheldon (1976) analyzed recent census data and reported that many women are reducing family size expectations (*reduction of the total number of role contacts*); they also found an increase in the number of women who are choosing not to bear children (*reduction of the number of statuses in the status set*).

Two studies have attempted to evaluate various methods of coping. Hall (1972a) classified 16 common coping strategies into one of three types: Type I, or *structural role redefinition*, which involves changing the expectations imposed on the woman by others (e.g., husband, children, employers); Type II, or *personal role redefinition*, which involves the woman's changing her own behavior and expectations, without attempting to change the environment; and Type III, or *reactive role behavior*, which attempts to meet all role demands and, thus, please everyone (the "superwoman" syndrome). O'Leary (1977) speculated that Type I coping was probably the most effective means of dealing with role conflict, but also the most difficult to implement, as it involves obtaining the approval of role senders, which may be quite difficult.

Hall (1972b) examined the relationship between these coping styles and satisfaction among women. He found that the association between

Type I coping and satisfaction was positive, although it did not reach the usual standards of statistical significance. There was a negative relationship between Type III coping and satisfaction. Kroeker (1963) has suggested that attempts to respond to all the demands of multiple roles reflect defensiveness, rather than coping. Hall (1972b), following this interpretation, labeled Type III coping as maladaptive. O'Leary (1977) agreed, but noted that she has yet to meet a professional married woman with children familiar with Hall's typology who does not consider herself a Type III coper!

Gray (1980b) suggested that Hall's categories were not mutually exclusive, and therefore, investigated the linkages between individual coping strategies and satisfaction. She analyzed the results of a questionnaire completed by 232 married professional women and found strong positive associations between satisfaction and the strategies of having family members share household tasks (delegation), reducing standards within certain roles, and considering personal interests important. Gray (1979) reported that certain strategies were negatively related to satisfaction, including overlapping roles, keeping roles totally separate, attempting to meet all expectations, eliminating entire roles, and the absence of a conscious strategy for dealing with role conflict. These results suggest that at least one of Epstein's (1970) coping mechanisms (i.e., reduction of total number of statuses) may not be functional for all women.

SUMMARY

This chapter has surveyed the literature on the home–work interface. Although much of the research is contradictory, due to poor conceptualizations and the ubiquity of sex role expectations, it is possible to propose some tentative conclusions. Women who work appear to be at a psychological advantage compared to their nonworking counterparts, particularly when they work because they wish to do so. This advantage translates into increased power and influence in their marital relationships and into higher levels of self-esteem. Although the home–work interface appears to be quite difficult to negotiate, particularly when there are children involved, there is little evidence that husbands and children of working wives suffer any deleterious effects. The lack of systematic and high-quality child care programs in this country make it quite difficult to appropriately evaluate nonmaternal care during the preschool years. However, it seems clear that school-age and adolescent children of working mothers do better on a variety of indicators. This is particularly true for female children.

Working women do indeed work very hard, and they retain the great majority of the household and child care tasks performed by their counterparts who do not engage in paid employment. Although the research on coping suggests that attempts to meet all expectations at home and work (i.e., the superwoman syndrome) is not healthy for women, many do engage in this pattern. We conclude that strong involvement in both career and family roles is very difficult to "pull off," given present cultural conditions, and suggest that the perceived primacy of women's biological roles is the most salient (and pernicious) barrier to their career adjustment.

DUAL-CAREER COUPLES

The focus of the last several years on the combination of work and family responsibilities for an increasing number of women has culminated in the study of the phenomenon of the "dual-career" couple. Initially coined by Rapoport and Rapoport (1971), this term is generally used to refer to a married couple, each member of which pursues a professional career through choice rather than economic necessity. As interest in this topic has grown both in the social sciences (Rapoport & Rapoport, 1971, 1976; Holmstrom, 1972; Poloma & Garland, 1971; Hall & Hall, 1978, 1980; and others) and in popular literature (Bird, 1979) and research has proliferated, various definitions, both operational and literary, have been used, few of which are operationally identical. For example, Rice (1979) specified that the dual-career couple must be legally married to each other, although Hall and Hall (1980) disagree. The Rapoport's original definition included the presence of at least one child, while other researchers have investigated the *effect* of the presence or absence of children on the marital and career adjustment of the couple. Finally, the distinction between dual-career couples and *dual-worker* couples has been proposed, but, in practice, often ignored. Dual-worker couples are usually thought to be those in which the wife works out of necessity rather than choice. Other formulations (e.g., Aldous, 1982; and others) would suggest, however, that the distinction between two-career and two-worker families arises from the nature of the work undertaken; if it is developmental in nature, leading to increasing levels of responsibility, the couple is a career couple. If not, then they are classified as dual-worker, dual-job, two-paycheck, and the like. This definitional confusion has resulted in a large body of research which is plagued by conflicting findings and an inability to draw supportable conclusions concerning this life pattern. In addition, the majority of the research in this area has been conducted by sociologists, and reflects that discipline's focus on marital structure, roles, power distribution, status, and so forth; to date, there has been less focus on the more psychological variables (e.g., individual differences in personality characteristics, sex role attitudes, self-esteem), although there are indications that this may be changing [see, for example, Hardesty & Betz (1980) and Sekharan (1982)].

In reviewing the literature, we have found the definition offered by Hall and Hall (1980) to be the closest to our own. These writers define dual-career couples as two people who share a life-style that includes cohabitation, separate work roles, and a love relationship that supports and facilitates both. It is these definitional criteria that we have employed in selecting the literature reviewed in the present chapter. In addition, we focus our attention primarily, although not exclusively, on the sociological literature; the more psychological correlates of dual-career marriage, including role conflict, coping, satisfaction, and the like, are discussed in Chapters 11 and 12. This arrangement appeared logical in that the present chapter is devoted exclusively to dual-*career* couples, whereas the psychological variables are also relevant to the study of dual-*worker* couples.

We begin by discussing, in some depth, the classic investigations in this area (i.e., Rapoport & Rapoport, 1969, 1971; Epstein, 1971; Holmstrom, 1972; and those of Poloma, 1972; and Garland, 1972). The various typologies of dual-career families are explored, along with variations on the basic dual-career pattern (e.g., job-sharing couples). In addition, the organizational impact of this rapidly emerging life pattern is examined. Finally, we attempt to summarize the costs and benefits of this life-style, with particular reference to its influence on women's career development.

DUAL CAREERS: THE CLASSIC STUDIES

The term *dual-career family* was coined in 1969 by Rhona and Robert Rapoport, defined by them as families in which both husband and wife pursue careers ["jobs which are highly salient personally, have a developmental sequence and require a high degree of commitment" (p. 3)], and operationalized as professional couples with at least one child. As part of a larger investigation of the work force participation of highly trained women in Great Britain (Fogarty, Rapoport, & Rapoport, 1971), they interviewed 13 functioning dual-career couples, and 3 in which the wife had broken off her career, reporting their results in an article focusing on the stresses of this life-style (Rapoport

& Rapoport, 1969) as well as in a book that presented 5 in-depth case studies of families drawn from their original sample (Rapoport & Rapoport, 1971).

These authors noted that the couples in their study were subject to stress arising from several sources. *Overload dilemmas* were common and were seen as a function of the degree of the couple's investment in their children and family life, aspirations to a high standard of domestic living, difficulties in obtaining and retaining adequate support services (e.g., housekeepers and child care workers), and psychological conflicts surrounding various aspects of their (at the time) deviant life-style.

In addition, dilemmas arose from the *discrepancy between the couples' personal norms and the norms of the surrounding society,* that is, the difficulties of being "different," nontraditional, and so forth. [This source of stress was subsequently labeled *environmental sanctions* (Rapoport & Rapoport, 1971).] Thirdly, stress arose from what the Rapoports termed *dilemmas of identity* (personal conflict over sex role-inappropriate behavior), *social network dilemmas* (difficulties in dealing with family members and colleagues who hold more traditional life views), and *role-cycling dilemmas* (difficulties in sequencing and coordinating various stages of career and family development). In their book, the Rapoports (1971) pointed out the advantages that reduction in sex role stereotyping, improvements in child care facilities, various forms of environmental engineering, and the social legitimization of heterogeneous family patterns would have for these families.

The study by Epstein (1971) was the first to concentrate on what would later be termed *coordinated career couples* (Butler & Paisley, 1980), in this case, the husband-and-wife legal partnership. Conceptualizing this particular life pattern as a direct descendent of preindustrial society, in which the married couple working together in the home were the core economic unit, Epstein conducted in-depth interviews with 12 women who were in legal practice with their husbands in and around the New York City area. Like the Rapoport studies, the data were qualitative in nature and no statistical analysis was performed. The themes that Epstein "teased out" of her interviews, however, have subsequently been borne out by more quantitatively oriented investigations.

Epstein discussed the functional nature of the joint partnership for these women in a time when the legal profession was not as accessible to women as it is today. The opportunity for part-time employment, for interrupting and reentering practice to coincide with child care responsibilities, and for equal financial remuneration made this arrangement an attractive one in many ways. Epstein reported, however, that "The joint partnerships studied here did not show much evidence of an ideology of equality" (p. 550). Rather, the women chose, or were relegated to, the less visible and less prestigious work areas: research and library work, and specialties such as probate work, family law, and real estate. Additionally, many of the women reported performing the practices' nonlegal administrative tasks, such as managing the office, keeping the calendar, and supervising the secretaries. In this regard, Epstein noted that the women, for the most part, defined their roles as "husband's helpmate," thus compatible with the dominant cultural image of the wife. Although this strategy has some obvious advantages, it is also true that it does not develop the lawyer's career skills, and may be personally frustrating. As one respondent commented about a female judge formerly in partnership with her husband, "She complained. . . that it was always 'darling, get me this from the file or that from the file' till she was so disgusted she went out and got herself a judgeship" (p. 554).

Division of labor within the homes of these couples was quite traditional, with the wife retaining the entire responsibility for maintaining the household and children. Although the husbands seemed to "exhibit interest in their children, and spend time with them" (p. 560) and appeared to be aware of the strain imposed on the wives by their dual responsibilities, Epstein noted that "despite this awareness, the women lawyers with whom we spoke were not in any *significant* way aided by their husbands in the home sphere" (p. 560; emphasis in the original). Indeed, the women in this study apparently felt very strongly the need to demonstrate to the interviewer their competency and proficiency in the traditional feminine sphere.

Epstein's (1971) investigation of attorneys was followed barely a year later by the first American study of the general dual-career family (Holmstrom, 1972). Her investigation, again using a semistructured interview technique, focused on 20 married couples in the greater Boston area in which the wife possessed the Ph.D. in the physical or social sciences or the humanities, and compared them with seven similar couples in which the wife had given up her career. This investigation of *professional* versus *traditional* families was the first to utilize an implicitly feminist analysis, wherein the results were discussed in terms of the then current explicit acceptance of masculine superiority and the effect this had on the family's management of dual-career issues. Holmstrom (1972) concluded that although the professional wives had much more equitable relationships than the traditional wives, they still suffered by comparison to men—specifically, their husbands. She noted that, typically, the man's career was more important, as measured by career decisions, mobility, allocation of time, and responsibility for household and child care responsibilities. She concluded, "Thus, within the professional group, dilemmas resulting from two careers in one family were resolved more in favor of the husband than the wife. This outcome is in keeping with the current cultural expectation that this is the way it should be. In summary, two general conclusions can be drawn. On the one hand, the two career couples deviated a great deal from middle-class norms. On the other hand, they were still a long way from equality of the sexes" (p. 155). Holmstrom provided an interesting analysis of the barriers encountered by the couple that are traceable to the rigidity and inflexibility of organizations and professional roles (e.g., the dubious status of less than full-time employment).

The final investigation in this generation of seminal studies was that of Poloma and Garland (Poloma, 1972; Garland, 1972; Poloma & Garland, 1971). Based on coordinated doctoral dissertations completed in 1970, this research focused on a sample of 53 professional married couples in which the wife was an attorney, a physician, or a college professor. These occupations were chosen because of the extensive training and high degree of commitment they demand and because, though representing diverse fields, they were all male-dominated professions. The findings were discussed in a series of papers focusing on the conflicts and role strain experienced by the wife as well as strategies for dealing with them (Poloma, 1972), the attitudes of the husbands toward their life patterns (Garland, 1972), and the degree to which the wives subjugated their careers to their family involvement (Poloma & Garland, 1971), a situation the authors label the "tolerance of domestication." These four investigations constitute what Rapoport and Rapoport (1980) call the *pivotal* generation of research on the dual-career phenomenon.

TYPOLOGIES

From the inception of research on dual-career families, writers have noted that they are not all alike. Even given a definition which specifies commitment to a demanding profession on the part of both partners, differences in the relative emphasis given to family versus career have been noted by most of the major researchers in the field. For example, Poloma and Garland (1971) divided their sample into traditional, neotraditional, and egalitarian families. The *traditional* families ($N = 25$) were characterized by extreme sex segregation of family responsibilities. Despite the fact that the women in this study were physicians, attorneys, or academicians, these traditional wives were just that—very traditional. They described their careers as clearly secondary to caring for the needs of their families. One woman professor, married to a physician, provided an illustration: When asked whether she would consider her own career plans if her husband were to wish to move out of town, she replied, "I wouldn't give any consideration to my position" (p. 534). Further, she remarked, "I know I wouldn't do it (work), if my husband didn't want me to" (p. 534). Clearly, these couples saw the home and family responsibilities as belonging to the wife, while breadwinning responsibilities belonged to the husband. The wife's income was not considered necessary to the family, and both husbands and wives were clearly committed to this traditional pattern.

The *neotraditional* couples ($N = 27$) were similar in their allocation of household responsibilities. However, in these families, the wife's income was needed to maintain the family's standard of living, and thus, her career assumed some importance in family decisions, particularly concerning issues of moving to another location.

In the entire sample of 53 couples, only one could be classified as *egalitarian*, implying that work and family responsibilities were shared equally. The wife's career activities and her breadwinning responsibilities were considered as serious as those of her husband, who participated equally in the running of the household.

The Rapoports (1971) suggested four prototypes of dual-career couples: familistic, careeristic, conventional, and coordinate. In the *familistic* couples, both husband and wife emphasize family as the major source of their satisfaction; *careeristic* couples are those in which both members emphasize career; and *conventional* couples are those in which the husband emphasizes career, while the wife emphasizes family interests. The Rapoports' typology does not contemplate the possibility of an *unconventional* pattern, but rather offers the *coordinate* type, in which the wife has a career orientation, but the husband values family life as well as career. It is this latter position that is represented in the Rapoport (1971) case studies. They noted that the potential for life satisfaction is not significantly different for any of the couple patterns except the careerist, in which there is a significant decrease in the level of marital happiness.

Bird (1979) based her typology of marriage on the various combinations of husband/wife agreement or disagreement concerning whether or not the wife works. Only two of her resulting eight patterns could be considered dual-career in nature, that is, the couples characterized by a *defiant* working wife (one who pursues a career over the objections of her husband) and the *contemporary* working wife, who engages in her career pursuits with her husband's encouragement and approval. The remaining six types of relationships are listed in two categories: homemakers, who can be traditional, defiant, submissive, or reluctant; or workers, who can be submissive, or reluctant.

Perhaps the most complete statement of this type is that of Hall and Hall (1980). They constructed a fourfold typology that recalls in some respects that proposed earlier by the Rapoports. In their schema, Type I couples are characterized as *accomodators*, one partner being heavily invested in career pursuits, while the other evinces high involvement in the home. They noted that the career-oriented partner can be either the husband or the wife, a feature that differentiates this type from the conventional couples described by the Rapoports, to whom they are otherwise similar. Type II partners are labeled *adversaries*. These husband and wife pairs are both strongly career oriented in nature (similar to the Rapoports' careeristic families). The adversarial nature of the relationship derives from the fact that both partners are also strongly invested in having a well-ordered home, but neither is willing to devote time to providing it. Thus, there arises considerable competition and stress over support demands. Partners in the Type III model are best understood as *allies*, with both being intensively involved in career pursuits with little concern about the home, or, alternatively, both being heavily invested in their family life, with correspondingly little priority given to career demands. The Type IV couple is labeled by the Halls as *acrobats*. With both partners deeply involved in home *and* family roles, this high-stress life-style seems aptly characterized.

The Halls moved their discussion to another level when they noted that both relationships and careers can be either traditional, or *protean*, in nature. The term protean is taken from the Greek mythological figure Proteus, who was able to change his form at will. A protean career or relationship is characterized by a great deal of inner-directedness, flexibility, and willingness to innovate in the quest for fulfillment. In a relationship, this might mean trying new life-styles, such as a commuter marriage, or a role reversal in which the husband takes on the domestic role while the wife works. A protean career might involve changing jobs or organizations, job sharing, or even dropping out of the work force for a while. The key note is that the relationship and/or career are based on individual or couple-based values, rather than the norms of society. These concepts yield a second-order typology, representing various combinations of traditional and protean careers and relationships. The Halls suggested that the life-style characterized by a traditional relationship and traditional career for both partners is probably very stressful in nature, as neither the career nor family system offers much "slack" or flexibility, and the demands are high. By way of contrast, those life-styles characterized by protean relationships *and* protean careers may be too ambiguous to be tolerated by many people for any extended period of time. The Halls offered several interesting hypotheses concerning dual-career couples (e.g., couples in the same or similar fields will experience less stress than those in very different fields) that offer a rich field for investigations which should considerably enhance our understanding of this phenomenon.

COORDINATORS AND COMMUTERS: VARIATIONS ON A BASIC PATTERN

As dual-career families have become more numerous and research on this life-style has advanced, some investigators have turned their attention to special cases, or variations on the basic pattern. Three such variations considered here are *coordinated career couples*, in which the husband–wife pair are members of the same profession; *job-sharing couples*, in which each partner works half the time, sharing the same position; and *commuter career couples*, a small but growing number of couples in which the partners maintain separate residences for various periods of time, commuting to be together on weekends, vacations, or whenever their schedules allow.

COORDINATED CAREER COUPLES

Probably the first well-known study of coordinated career couples was that of Epstein (1971), described earlier. This intensive interview investigation of female attorneys who were in practice with their attorney husbands revealed that these women, while probably better off than other female attorneys of the period in terms of employment and remuneration, were congregated in the less visible and less prestigious law specialties, were often treated as adjuncts and assistants to their husbands, and still retained the majority of responsibility for homemaking and child care. More recent studies of other professional pairs (e.g., sociologists and psychologists), using a more quantitative methodology, reflect a similar picture.

Martin, Berry, and Jacobsen (1975) set out to test an implication of the Parsonian dictum that marriage between professionals would be both personally and professionally destructive to the couples involved. They examined the career patterns of 86 married sociologist pairs, and those of a comparison group of 751 female sociologists *not* married to another sociologist, in order to "tease out" the influence of sex and coordinate marriage on the careers of these professionals. The data were gathered from five consecutive issues of the American Sociological Association's *Guide to Graduate Departments of Sociology,* 1969 to 1974. Thus, the sample consisted entirely of academic sociologists, which is, of course, the primary source of employment for sociologists in this country. Dependent variables included the possession of the Ph.D., academic rank, frequency of promotion, degree of employment, and career longevity. The results indicated that the husbands were better off on every indicator except promotion; however, since 40% of the men achieved the rank of full professor during the 5 years covered by the study, compared with 15.1% of the sociologist wives and 10% of the non-wives, and thus could not be promoted further, this outcome indicator is artificially depressed for this group. The wives were more likely than their non-wife counterparts to receive the Ph.D. (78% versus 64%) and were slightly more likely to be found in the higher academic ranks. On the other hand, the wives were twice as likely to be working only half-time, and were much more likely to drop out of academic sociology altogether. The authors concluded, "In sum, then, professional marriage seems to reduce the probability that the wife will be a full time professional; increase the probability of a wife's half time pursuit of a career; and offers no significant relief or aggravation to the general rate of unemployment experienced by all females in the profession" (pp. 737–738).

This study of sociologists was followed shortly by a large-scale investigation of husband/wife pairs in psychology (Bryson & Bryson, 1980; Heckman, Bryson, & Bryson, 1977). Rather than utilizing archival data, these investigators sent questionnaires to the 605 persons who claimed "husband–wife" credit on the American Psychological Association (APA) dues statement in 1972. This list was presumed to define a set of "professional pairs," or husbands and wives who shared common professional identities. The final sample consisted of 200 couples who completed the data packet, which consisted of separate questionnaires for the husbands and wives, as well as a third questionnaire for them to fill out as a couple. In addition, an abbreviated form of the questionnaire was mailed to a comparison group of 150 men and 150 women who were randomly selected from the APA directory, but who were not married to each other. Review of the demographic data on this sample reveals a pattern of results strikingly similar to those of Martin *et al.* (1975), reported above. Psychologist husbands were more likely than any other group to hold the Ph.D. [90.5%, compared to other male psychologists (82.2%), psychologist wives (79.5%), and other female psychologists (62.9%)]. The wives, on the other hand, had held their jobs for the shortest period of time, were less likely to be employed than were female comparison subjects, more likely to be employed part-time, and received a lower annual income than any other group. The income differential between husbands and wives was related to the expected variables such as length of wives' employment and number of publications, but was also significantly related to the number of children in the family ($r = .21$) and was substantially affected by the amount of responsibility for household duties that the husband accepted ($r = -.28$). The husbands were the most productive group in terms of all measures (publications, papers, books, and grants) while wives exceeded female comparison subjects in all categories and equaled male comparison subjects in numbers of grants received. In other words, the psychologist wives published more, but were less highly employed and made less money than did female colleagues who were *not* married to other psychologists. Not surprisingly, these psychologist wives reported less satisfaction in a number of areas than did their husbands. Specifically, the wives in professional pairs reported less satisfaction with the amount of time they have for domestic, avocational, and professional activities; rate of advancement; opportunities for collegial interaction; and freedom to pursue long-range job goals. Bryson and Bryson (1980) concluded:

> Taken together, our findings regarding salary, productivity, and satisfaction form a rather complex picture. The effects of dual career status for the husband seem uniformly positive: He tends to be more productive, to earn more, and to report a level of satisfaction with professional and personal life equal to or greater than that of any other group. For the wives, however, the effects of dual-career status are less uniform. Although they are, as a group, more productive than their same sex counterparts, this productivity is not reflected in job stability or income. As a result, they report lower satisfaction than any other group. (pp. 252–253)

Butler and Paisley (1977) referred to this pattern as the "professional couple syndrome" and set out to examine three commonly accepted assumptions that purport to explain observed status differences between husband–wife professional pairs. According to Butler and Paisley, "Myth 1 says husbands appear to be more successful than their wives because they are older and/or graduated first and have

more professional years. . . Myth 2 says husbands are more successful than their wives because they have graduated from higher status
universities. . . Myth 3 says husbands are more successful than their
wives because they have higher degrees" (p. 309). To examine these
assumptions and to determine what, if any, changes have occurred
over time, these researchers identified 139 husband–wife pairs from
the 1958 APA membership directory and 322 couples for the 1973
directory. The couples were coded for sex, birth year, year of graduation, status of university where highest degree was earned, current
employer, status of employer if an academic institution, and current
position. The data indicated that in both subsets of the sample, the
women and men were close in chronological as well as professional
age. For the 1958 sample, the median ages for the women and men
were 42 and 43, respectively; corresponding data for the 1973 sample
were 45 and 48. Data on "professional age" indicated that the 1958
couples received their degrees 1 year apart (median of 10 and 11 years
previously, for wives and husbands, respectively), while those in the
1973 sample were 4 years apart (sample median = 14 and 18). In
neither chronological nor professional age was there enough difference to account for the greater success of husbands, thus dispelling
Myth 1.

Similarly, the data showed no support for Myth 2, as approximately
equal numbers of women and men graduated from major universities
(67% and 64% in 1958, and 43% and 42% in 1973). Finally, these
researchers found no support for Myth 3. Although more men (89%)
than women (75%) did receive the doctorate, when couples with the
same highest degree were analyzed separately, the husbands held the
higher positions, and were more often supervisors, administrators, or
chairpersons. Butler and Paisley (1977) concluded, "Differences in
success between husbands and wives cannot be attributed to age,
training, degree, or place of employment. The remaining explanation
is sex discrimination, including discrimination in the form of sex role
socialization, which creates self-fulfilling prophecies concerning
women's professional careers" (p. 318).

What then, is the effect of a coordinate marriage on the career of the
professional woman? Bryson and Bryson (1980) concluded wryly,
"The easiest advice we can offer. . . is to suggest that, if you are a
male psychologist, you should marry a female psychologist. However,
if you are a female psychologist, you should not even consider marry-
ing a male psychologist" (p. 253). We agree with these authors that the
inherent asymmetry in this advice makes it somewhat unhelpful, but
find it tempting to speculate as to whether it is not the "best and the
brightest" of women who marry into their profession, only to find that

coordinate marriage decreases their professional viability, even as the intellectual stimulation and professional support they provide creates an "enriched" environment in which their husbands thrive and grow. Obviously, this is only speculation; however, as a hypothesis, it does fit the existing data and deserves to be directly examined in further research.

JOB-SHARING COUPLES

The second variation of the dual-career pattern to be considered here is that of the job-sharing couple. Defined by Dickson (1975) as "dividing a job with each taking responsibility for half the total work—splitting the total workload of a single job" (p. 244), job sharing is one way of integrating the usually separate domains of work and family. According to Arkin and Dobrovsky (1978), "job sharing is permanent, high quality, part-time employment without the exploitive dynamics of low status, low wages, job insecurity and absence of fringe benefits which have been characteristics of most part time jobs" (p. 122). They noted that job sharing attempts to capture the good aspects of the part-time work situation, such as flexible time, while eliminating the undesirable, marginal quality that such employment has previously implied. Additionally, job sharing can be a creative response to the stress of managing a full-time family and two full-time careers.

Little is known about this life-style, although it has received some attention in the popular press (Anderson, 1972; Bagchi, 1976; Closson, 1976a,b; Gallese, 1974) and occasional case studies have appeared (Rosenberg & Rosenberg, 1978). Since the shared-role ideology exemplified by job sharing runs directly counter to Western cultural norms of individuality, work commitment, and occupational status, it is perhaps not surprising that such a pattern is only rarely attempted in this country.[1] The study by Arkin and Dobrovsky (1978) provided one of the few formal pieces of research that has so far emerged. Through a networking technique, these investigators identified a sample of 21 job-sharing couples in three different occupations: the clergy, academia, and journalism. As in other dual-career, and particularly coordinate career, studies, academicians were overrepresented; it appears that the particular characteristics (high educational level, flexible schedule) and limitations (limited number of positions, antinepotism

[1] Gronseth (1978) provided a fascinating account of work sharing in Norway, a country with a tradition of liberal and innovative social policies, wherein such practices were encouraged and studied by the Norwegian Family Council.

policies) of academia produce a situation uniquely suited to the crea-
tion of innovative dual-career patterns. The majority (77%) of these
couples reported that job sharing held more advantages than a traditional pattern; fewer than one in ten reported fewer advantages. The
women were slightly more favorable than the men, and there were no
complaints of work and family conflicts. Stresses there were; however,
they appeared to be related to the unusual nature of the couple's
occupational involvement rather than the role overload and consequent lack of time usually reported by dual-career couples. The subjects reported three such areas of stress: sexism, part-time stigma, and
economic exploitation. Stresses related to a traditional sex role ideology derived from the reactions of colleagues who, for example, treated
the male as the *real* professional (emphasis in original), while the part-
time stigma stemmed from perceptions of the couple as less than fully
qualified or functioning members of their occupational group. Arkin
and Dobrovsky (1978) reported, "The stigma of traditional part-time
employment with its low status seems to prevail in interactions with
members of both social and work groups. Couples also report that
others tend to perceive their job-sharing arrangement as temporary
and the result of being unable to find two 'regular' jobs. These perceptions and their impact stigmatize the individuals as lacking in occupational commitment or motivation; as less than fully qualified" (p. 131).
It was most likely reactions such as these that led to what Arkin and
Dobrovsky labeled economic exploitation, but which may more parsi-
moniously be described as overcompensation on the part of the
couple to demonstrate to employers and colleagues the legitimacy of
the arrangement. Most members of most couples do a great deal more
than half-time employment requires. Other writers have noted that
job-sharing "workers produce not half, but 80 percent as much as their
full-time counterparts" (Closson, 1976a, p. 36). One solution that
has been suggested is for couples to share 1½ jobs as opposed to the
single position.

It is presently unclear whether or not job sharing will emerge as a
viable option for more than a very small number of couples. However,
its flexibility, cooperation, and opportunity for interplay among marital, family, and work relations make it one of the most creative and
attractive patterns of dual-career living that has yet emerged.

COMMUTER COUPLES

In striking contrast to the interdependence of the job-sharing
couple is the marked individuation of the commuter couple, who
maintain separate residences during the week or month, or more or

less on a permanent basis. Despite growing attention in the popular press (Baldridge, 1977; Drachman, Schwartz, & Schwebs, 1976; Haddad, 1978; Rule, 1977; Saul, 1976), very little research has yet accumulated on this particular life-style. As with other areas of investigation which have yet to mature, most studies have been qualitative and impressionistic in nature.

One of the first reports of this sort to appear was that of Farris (1978), who interviewed ten commuting couples of various professional and family backgrounds to investigate such questions as why these couples commute, how they decided to do so, and what are the benefits and costs associated with this particular pattern. She noted that the commuters in her sample had exceptionally high educational qualifications, with all but two possessing graduate training. University professors were disproportionately represented, a finding also reported by Gross (1980). Farris noted that the typical arrangement was characterized by weekly separations and weekend reunions, although there were also other patterns. Typically, work and family lives were highly compartmentalized, with the commuter devoting extremely long hours to work demands during the week, while the weekends were filled with family activities. Farris noted, however, that even in this most nontraditional of arrangements, "the wife's weekends were often spent in household work and organization, rather than in recuperating from the previous week" (p. 102). The decision to commute was solely motivated by career concerns, typically those of the wife, at some crucial point in her vocational development.

With regard to the issues faced by these couples, Farris noted that the younger, childless couples primarily expressed concern with emotional and interpersonal issues: fears of growing apart, of outside sexual involvement, of divorce. For older couples and those with children, logistical problems concerning housework and child care predominated. In examining any possible effect of this variant family pattern on the children, Farris reported that the parents believed the effect to be a positive one, describing their children as independent, resourceful, and competent, an impression shared by the researcher herself. She concluded that the major benefits were the intrinsic ones of high-level career involvement and satisfaction, while the major cost was just that—the cost of maintaining separate residences and a heavy travel budget. Farris noted that the families involved were quite positive and enthusiastic about their own choice of this life-style, though cautioning that it was probably not viable as a general model, due to the high degree of independence, self-reliance, and career commitment required.

Gross (1980) took a somewhat less positive tone in her study of 43 commuter spouses living in or around the greater Chicago metropolitan area. Also utilizing an in-depth interview approach, Gross noted that these commuter spouses seemed to be intuitively comparing their marriages to the traditional model they had consciously rejected, and feeling either somewhat guilty about their "special privileges" (the wives) or somewhat deprived by the loss of their unquestioned precedence (the husbands). Like Farris (1978), Gross suggested that career involvement and satisfaction are the greatest benefits to be derived from this pattern, while emotional conflict represented the greatest disadvantage. She sorted her sample into two groups: members of *adjusting couples,* who were younger, childless, and somewhat concerned about whose career had or should have ascendency; and members of *established couples,* who were older, had children, and, like the older couples in the Farris (1978) study, were more likely to report difficulty over child care and domestic responsibilities. She concluded that couples who possessed certain characteristics were likely to find the life-style to be less stressful; specifically, older couples, who had been married longer and were freed from childrearing responsibilities, and in which at least one spouse already had a well-established career. Even so, she noted, "The decision to live apart produces a lifestyle that is difficult at best, endured in the service of career or other goals, but not one endorsed enthusiastically" (p. 569).

Douvan and Pleck (1978) offered an alternative to this somewhat negative picture. In a thoughtful paper, they proposed that, rather than being a stress on the dual-career marriage, separation often provides a support for dual-career relationships, and can be seen as one of a number of 'enabling' processes in family life (Rapoport & Rapoport, 1973). Noting that even very traditional marriages require regular periods of separation and coming together, they suggested that such rhythm and punctuation may be necessary for the marital relationship. Extending this thesis, they presented three case studies to illustrate the positive influence geographic separation can exert on the growth of one of the partners and on the relationship itself. Interestingly, all three cases focus on a professional wife, who copes with a developmental or structural need for individuation by instituting some form of time-limited or geographically structured separation.

This leads us to the observation that the recent interest in commuter couples obscures the fact that such commuting has long been common in this, and other, cultures. Long-distance truck drivers and traveling salesmen are traditionally away from home a majority of the time. Douvan and Pleck (1978) pointed out that military families take for granted periodic separations, of either an abbreviated or more extended nature, and airline pilots and sailors also find such separations a routine part of their lives. Gross (1980) noted that politicians, professional ball players, actors, and construction workers have long been required by their occupations to engage in more or less lengthy periods of marital separation. What is new and unusual is not the commuting itself, but the fact that it is often the wife who is doing it. Thus, once again, it is the departure from traditional sex roles that stimulates a flurry of research designed to investigate the costs, the benefits, and the effects on the marriage and the children, a tribute once more to the power of the nonconscious ideology described by Bem and Bem (1976) over a decade ago.

DUAL-CAREER COUPLES: ORGANIZATIONAL PERSPECTIVES

Until very recently, the research on dual-career couples has focused exclusively on the determinants, styles, costs, and benefits of this life choice for such families themselves, either for the various individuals involved or for the family as a unit. More recently, however, attention has turned to the organizations and institutions which employ members of dual-career couples, and research has been initiated to investigate the impact of this life-style on the employer, and the policies, if any, instituted to address this impact.

EARLY RESEARCH

In one of the first studies of this kind, Pingree, Butler, Paisley, and Hawkins (1978) sent questionnaires to the chairperson of either the psychology or sociology departments of every college or university in the United States. Three hundred twenty-nine responses were received (16%); however, the response rate for the 34 designated "major departments" was 62%, with one follow-up. The questionnaire asked the chairs to describe the advantages and disadvantages to the department of hiring both members of a dual-career couple, as well as to respond to the question "Overall, how likely is it you would support the hiring of a professional couple?"

The results indicated that the respondents were more likely to mention disadvantages than advantages, the most commonly mentioned being

1. Difficulty in departmental faculty evaluation (31%)
2. The possibly disruptive effect on the department of any marital and emotional problems experienced by the couple (22%)

3. The couple's disproportionate or adverse influence on departmental politics (22%)
4. The possibility that dissatisfaction on the part of the couple
   would result in two vacancies at the same time (18%)

In terms of possible benefits to the department, these chairpersons
were more likely to mention

1. The possibility that the strong interface between the couple's
   personal and professional lives would enhance the department
   (23%)
2. The department's greater ability to coordinate faculty professional and research activities (14%)
3. The department's greater stability of personnel (12%)

Slightly more than one third of the subjects opposed the hiring of such
couples, while approximately the same percentage supported it, and
about 25% were neutral.

The Pingree *et al.* (1978) study, while offering some beginning in-
sights into organizational perspectives on the dual-career couple, possesses unique characteristics that limit its usefulness for more general
purposes. First, it investigates academic institutions, which do not
share some of the more pressing problems of private-sector, for-profit
corporations; for example, employee resistance to transfer. Secondly,
and possibly of greater importance, it focuses on a somewhat singular
population, that subset of dual-career couples who are employed in
the same unit by the same institution.

CORPORATE FINDINGS

Research focused more directly on organizations' perceptions of
and reactions to the dual-career issue was undertaken by the staff of
Catalyst Career and Family Center (Catalyst, 1981) and that of RE-
SOURCE: Careers (RESOURCE, 1983), both of which are nonprofit
organizations dedicated to fostering the career development of
women in the private sector. Operating under a grant from the Exxon
Corporation, Catalyst surveyed 374 of the Fortune 1300 companies,
representing a national sample of large and small companies, and 815
couples, in which the wife had a career within the business community. (The husband, however, could be employed in any professional
field.) The corporate survey addressed whether or not corporations
believed recruitment, productivity, and so forth were affected by the
problems of two-career families; what, if any, specific practices these

companies were instituting to alleviate these problems; their degree of satisfaction with these practices; and plans for the future. Using essentially the same questionnaire, and funded by grants from The Cleveland Foundation, the RESOURCE (1983) staff conducted an intensive investigation of 156 northeastern Ohio corporations of various sizes, and 392 couples who were professionally employed in the area. Interestingly enough, although the samples were different and the methodologies differed somewhat (Catalyst mailed their questionnaires to the Chief Executive Officer and Chief Financial Officer of each company, while RESOURCE conducted telephone interviews with human resource professionals within each organization), the results were quite similar, adding to the confidence that can be placed in them.

The main conclusion that can be drawn from these studies is that corporations have definitely felt the impact of the growth of the two-career life-style and expect to be even more affected in the future; however, there appears to be some uncertainty as to how to go about addressing the issue. Indeed, these organizations were much more likely to *favor* innovative personnel practices that would benefit the dual-career couple (e.g., flexible work schedules, in-house child care, career assistance to the spouse of a transferred employee, or "cafeteria style" benefits) than they were to actually *institute* such practices. Couples in both surveys, although professing a belief in an egalitarian life-style, were in practice somewhat more traditional; for example, in the Catalyst study, almost twice as many husbands (40%) as wives (21%) had relocated for their own jobs; and wives ranked "job for spouse" as the most important factor in choosing where to locate, while husbands gave first place to "job for self." In fact, "job for spouse" was chosen as a location factor by only 33% of the husbands in this sample.

The data from these two large-scale studies are both extremely rich and quite extensive, too extensive to be adequately reviewed in the space available. However, it is possible to extrapolate from them "areas of impact" to which corporations will have to attend if they wish to retain high-performance members of professional pairs. These areas are also addressed by Stringer-Moore (1981), who labeled them hiring procedures, working conditions, and personal considerations.

Areas of Organizational Impact: Issues and Practices

With respect to hiring practices, Stringer-Moore (1981) noted that the legislation which has been enacted to counteract discrimination can sometimes be problematic in hiring dual-career couples. For example, the legal necessity to post and advertise openings makes questionable the practice of hiring one spouse and creating a position for the second. Similarly, marital status may neither be elicited in the employment interview nor considered in the hiring decision, which may work to the disadvantage of dual-career couples. Finally, antinepotism policies are still formally and informally enforced in many situations, to the detriment to the female member of the two-career pair. Stringer-Moore suggested that companies combat these problems by advertising several positions at the same time, while also publicly advertising their interest in hiring two-career couples, by exploring alternative work patterns, such as job sharing, by examining their antinepotism policies, and by sharing ideas and innovative practices with other companies. Along these lines, Catalyst reported that 56% of their corporate sample expressed interest in participating in a geographically based consortium that would pool positions available in an attempt to help two-career couples with relocation problems.

With regard to working conditions, the issue of relocation, transfer, mobility, and the like emerges by far the most salient for employers. The RESOURCE (1983) study reported that 42% of their corporate subjects reported an increase in employee resistance to transfers; a parallel figure from the Catalyst (1981) report is 67%. Additional data are found in a 1975 report by Dun and Bradstreet, which noted that in their survey of 617 firms, employees at 42% of the companies refused to relocate, while Maynard and Zawacki (1979) quoted the New York firm of Gilbert Tweed Associates to the effect that one in three executives cannot or will not relocate, because it would interfere with the career or studies of a spouse. Although financial considerations obviously play a large part in the relocation decision, most research indicates that family resistance, particularly the career considerations of the spouse, is one of the largest factors in refusal to transfer. It is commonplace for companies to offer financial assistance to couples faced with relocation; spousal career assistance is, however, far less common. Both Catalyst and RESOURCE suggest such assistance, including job counseling, referral, resume preparation, and the like. Maynard and Zawacki (1979) suggested alternatives to relocation such as the simulation of field experience in local training, temporary assignments; the shortening of work weeks and staggering of schedules to allow for commuting, limiting the geographical area of training moves, and the increased use of communications media as an alternative to relocation.

The final "area of impact" on corporations is that which Stringer-Moore (1981) labeled *personal considerations,* the most important of which is child care. More than any other corporate/dual-career issue, the problem of child care exerts an enormous influence on women's career adjustment, satisfaction, productivity, retention, and so forth. It is on women, of course, whatever their level of training or responsibility, that the burden (both psychological and practical) of child care largely falls. Stringer-Moore (1981) noted that the United States is the only developed country in the world without a national child care policy, while only 1% of the Catalyst corporations reported either on-site child care or subsidies for child care, 19% provided monetary support of community-based child care facilities, and less than 30% provided employee sick leave for children's illnesses. Clearly, this is an area in which corporate involvement could and should be increased, for the benefit of both the organization and the woman employee. Stringer-Moore (1981) presented an extremely provocative discussion of innovative practices in this area.

SUMMARY

Although research into the organizational impact of the dual-career life-style is in its infancy, several issues are emerging as critical to both organizational and individual well-being. It is also clear that dual-career problems are primarily women's problems. Thus, the perennial issues of child care, career permanence in the face of husband's transfer, and the like remain. Evidence suggests that the growth of the two-career life-style has resulted in (very slowly) increasing male involvement in childrearing and concomitant concern for the quality of life of the family as a unit. Organizations will ignore this, to their detriment. As the staff of RESOURCE remarked, "If one's organization does not take steps to react to the changing environment, other organizations will" (RESOURCE, 1983, unpaginated). Recent writings (e.g., Sekaran, 1986) indicate that organizational interest in these issues is beginning to be awakened.

SEXUAL HARASSMENT

INTRODUCTION AND OVERVIEW

No discussion of women and work would be complete without an analysis of that complex and pervasive set of behaviors that have come to be known as sexual harassment. Although only recently reaching public and scholarly awareness as an important issue, sexual harassment of women workers has been a problem for as long as women have worked outside the home. Goodman (1981) noted that "The history of sexual harassment dates back at least to the time women first traded their labor in the marketplace" (p. 449). In 1908, *Harper's Bazaar* published a collection of stories documenting the experiences of women who had migrated to the city at the turn of the century to find work. These stories revealed widespread and extensive harassment. Bularzik (1978), in a fascinating historical account of the phenomenon, told of a broom factory in which women carried knives to protect themselves! Contemporary accounts, while usually less dramatic, are no less compelling; according to Goodman (1981), many of the essential facts about sexual harassment, particularly its frequency, are as true today as they were at the turn of the century. The present chapter presents an analysis of sexual harassment, including definitions, extent, and consequences, in both occupational and educational settings. Following this, various explanatory models of sexual harassment will be considered.

SEX AT WORK: THE SEXUAL HARASSMENT OF WOMEN WORKERS

Definitions

As we have noted elsewhere (Fitzgerald & Betz, 1983), there is less than complete agreement on what constitutes sexual harassment. Harragan (1977) suggested the terms sexual molestation, sexual exploitation, and civil rape—but does not explicitly define the behaviors to which these terms refer. She does note, however, that the behavior is most often verbal, including comments on the woman's physical characteristics, as well as invitations to sexual contact. Physical molestation, when it occurs, is even more devastating. Harrigan suggested that the typical victim is a woman who is financially vulnerable and that the perpetrator is necessarily a male supervisor or employer who wields economic power over her. If the woman refuses a sexual relationship, she may be fired or her performance evaluation downgraded, suggesting she is incompetent. Because Harragan's discussion implies that harassment is possible only when the perpetrator is superior in position to the victim, she minimizes the equally serious effects of persistent, offensive, and unwelcome sexual advances by peers.

A broader definition of sexual harassment is provided by Farley (1978), who wrote

> Sexual harassment is best described as unsolicited nonreciprocal male behavior that asserts a woman's sex role over her function as worker. It can be any or all of the following: staring at, commenting upon, or touching a woman's body; requests for acquiescence in sexual behavior; repeated nonreciprocal propositions for dates; demands for sexual intercourse; and rape. (pp. 14–15)

Whereas Farley acknowledged that sexual harassment may involve inequities in the positions of the perpetrator versus the victim, she also pointed out that men have inherently higher societal status by virtue of being male, usually outnumber women in the organizational setting, and can penalize noncooperative women even when positions are equal in status (e.g., through noncooperation or verbal denigration). Farley's definition obviously encompasses a much wider range of behaviors, and has been occasionally criticized on the grounds that almost any social approach made by a man to a female coworker or subordinate could be construed as sexual harassment.

The most explicit, and probably most influential, definition of sexual harassment was set forth in 1980 by the Equal Employment Opportunity Commission (EEOC), the federal agency responsible for enforcement of Title VII of the Civil Rights Act, which is that portion of the act that prohibits discrimination in the employment situation. The EEOC (1980) stated

> Unwelcome sexual advances, requests for sexual favors, and other verbal or physical conduct of a sexual nature constitute sexual harassment when:
> (1) submission to such conduct is made either explicitly or implicitly a term or condition of an individual's employment;
> (2) submission to or rejection of such conduct by an individual is used as the basis for employment decisions affecting such individual or

(3) such conduct has the purpose or effect of substantially interfering with an individual's performance, or creating an intimidating, hostile, or offensive work environment.

This decision is precise enough to be workable, and has had great influence in widening the legal definition from one that depends solely on a *quid pro quo* (the woman is required to engage in sexual behavior or suffer some negative employment consequence) to one that includes a *condition of work* interpretation (the woman's work environment is permeated with unpleasant and inappropriate sexual behavior; however, sexual cooperation is not necessarily required of her).

EXTENT OF SEXUAL HARASSMENT

Although sexual harassment has been thought to have serious negative effects on women's career development, data regarding the prevalence of the phenomenon have, until recently, been scarce. Harragan (1977) suggested the magnitude of the problem when she stated that more women are refused employment, fired, or forced to quit salaried jobs as the result of sexual demands than for any other single cause. She based her remarks on the work of Farley (1978), who cited two systematic studies that were conducted on working women in the private sector. In May of 1975, the Women's Section of the Human Affairs Program at Cornell University surveyed a sample of New York women concerning sexual harassment, which they defined as any repeated or unwanted sexual comments, looks, suggestions, or physical contact that were found to be objectionable or offensive and caused discomfort on the job. Of the 155 respondents, 92% described sexual harassment as a serious problem; 70% had personally experienced some form of harassment, and of these, 56% reported physical harassment. Farley noted that the incidents occurred among all job categories, ages, marital statuses, and pay ranges.

Farley also cited the results of a survey conducted by *Redbook* magazine (*Redbook*, 1976) in which responses from over 9,000 women were obtained. Of these women, 92% reported sexual harassment as a problem and 90% reported that they had personally experienced one or more forms of unwanted sexual attention on the job. This study has been criticized due to its dependence on the self-selection of the respondents, which is thought to result in the overrepresentation of the incidence of harassment.

Two large-scale formal studies lend support to the results of this early work. In 1980, the first comprehensive national survey of sexual harassment was initiated by the U.S. Merit Systems Protection Board.

Data were collected from a stratified, random sample of federal employees listed in the Central Personnel Data File of the Office of Personnel Management. Usable data were obtained from 83.8% of the 23,964 persons who received the questionnaire. The final sample contained 10,644 women. Forty-two percent of these women reported being the target of overt sexual harassment at some point in the 2-year period covered by the study. As Chapman (1981) pointed out, this is likely to be an underestimate, given the somewhat narrow definition of sexual harassment employed. Even so, it projects to roughly *18 to 19 million employees* in the total U.S. labor force in 1980.

Similarly, in a large survey of a representative sample of private-sector workers in the Los Angeles area (Gutek, 1981), 53.1% of the women respondents reported experiencing at least one incident that they consider sexual harassment during their working lives. Again, this is very likely an *underestimate,* as it includes only those behaviors that the respondents personally labeled as sexual harassment. Clearly, sexual harassment is so widespread as to touch almost every woman at some point in her working life.

CONSEQUENCES OF SEXUAL HARASSMENT

Given that the phenomenon of sexual harassment is so ubiquitous, what can be said about its effects on women, and in what ways does it constitute a barrier to their career development? Farley (1978) cited a study conducted at the United Nations in which over 50% of the female respondents reported that they had personally experienced sexual pressure or knew other women who had experienced such pressure in situations involving promotion, recruitment, obtaining a permanent contract, transfer, and going on missions. Thirty-one percent of the women in Gutek's (1981) study had experienced some negative employment consequence, including being fired. Negative consequences in the Merit System study included emotional or physical difficulties, negative feelings about work, and poor job performance. Goodman (1981) wrote that

> The picture of sexual harassment that emerges as understanding of the phenomenon grows is not only one of a common experience, but also a damaging one. Physical symptoms like headache, backache, nausea, weight loss or gain, and psychological reactions, like insomnia, depression, and nervousness, are common. A study by Working Women's Institute (Crull, 1979) found sixty-three percent of the women who were sexually harassed suffered physical symptoms and ninety-six percent suffered symptoms of emotional stress. These reactions in turn cause loss of motivation, absenteeism, and, in the end, diminished productivity, as women lose their desire and ability to work efficiently. (p. 456)

Goodman went on to cite evidence that plaintiffs in many of the early sexual harassment cases were women who were fired from their jobs. Adrienne Tomkins was fired after lodging a complaint against her boss (*Tomkins v. PSE & G Co.*, 1977); Diane Williams was fired from the U.S. Department of Justice 9 days after filing a complaint asserting that she was humiliated and harassed for rejecting her supervisor's sexual advances (*Williams v. Saxbe*, 1976); Margaret Miller received a "superior" performance rating and a raise from her employer, the Bank of America, and then was promptly fired for refusing to have sex with her supervisor (*Miller v. Bank of America*, 1979); and Paulette Barnes' job was abolished shortly after she refused to grant her supervisor sexual favors (*Barnes v. Costle*, 1977). The list goes on. It is difficult to escape the conclusion that sexual harassment constitutes one of the most, if not *the* most, ubiquitous and damaging barriers to women's success and satisfaction. Nor is it limited to the workplace. The following section of the chapter will examine the sexual harassment of women students in higher education, and how it operates to discourage women from education and careers, both traditional and nontraditional.

SEXUAL HARASSMENT IN EDUCATION: A SPECIAL CASE

The sexual harassment of students by their professors has been called "a hidden issue" (Project on the Status and Education of Women, 1978). According to a recent book devoted to the topic, "Sexual harassment of college students by their professors is a fact of campus life that many educators learn to ignore, and, in their silence, accept" (Dzeich & Weiner, 1984, p. 1). Although it has only recently been recognized and named, such harassment is not a new problem, but one that women students have always faced. Writing for the Modern Language Association's Commission on the Status of Women, Phyllis Franklin and her colleagues suggested, "On occasion, in certain forms, it appeared as romance: the naive student swept into bed by her brilliant professor. . . . Charlotte Bronte wrote about it more than a hundred years ago; in the popular confessions magazines, authors write about it still. In fictional form, it remains the stuff that fantasies are made of, fantasies that reflect and reinforce the tendency of our society to limit the definition of women to the sexual and domestic spheres and to soften . . . the linking of sexual dominance with the powerful and of sexual submission with the powerless" (Franklin, Moglen, Zatling-Boring, & Angress, 1981, p. 3).

In recent years, the growing interest in sexual harassment in the workplace and the accumulating body of case law have led to a parallel interest in defining and documenting the phenomenon in institutions of higher learning. As Crocker and Simon (1981) have noted, "Formal education is, in the United States, an important factor in an individual's career possibilities and personal development, therefore stunting or obstructing that person's educational accomplishment can have severe consequences" (p. 542). Thus, to the degree that sexual harassment exists in academic settings, and leads to negative consequences for women students, it can be considered a serious external barrier to women's career development. This section of the chapter will examine sexual harassment as a manifestation of sex discrimination in education.

Definitions

According to Somers (1982), many of the problems concerning sexual harassment in academic settings arise from "the lack of a clear, concise, widely accepted definition of sexual harassment" (p. 23). As is the case in industrial and organizational settings, there has been a great deal of disagreement concerning the nature of sexual harassment, as well as a general reluctance to define any but the most serious offenses as harassment. As Dzeich and Weiner (1984) pointed out, "Men and women faculty and administrators assume, are led to believe, or find it convenient to make sexual harassment a confusing topic. . . attention is quickly distracted from the fundamental issues surrounding sexual harassment to debatable, speculative, trivial ground. Some people, especially men, worry that sexual harassment is too vague and ill-defined that they personally will suffer if the problem is confronted vigilantly" (pp. 17–18).

Much of the confusion concerning academic harassment can be attributed to the newness of the concept, as well as its status as an actionable offense under the law. If sexual harassment is a legal offense, there is obviously a need for clear and precise definition. It has become increasingly clear that sexual harassment is indeed sex discrimination within the legal definition, and thus prohibited in the academic setting by Title IX of the 1972 Educational Amendments, administered by the Office for Civil Rights (OCR). According to OCR,

Sexual harassment consists of verbal or physical conduct of a sexual nature, imposed on the basis of sex, by an employee or agent of a recipient (of federal funds) that denies, limits, provides different, or conditions the provision of aid, benefits, services, or treatment protected under Title IX. (Califa, 1981)

Other definitions that have been influential in shaping the parameters of the issue have been more denotative. For example, the Association of American Colleges' (AAC) Project on the Status and Education of Women (1978) provided the following list of behaviors:

1. Verbal harassment or abuse
2. Subtle pressure for sexual activity
3. Sexist remarks about a woman's clothing, body, or sexual activities
4. Unnecessary touching, patting or pinching, leering, or ogling at a woman's body
5. Constant brushing against a woman's body
6. Demanding sexual favors accompanied by implied or overt threats, concerning one's job, grades, letters of recommendation, and so forth
7. Physical assault

Writing for the Modern Language Association's Committee on the Status of Women in the Profession, Franklin *et al.* (1981) distinguish between *gender harassment* and other, more dramatic forms of sexual harassment. Gender harassment consists principally of verbal behavior—remarks, jokes, innuendos—directed at someone because of gender, and is not necessarily aimed at eliciting sexual cooperation. Rather, it is directed at a group that the initiator deems inferior, and, as such, resembles racial slurs, epithets, and other, similar behaviors.

Possibly the most clear and useful definition, which has the additional advantage of being data based, is that of the National Advisory Council on Women's Educational Programs. In 1980, based on their national survey, they wrote:

> Academic sexual harassment is the use of authority to emphasize the sexuality or sexual identity of a student in a manner which prevents or impairs that student's full enjoyment of educational benefits, climate or opportunities. . . [Sexual harassment includes]
>
> 1. generalized sexist remarks or behavior;
> 2. inappropriate and offensive, but essentially sanction-free, sexual advances;
> 3. solicitation of sexual activity or other sex-linked behavior by promise of rewards;
> 4. coercion of sexual activity by threat of punishment; and
> 5. assault. (Till, 1980)

Till's (1980) definition presages Franklin *et al.*'s (1981) distinction of gender harassment (Level 1 in the Till system) and condenses the AAC's seven behavioral indicators into five nonoverlapping and distinct categories arranged on a continuum of severity from verbal harassment (Level 1) to physical assault (Level 5). The distinguishing characteristic of Level 2 is its focus on seduction without promise of reward (Level 3) or threat of punishment (Level 4). The precise, non-overlapping nature of the categories lends itself to objective measurement, and is the basis of the Sexual Experiences Questionnaire (Fitzgerald & Shullman, 1985), discussed below.

EXTENT OF SEXUAL HARASSMENT OF STUDENTS

The data concerning the frequency and extent of sexual harassment of college students vary depending on the definition used. When definitions include verbal or gender harassment, the incidence rate reaches close to 70% (Adams, Kottke, & Padgitt, 1983; Lott, Reilly, & Howard, 1982); limiting the definition to explicit sexual advances (either verbal or physical), bribery, or sexual assault predictably lowers the reported incidence. Wilson and Kraus (1983) reported that 8.9% of the female students in their survey had received verbal sexual advances, 13.6% had received (sexual) invitations, 6.4% had been subjected to physical advances, and 2% had received direct sexual bribes. In an earlier study conducted at the Berkeley campus of the University of California, and published in 1982, Benson and Thompson (1982) reported that 30% of senior women reported receiving unwanted sexual attention from at least one male instructor during their four years at college. Dzeich and Weiner (1984) in the most comprehensive treatment of the subject to date, note that this 30% figure appears to be quite reliable.

> These individual campus or organizational studies employed different research techniques and slightly different definitions of sexual harassment. Some used random sampling; others reported on self-selected respondents. . . . Yet despite the variations in the surveys, the results are remarkably similar: again and again 20 to 30 percent of women students report they have been sexually harassed by male faculty during their college years. Campus administrators, student affairs staff, ombudsmen, and consultants who have done workshops on individual campuses affirm the pattern: 20 to 30 percent experience sexual harassment. (pp. 14–15)

Although these figures are markedly lower than the 70–90% estimated in industrial and organizational research, the magnitude of the problem was underscored by these authors when they pointed out that 20% of female students equals over *one million women*. Clearly, the problem is of near-epidemic proportion. Dzeich and Weiner (1984) called for the development of a standardized survey instrument that individual campuses could use to measure frequency so that a national profile can be drawn.

One such instrument is the Sexual Experience Questionnaire (SEQ)
Fitzgerald & Shullman, 1985). Designed to provide an objective and
standardized measurement technique which can be used on any campus and thus provide comparable data across studies, the SEQ is a 28-
item inventory based on Till's (1980) five levels of sexual harassment.
The instrument was constructed to provide scores on five scales:

1. *Gender harassment:* Generalized sexist remarks and behavior
2. *Seductive behavior:* Inappropriate and offensive but essentially
sanction-free sexual advances
3. *Sexual bribery:* Solicitation of sexual activity or other sex-linked
behavior by promise of rewards
4. *Sexual coercion:* Coercion of sexual activity by threat of punishment
5. *Sexual assault:* Gross sexual imposition or assault

The five scales, with a representative item from each, appear in Table
14.1.

TABLE 14.1   Definitions of and Representative Items from the Five Levels
of the SEQ

Level I: Gender harassment
Definition: Generalized sexist remarks and behavior.
Sample Item: "Have you ever been in a situation where a professor or instructor habitu-
ally told suggestive stories or offensive jokes?"
Level 2: Seductive behavior
Definition: Inappropriate and offensive, but essentially sanction-free sexual advances.
Sample Item: "Have you ever been in a situation where a professor or instructor made
unwanted attempts to draw you into a discussion of personal or sexual matters (e.g.,
attempted to discuss or comment on your sex life)?"
Level 3: Sexual bribery
Definition: Solicitation of sexual activity or other sex-linked behavior by promise of
rewards.
Sample Item: "Have you ever felt that you were being subtly bribed with some sort of
reward (e.g., good grades, preferential treatment) to engage in sexual behavior with a
professor or instructor?"
Level 4: Sexual coercion
Definition: Coercion of sexual activity by threat of punishment.
Sample Item: "Have you ever been *directly* threatened or pressured to engage in sexual
activity by threats of punishment or retaliation?"
Level 5: Sexual assault
Definition: Gross sexual imposition or assault.
Sample Item: "Have you ever been in a situation where a professor or instructor made
forceful attempts to touch, fondle, kiss, or grab you?"

One notable feature of the instrument is that all items are written in behavioral terms, and the words "sexual harassment" do not appear until the end of the questionnaire. This avoids the necessity for the subject to make a subjective judgment as to whether or not she has been harassed before she can respond. Much research exists that documents extensive individual differences in the perceptions and personal definition of sexual harassment, which leads to some confusion on the part of the victims as to whether or not they have "really been harassed."

The SEQ avoids this problem by eliminating the subjectivity involved in making such a judgment. For each item, the subjects are instructed to circle the response which most closely describes their own experience. The response options are: (1) Never, (2) Once, and (3) More than once. If the subject circles (2) or (3), they are further instructed to indicate whether the person involved was a man or a woman (or both, if it happened more than once) by circling M, F, or B.

Following the initial construction of the inventory, it was piloted on a sample of 468 students, both graduate and undergraduate, male and female. These students were asked to respond to the SEQ, and to comment on the items, their clarity, relevance, and so forth. This feedback was used to refine the instrument and put it into final form. Initial psychometric analysis, using Cronbach's *alpha,* on a sample of 1,395 subjects (both male and female, graduate and undergraduate) yielded an internal consistency coefficient of .92 for the entire 28-item questionnaire. Test–retest stability on a small subsample of graduate students ($N = 46$) yielded a stability coefficient of .86 over a 2-week period. Thus, the instrument appears to possess acceptable reliability for general use.

Three validity strategies were utilized. First, content validity was built in through basing item construction on Till's (1980) empirically derived categories. Second, the correlation of each item with the criterion item ("I have been sexually harassed") was examined. With the exception of two items on Scale 3 which had very little variance, and one item on Scale 1, all items were significantly positively correlated with the criterion item. In addition, the average item–criterion correlations for the five levels of sexual harassment conformed, with some exception, to theoretical expectation, ranging from .15 for Level 1 to .37 for Level 4. [The coefficient for Level 5 was lower than expected ($r = .20$) most likely because several items showed very little variance.] In general, it appears that the instrument possesses an acceptable degree of criterion-related validity.

Finally, factor analysis was performed to examine the structure of the instrument and the dimensions of the construct. An alpha-factor analysis with a varimax rotation was utilized, yielding three meaningful factors accounting for approximately 50% of the total variance. Factor 1, which included all of the Level 2 items (seduction) as well as the Level 5 items (sexual imposition/assault), accounted for slightly over 27% of the variance and was labeled Sexual Harassment. Factor 2, accounting for about 9% of the variance, included most of the items in Levels 3 and 4 (bribery and threat, respectively) and was labeled Sexual Coercion. The final factor, accounting for somewhat over 7% of the variance, included all items in Level 1, and was thus labeled Gender Harassment. In general, the factor structure appears substantively interpretable and theoretically meaningful, thus lending further support to the overall construct validity of the inventory.

Using this final version of the inventory and a stratified random sample of 902 undergraduate and graduate student women enrolled in over 70 academic disciplines, Fitzgerald, Shullman, et al. (1986) obtained the following results. Four hundred and forty-eight women, or 50%, answered at least one of the items in the positive direction. The items, and their percentage of endorsement, separately by graduate and undergraduate women, appear in Table 14.2.

As expected, the most frequently reported situations were those involving gender harassment, or seductive behavior. Of the ten most frequently endorsed items, all were Level 1 or Level 2 situations. However, over 8% of the sample reported having been subjected to unwanted stroking or fondling, 8% had been directly propositioned, and nearly 5% of the total sample had been either subtly bribed or threatened with retaliation for refusing sexual advances. Lest these percentages seem trivial, it should be pointed out that 5% generalizes to hundreds of thousands of the college women in this country. Given the severity of many of these situations (e.g., touching, fondling, propositions, threats), it was surprising to find that only 4% of the sample indicated that they believed they had been sexually harassed! It is an unfortunate tribute to the strength of the socialization process that less than half of these women who had been propositioned or fondled by their professors labeled their experiences as sexual harassment.

Another form of the inventory (SEQ–F2) is available for use with employed women (Shullman & Fitzgerald, 1985). A complete description of the research program is available in Fitzgerald, Shullman et al. (1986). These instruments show promise of providing researchers a reliable and valid measurement technique for large-scale investigations of sexual harassment and for reliable comparisons across studies.

TABLE 14.2   Percentage of Graduate and Undergraduate Student Women Who Endorsed Each Item on the SEQ

Item	Undergraduate women	Graduate women
1. Treated "differently" because I am a woman	47.5	47.3
2. Suggestive stories and offensive jokes	42.3	38.0
3. Sexist remarks about women's career options	38.0	36.0
4. Crudely sexual remarks	31.0	26.0
5. Staring, leering, or ogling	27.0	23.8
6. Seductive behavior (requests for dates, drinks, backrubs, etc.)	20.0	20.6
7. Seductive remarks	17.2	21.6
8. Unwanted sexual attention	16.0	19.0
9. Suggestive or pornographic teaching materials	16.0	15.0
10. Unwanted discussion of personal or sexual matters	10.0	12.1
11. Attempts to establish a romantic sexual relationship	8.0	12.0
12. Unwanted stroking or fondling	8.0	8.6
13. Propositions	7.5	8.6
14. Subtle offers of reward	5.0	3.8
15. Subtle threats	5.0	3.7
16. Forceful attempts to kiss or grab	2.5	3.7
17. Punished for refusal	2.5	2.0
18. Direct bribes	<1.0	<1.0
19. Rewarded for social or sexual cooperation	<1.0	<1.0
20. Direct threats of punishment for refusal	<1.0	<1.0
21. Engaged in unwanted sexual behavior due to promise of reward or threat of punishment	<1.0	<1.0

Note. Five items, each describing situations of extreme physical harassment, were not endorsed by any of the sample. $N = 903$ (graduate = 351, undergraduate = 552). From Fitzgerald, Shullman *et al.* (1986).

THE EFFECTS OF SEXUAL HARASSMENT ON WOMEN STUDENTS

Contrary to much contemporary mythology, which asserts that sexual harassment is a trivial matter, or an instance of "natural" erotic byplay between the sexes, evidence exists that sexual harassment can result in serious psychological and practical consequences for women students. According to Dzeich and Weiner (1984), such harassment often "forces a student to forfeit work, research, educational comfort, or even career. Professors withhold legitimate opportunities from those who resist, or students withdraw rather than pay certain prices" (p. 10). The practical costs of harassment to the victim are quite stunning, and have been documented by both survey and qualitative research efforts. For example, a 1983 study conducted at Harvard University, and reported in the *Chronicle of Higher Education* indicated that 15% of the graduate and 12% of the undergraduate student victims in this survey changed their major or educational program as a result of the harassment. Similarly, Meek and Lynch (1983) reported, "[A] common reaction to sexual harassment is an attempt to escape the situation in order to avoid the harasser. Some students do this by dropping courses; others withdraw from school; still others change majors or alter career plans because of harassment" (p. 30). Similar reactions were reported by Till (1980), while 13% of the women students in the Adams *et al.* (1983) survey said they had avoided taking a class or working with certain professors because of the risk of being subjected to sexual advances.

The psychological consequences can be even more devastating. Sandler (1981) reported that emotional and physical reactions to academic sexual harassment include depression, decreased motivation, listlessness, a sense of helplessness, insomnia, headaches, and other physiological complaints. Similarly, in a recent survey conducted at the Davis campus of the University of California, 43% of the undergraduate and 87% of the graduate student victims reported that the harassment had created an intimidating, hostile, or offensive environment, while 40% of the overall sample indicated that they felt embarrassed, uneasy, tense, frustrated, pressured, and nervous (Whitmore, 1983). Clearly, the consequences of sexual harassment are quite serious, and provide support for the notion that such experiences constitute a formidable barrier to women's career development.

THEORETICAL FRAMEWORKS FOR UNDERSTANDING SEXUAL HARASSMENT

Although much of the extant research on sexual harassment has been descriptive in nature, some theoretical work has recently appeared. Tangri, Burt, and Johnson (1982) proposed three alternative models of sexual harassment: the natural/biological model, the organizational model, and the socio cultural model.

The natural/biological model posits that what has been called sexual harassment is, in actuality, natural sexual attraction between the sexes. This model suggests that harassing behavior is not *meant* or *intended* to be offensive, but is merely a logical result of biological urges, possibly reflecting men's stronger sex drive. Tangri *et al.* (1982) pointed out that if this model is true, certain conditions should be present; for example, victims should be similar to their harassers in age, race, and occupational status, they should be unmarried, the behaviors should resemble courtship behaviors, and should stop if the victim shows disinterest. The victims should be flattered by the behavior or, at least, not offended. According to this view, sexual harassment is really most appropriately viewed as courtship behavior.

The organizational model asserts that sexual harassment results from the opportunities presented by power and authority relations that derive from the hierarchical structure of organizations. Thus, though harassment is seen as a power issue, the power is organizational and not personal in nature. "Since work organizations are characterized by vertical stratification, individuals can use their power and position to extort sexual gratification from their subordinates. Although typically males harass females, in principle, it is possible for females to sexually harass males. It is less likely only because women tend to be employed in occupations subordinate to men" (Tangri *et al.*, 1982, p. 37).

The sociocultural model asserts that sexual harassment is only one manifestation of the larger patriarchal system in which men are the dominant group. Thus, sexual harassment is an example of men asserting their *personal* power, based on their gender; according to this model, *gender* would be a better predictor of both victim and initiator status than is organizational position. Women should be much more likely to be victims, especially in nontraditional occupations in which they are somewhat of a rarity.

Tangri and her colleagues derived several hypotheses from each model and tested them with the data from the U.S. Merit Protection Board study described above. Although not clear-cut, their results provide more support for Models 2 and 3 than for Model 1. These authors concluded that sexual harassment is possibly multidetermined but also that the base rates are so high that it may not be possible to develop reliable predictors. They noted, "If sexual harassment is as widespread as the results of the MSPB survey indicate, it may approximate a random event in women's working lives—something that is highly likely to happen at some time with just when, where, and how being so multidetermined that prediction is difficult. This very fact supports the cultural model in some ways, but it also implies that finding empirical support for the cultural model will not be easy, if only because few, if any, circumstances exist where the dominant culture does not exert its influence" (p. 52–53).

Gutek and Morasch (1982) proposed another perspective. They suggested that sexual harassment of women at work is a product of *sex role spillover*, defined as the carry-over into the workplace of gender-based expectations of behavior. This spillover, predicated on skewed sex ratios in the workplace, is of two types. Women who are employed in nontraditional occupations, in which they operate under a "token" status, will be treated as role deviates; their sex will be particularly salient because of its singularity, and they will be treated differently from their male counterparts. According to Gutek and Morasch (1982), such women are aware of this differential treatment, and they think it is directed at them as women. They should be more likely to report sexual harassment as a problem at work. On the other hand, women in female-dominated work will experience a different kind of sex role spillover. Their work role parallels their sex role. Since most of the workers are female and they are treated similarly, they should be unaware that their treatment is based on their sex. This group should be less likely to report sexual harassment as a problem at work.

Although Gutek and Morasch (1982) interpreted their data as providing some support for their ideas, it should be pointed out that their notions are not incompatible with the sociocultural model of sexual harassment. They stated, "According to the power differential (i.e., sociocultural, in the Tangri *et al.* system) hypothesis, sexual harassment will always be perceived as sexual harassment" (p. 72). The basis for this assertion is not clear, as they provided no referent for their contention, nor was such a statement located in an extensive search of the literature. Rather, the confusing and mystifying nature of much of the more subtle forms of sexual harassment appears to be the rule. Therefore, the finding by Gutek and Morasch that women in nontraditional jobs are more likely to label a given behavior as sexual harassment does not bear on the power differential hypothesis; this sensitivity to the issue most likely reflects these women's higher levels of education, self-esteem, and nontraditional attitudes toward women's roles.

This is not to imply that the sex ratio of jobs is an insignificant consideration. Data indicating the greater incidence of harassment of women in nontraditional areas is available from many sources (see, for example, Till, 1980, and others). Rather, it is suggested here that the power differential hypothesis, as articulated in the sociocultural model of Tangri and her colleagues (1982) subsumes the sex role spillover hypothesis in its formulation.

CONCLUSION

Although the theoretical models discussed above are promising, much remains to be done in this area before a clear understanding of the complex dynamics of sexual harassment emerges. Interestingly enough, this appears to be one of the rare areas in which there are more data than theory! After reviewing both available data and theory, we conclude that sexual harassment is a pervasive and noxious experience, the ultimate but inevitable outcome of the persistent inability (or refusal) to separate women's sexual/biological role from their work role. Often more subtle than the "traditional" forms of discrimination (i.e., selection, promotion, and compensation, its effects are even more pernicious, none the less so because of the low level of awareness on the part of many victims that they are indeed victims. As Fitzgerald and Shullman (1985) suggested, "It would seem to be the ultimate victimization to be sexually insulted, manipulated, or exploited not only without one's consent, but even without one's awareness—a situation not unlike that shared by many battered women and victims of acquaintance or date rape" (p. 7). In this context, we submit that studies examining *perceptions* of sexual harassment (e.g., "In your opinion, is this situation sexual harassment or not?") are to some degree asking the wrong question and may well lead to a "blaming the victim" phenomenon. For example, Reilly, Carpenter, Dull, & Bartlett (1982) found that subjects at the Santa Barbara campus of the University of California were much less likely to label a situation as sexual harassment when the woman was portrayed as provocatively dressed, or as having a previous relationship with her harasser. (The parallel with rape research is quite striking here, as are other aspects of the sexual harassment phenomenon.) Other studies seem to imply that if a behavior is not *perceived* to be harassment, then it is not. Such interpretations are clearly incorrect. Sexual harassment is well defined in legal terms, and the behaviors defined as harassment are just that, whatever one's "perceptions" may be. Research in this area should take care to point this out, lest important and theoretically meaningful data on individual differences in perceptions be misconstrued to dismiss or trivialize this extremely important barrier to women's career adjustment.

IV

SUMMARY AND RECOMMENDATIONS

SUMMARY AND IMPLICATIONS FOR THEORY, RESEARCH, AND INTERVENTION

The present chapter will summarize and integrate the preceding chapters focusing on issues in women's career choice and career adjustment. The discussion will focus on needs for further research and theory development and for interventions having the potential to facilitate the career development of women. As in the preceding chapters, the discussion will be organized under the headings "Career Choice" and "Career Adjustment."

CAREER CHOICE

Chapters 1 through 9 reviewed issues in and factors influencing the career choices of women. Problematic aspects of the choices of women included underutilization of their abilities, their overconcentration in a small number of traditionally female-dominated (and also generally low-paying) occupations and resulting underrepresentation in an extensive variety of traditionally male-dominated (and generally higher-paying) fields, and their avoidance of coursework in mathematics, resulting in externally forced limitations in their career options.

As stated in the summary of Part I, there seems ample reason to contend that most women, like most men, should be encouraged to pursue rewarding careers. Men have never had to "choose between home and family," and the possibility of combining important life roles is just as vital to women as it is to men. In their pursuit of careers, women's choices should represent better matching of their individual characteristics to the level and nature of the chosen field. The waste of female talent and ability when women seriously underutilize their abilities in career choices is a significant personal and societal problem and needs to be counteracted. Women's career choices should be made in the context of a broad range of perceived and real *options* rather than by default—thus, options should more often include careers in traditionally male-dominated fields, particularly those in mathematical, scientific, and technical areas. Women's career choices, then, should utilize rather than waste women's abilities and talents and should represent the full range of occupational possibilities rather than the restricted range of female-dominated professions and "pink-collar" jobs.

Given these general goals, there are several areas needing further theoretical and research attention. There is as yet no satisfactory theory of the career development of women. Although theories such as those of Holland, Roe, Super, and others have some relevance to the understanding of women's career behavior, they were developed with men rather than women in mind. Although approaches such as those of Astin (1984), Farmer (1985), Gottfredson (1981), Hackett and Betz (1981), and Harmon (1977) represent worthy attempts to address the lack of work focusing specifically on women, additional and, in particular, more comprehensive theories are needed. Further advances in our knowledge of women's career development will require theoretical innovation and synthesis.

Probably the most comprehensive attempts to date to explain women's career choices from the standpoint of empirical data are the multidimensional models of Farmer (1985) and of Fitzgerald and Betz, as tested by Fassinger (1985). These models have the advantage of incorporating available research findings yet of advancing knowledge by postulating and testing causal relationships among systems of variables previously examined only in bivariate relationship to one another. Although research must begin at a relatively simple level, the most important phenomena require multivariate explanations. Thus, research investigating women's career choices must now rely more on multivariate models and analyses. In addition, use of methods providing causal inferential possibilities advances theory development; since theory development can be said to begin with nomological networks explicating constructs or other important phenomena (Betz & Weiss, 1976; Cronbach & Meehl, 1955), a causal or structural diagram provides the basis of a theory of behavior. Thus, more sophisticated methods of analysis will facilitate the use of appropriately complex, multivariate examinations and will also provide an impetus for new theory construction.

In addition to theory construction and explication, research investigating the following topics is needed. First, further work on women's continued avoidance of many male-dominated careers is needed. Second, the impact of current social changes on young women is not well understood. For example, there is more emphasis on the work role of the adult woman but, it seems, without a corresponding reduction in emphasis on the importance of home and family roles. Thus, the extent to which young women perceive a new cultural imperative of combining full-time career pursuits with the traditional responsibility for managing home and children needs investigation, as do the potential effects of such perceptions on career choices and mental health. Also needing study are the problems of conflicts in a society which continues to teach young women that their worth is contingent on the value of a man; this and other detrimental aspects of the female role cannot be assumed to have lessened in impact just because a new role has been introduced. Clearly, further research concerned with factors influencing the development of strong, noncontingent self-concepts is needed. It is the belief of the present authors that truly free, truly "fitting" career choices are possible only in the context of self-knowledge and positive self-valuation.

Given these goals, the research reviewed was summarized as suggesting some facilitators of and barriers to women's career development. Table 9.1 summarized those factors *generally* found to enhance the quality of women's career choices and the extent of their career achievements. In examining the table, it should be noted that family background characteristics (or any other variables) found to characterize career-oriented women or women in male-dominated fields obviously do not characterize all such women. There are certainly many highly achievement- and career-oriented women whose mothers were homemakers, who did not obtain high levels of education, etc. However, these factors do characterize women in general and, as such, offer the best odds for the enhancement of women's career development.

A final point regarding Table 9.1 is that the factors influencing women's career development will almost surely change as societal attitudes and norms change and as increasing numbers of women enter the work force. If girls and women, like boys and men, begin to assume that career pursuits will be an integral part of their lives, we may see changes in the nature of the influences on women's career choices. As summarized by Osipow (1983), the rapidity and magnitude of social change render definitive conclusions and attempts at generalization unwarranted. Thus, the study of women's career choices will be a continuing and challenging endeavor.

IMPLICATIONS FOR COUNSELING WOMEN

Although further research, particularly integrative in nature, on the factors influencing women's career development is needed, several recommendations for educational and counseling interventions can also be made. First, previous chapters reviewed the issues regarding sexism and sex bias in the educational system (Chapter 4) and in counseling (Chapter 5). Of particular importance as well are the theoretical issues reviewed in Chapter 5, for example, the theoretical models of Gottfredson (1981) and Astin (1984), and the concept of the "null environment" (Freeman, 1975) discussed in Chapter 4.

As discussed in Chapter 4, women develop in a sexist, biased environment that begins early in life to "stack the deck" in favor of stereotyped, traditionally feminine career options and against nontraditional choices, choices which in many cases represent the best "match" with individual difference variables. The failure to counteract this biased, or in Freeman's (1975) terms "null" environment, is a form of discrimination against women. Although humanistic psychology has long endorsed the ideal of individual self-determination, and thus has tried to avoid "undue influence" over clients, psychology also needs to confront the fact that leaving a women to "do what she thinks best" actually results in abandoning her to fight societal sex stereotypes alone—society is only too ready to influence her in stereotypic directions. Thus, failure to actively support women's career development may in effect be a vote for traditional roles and occupations. It is, in essence, impossible to remain neutral, so the actions or lack of action of psychologists and counselors, educators, and organizational consultants have massive and undeniable effects.

Keeping in mind, then, the necessity for action on the part of the counseling profession, a number of recommendations for counseling practice have been made by Betz (1982) and Fitzgerald (1980, 1986). Particularly important guidelines for career counseling, as suggested by Betz (1982), include the following:

1. Counselors should be knowledgeable in the area of women's career development, including knowledge of research on factors influencing that development and of counselor and test biases which perpetuate stereotyped roles and limited options for women.

2. Counselors should avoid sexist assumptions and sex-restrictive vocational interest inventories.

3. Counselors should actively encourage the development of nontraditional interests and competencies, so that choices will be truly "free."

4. Counselors should in particular encourage continuation in mathematics, so that career options will not be prematurely and unnecessarily restricted.

5. Counselors should counteract socialized stereotypes and beliefs which serve to restrict a woman's range of options, for example, "I can't do both," "I can't do math," and "Highly achieving women lose their femininity."

6. Counselors should help women deal with realistic issues and fears, for example, "But I'll be the only woman in that profession— how will I survive?," and "But I didn't think that women could be apprentices."

7. Counselors should use materials which help to expand rather than restrict a woman's range of options, for example, nonsexist interest inventories, vocational card sorts (Dewey, 1974), and occupational information.

8. Counselors should encourage women to obtain quality education and/or training and to gain needed skills in job-hunting, resume-writing, interviewing, assertion, and information-seeking.

9. Counselors and educators should support women studying in null (or worse) environments by helping them locate support systems, role models, and mentors.

10. Counselors should help women deal with discrimination, sexual harassment, etc., when necessary.

For purposes of increasing interests and competencies in nontraditional areas, the model shown in Fig. 7.1 should be recalled. Specifically, Hackett and Betz' (1981) application of Bandura's (1977) theory of self-efficacy expectations in women's career development implies four sources of information useful in increasing women's career-related self-efficacy expectations. Self-efficacy expectations can be strengthened by facilitating performance accomplishments, providing exposure to female role models, assisting girls and women to manage, if not conquer, anxiety with respect to nontraditional domains, and providing active support and encouragement of girls' and women's efforts to increase the extent and range of their feelings of competency.

For example, application of self-efficacy theory to the improvement of mathematics-related self-efficacy expectations would include providing opportunities for successful experiences learning and performing math, providing females with models of mastery of mathematics, for example, women mathematicians and engineers as guest speakers in schools, providing support and encouragement for math-approach behaviors, and helping women learn to manage math-related anxiety and fear.

In addition to these recommendations, there is ample research evidence now to support the contention that education is *the key* to improving women's place in the labor force. Thus, attention to increasing sex equity in education (see Klein & Simonson, 1984, for a number of suggestions for doing this) is particularly crucial. Finally, further discussion of ways in which counselors and educators can facilitate the career development of women can be found in articles by Fitzgerald (1986), Rodenstein, Pfleger, and Colangelo (1977), and Stake (1981).

As women make better career choices, it can be hoped that their adjustment vocationally will also be facilitated. At present, however, the following areas of emphasis in the investigation and improvement of vocational adjustment are of particular importance.

ISSUES IN VOCATIONAL ADJUSTMENT

As with vocational psychology in general, the literature on women's vocational behavior has until recently been concerned almost exclusively with choice; only in the last several years has systematic attention been paid to the career development of women after they enter the world of work. Although research and writing has focused on specific "hot issues" (e.g., discrimination, pay inequities, and so forth) and at least one book has appeared which discusses a broader range of work behaviors (i.e., Nieva & Gutek, 1981), most of this work has taken place within the framework of industrial psychology, economics, and occupational sociology. To our knowledge, the present volume represents the first attempt to systematically examine what is known about women's career adjustment, cast within the frame of traditional vocational psychology (Crites, 1969; Walsh & Osipow, 1983a,b). Given this state of affairs, it is not surprising to find that the research in this area is less mature and characterized by what can perhaps best be described as a certain "unevenness" of quality. This last section of the book will attempt to briefly summarize what has been reviewed in the preceding chapters, to identify salient research *issues* (as opposed to conclusions), and to discuss possible approaches to intervention.

Chapters 10 and 11 represented an initial attempt to examine women's postchoice vocational behavior in terms of the two preeminent adjustment paradigms: the *process* model of Crites (1969, 1976) and the more *content*-oriented, trait-and-factor approach of the Work Adjustment Project (Lofquist & Dawis, 1969; Dawis & Lofquist, 1983). Probably the most parsimonious conclusion that can be drawn from the research in this area is that, while women appear very similar to men in terms of the fundamental psychological *processes* of vocational adjustment, they do face unique barriers, and they achieve far lower levels of reward. It seems reasonable to state that, in process terms, women as a group are as vocationally adjusted as men; however, with respect to the traditional *outcome* criteria, women fare far less well, at least in terms of economic and organizational success. (The data on satisfaction are, as we noted above, so riddled with conceptual and methodological problems that it is not possible to draw conclusions at this time.)

The primary reason for this situation appears to inhere in the persistent and pernicious intertwining of women's sexual/biological role with the role of worker, in a manner that is simply not salient for men. It is this one factor which most clearly differentiates the career development and vocational behavior of the sexes. Support for this assertion can be found in every area of the vocational psychology of women. With respect to adjustment issues, it arises in the effect of sex role stereotypes on perceptions of performance, the coping roles that are sometimes adopted by women, the difficulties posed by role overload and role conflict (variables practically unknown in the vocational psychology of men) and, most dramatically and shockingly, in the manner in which millions of women are sexually harassed, both in academia and on the job. This is to name but a few.

Chapters 12 through 14 examined in-depth three areas in which the sex role–work role interface appears most salient: the home–work place interplay, with particular emphasis on the effect of women's working on their traditional responsibilities, as well as the reverse; the particular issues raised by living and working in a dual-career relationship; and the incidence and consequences of sexual harrassment. We conclude that, while there is no clear-cut evidence that a woman's employment has any detrimental effects on her husband and/or children, the reverse, unfortunately is not true. While full-time employment confers many benefits on women, both tangible and psychological, it is still true that most women who supposedly work "full-time" in actuality work a great deal more than that, particularly when there are children involved. The practical and psychological impossibility of satisfying two complete, separate, and often opposing, roles is, we feel, not fully appreciated in the literature, although some interesting work has appeared that examines coping mechanisms.

The body of research that has emerged examining dual-career families represents, in some ways, the most well-developed effort to investigate the home–career interface, at least for that essentially middle-class subset of working couples who qualify for this rubric. Even so, the work has not progressed much beyond the classification stage and is often plagued by definitional imprecision and confusion.

Nowhere is fusion of sex role with work role demonstrated with greater clarity than in the emerging literature on sexual harassment. It is here that the issue stands in bold relief, clearly demonstrating the great personal and societal cost of the inability or refusal to view women in nonsexual terms. We agree with Tangri *et al.* (1982) that the base rate incidence of sexual harassment is so great that attempting to predict its occurrence is probably not useful. The best prediction, quite simply, is that it will occur. Even so, this is an issue that is not yet understood, or often even acknowledged by either the public or the scholarly community. This was demonstrated dramatically, if informally, when an eminent psychologist remarked in a discussion of the present volume, "Sexual harassment? What does that have to do with women's career development?" Rather than continuing to focus on incidence rate and prediction, the research in this area might profitably progress to demonstrations of psychological and practical costs, investigation of harassment-supportive attitudes, and identification of effective coping responses. Studies of men who harass, while difficult to conduct, might eventually prove particularly enlightening. [See Fitzgerald, Gold, Ormerod, & Weitzman (1986) for a beginning effort.]

METHODOLOGICAL ISSUES

While the sex role–work role interaction clearly appears to be the most salient theoretical issue in the vocational adjustment of women, several other, more methodological issues require attention. The first is the persistent tendency of many researchers to ignore individual difference variables when examining the vocational behavior of women. In particular, studies conducted from a sociological perspective tend to ignore much of the work on "person" variables, preferring to focus on more structural considerations. Other investigations rely too heavily on economic formulations of behavior to the detriment of other, more psychological variables. Finally, as Nieva and Gutek (1981) pointed out, the work variable is often only weakly operationalized, usually through a simple working/not working dichotomy, occasionally enriched by a part-time/full-time distinction. The result is a plethora of "broad-band" investigations which are not only not useful for understanding the behavior of individual women, but have the additional disadvantage of often conflicting with one another, due to inadequate conceptualization of the independent variables.

We suggest that this persistent tendency to "lump" women together is likely not unrelated to the power of the sex role spillover (sex role–work role interface) discussed above. The mere fact that a woman is working is apparently assumed by some researchers to be powerful enough to render uninteresting or impotent any other variable. While many studies, particularly in the more classical vocational psychology tradition, do indeed include sophisticated analysis of individual differences, we are struck by the frequent absence, in our review, of such analysis. This is a major shortcoming in the literature.

A related issue is the difficulty that is often experienced by researchers in attempting to operationalize their *dependent* variables. As was pointed out in Chapter 12, the research that is labeled as investigating the "consequences of maternal employment" can be more accurately characterized as the consequences of inadequate day care. The implications of the former rubric are much different than are those of the latter.

Finally, we suggest that the *choice* of what variable to study makes some fairly clear value statements, as well as influencing our body of knowledge in systematic, if nonconscious ways. Smith (1981) made this point when she suggested that by choosing to study mothering instead of, say, fathering, researchers unconsciously reinforce the motherhood mandate. An equally apt example is the research on how women "cope" with role overload. By choosing to study women's coping behavior, we make it quite clear where we believe the responsibility for the problem lies. While we are not suggesting that such research is unimportant, we do believe that it needs to be balanced by other sorts of inquiry. Gilbert's (1985) discussion of dual-career husbands and the Catalyst/RESOURCE studies of organizational response to dual-career families are examples of such work, making clear as they do that this is a *societal* issue, not just a *women's* issue.

INTERVENTIONS

As Nieva and Gutek (1981) have noted, "the model that one adopts to explain women's work situation dictates one's prescription for change." They identified four models or paradigms, each of which leads to differing interventions. The *individual model* suggests that deficiencies in women's vocational adjustment are rooted in personal deficiencies in women themselves (i.e., in education, skills, or other work related behaviors and attitudes). This conception would logically suggest that intervention strategies are most appropriately focused on self-improvement training programs, and it is, indeed, this approach that is currently most widespread.

In contrast, the *structural model* suggests that the problem lies in the structure of the work organization, rather than in the individual. Thus, sex segregation of occupations and jobs, blocked career paths, and all forms of sex discrimination are the appropriate targets of intervention under this model. It is here that affirmative action programs, human resource development programs, and relevant legislation come into play.

The *sex role* model posits that the differential vocational experience of men and women is a result of societally sanctioned sex role norms, a position most similar to the one proposed in the current volume. Interventions for change would thus focus on relaxing sex role definitions, enlarging masculine involvement in the domestic sphere, and generally attempting to move toward a more androgynous model of human behavior. While admirable in purpose, and probably eventually necessary for fundamental change to occur, such transitions are an extremely long-term proposition.

The final model is labeled as the *intergroup model* and posits that, by virtue of group membership, the interaction between the sexes is characterized by factors related to such membership. The result is that intergroup differences are emphasized, while between-group similarities are downplayed or ignored. In addition, one group is viewed as clearly superior to the other. Although this description appears to capture well the views of many, it is difficult to suggest interventions to alleviate the situation. Complete homogenization of the sexes is likely neither possible nor desirable—however, a research focus on gender similarities might produce a healthy complement to the body of work that seeks to examine gender differences.

It is suggested here that the four types of interventions, rather than being in any sense mutually exclusive, are actually complementary. Training programs for women (Fitzgerald & Shullman, 1984), organizational interventions (Nieva & Gutek, 1981), sex role flexibility, and strategies aimed at effecting fundamental social change are all necessary to improve women's vocational adjustment.

In closing this chapter, and this book, we are reminded of the dedication of a recent volume on the psychology of women. It read, "To every woman who didn't get what she deserved." The fundamental aim of all work in the vocational psychology of women is, in some way, focused on finally eradicating the situation that stimulated that inscription.

REFERENCES

Abrahams, B., Feldman, S. S., & Nash, S. C. (1978). Sex role, self-concept, and sex role attitudes: Enduring personality characteristics or adaptations to changing life situations? *Developmental Psychology*, **14**, 399–400.

Abramowitz, C. V., & Dokecki, P. R. (1977). The politics of clinical judgment: Early empirical returns. *Psychological Bulletin*, **84**, 460–476.

Abramowitz, S. I., & Abramowitz, C. V. (1978). *Sex bias in psychotherapy: A review of reviews.* Paper presented at the meeting of the Western Psychological Association, San Francisco, April.

Adams, J. (1984). Women at West Point: A three year perspective. *Sex Roles*, **11**, 525–542.

Adams, J. W., Kottke, J. L., & Padgitt, J. S. (1983). Sexual harassment of university students. *Journal of College Student Personnel*, **24**, 484–490.

Ahrons, C. R. (1976). Counselors' perceptions of career images of women. *Journal of Vocational Behavior*, **8**, 197–207.

Albrecht, S. L., Bahr, H. M., & Chadwick, B. A. (1977). Public stereotyping of roles, personality characteristics, and occupations. *Sociology and Social Research*, **61**, 223–240.

Aldous, J. (Ed.) (1982). *Two paychecks: Life in dual-earner families*, Beverly Hills: Sage.

Allport, G. (1954). *The nature of prejudice.* Cambridge, MA: Addison-Wesley.

Almquist, E. M. (1974). Sex stereotypes in occupational choice: The case for college women. *Journal of Vocational Behavior*, **5**, 13–21.

Almquist, E. M. (1979). Black women and the pursuit of equality. In J. Freeman (Ed.), *Women: A feminist perspective* (pp. 430–450). Palo Alto, CA: Mayfield.

Almquist, E. M., & Angrist, S. S. (1970). Career salience and atypicality of occupational choice among college women. *Journal of Marriage and Family*, **32**, 242–249.

Almquist, E. M., & Angrist, S. S. (1971). Role model influences on college women's career aspirations. *Merrill-Palmer Quarterly*, **17**, 263–279.

Altman, S. L., & Grossman, F. K. (1977). Women's career plans and maternal employment. *Psychology of women Quarterly*, **1**, 365–376.

AMEG Commission on Sex Bias in Measurement (1977). A case history of change: A review of responses to the challenge of sex bias in interest inventories. *Measurement and Evaluation in Guidance*, **10**, 148–152.

American Medical Association (1977). Undergraduate medical education. *Journal of the American Medical Association*, **238**, 2767–2780.

Anastasi, A. (1958). *Differential psychology* (3rd ed.). New York: Macmillan.

Anastasi, A. (1982). *Psychological testing* (5th ed.). New York: Macmillan.

Andberg, W. I., Follett, C. V., & Hendel, D. D. (1979). Career influences, educational experiences, and professional attitudes of women and men in veterinary medicine. *Journal of College Student Personnel*, **20**, 158–165.

Anderson, J. (1972). A new way of sharing—one job for two. *San Francisco Chronicle*, **Spring.**

Angle, H. L., & Wissman, D. A. (1983). Work experience, age and gender discrimination. *Social Science Quarterly*, **64**, 66–84.

Angrist, S. S. (1972). Variations in women's adult aspirations during college. *Journal of Marriage and Family*, **34**, 465–468.

Angrist, S. S. (1974). The study of sex roles. In C. Perucci & D. Targ (Eds.), *Marriage and the family: A critical analysis and proposal for change* (pp. 182–188). New York: McKay.

Angrist, S. S., & Almquist, E. M. (1975). *Careers and contingencies.* New York: Dunellen.

Antill, J. K., & Cunningham, J. D. (1979). Self-esteem as a function of masculinity in both sexes. *Journal of Consulting and Clinical Psychology, 47,* 783–785.

Arkin, R. M., & Johnson, K. S. (1980). Effects of increased occupational participation by women on androgynous and non-androgynous individuals' ratings of occupational attractiveness. *Sex Roles, 6,* 593–606.

Arkin, W., & Dobrovsky, W. R. (1978). Job sharing, In R. Rapoport and R. Rapoport (Eds.), *Working couples.* London: Routledge & Kegan Paul.

Armstrong, J. M. (1985). A national assessment of participation and achievement of courses in mathematics. In S. F. Chipman, L. R. Brush, & D. M. Wilson (Eds.), *Women and mathematics* (pp. 59–94). Hillsdale, NJ: Erlbaum.

Arvey, R. D. (1979a). Unfair discrimination in the employment interview: Legal and psychological aspects. *Psychological Bulletin, 86,* 736–765.

Arvey, R. D. (1979b). *Fairness in selecting employees.* Reading, MA: Addison-Wesley.

Astin, A. W. (1977). *Four critical years.* San Francisco: Jossey-Bass.

Astin, H. S. (1967). Factors associated with the participation of women doctorates in the labor force. *Personnel and Guidance Journal, 46,* 240–246.

Astin, H. S. (1968). Career development of girls during the high school years. *Journal of Counseling Psychology, 15,* 536–540.

Astin, H. S. (1969). *The woman doctorate in America.* New York: Russell Sage Foundation.

Astin, H. S. (1984). The meaning of work in women's lives: A sociopsychological model of career choice and work behavior. *The Counseling Psychologist, 12,* 117–126.

Astin, H. S., & Bayer, A. E. (1972). Sex discrimination in academe. *Educational Record, 54,* 101–118.

Astin, H. S., & Myint, T. (1971). Career development of young women during the post high school years. *Journal of Counseling Psychology Monograph, 18,* 369–393.

Atkinson, J. W. (Ed.) (1958). *Motives in fantasy, action and society.* Princeton, NJ: Van Nostrand-Reinhold.

Atkinson, J. W., & Feather, N. T. (Eds.)(1966). *A theory of achievement motivation.* New York: Wiley.

Atkinson, J., & Huston, T. L. (1984). Sex role orientation and division of labor early in marriage. *Journal of Personality and Social Psychology, 46,* 330–345.

Atkinson, J. W., & Raynor, J. O. (Eds.) (1974). *Motivation and achievement.* Washington, DC: Winston.

Axelson, L. (1963). The marital adjustment and marital role definitions of husbands of working and nonworking wives. *Marriage and Family Living,* **May.**

Bachtold, L. M. (1976). Personality characteristics of women of distinction. *Psychology of Women Quarterly, 1,* 70–78.

Bachtold. L. M., & Werner, E. E. (1970). Personality profiles of gifted women: Psychologists. *American Psychologist, 25,* 234–243.

Bachtold, L. M., & Werner, E. E. (1972). Personality characteristics of women scientists. *Psychological Reports, 36,* 391–396.

Bachtold, L. M., & Werner, E. E. (1973). Personality profiles of creative women. *Perceptual and Motor Skills, 36,* 311–319.

Bagchi, P. (1976). Job sharing. *Peninsula Magazine,* (4), 12–15.

Bahr, S. J. (1974). Effects on power and division of labor in the family. In L. W. Hoffman & F. I. Nie (Eds.), *Working mothers.* San Francisco: Jossey-Bass.

Bailey, S., & Burrell, B. (1981). Harvard graduate women's unequal career development. *Second Century Radcliffe News,* **January,** 15–17.

Bailyn, L. (1970). Career and family orientations of husbands and wives in relation to marital happiness. *Human Relations*, **23**, 97–113.

Bakan, D. (1966). *The duality of human existence: An essay on psychology and religion.* Chicago: Rand McNally.

Baldridge, L. (1977). For some it's a tale of two home cities. *Chicago Daily News*, **March 25**, p. 51.

Bandura, A. (1977). Self-efficacy: Toward a unifying theory of behavioral change. *Psychological Review*, **84**, 191–215.

Bannon, J. A., & Southern, M. L. (1980). Father-absent women: Self-concept and modes of relating to men. *Sex Roles*, **6**, 75–84.

Barnes v. Costle, 561 F.2d at 983, 989, n. 49 (D. C. Circuit 1977).

Bart, P. (1971). Depression in middle-aged women. In V. Gornick & B. K. Moran (Eds.), *Woman in sexist society* (pp. 163–186). New York: Basic Books.

Bar-Tal, D., & Saxe, L. (1976). Physical attractiveness and its relationship to sex-role stereotyping. *Sex-Roles*, **2**, 123–134.

Bartol, K. M., & Manhardt, P. J. (1979). Sex differences in job outcome preferences: Trends among newly hired college graduates. *Journal of Applied Psychology*, **64**, 477–482.

Baruch, G. K. (1966). *The achievement motive in women: A study of the implications for career development.* Unpublished doctoral dissertation, Harvard University.

Baruch, G. K. (1972). Maternal influences upon college women's attitudes toward women and work. *Developmental Psychology*, **6**, 32–37.

Baruch, G. K. (1976). Girls who perceive themselves as competent: Some antecedents and correlates. *Psychology of Women Quarterly*, **1**, 38–49.

Basow, S. A., & Howe, K. G. (1978). Model influences on career choices of college students. *Vocational Guidance Quarterly*, **27**, 239–243.

Basow, S. A., & Howe, K. G. (1980). Role model influence: Effects of sex and sex-role attitude in college students. *Psychology of Women Quarterly*, **4**, 558–572.

Bass, B. M., Krusell, J., & Alexander, R. A. (1971). Male manager's attitudes toward working women. *American Behavioral Scientist*, **15**, 221–236.

Beale, F. (1970). Double jeopardy: To be black and female. In T. Cade (Ed.), *The black woman: An anthology* (pp. 90–100). New York: New American Library.

Bebbington, P., Hurry, J., Tennant, C., Sturt, E., & Wing, J. K. (1981). Epidemiology of mental disorders in Camberwell. *Psychological Medicine*, **11**, 561–580.

Beere, C. A. (1979). *Women and women's issues: A handbook of tests and measures.* San Francisco: Jossey Bass.

Beere, C. A., King, D. W., Beere, D. B., & King, L. K. (1984). The sex role egalitarianism scale: A measure of attitudes toward equality between the sexes. *Sex Roles*, **10**, 563–576.

Bem, S. L. (1974). The measurement of psychological androgyny. *Journal of Consulting and Clinical Psychology*, **42**, 155-162.

Bem, S. L. (1977). On the utility of alternate procedures for assessing psychological androgyny. *Journal of Consulting and Clinical Psychology*, **45**, 196-205.

Bem, S. L. (1981). Gender schema theory: A cognitive account of sex typing. *Psychological Review*, **88**, 354–364.

Bem, S. L., & Bem, D. J. (1976). Case study of a nonconscious ideology: Training the woman to know her place. In S. Cox (Ed.), *Female psychology* (pp. 180–191). Chicago: Science Research Associates.

Benbow, C. P. & Stanley, J. C. (1980). Sex differences in mathematical ability: Fact or artifact? *Science*, **210**, 1262–1264.

Benson, D. J., & Thomson, G. E. (1982). Sexual harassment on a university campus: The confluence of authority relations, sexual interest and gender stratification. *Social Problems*, **29**, 236–251.

Bentler, P. M. (1980). Multivariate analaysis with latent variables: Causal modeling. *Annual Review of Psychology*, **31**, 419–456.

Bergman, J. (1974). Are little girls being harmed by Sesame Street? In J. Stacey, S. Bereand, & J. Daniels (Eds.), *And Jill came tumbling after: Sexism in American education.* New York: Dell.

Berk, R., & Berk, S. F. (1979). *Labor and leisure at home.* Beverly Hills: Sage.

Bernard, J. (1971). The paradox of the happy marriage. In V. Gornick & B. K. Moran (Eds.), *Woman in sexist society.* New York: Mentor.

Bernard, J. (1972). *The future of marriage.* New York: Bantam.

Bernard, J. (1976). Where are we now? Some thoughts on the current scene. *Psychology of Women Quarterly*, **1**, 21–37.

Berscheid, E., & Walster, E. H. (1974). In L. Berkowitz (Ed.), *Advances in experimental social psychology* (Vol. 7). New York: Academic Press.

Best, F. (1981). Changing sex roles and worklife flexibility. In S. S. Tangri & J. Wirtenberg (Eds.), *Women and the Future. Special Issue of Psychology of Women Quarterly*, **6**, 55–71.

Betz, E. L. (1982). Need fulfillment in the career development of women. *Journal of Vocational Behavior*, **20**, 53–66.

Betz, E. L. (1984a). A study of career patterns of college graduates. *Journal of Vocational Behavior*, **24**, 249–264.

Betz, E. L. (1984b). Two tests of Maslow's theory of need fulfillment. *Journal of Vocational Behavior*, **24**, 204–220.

Betz, N. E. (1978). Prevalance, distribution, and correlates of math anxiety in college students. *Journal of Counseling Psychology*, **25**, 441–448.

Betz, N. E. (1982). *Guidelines for career counseling with women.* Unpublished manuscript, Department of Psychology, Ohio State University, Columbus.

Betz, N. E., & Hackett, G. (1981). The relationship of career-related self-efficacy expectations to perceived career options in college women and men. *Journal of Counseling Psychology*, **28**, 399–410.

Betz, N. E., & Hackett, G. (1983). The relationship of mathematics self-efficacy expectations to the selection of science-based college majors. *Journal of Vocational Behavior*, **23**, 329–345.

Betz, N. E., & Weiss, D. J. (1986). Validity. In B. Bolton (Ed.), *Handbook of measurement and evaluation in rehabilitation* (2nd ed.). Baltimore: Paul Brookes.

Beutell, N. J., & Brenner, O. C. (1986). Sex differences in work values. *Journal of Vocational Behavior*, **28**, 29–41.

Bingham, W. C., & House, E. W. (1973a). Counselors view women and work: Accuracy of information. *Vocational Guidance Quarterly*, **21**, 262–268.

Bingham, W. C., & House, E. W. (1973b). Counselor's attitudes towards women and work. *Vocational Guidance Quarterly*, **22**, 16–32.

Bingham, W. C., & Turner, C. J. (1981). Modified questionnaire on the occupational status of women. *Educational and Psychological Measurement*, **41**, 909–915.

Bingham, W. V. & Freyd, M. (1926). *Procedures in employment psychology.* Chicago: Shaw.

Bird, C. (1968). *Born female.* New York: McKay.

Bird, C. (1979). *The two-paycheck marriage: How women at work are changing life in America.* New York: Pocket Books.

Birk, J. M., Tanney, M. F., & Cooper, J. F. (1979). A case of blurred vision: Stereotyping in career information illustrations. *Journal of Vocational Behavior*, **15**, 247–257.

Birnbaum, J. A. (1975). Life patterns and self-esteem in gifted family-oriented and career-committed women. In M. Mednick, S. Tangri, & L. Hoffman (Eds.), *Women and achievement*. New York: Hemisphere.

Blaska, B. (1978). College women's career and marriage aspirations: A review of the literature. *Journal of College Student Personnel, 19*, 302–306.

Blau, P. M., & Duncan, O. D. (1967). *The American occupational structure*. New York: Wiley.

Blaxall, M., & Reagan, B. (Eds.) (1976). *Women and the workplace*. Chicago: University of Chicago Press.

Block, J. H. (1976). Issues, problems, and pitfalls in assessing sex differences. *Merrill-Palmer Quarterly, 22*, 283–308.

Blood, R. O., Jr. (1963). The husband-wife relationship. In F. I. Nye & L. W. Hoffman (Eds.), *The employed mother in America*. Chicago: Rand McNally.

Blood, R. O. (1965). Long-range causes and consequences of the unemployment of married women. *Journal of Marriage and the Family, 27*, 43–47.

Blum, C., & Givant, S. (1982). Increasing the participation of college women in mathematics-related fields. In S. M. Humphreys (Ed.), *Women and minorities in science* (pp. 119–138). Boulder, CO: Westview Press.

Blumrosen, R. G. (1979). Wage discrimination, job segregation, and Title VII of the Civil Rights Act of 1964. *University of Michigan Journal of Law Reform, 12*, 399–502.

Bock, R. D., & Kolakowski, D. (1973). Further evidence of sex-linked major gene influence on human spatial visualizing ability. *American Journal of Human Genetics, 25*, 1–14.

Bond, J. R., & Vinache, W. E. (1961). Coalitions in mixed-sex triads. *Sociometry, 24*, 61–75.

Booth, A. (1977). Wife's employment and husband's stress: A replication and refutation. *Journal of Marriage and the Family, 39*, 645–650.

Boswell, S. L. (1985). The influence of sex-role stereotyping on women's attitudes and achievement in mathematics. In S. F. Chipman, L. R. Brush, & D. M. Wilson (Eds.), *Women and mathematics* (pp. 175–198). Hillsdale, NJ: Erlbaum.

Bouchard, T. (1976). *Sex differences in human spatial ability: Not an x-linked recessive gene*. Unpublished manuscript, Department of Psychology, University of Minnesota.

Bowlby, J. (1982). *Attachment and loss*. (2nd ed.). New York: Basic Books.

Bowman, G. W., Worthy, N. B., & Greyser, S. A. (1965). Problems in review: Are women executives people? *Harvard Business Review, 43*, 52–67.

Brief, A. P., & Aldag, R. J. (1975). Male-female differences in occupational attitudes within minority groups. *Journal of Vocational Behavior, 6*, 305–314.

Brief, A. P., & Oliver, R. L. (1976). Male-female differences in work attitudes among retail sales managers. *Journal of Applied Psychology, 61*, 526–528.

Brief, A. P., Rose, G. L., & Aldag, R. J. (1977). Sex differences in preferences for job attitudes revisited. *Journal of Applied Psychology, 62*, 645–646.

Brito, P. K., & Jusenius, C. L. (1978). A note on women's occupational expectations for age 35. *Vocational Guidance Quarterly, 27*, 165–175.

Brogden, H. E., & Taylor, E. K. (1950). The theory and classification of criterion bias. *Educational and Psychological measurement, 10*, 159–186.

Brookhart, J., & Hock, E. (1976). The effects of experimental context and experimental background on infants behavior toward their mothers and a stranger. *Child Development, 47*, 333–340.

Broverman, I. K., Broverman, D. M., Clarkson, F. E., Rosenkrantz, P., & Vogel, S. R.

(1970). Sex-role stereotypes and clinical judgments of mental health. *Journal of consulting and Clinical Psychology, 34,* 1–7.

Brown, D. (1970). *Students' vocational choices: A review and critique.* Boston: Houghton Mifflin.

Brown, G. W., & Harris, T. (1978). *Social origins of depression: A study of psychiatric disorder in women.* London: Tavistock.

Brown, J. W., Aldrich, M. L., & Hall, P. Q. (1978). *Report on the participation of women in scientific research.* Washington, D. C.: National Science Foundation.

Brown, S. M. (1979). Male versus female leaders: A comparison of empirical studies. *Sex Roles, 5,* 595–611.

Bruning, N. S., & Snyder, R. A. (1983). Sex and position as predictors of organizational commitment. *Academy of Management Journal, 26,* 485–491.

Brush, L. R. (1985). Cognitive and affective determinants of course preferences and plans. In S. F. Chipman, L. R. Brush, & D. M. Wilson (Eds.), *Women and mathematics: Balancing the equation* (pp. 123–150). Hillsdale, NJ: Erlbaum.

Bryson, J., Bryson, R., & Licht, B. G. (1975). *Professional pairs: Relative career values of wives and husbands.* Paper presented at American Psychological Association Meeting.

Bryson, J. B., & Bryson, R. (1980). Salary and job performance differences in dual career couples. In F. Pepitone-Rockwell (Ed), *Dual-career couples.* Beverly Hills: Sage.

Bryson, R. B., Bryson, J. B., Licht, M. H., & Licht, B. G. (1976). The professional pair: Husband and wife psychologists. *American Psychologist, 31,* 10–16.

Buczek, T. A. (1981). Sex biases in counseling: Counselor retention of the concerns of a female and male client. *Journal of Counseling Psychology, 28,* 13–21.

Buffery, A. W. H., & Gray, J. A. (1972). Sex differences and the development of spatial and linguistic skills. In C. Ounsted & D. C. Taylor (Eds.), *Gender differences: Their ontogeny and significance.* Edinburgh: Churchill Livingstone.

Bularzik, M. (1978). Sexual harassment at the workplace: Historical notes. *Radical America, 12,* 25–43.

Burke, R. J., & Weir, T. (1976). Relationship of wives employment status to husband, wife, and pair satisfaction and performance. *Journal of Marriage and the Family, 38,* 279–287.

Burlew, A. K. (1982). The experiences of black females in traditional and non-traditional professions. *Psychology of Women Quarterly, 6,* 312–236.

Burlin, F. (1976). The relationship of parental education and maternal work and occupational status to occupational aspiration in adolescent females. *Journal of Vocational Behavior, 9,* 99–106.

Burns, R. B. (1979). *The self-concept.* London: Longman.

Busby, L. J. (1975). Sex role research on mass media. *Journal of Communication, 25,* 107–137.

Butler, M., & Paisley, W. (1977). Status of professional couples in psychology. *Psychology of Women Quarterly, 1,* 307–318.

Butler, M., & Paisley, W. (1980). Co-ordinated career couples: Convergence and divergence. In F. Pepitone-Rockwell (Ed.), *Dual-career couples.* Beverly Hills: Sage.

Caldwell, B. M., Wright, C. M., Honig, A. S., & Tannebaum, J. (1970). Infant day care and attachment. *American Journal of Orthopsychiatry, 40,* 397–412.

Campbell, A., Converse, P. E., & Rodgers, W. L. (1976). *The quality of American life.* New York: Russell Sage Foundation.

Campbell, A., Converse, P. E., & Rodgers, W. L. (1976). *The quality of American life.* New York: Russell Sage Foundation.

Campbell, P. B. (1976). Adolescent intellectual decline. *Adolescence,* **11,** 631–635.

Carbonell, J. L. (1984). Sex roles and leadership revisited. *Journal of Applied Psychology,* **69,** 44–49.

Card, J. J., Steel, L., & Abeles, R. P. (1980). Sex differences in realization of individual potential for achievement. *Journal of Vocational Behavior,* **17,** 1–21.

Carnegie Commission on Higher Education (1973). *Opportunities for women in higher education.* New York: McGraw-Hill.

Cartwright, L. K. (1972). Conscious factors entering the decisions of women who study medicine. *Journal of Social Issues,* **28,** 201–215.

Cash, T. F., Begley, P. J., McCown, D. A., & Weise, B. C. (1975). When counselors are heard but not seen: Initial impact of physical attractiveness. *Journal of Counseling Psychology,* **22,** 273–279.

Cash, T. F., Gillen, B., & Burns, D. S. (1977). Sexism and "beautyism" in personnel consultant decision-making. *Journal of Applied Psychology,* **62,** 301–310.

Cash, T. F., Kehr, J., Polyson, J., & Freeman, V. (1977). The role of physical attractiveness in peer attributions of psychological disturbance. *Journal of Consulting and Clinical Psychology,* **45,** 98–993.

Castle, C. S. (1913). A statistical study of eminent women. *Archives of Psychology,* **27,** 20–34.

Catalyst Career and Family Center (1981). *Corporation and two-career families: Directions for the future.* New York: Author.

Cattell, R. B. (1949). *Manual for Forms A and B: Sixteen Personality Factor Questionnaire.* Champaign, IL: Institute for Personality and Ability Testing.

Cattell, R. B., Eber, H. W., & Tatsuoka, M. M. (1970). *Handbook for the 16PF.* Champaign, IL: Institute for Personality Testing.

Chapman, G. R. (Ed.) (1981). *Harassment and discrimination of women in employment.* ERIC Document N. ED 225054.

Chapman, J. B. (1975). Comparison of male and female leadership styles. *Academy of Management Journal,* **18,** 645–650.

Chesler, P. (1972). *Women and madness.* Garden City, NY: Doubleday.

Chipman, S. F., Brush, L. R., & Wilson, D. M. (1985). *Women and mathematics: Balancing the equation.* Hillsdale, NJ: Erlbaum.

Chipman, S. F., & Thomas, V. G. (1985). Women's participation in mathematics: Outlining the problem. In S. F. Chipman, L. R. Brush, & D. M. Wilson (Eds.), *Women and mathematics* (pp. 1–24). Hillsdale, NJ: Erlbaum.

Chipman, S. F., & Wilson, D. M. (1985). Understanding mathematics course enrollment and mathematics achievement: A synthesis of the research. In S. F. Chipman, L. R. Brush, & D. M. Wilson (Eds.), *Women and mathematics* (pp. 275–328). Hillsdale, NJ: Erlbaum.

Clay, W. L. (1975). The socioeconomic status of blacks. *Ebony,* **29,** 40–44.

Closson, M. (1976a). The joys of job sharing. *Human Behavior,* **November,** 36.

Closson, M. (1976b). Company couples flourish. *Business Week,* **25,** October, p. 112e.

Cohen, S. E. (1978). Maternal employment and mother-child interactions. *Merrill-Palmer Quarterly,* **24,** 189–197.

Cohen, S. L., & Bunker, K. A. (1975). Subtle effects of sex role stereotypes on recruiters hiring decisions. *Journal of Applied Psychology,* **60,** 566–572.

Cole, N. S., & Hanson, G. R. (1975). Impact of interest inventories on career choice. In E. E. Diamond (Ed.), *Issues of sex bias and sex fairness in career interest measurement.* Washington: DC: National Institute of Education.

Colwill, N. L., & Ross, N. P. (1978). Debunking a stereotype: The female medical student. *Sex Roles,* **4,** 717–722.

Constantini, E., & Craik, K. H. (1972). Women as politicians: The social background, personality, and political careers of female party leaders. *Journal of Social Issues,* **28,** 217–236.

Constantinople, A. (1973). Masculinity-femininity: An exception to the famous dictum. *Psychological Bulletin,* **80,** 389–407.

Conway, C. Y., & Niple, M. L. (1976). The working patterns of mothers and grandmothers of freshmen women at the Ohio State University, 1955 and 1965. *Journal of the National Association of Women Deans and Counselors,* **29,** 167–170.

Cook, E. P. (1985). *Psychological androgyny.* New York: Pergamon.

Cook, T. D., & Campbell, D. T. (1979). *Quasi-experimentation: Design and analysis issues for field settings.* Chicago: Rand McNally.

Coopersmith, S. (1967). *The antecedents of self-esteem.* San Francisco: Freeman.

Coser, R. L., & Rokoff, G. (1971). Women in the occupational world: Social disruption and conflict. *Social Problems,* **18,** 535–554.

Crandall, V. C. (1969). Sex differences in expectancy of intellectual and academic reinforcement. In C. P. Smith (Ed.), *Achievement-related motives in children.* New York: Russell Sage Foundation.

Crandall, V. C. (1978). *Expecting sex differences and sex differences in expectancies: A developmental analysis.* Paper presented at the annual convention of the American Psychological Association, Toronto, August.

Crawford, J. D. (1978). Career development and career choice in pioneer and traditional women. *Journal of Vocational Behavior,* **12,** 129–139.

Crissy, W. J., & Daniel, W. J. (1939). Vocational interest factors in women. *Journal of Applied Psychology,* **34,** 488–494.

Crites, J. O. (1969). *Vocational psychology.* New York: McGraw-Hill.

Crites, J. O. (1976). A comprehensive model of career development in early adulthood. *Journal of Vocational Behavior,* **9,** 105–118.

Crites, J. O. (1979). Validation of the diagnostic taxonomy of adult career problems: A pilot study. In R. E. Campbell, J. V. Cellini, P. E. Shaltry, A. E. Long, & D. Pinkos (Eds.), *A diagnostic taxonomy of adult career problems.* Columbus, OH: National Center for Research on Vocational Education.

Crites, J. O. (1981). *Career counseling: Models, methods, and materials.* New York: McGraw-Hill.

Crocker, P. L., & Simon, A. E. (1981). Sexual harassment in education. *Capitol University Law Review,* **10,** 541–584.

Cronbach, L. J., & Meehl., P. E. (1955). Construct validity in psychological tests. *Psychological Bulletin,* **52,** 281–302.

Cronkite, R. C., & Perl, T. H. (1982). A short-term intervention program: Math-science conferences. In S. M. Humphreys (Ed.), *Women and minorities in science* (pp. 65–86). Boulder, CO: Westview Press.

Crosby, F., Golding, J., & Resnick, A. (1983). Discontent among male lawyers, female lawyers, and female legal secretaries. *Journal of Applied Social Psychology,* **13,** 183–190.

Crowley, J., Levitin, T. E., & Quinn, R. P. (1973). Seven deadly half-truths about women. In C. Tavris (Ed.), *The female experience.* Del Mar, CA: CRM.

Crull, P. (1979). *The impact of sexual harassment on the job: A profile of the experiences of 92 women.* Working Women's Institute Research Series, Report No. 3.

Cumming, E., Lazer, C., & Chisholm, L. (1975). Suicide as an index of role strain among employed and non employed married women in British Columbia. *Canadian Review of Sociology and Anthropology,* **12,** 462–470.

Darley, J. G. (1941). *Clinical aspects and interpretation of the Strong Vocational Interest Blank*. New York: Psychological Corporation.

Dawis, R. V., & Lofquist, L. H. (1984). *A psychological theory of work adjustment*. Minneapolis: University of Minnesota Press.

Day, D. R., & Stogdill, R. M. (1972). Leader behavior of male and female supervisors: A comparative study. *Personnel Psychology, 25,* 353–360.

Deaux, K. (1984). From individual differences to social categories: Analysis of a decade's research on gender. *American Psychologist, 39,* 105–116.

Deaux, K., & Emswiller, T. (1974). Explanations of successful performance on sex-linked tasks: What is skill for the male is luck for the female. *Journal of Personality and Social Psychology, 29,* 80–85.

Deaux, K., & Farris, E. (1977). Attributing causes for one's own performance: The effects of sex, norms, and outcome. *Journal of Research in Personality, 11,* 59–72.

Deaux, K., & Taynor, J. (1973). Evaluation of male and female ability: Bias works two ways. *Psychology Reports, 31,* 20–31.

DeFries, J. C., Ashton, G. C., Johnson, R. C., Kuse, A. R., McClearn, G. E., Mi, M. P., Rashad, M. N., Vanderberg, S. G., & Wilson, J. R. (1976). Parent-offspring resemblance for specific cognitive abilities in two ethnic groups. *Nature (London), 261,* 131–133.

Del Vento Bielby, D. (1978). Maternal employment and socioeconomic status as factor in daughters' career salience: Some substantive refinements. *Sex Roles, 4,* 249–266.

Demo, D. H. (1985). The measurement of self-esteem: Refining our methods. *Journal of Personality and Social Psychology, 48,* 1490–1502.

Denmark, F. L., & Diggory, J. C. (1966). Sex differences in attitudes toward leaders' display of authoritarian behavior. *Psychological Reports, 18,* 863–872.

Dermer, M., & Thiel, D. L. (1975). When beauty may fail. *Journal of Personality and Social Psychology, 31,* 1168–1176.

Deutsch, H. (1944). *The psychology of women: A psychoanalytic interpretation (Vol. 1)*. New York: Grune & Stratton.

Deutsch, H. (1945). *The psychology of women: A psychoanalytic interpretation (Vol. 2)*. New York: Grune & Stratton.

DeVries, D. L., Morrison, A. M., Shullman, S. L., & Gerlach, M. L. (1981). *Performance appraisal on the line*. New York: Wiley.

Dew, K. M. H., Galassi, J. P., & Galassi, M. D. (1983). Math anxiety: Some basic issues. *Journal of Counseling Psychology, 30,* 443–446.

Dewey, C. R. (1974). Exploring interests: A non-sexist method. *Personnel and Guidance Journal, 52,* 311–215.

Diamond, E. E. (1975). Guidelines for the assessment of sex bias and sex fairness in career interest inventories. *Measurement and Evaluation in Guidance, 8,* 7–11.

Dickson, P. (1975). *The future of the work place*. New York: Weybright & Talley.

Dion, K. K., Berscheid, D., & Walster, F. (1972). What is beautiful is good. *Journal of Personality and Social Psychology, 24,* 285–290.

Dipboye, R. L., Arvey, R. D., & Terpstra, D. E. (1977). Sex and physical attractiveness of raters and applicants as determinants of resume evaluations. *Journal of Applied Psychology, 62,* 288–294.

Dipboye, R. L., Fromkin, H. L., & Wiback, K. (1975). Relative importance of applicant sex, attractiveness, and scholastic standing in evaluation of job applicant resumes. *Journal of Applied Psychology, 60,* 39–43.

DiSabatino, M. (1976). Psychological factors inhibiting women's occupational aspirations and vocational choices. *Vocational Guidance Quarterly, 25,* 43–49.

Doherty, E. G., & Culver, C. (1976). Sex-role identification, ability, and achievement among high school girls. *Sociology of Education*, **49**, 1–3.

Dolliver, R. H. (1967). An adaptation of the Tyler Vocational Card Sort. *Personnel and Guidance Journal*, **45**, 916–920.

Donahue, T. J. (1976). Discrimination against young women in career selection by high school counselors. *Dissertation Abstracts International*, (University Microfilms No. 76–18612).

Donahue, T. J. (1979). Counselor discrimination against women: Additional information. *Journal of Counseling Psychology*, **26**, 276–278.

Donahue, T. J., & Costar, J. W. (1977). Counselor discrimination against young women in career selection. *Journal of Counseling Psychology*, **24**, 481–486.

Douvan, E. (1976). The role of models in women's professional development. *Psychology of Women Quarterly*, **1**, 5–20.

Douvan, E., & Pleck, J. (1978). Separation and support. In R. Rapoport & R. N. Rapoport (Eds.), *Working couples*. London: Routledge & Kegan Paul.

Dowling, D. M. (1978). *The development of a mathematics confidence scale and its application in the study of confidence in women college students.* Unpublished Ph.D. Dissertation, Ohio State University.

Doyle, A. B. (1975). Infant development in daycare. *Developmental Psychology*, **11**, 655–656.

Drabman, R. S., Robertson, S. J., Patterson, J. N., Jarvie, G. J., Hammer, D., & Cordua, G. (1981). Children's perception of media-portrayed sex roles. *Sex Roles*, **7**, 379–390.

Drachman, V., Schwartz, M. C., & Schwebs, C. (1976). Weekend marriage. *Vogue*, **November,** 278–280.

Dreyer-Arkin, N. (1976). *Delaying behavior in seeking diagnosis for suspected cervical cancer.* Unpublished Master's Thesis, School of Public Health, University of North Carolina.

Dreyer, N. A., Woods, N. F., & James, S. A. (1981). ISRO: A scale to measure sex-role orientation. *Sex Roles*, **7**, 173–182.

Dunton, N. E., & Featherman, D. L. (1983). Social mobility through marriage and career. In J. T. Spence (Ed.), *Achievement and achievement motives* (pp. 285–320). San Francisco: Freeman.

Dweck, C., Davidson, W., Nelson, S., & Enna, B. I. (1978). Sex differences in learned helplessness: II. The contingencies of evaluative feedback in the classroom; III. An experimental analysis. *Developmental Psychology*, **14**, 268–276.

Dzeich, B. W., & Weiner, L. (1984). *The lecherous professor: Sexual harassment on campus.* Boston: Beacon Press.

Eagly, A. H., & Steffen, V. J. (1980). Gender stereotypes stem from the distribution of women and men into social roles. *Journal of Personality and Social Psychology*, **46**, 735–754.

Eccles, J. (1983). Sex differences in mathematics participation. In M. Steinkamp & M. Maehr (Eds.), *Women in science* (pp. 80–110). Greenwich, CT: JAI Press.

Eccles, J., Adler, T., & Meece, J. L. (1984). Sex differences in achievement: A test of alternate theories. *Journal of Personality and Social Psychology*, **46**, 26–43.

Eccles, J. E., Adler, T. F., Futterman, R., Goff, S. B., Kaczala, C. M., Meece, J. I., & Midgley, C. (1983). Expectations, values, and academic behaviors. In J. T. Spence (Ed.), *Achievement and achievement motives* (pp. 75–145). San Francisco: Freeman.

Edwards, A. L., & Cronbach, L. J. (1952). Experimental design for research in psychotherapy. *Journal of Clinical Psychology*, **8**, 51–59.

Edwards, C. N. (1969). Cultural values and role decisions. *Journal of Counseling Psychology*, **16**, 36–40.

English, H. B., & English, A. C. (1958). *A comprehensive dictionary of psychological and psychoanalytical terms*. New York: McKay.

Epstein, C. F. (1968). *Women and professional careers: The case of the woman lawyer*. Unpublished Ph.D. dissertation, Columbia University.

Epstein, C. F. (1970a). Encountering the male establishment: Sex-status limits on womens' careers in the professions. *American Journal of Sociology*, **75**, 965–982.

Epstein, C. F. (1970b). *Woman's place*. Berkeley, CA: University of California Press.

Epstein, C. F. (1971). Law partners and marital partners. *Human Relations*, **24**, 549–564.

Epstein, C. F. (1973). Positive effects of the multiple negative. *American Journal of Sociology*, **78**, 912–935.

Epstein, C. F. (1976). Sex role stereotyping, occupations and social exchange. *Women's Studies*, **3**, 185–194.

Equal Employment Opportunity Commission, Civil Service Commission, Department of Labor, and Department of Justice (1978). Adoption by four agencies of uniform guidelines on employee selection procedures. *Federal Register*, **43**, 38290–38315.

Equal Employment Opportunity Commission (1980). Discrimination because of sex under Title VII of the Civil Rights Act of 1964, as ammended: Adoption of interim interpretive guidelines—Sexual harassment. *Federal Register*, **45**, 25024–25025.

Ernest, J. (1976). Mathematics and sex. *The American Mathematical Monthly*, **83**, 595–614.

Eskilson, A., & Wiley, M. G. (1976). Sex composition and leadership in small groups. *Sociometry*, **39**, 183–194.

Etaugh, C. (1974). Effects of maternal employment on children: A review of recent research. *Merrill-Palmer Quarterly*, **20**, 71–98.

Etaugh, C. (1980). Effects of nonmaternal care on children: Research evidence and popular views. *American Psychologist*, **35**, 309–319.

Etaugh, C., & Hall, P. (1980). Is preschool education more highly valued for boys than girls? *Sex Roles* **6**, 339–344.

Evan, W. M. (1963). Peer group interaction and organizational socialization: A study of employee turnover. *American Sociological Review*, **28**, 436–440.

Eyde, L. D. (1962). *Work values and background factors as predictors of women's desire to work*. (Research Monograph No. 108.) Columbus, OH: Bureau of Business Research, Ohio State University.

Eyde, L. D. (1970). Eliminating barriers to career development in women. *Personnel and Guidance Journal*, **49**, 24–29.

Eysenck, H. J., & Cookson, D. (1970). Personality in primary children: III—Family background. *British Journal of Educational Psychology*, **40**, 117–131.

Fagot, B. (1981). Male and female teachers: Do they treat boys and girls differently? *Sex Roles*, **7**, 263–272.

Fairhurst, G. T., & Snavely, B. K. (1983). Majority and token minority group relationships: Power acquisition and communication. *Academy of Management Review*, **8**, 292–300.

Falk, W. W., & Cosby, A. G. (1978). Women's marital-familial statuses and work histories: Some conceptual considerations. *Journal of Vocational Behavior*, **13**, 126–140.

Falk, W. W., & Salter, N. J. (1978). The stability of status orientations among young white, rural women from three southern states. *Journal of Vocational Behavior*, **12**, 20–32.

Falkowski, C. K., & Falk, W. W. (1983). Homemaking as an occupational plan: Evidence from a national longitudinal study. *Journal of Vocational Behavior*, **22**, 227–242.

Fannin, P. M. (1979). The relations between ego-identity status and sex-role attitude, work-role salience, atypicality of major, and self-esteem in college women. *Journal of Vocational Behavior*, **14**, 12–22.

Farley, L. (1978). *Sexual shakedown: The sexual harassment of women on the job.* New York: McGraw-Hill.

Farmer, H. S. (1976). What inhibits achievement and career motivation in women? *The Counseling Psychologist*, **6**, 12–14.

Farmer, H. S. (1980). Environmental, background, and psychological variables related to optimizing achievement and career motivation for high school girls. *Journal of Vocational Behavior*, **17**, 58–70.

Farmer, H. S. (1983). Career and homemaking plans for high school youth. *Journal of Counseling Psychology*, **30**, 40–45.

Farmer, H. S. (1984a). A shiny fresh minted penny. *The Counseling Psychologist*, **12**, 141–144.

Farmer, H. S. (1984b). Development of a measure of home-career conflict related to career motivation in college women. *Sex Roles*, **10**, 663–676.

Farmer, H. S. (1985). Model of career and achievement motivation for women and men. *Journal of Counseling Psychology*, **32**, 363–390.

Farmer, H. S., & Bohn, M. J. (1970). Home-career conflict reduction and the level of career interest in women. *Journal of Counseling Psychology*, **17**, 228–232.

Farran, D. C., & Ramey, C. T. (1977). Infant daycare and attachment behaviors toward mothers and teachers. *Child Development*, **48**, 1112–1116.

Farris, A. (1978). Commuting. In R. Rapoport & R. N. Rapoport (Eds.), *Working couples.* London: Routledge & Kegan Paul.

Fassinger, R. E. (1985). A causal model of career choice in college women. *Journal of Vocational Behavior*, **27**, 123–153.

Feld, S. (1963). Feelings of adjustment. In F. I. Nye & L. W. Hoffman (Eds.), *The employed mother in America.* Chicago: Rand McNally.

Feldberg, R., & Glenn, E. (1979). Male and female: Job versus gender models in the sociology of work. *Social Problems*, **26**, 524–535.

Feldman, S. D. (1974). *Escape from the doll's house: Women in graduate and professional school education.* New York: McGraw-Hill.

Fennema, E., & Sherman, J. A. (1976). Fennema-Sherman Mathematics Attitudes Scales: Instruments designed to measure attitudes toward the learning of mathematics by males and females. *Catalog of Selected Documents in Psychology* **6**, 31 (MS. 1225).

Fennema, E., & Sherman, J. A. (1977). Sex-related differences in mathematics achievement, spatial visualization, and affective factors. *American Educational Research Association Journal*, **14**, 51–71.

Ferraro, G. A. (1984). Bridging the wide gap: Pay equity and job evaluations. *American Psychologist*, **39**, 1166–1170.

Fidell, L. S. (1970). Empirical verification of sex discrimination in hiring practices in psychology. *American Psychologist*, **25**, 1094–1098.

Finn, J. D. (1980). Sex differences in educational outcomes: A cross-national study. *Sex Roles*, **6**, 9–26.

Finn, J. D., Dulberg, L., & Reis, J. (1979). Sex differences in educational attainment: A cross-national perspective. *Harvard Educational Review*, **49**, 477–503.

Fishel, A., & Pottker, J. (1977). *National politics and sex discrimination in education.* Lexington, MA: Health.

Fitzgerald, L. F. (1980). Nontraditional occupations: Not for women only. *Journal of Counseling Psychology, 27,* 252–259.

Fitzgerald, L. F. (1984). *The developmental process of career adjustment.* Paper presented to the annual meeting of the American Psychological Association, Toronto.

Fitzgerald, L. F. (1985). *Education and work: The essential tension.* Columbus, OH: National Center for Research in Vocational Education.

Fitzgerald, L. F. (1986). Career counseling women: Principles, problems, and practice. In Z. Leibowitz & D. Lee (Eds.), *Adult career development.* Washington, DC: National Vocational Guidance Association.

Fitzgerald, L. F., & Betz, N. E. (1983). Issues in the vocational psychology of women. In W. B. Walsh & S. H. Osipow (Eds.), *Handbook of vocational psychology* (Vol. I). Hillsdale, NJ: Erlbaum.

Fitzgerald, L. F., & Betz, N. E. (1984). Astin's model in theory and practice: A technical and philosophical critique. *The Counseling Psychologist, 12,* 135–138.

Fitzgerald, L. F., & Cherpas, C. (1985). On the reciprocal relationship between gender and occupation: Rethinking the assumptions concerning masculine career development. *Journal of Vocational Behavior, 27,* 109–122.

Fitzgerald, L. F., & Crites, J. O. (1980). Toward a career psychology of women: What do we know? What do we need to know? *Journal of Counseling Psychology, 27,* 44–62.

Fitzgerald, L. F., & Shullman, S. L. (1984). The myths and realities of women in organizations. *Training and Development Journal, 38,* 65–70.

Fitzgerald, L. F., & Shullman, S. L. (1985). *The development and validation of an objectively scored measure of sexual harassment.* Paper presented at the convention of the American Psychological Association.

Fitzgerald, L. F., Gold, Y., Ormerod, M., & Weitzman, W. (1986). *The lecherous professor: A study in power relations.* Paper presented at the convention of the American Psychological Association, Washington, DC.

Fitzgerald, L. F., Shullman, S. L., et al. (1986). The extent and dimensions of sexual harassment in academia and the workplace. (Submitted for publication.)

Flanagan, J. (1954). The critical incident technique. *Psychological Bulletin, 51,* 327–358.

Flanagan, J. C. (1971). *Project TALENT: Five years after high school and appendix II. Final Report.* Pittsburg: University of Pittsburg, American Institute for Research.

Fleener, D. E. (1973). Experimental production of infant-maternal attachment behaviors. *Proceedings of the 81st Annual Convention of the American Psychological Association, 8,* 57–58.

Fleming, J. (1982). Fear of success in black male and female graduate students. *Psychology of Women Quarterly, 6,* 327–341.

Fogarty, M. P., Rapoport, R., & Rapoport, R. N. (1971). *Sex, career, and family.* Beverly Hills, CA: Sage.

Fottler, M. D., & Bain, T. (1980). Managerial aspirations of high school seniors: A comparison of males and females. *Journal of Vocational Behavior, 16,* 83–95.

Fox, L. H., Brody, L., & Tobin, D. (1980). *Women and the mathematical mystique.* Baltimore: Johns Hopkins University Press.

Fox, L. H., Brody, L., & Tobin, D. (1985). Women and mathematics: The impact of early intervention programs upon course-taking and attitudes in high schools. In S. F. Chipman, L. R. Brush, & D. M. Wilson (Eds.), *Women and mathematics.* Hillsdale, NJ: Erlbaum.

Franklin, P., Moglen, H., Zatling-Boring, P., & Angress, R. (1981). *Sexual and gender harassment in the academy.* New York: Modern Language Association.

Freeman, J. (1975). How to discriminate against women without really trying. In J. Freeman (Ed.), *Women: A feminist perspective*, pp. 194–208. Palo Alto, CA: Mayfield.

Freun, M. A., Rothman, A. I., & Steiner, J. W. (1974). Comparison of characteristics of male and female medical school applicants. *Journal of Medical Education, 49*, 137–145.

Friedersdorf, N. W. (1970). A comparative study of counselor attitudes toward the further education and vocational plans of high school girls. *Dissertation Abstracts International, 30*, 4220–4221.

Frieze, I. H., Parsons, J. E., Johnson, P. B., Ruble, D. N., & Zellman, G. L. (1978). *Women and sex roles: A social psychological perspective*. New York: Norton.

Frieze, I. H., Whitley, B. E., Jr., Hanusa, B. H., & McHugh, M. C. (1982). Alternative theoretical models for sex differences in causal attributions for success and failure. *Sex Roles, 8*, 333–343.

Frieze, I. R., Fisher, J., Hanusa, B., McHugh, M. C., & Valle, V. A. (1981). Attributions of the causes of success and failure as internal and external barriers to achievement in women. In J. Sherman & F. Demmark (Eds.), *Psychology of women: Future directions in research*. New York: Psychological Dimensions.

Frost, F., & Diamond, E. E. (1979). Ethnic and sex differences in occupational stereotyping by elementary school children. *Journal of Vocational Behavior, 15*, 43–54.

Frueh, T., & McGhee, P. E. (1975). Traditional sex role development and amount of time spent watching television. *Developmental Psychology, 11*, 109.

Frye, J. (1984). *Success and satisfaction: Does it make a difference who you ask?* Paper presented at the convention of the American Psychological Association, Toronto.

Furniss, W. T., & Graham, P. A. (1974). *Women in higher education*. Washington, DC: American Council on Education.

Gackenbach, J. (1978). The effect of race, sex, and career goal differences on sex role attitudes at home and at work. *Journal of Vocational Behavior, 12*, 93–101.

Gaddy, C. D., Glass, C. R., & Arnkoff, D. B. (1983). Career development of women in dual career families: The influence of sex role identity. *Journal of Counseling Psychology, 30*, 388–394.

Gallese, L. R. (1974). Two for the price of one: Colleges say they get more for their money by hiring a couple to share one faculty job. *The Wall Street Journal, 19 April*, p. 30.

Garbin, A. P., & Stover, R. G. (1980). Vocational behavior and career development, 1979: A review. *Journal of Vocational Behavior, 17*, 125–170.

Garland, T. N. (1972). The better half: The male in the dual career family. In C. Safilios-Rothschild (Ed.), *Toward a sociology of women*. Lexington, MA: Xerox College Publishing.

Gettys, L. D., & Cann, A. (1981). Children's perceptions of occupational sex stereotypes. *Sex Roles, 7*, 301–308.

Ghiselli, E. E. (1971). *Explorations in managerial talent*. Pacific Palisades, CA: Goodyear Publishing.

Gianopulos, A., & Mitchell, H. (1975). Marital disagreement in working wife marriage as a function of husband's attitude toward wife's employment. *Marriage and Family Living, November*.

Gigy, L. L. (1980). Self-concept in single women. *Psychology of Women Quarterly, 5*, 321–340.

Gilbert, L. A. (1984). Comments on the meaning of work in women's lives. *The Counseling Psychologist, 12*, 129–130.

Gilbert, L. A. (1985). Measures of psychological masculinity and femininity: A comment on Gadd, Glass, and Arnkoff. *Journal of Counseling Psychology, 32*, 163–166.

Gilkes, C. T. (1982). Successful rebellious professionals: The black woman's professional identity and community commitment. *Psychology of Women Quarterly*, **6**, 289–311.

Gillen, B. (1975). *Physical attractiveness as a determinant of perceived sex-role appropriateness*. Paper presented at the meeting of the Southeastern Psychological Association, Atlanta, March.

Gilligan, C. (1982). *In a diferent voice*. Cambridge, MA: Harvard University Press.

Gilmer, B. (1961). *Industrial psychology*. New York: McGraw-Hill.

Ginzberg, E., Berg, I., Brown, C., Herma, L., Yohalem, A., & Gorelick, S. (1966). *Lifestyles of educated women*. New York: Columbia University Press.

Gitelson, I., Petersen, A., & Tobin-Richards, M. (1982). Adolescents' expectancies of success, self-evaluations, and attributions about performance on spatial and verbal tasks. *Sex Roles*, **8**, *411–419*.

Gold, A. R., Brush, L. R., & Sprotzer, E. R. (1980). Developmental changes in self-perceptions of intelligence and self-confidence. *Psychology of Women Quarterly*, **5**, 231–239.

Gold, D., & Andres, D. (1978). Developmental comparisons between ten-year old children with employed and nonemployed mothers. *Child Development*, **49**, 75–84.

Goldberg, P. A. (1968). Are women prejudiced against women? *Transaction*, **April**, 28–30.

Golding, J., Resnick, A., & Crosby, I. (1983). Work satisfaction as a function of gender and job status. *Psychology of Women Quarterly*, **7**, 286–290.

Goldman, R. D., & Hewitt, B. N. (1976). The scholastic aptitude test "explains" why college men major in science more often than college women. *Journal of Counseling Psychology*, **23**, 50–54.

Goldman, R. D., Kaplan, R. M., & Platt, B. B. (1973). Sex differences in the relationship of attitudes toward technology to choice of field of study. *Journal of Counseling Psychology*, **20**, 412–418.

Goldsen, R. K., Rosenberg, M., Williams, R. M., & Suchman, E. A. (1960). *What college students think*. Princeton, NJ: Van Nostrand-Reinhold.

Goldstein, E. (1979). Effects of same-sex and cross-sex role models on the subsequent academic productivity of scholars. *American Psychologist*, **34**, 407–410.

Goodale, J. G., & Hall, D. T. (1976). Inheriting a career: The influence of sex, values, and parents. *Journal of Vocational Behavior*, **8**, 19–30.

Goodman, J. L. (1981). Sexual harassment: Some observations on the distance traveled and the distance yet to go. *Capitol University Law Review*, **10**, 445–469.

Gottfredson, L. (1978). An analytical description of employment according to race, sex, prestige, and Holland-type of work. *Journal of Vocational Behavior*, **13**, 210–221.

Gottfredson, L. S. (1981). Circumscription and compromise: A developmental theory of occupational aspirations. *Journal of Counseling Psychology*, **28**, 545–579.

Gottfredson, G. D., Holland, J. L., & Gottfredson, L. S. (1975). The relation of vocational aspirations and assessments to employment reality. *Journal of Vocational Behavior*, **7**, 135–148.

Gover, P. A. (1963). Socio-economic differentials in the relationship between marital adjustment and wife's employment status. *Marriage and Family Living*, **25**, 452–456.

Gough, H. G. (1957). *Manual for the California Psychological Inventory*. Palo Alto, CA: Consulting Psychologists Press.

Graddick, M. M., & Farr, J. L. (1983). Professionals in scientific disciplines: Sex related differences in working life commitments. *Journal of Applied Psychology*, **68**, 641–645.

Graham, P. A. (1978). Expansion and exclusion: A history of women in higher education. *Signs, 3*, 759–773.

Grant, W. V., & Eiden, L. J. (1981). *Digest of education statistics.* Washington, DC: National Center for Education Statistics.

Gray, J. D. (1979). *Role conflicts and coping strategies in married professional women.* Unpublished doctoral dissertation, University of Pennsylvania.

Gray, J. D. (1980a). Counseling women who want both a profession and a family. *Personnel and Guidance Journal, 59*, 43–45.

Gray, J. D. (1980b). Role conflicts and coping strategies in married professional women. *Dissertation Abstracts International, 40*, 3781–A.

Green, D. R. (1974). *The aptitude-achievement distinction.* New York: McGraw-Hill.

Greenfield, S., Greiner, L., & Wood, M. M. (1980). The "Feminine Mystique" in male-dominated jobs: A comparison of attitudes and background factors of women in male-dominated versus female-dominated jobs. *Journal of Vocational Behavior, 17*, 291–309.

Greenglass, E. R., & Devins, R. (1982). Factors related to marriage and career plans in unmarried women. *Sex Roles, 8*, 57–72.

Greenhaus, J. H. (1971). An investigation of the role of career salience in vocational behavior. *Journal of Vocational Behavior, 1*, 209–216.

Greenhaus, J. H., & Simon, W. E. (1976). Self-esteem, career salience, and the choice of an ideal occupation. *Journal of Vocational Behavior, 8*, 51–58.

Griggs v. Duke Power Co., 401 U.S. 424 (1971).

Grimm, J., & Stearn, R. (1974). Sex roles and internal labor market structure: The female semi-professions. *Social Problems, 21*, 690–705.

Gronseth, E. (1978). Work sharing: A Norwegian example. In R. Rapoport & R. Rapoport (Eds.), *Working couples.* London: Routledge & Kegan Paul.

Gross, H. E. (1980). Dual-career couples who live apart: Two types. *Journal of Marriage and the Family, 42*, 567–576.

Gump, J., & Rivers, L. (1975). A consideration of race in efforts to end sex bias. In E. Diamond (Ed.), *Issues of sex bias and sex fairness in career interest measurement.* Washington, DC: National Institute of Education.

Gunther v. County of Washington, 452 U.S. 161, 101 S.Ct. 2242, 68 L.Ed. (1981).

Gutek, B. A. (1981). *Experiences of sexual harassment: Results from a representative survey.* Paper presented at the 89th Annual Convention of the American Psychological Association. Los Angeles, August.

Gutek, B. A., & Morasch, B. (1982). Sex-ratios, sex-role spillover, and sexual harassment of women at work. *Journal of Social Issues, 38*, 55–74.

Guttentag, M., & Bray, H. (1976). *Undoing sex stereotypes: Research and resources for educators.* New York: McGraw-Hill.

Gysbers, N. C., Johnston, J. A., & Gust, T. (1968). Characteristics of homemaker and career-oriented women. *Journal of Counseling Psychology, 15*, 541–546.

Haavio-Mannila, E. (1972). Sex-role attitudes in Finland, 1960–1970. *Journal of Social Issues, 28*, 93–110.

Haber, S. (1980). Cognitive support for the career choices of college women. *Sex Roles, 6*, 129–138.

Haccoun, C. M., Haccoun, R. R., & Sallay, G. (1978). Sex differences in the appropriateness of supervisory styles: A nonmanagement view. *Journal of Applied Psychology, 63*, 124–127.

Hackett, G. (1985). Role of mathematics self-efficacy in the choice of math-related majors of college women and men: A path analysis. *Journal of Counseling Psychology, 32*, 47–56.

Hackett, G., & Betz, N. E. (1981). A self-efficacy approach to the career development of women. *Journal of Vocational Behavior, 18*, 326–339.

Hackett, G., & Campbell, N. K. (1984). *A test of the self-efficacy approach to career development*. Paper presented at the annual convention of the American Psychological Association, Toronto.

Haddad, G. M. (1978). Married but living apart. *Players*, **February**, 30, 32, 51.

Haefner, J. E. (1977). Sources of discrimination among employees: A survey investigation. *Journal of Applied Psychology, 62*, 265–270.

Hagen, R. I., & Kahn, A. (1975). Discrimination against competent women. *Journal of Abnormal and Social Psychology, 5*, 362–376.

Hall, D. T. (1972a). A model of coping with role conflict: The role behavior of college educated women. *Administrative Science Quarterly, 17*, 471–489.

Hall, D. T. (1972b). *Role and identity processes in the lives of married women*. Unpublished paper. Quoted in O'Leary, V. E. (1977). *Toward understanding women*. Monterey, CA: Brooks/Cole.

Hall, D. T., & Hall, F. E. (1980). Stress and the two-career couple. In C. L. Cooper & R. Payne (Eds.), *Current concerns in occupational stress*. New York: Wiley.

Hall, F. E., & Hall, D. T. (1978). Dual careers—How do couples and companies cope with the problems? *Organizational Dynamics, 6*, 57–77.

Hall, O. (1948). The stages of a medical career. *American Journal of Sociology, 53*, 327–336.

Handley, H. M., & Hickson, J. F. (1978). Background and career orientations of women with mathematical aptitude. *Journal of Vocational Behavior, 13*, 255–262.

Hansen, D. (1974). *Sex differences and supervision*. Paper presented at the annual meeting of the American Psychological Association.

Hansen, J. C. (1984). Response to the meaning of work in women's lives. *The Counseling Psychologist, 12*, 147–150.

Hansen, R. D., & O'Leary, V. E. (1985). Sex-determined attributions. In V. E. O'Leary, R. K. Unger, & B. S. Wallston (Eds.), *Women, gender, and social psychology* (pp. 67–100). Hillsdale, NJ: Erlbaum.

Hanson, G., Prediger, D., & Schussel, R. (1977). *Development and validation of sex-balanced interest inventory scales* (ACT Research Report No. 78). Iowa City, IA: American College Testing Program.

Hansson, R. O., Chernovetz, M. E., & Jones, W. H. (1977). Maternal employment and androgyny. *Psychology of Women Quarterly, 2*, 76–78.

Hardesty, S. A., & Betz, N. E. (1980). The relationships of career salience, attitudes towards women, and demographic and family characteristics to marital adjustment in dual-career couples. *Journal of Vocational Behavior, 17*, 242–248.

Hare-Mustin, R. T., Bennett, S. K., & Broderick, P. C. (1983). Attitude toward motherhood: Gender, generational, and religious comparisons. *Sex Roles, 9*, 643–660.

Haring-Hidore, M., & Beyard-Tyler, K. (1984). Counseling and research on nontraditional careers: A caveat. *The Vocational Guidance Quarterly, 33*, 113–119.

Harmon, L. R. (1978). *A century of doctorates: Data analyses of growth and change*. Washington, DC: National Academy of Sciences.

Harmon, L. W. (1967). Women's working patterns related to their SVIB housewife and "own" occupational scores. *Journal of Counseling Psychology, 14*, 299–301.

Harmon, L. W. (1970). Anatomy of career commitment in women. *Journal of Counseling Psychology, 17*, 77–80.

Harmon, L. W. (1977). Career counseling for women. In E. Rawlings & D. Carter (Eds.), *Psychotherapy for women*. Springfield, IL: Thomas.

Harmon, L. W. (1980). *Life and career plans of young adult college women: A follow-up study.* Paper presented at the annual convention of the American Psychological Association, Montreal.

Harmon, L. W. (1984). What's new? A response to Astin. *The Counseling Psychologist,* **12,** 127–128.

Harragan, B. L. (1977). *Games mother never taught you: Corporate gamesmanship for women.* New York: Warner Books.

Harris, D. V. (1976). Physical sex differences. *The Counseling Psychologist,* **6,** 9–11.

Harrison, A. O., & Minor, J. H. (1982). Interrole conflict, coping strategies, and role satisfaction among single and married employed mothers. *Psychology of Women Quarterly,* **6,** 354–360.

Hawley, P. (1972). Perceptions of male models of femininity related to career choice. *Journal of Counseling Psychology,* **19,** 308–313.

Heckman, N. A., Bryson, R., & Bryson, J. (1977). Problems of professional couples: A content analysis. *Journal of Marriage and the Family,* **39,** 323–330.

Heilman, M. E. (1979). High school students' occupational interest as a function of projected sex ratios in male-dominated occupations. *Journal of Applied Psychology,* **64,** 275–279.

Heilman, M. E., & Saruwatari, L. R. (1979). When beauty is beastly: The effects of appearance and sex on evaluations of job applicants for managerial and nonmanagerial jobs. *Organizational Behavior and Human Performance,* **23,** 360–372.

Helmreich, R., & Stapp, J. (1974). Short Form of the Texas Behavior Inventory, an objective measure of self-esteem. *Bulletin of the Psychonomic Society,* **4,** 473–475.

Helmreich, R. L., & Spence, J. T. (1978). The Work and Family Orientation Questionnaire: An objective instrument to assess components of achievement motivation and attitudes toward family and career. *JSAS Catalog of Selected Documents in Psychology,* **8,** 35.

Helmreich, R. L., Beane, W. E., Lucker, G. W., & Spence, J. T. (1978). Achievement motivation and scientific attainment. *Personality and Social Psychology Bulletin,* **4,** 222–226.

Helmreich, R. L., Spence, J. T., Beane, W. E., Lucker, G. W., & Matthews, K. A. (1980). Making it in academic psychology: Demographic and personality correlates of attainment. *Journal of Personality and Social Psychology,* **39,** 896–908.

Helson, R. (1971). Women mathematicians and the creative personality. *Journal of Consulting and Clinical Psychology,* **36,** 210–221.

Helson, R. (1972). The changing image of the career woman. *Journal of Social Issues,* **28,** 33–46.

Hendel, D. D. (1980). Experiential and affective correlates of math anxiety in adult women. *Psychology of Women Quarterly,* **5,** 219–230.

Hendel, D. D., & Davis, S. O. (1978). Effectiveness of an intervention strategy for reducing mathematics anxiety. *Journal of Counseling Psychology,* **25,** 429–434.

Heneman, H. G. (1977). Impact of test information and applicant sex on applicant evaluation in a selection simulation. *Journal of Applied Psychology,* **62,** 524–526.

Hennig, M. (1973). Family dynamics and the successful woman executive. In R. Knudsin (Ed.), *Women and success.* New York: Morrow.

Herzog, A. R., Bachman, J. E., & Johnston, L. D. (1983). Paid work, child care, and housework: A national survey of high school seniors' preferences for sharing responsibilities between husband and wife. *Sex Roles,* **9,** 109–136.

Hesse-Biber, S. (1985). Male and female students' perceptions of their academic environment and future career plans. *Human Relations,* **38,** 91–105.

Hilton, T. L., & Berglund, G. W. (1974). Sex differences in mathematical achievement: A longitudinal study. *Journal of Educational Research, 67*, 231–237.

Hoffman, L. W. (1974a). Fear of success in males and females: 1965 and 1971. *Journal of Consulting and Clinical Psychology, 42*, 353–358.

Hoffman, L. W. (1974b). Effects of maternal employment on the child. *Developmental Psychology, 10*, 204–228.

Hoffman, L. W. (1977). Changes in family roles, socialization, and sex differences. *American Psychologist, 32*, 644–657.

Hoffman, L. W. (1979). Maternal employment: 1979. *American Psychologist, 34*, 859–865.

Hoffman, L. W., & Nye, F. I. (1974). *Working mothers.* San Francisco: Jossey-Bass.

Holahan, C. K. (1979). Stress experienced by women doctoral students, need for support, and occupational sex typing. *Sex Roles, 5*, 425–436.

Holland, J. (1972). *Professional manual for the self-directed search.* Palo Alto, CA: Consulting Psycholgists Press.

Holland, J. (1973). *Making vocational choices: A theory of careers.* New York: Prentice-Hall.

Holland, J. L. (1985). *Making vocational choices* (2nd ed.). New York: Prentice-Hall.

Hollinger, C. L. (1983). Self-perception and the career aspirations of mathematically talented female adolescents. *Journal of Vocational Behavior, 22*, 49–62.

Hollingshead, A. (1949). *Elmtown's youth.* New York: Wiley.

Holmstrom, L. L. (1972). *The two-career family.* Cambridge, MA: Schenkman.

Honig, A. S., Caldwell, B. M., & Tannebaum, J. (1970). Patterns of information processing used by and with young children in a nursery school setting. *Child Development, 41*, 1045–1065.

Horner, M. S. (1968). *Sex differences in achievement motivation and performance in competitive and non-competitive situations.* Unpublished doctoral dissertation, University of Michigan.

Horner, M. S. (1972). Toward an understanding of achievement-related conflicts in women. *Journal of Social Issues, 28*, 157–175.

House, W. C. (1974). Actual and perceived differences in male and female expectancies and minority goal levels as a function of competition. *Journal of Personality, 42*, 493–509.

Houseknecht, S. K. (1978). Voluntary childlessness: A social psychological model. *Alternative Lifestyles, 1*, 379–402.

Houseknecht, S. K. (1979). Timing of the decision to remain voluntarily childless: Evidence for continuous socialization. *Psychology of Women Quarterly, 4*, 81–96.

Houseknecht, S. K., & Spanier, G. B. (1980). Marital disruption and higher education among women in the United States. *The Sociological Quarterly, 21*, 375–389.

Houser, B. B., & Garvey, C. (1983). The impact of family, peers, and educational personnel upon career decision making. *Journal of Vocational Behavior, 23*, 35–44.

Houser, B. B., & Garvey, C. (1985). Factors that affect nontraditional vocational enrollment among women. *Psychology of Women Quarterly, 9*, 105–117.

Howe, F. (1979). Introduction: The first decade of women's studies. *Harvard Educational Review, 49*, 413–421.

Howe, L. K. (1977). *Pink collar workers.* New York: Putnam.

Hoyt, D. P., & Kennedy, C. E. (1958). Interest and personality correlates of career-motivated and homemaking-motivated college women. *Journal of Counseling Psychology, 5*, 44–49.

Hughes, E. (1945). Dilemmas and contradictions of status. *American Journal of Sociology*, **50**, 353–359.

Hughes, E. C. (1958). The study of occupations. In R. K. Merton, W. Broomand, & W. Cotrell (Eds.), *Sociology today*. New York: Basic Books.

Hughes, G. S. (1925). *Mothers in industry: Wage earning by mothers in Philadelphia*. New York: New Republic.

Hulin, C. L., & Smith, P. C. (1964). Sex differences in job satisfaction. *Journal of Applied Psychology*, **48**, 88–92.

Humphreys, S. M. (1982). *Women and minorities in science: Strategies for increasing participation*. Boulder, CO: Westview Press.

Hurwitz, R. E., & White, M. A. (1977). Effect of sex-linked vocational information on reported occupational choices of high school juniors. *Psychology of Women Quarterly*, **2**, 149–156.

Hutchins, E. B. (1966). *Minorities, manpower, and medicine*. Washington, DC: American Association of Medical Colleges.

Huth, C. M. (1978). Married women's work status: The influence of parents and husbands. *Journal of Vocational Behavior*, **13**, 255–262.

Hyde, J. S. (1981). How large are cognitive gender differences? *American Psychologist*, **36**, 892–901.

Hyde, J. S. (1985). *Half the human experience: The psychology of women* (3rd ed.). Lexington, MA: Heath.

Hyde, J. S., & Rosenberg, B. G. (1980). *Half the human experience: The psychology of women*. (2nd ed.). Lexington, MA: Heath.

Illfelder, J. K. (1980). Fear of success, sex role attitudes, and career salience and anxiety levels of college women. *Journal of Vocational Behavior*, **16**, 7–17.

Jeffries, D. (1976). Counseling for the strengths of the black woman. *The Counseling Psychologist*, **6**, 20–22.

Johnson, C. L., & Johnson, F. A. (1977). Attitudes toward parenting in dual-career families. *American Journal of Psychiatry*, **134**, 391–395.

Johnson, R. W. (1970). Parental identification and vocational interests of college women. *Measurement and Evaluation in Guidance*, **3**, 147–151.

Jones, J., & Welch, O. (1980). The black professional woman. *Journal of the National Association of Women Deans, Administrators, and Counselors*, **43**, 29–32.

Joreskog, K. G., & Sorbom, D. (1981). *LISRELVI*. Mooresville, IN: Scientific Software.

Joyce, N. C., & Hall, P. Q. (1977). Women researchers analyze education, job barriers, *Science*, **198**, 917–918.

Kagan, J., & Moss, H. A. (1962). *Birth to maturity: A study in psychological development*. New York: Wiley.

Kahl, A. (1983). Characteristics of job entrants in 1980–1981. *Occupational Outlook Quarterly*, **27**, 18–26.

Kahn, S. E. (1984). Astin's model of career development: The working lives of women and men. *The Counseling Psychologist*, **12**, 145–146.

Kaley, M. M. (1971). Attitudes toward the dual role of the married professional woman. *American Psychologist*, **26**, 301–306.

Kalin, R., & Tilby, P. (1978). Development and validation of a sex role ideology scale. *Psychological Reports*, **42**, 731–738.

Kanter, R. (1976). *Work and family in America: A critical review and research agenda*. Social Science Frontiers Monograph Series. New York: Sage.

Kanter, R. M. (1977). *Men and women of the corporation*. New York: Basic Books.

Kanungo, R. N. (1979). The concepts of alienation and involvement revisited. *Psychological Bulletin*, **86**, 119–138.

Karabel, J. (1972). Community colleges and social stratification. *Harvard Educational Review*, **42**, 521–562.

Kassner, M. W. (1981). Will both spouses have careers? Predictions of preferred traditional or egalitarian marriages among university students. *Journal of Vocational Behavior*, **18**, 340–355.

Katz, J. (1969). Career and autonomy in college women. In J. Katz (Ed.), *Class, character, and career*. Stanford, CA: Stanford University Press.

Kaufman, D., & Fetters, M. L. (1980). Work motivation and job values among professional men and women: A new accounting. *Journal of Vocational Behavior*, **17**, 251–262.

Kearney, H. R. (1979). Feminist challenges to the social structure and sex roles. *Psychology of Women Quarterly*, **4**, 16–31.

Key, M. R. (1975). Male and female in children's books. In R. K. Unger & F. L. Denmark (Eds.), *Woman: Dependent or independent variable* (pp. 55–70). New York: Psychological Dimensions.

Kimmel, E., Dickenson, J., & Topping, M. (1981). Curriculum revision for sex-fair elementary education: Analysis of an intervention model. *Peabody Journal of Education*, April, 154–160.

Klein, S. S., & Simonson, J. (1984). Increasing sex equity in education: Roles for psychologists. *American Psychologist*, **39**, 1187–1192.

Knapp, R. R., Knapp, L., & Knapp-Lee, L. (1985). Occupational interest measurement and subsequent career decisions. *Journal of Counseling Psychology*, **32**, 348–354.

Knaub, P. K., & Eversoll, D. B. (1983). Is parenthood a desirable adult role? An assessment of attitudes held by contemporary women. *Sex Roles*, **9**, 355–362.

Knell, S., & Winer, G. A. (1979). Effects of reading content on occupational sex-role stereotypes. *Journal of Vocational Behavior*, **14**, 78–87.

Komarovsky, M. (1982). Female freshmen view their future: Career salience and its correlates. *Sex Roles*, **8**, 299–314.

Krefting, L. A., & Berger, P. K. (1979). Masculinity–femininity perceptions of job requirements and their relationship to job sex types. *Journal of Vocational Behavior*, **15**, 164–174.

Krefting, L. A., Berger, P. K., & Wallace, M. J. (1978). The contribution of sex-distribution, job content, and occupational classification to job sex typing: Two studies. *Journal of Vocational Behavior*, **13**, 181–191.

Kreinberg, N. (1982). EQUALS: Working with educators. In S. M. Humphreys (Ed.), *Women and minorities in science* (pp. 39–54). Boulder, CO: Westview Press.

Kriedberg, G., Butcher, A. L., & White, K. M. (1978). Vocational role choice in 2nd and 6th grade children. *Sex Roles*, **4**, 175–182.

Kriger, S. F. (1972). Achievement and perceived parental childrearing attitudes of career women and homemakers. *Journal of Vocational Behavior*, **2**, 419–432.

Kroeker, T. (1963). Coping and defensive function of the ego. In R. W. White (Ed.), *A study of lives*. New York: Atherton.

Kutner, N. G., & Brogan, D. (1976). Sources of sex discrimination in educational systems: A conceptual model. *Psychology of Women Quarterly*, **1**, 50–69.

Kutner, N. G., & Brogan, D. R. (1980). The decision to enter medicine: Motivation, social support, and discouragements for women. *Psychology of Women Quarterly*, **5**, 321–340.

Lacy, W. B., Bokemeier, J. L., & Shepard, J. M. (1983). Job attribute preferences and work commitment of men and women in the United States. *Personnel Psychology, 36*, 315–329.

Lamouse, A. (1969). Family roles of women: A German example. *Journal of Marriage and the Family, 31*, 145–152.

Lanier, H. B., & Byre, J. (1981). How high school students view women: The relationship between perceived attractiveness, occupation, and education. *Sex Roles, 7*, 146–148.

Lantz, A. (1985). Strategies to increase mathematics enrollments. In S. F. Chipman, L. R. Brush, & D. M. Wilson (Eds.), *Women and mathematics: Balancing the equation* (pp. 329–354). Hillsdale, NJ: Erlbaum.

Lao, R. C., Upchurch, W. H., Corwin, B. J., & Crossnickle, W. F. (1975). Biased attitudes toward females as indicated by ratings of intelligence and likeability. *Psychology Reports, 37*, 1315–1320.

Lauver, P. J., Gastellum, R. M., & Sheehey, M. (1975). Bias in OOH illustrations? *Vocational Guidance Quarterly, 23*, 335–340.

Laws, J. L. (1979). *The second X: Sex role and social role.* New York: Elsevier.

Layton, W. L. (1958). *Counseling use of the Strong Vocational Interest Blank.* Minneapolis: University of Minnesota Press.

Lemkau, J. P. (1979). Personality and background characteristics of women in male-dominated occupations: A review. *Psychology of Women Quarterly, 4*, 221–240.

Lemkau, J. P. (1983). Women in male-dominated professions: Distinguishing personality and background characteristics. *Psychology of Women Quarterly, 8*, 144–165.

Lenney, E. (1977). Women's self confidence in achievement settings. *Psychological Bulletin, 84*, 1–13.

Levinson, R. M. (1975). Sex discrimination and employment practices: An experiment with unconventional job inquiries. *Social Problems, 22*, 533–542.

Levitt, E. S. (1972). Vocational development of professional women: A review. *Journal of Vocational Behavior, 1*, 375–385.

Levy, J. (1969). Possible basis for the evolution of lateral specialization of the human brain. *Nature (London), 224*, 614–615.

Levy-Agresti, J., & Sperry, R. W. (1968). Differential perceptual capacities in major and minor hemispheres. *Proceedings of the National Academy of Sciences of the U.S., 61*, 1151.

Lichtenberg, J. W., & Heck, E. J. (1983). Sex bias in counseling: A reply and critique. *The Personnel and Guidance Journal, 62*, 102–104.

Lipmen-Blumen, J., Handley-Isaksen, A., & Leavitt, H. J. (1983). Achieving styles in men and women. A model, an instrument, and some findings. In J. Spence (Ed.), *Achievement and achievement motives.* San Francisco: Freeman.

Llabre, M. M., & Suarez, E. (1985). Predicting math anxiety and course performance in college women and men. *Journal of Counseling Psychology, 32*, 283–287.

Lockheed, M. E., & Ekstrom, R. B. (1977). *Sex discrimination in education: A literature review and bibliography.* Princeton, NJ: Educational Testing Service.

Locksley, A. O. (1980). On the effects of wives' employment on marital adjustment and companionship. *Journal of Marriage and the Family, 42*, 337–346.

Lofquist, L. H., & Dawis, R. V. (1969). *Adjustment to work.* New York: Appleton.

Long, J. S. (1983). *Covariance structure models: An introduction to LISREL.* Beverly Hills, CA: Sage.

Looft, W. R. (1971). Sex differences in the expression of vocational aspirations by elementary school children. *Developmental Psychology, 5*, 366.

Lopata, H. Z. (1966). The life cycle of the social role of the housewife. *Sociology and Social Research*, **51**, 5–22.

Lott, B. (1985). The potential enrichment of social/personality psychology through feminist research and vice versa. *American Psychologist*, **40**, 155–164.

Lott, B., Reilly, M. E., & Howard, D. R. (1982). Sexual assault and harassment: A campus community case study. *Signs*, **8**, 296–319.

Lundberg, F., & Farnham, M. F. (1947). *Modern woman: The lost sex*. New York: Harper.

Lunneborg, C. E., & Lunneborg, P. W. (1984). Contribution of sex-differentiated experience to spatial and mechanical reasoning abilities. *Perceptual and Motor Skills*, **59**, 107–113.

Lunneborg, P. W. (1977). Construct validity of the Strong-Campbell Interest Inventory and the Vocational Interest Inventory among college counseling clients. *Journal of Vocational Behavior*, **10**, 187–195.

Lunneborg, P. W. (1979). Service vs. technical interest—Biggest sex difference of all? *Vocational Guidance Quarterly*, **28**, 146–153.

Lunneborg, P. W. (1980). Reducing sex bias in interest measurement at the item level. *Journal of Vocational Behavior*, **16**, 226–234.

Lunneborg, P. W., & Lillie, C. (1973). Sexism in graduate admissions: The letter of recommendation. *American Psychologist*, **28**, 188–189.

Lunneborg, P. W., & Lunneborg, C. E. (1986). Everday Spatial Activities Test for studying differential experience and vocational behavior. *Journal of Vocational Behavior*, **28**, 135–141.

Lyson, T. A., & Brown, S. S. (1982). Sex-role attitudes, curriculum choice, and career ambition: A comparison between women in typical and atypical college majors. *Journal of Vocational Behavior*, **20**, 366–375.

Maccoby, E. E., & Jacklin, C. N. (1974). *The psychology of sex differences*. Stanford, CA: Stanford University Press.

MacKay, W. R., & Miller, C. A. (1982). Relations of socio-economic status and sex variables to the complexity of worker functions in the occupational choices of elementary school children. *Journal of Vocational Behavior*, **20**, 31–37.

MacKinnon, D. A. (1978). *Sexual harassment of working women*. New Haven, CT: Yale University Press.

Maier, N. R. (1970). Male versus female discussion leaders. *Personnel Psychology*, **23**, 445–461.

Malkiel, B. G., & Malkiel, J. A. (1973). Male-female pay differentials in professional employment. *American Economic Review*, **63**, 693–704.

Manhardt, R. J. (1972). Job orientation of male and female college graduates in business. *Personnel Psychology*, **25**, 361–368.

Mannheim, B. (1983). Male and female industrial workers: Job satisfaction, work role centrality and work place preference. *Work and Occupations*, **10**, 413–436.

Maracek, J., & Frasch, C. (1977). Locus of control and college women's role expectations. *Journal of Counseling Psychology*, **24**, 132–136.

Marawski, J. G. (1982). On thinking about history as social psychology, *Personality and Social Psychology Bulletin*, **8**, 383–401.

Maret-Havens, E. (1977). Developing an index to measure female labor force attachment. *Monthly Labor Review*, **100**, 35–38.

Marini, M. M. (1978). Sex differences in the determination of adolescent aspirations: A review of research. *Sex Roles*, **4**, 723–754.

Marshall, S. J., & Wijting, J. P. (1980). Relationships of achievement motivation and sex role identity to college women's career orientation. *Journal of Vocational Behavior,* **16,** 299–311.

Martin, J. R. (1982). Excluding women from the educational realm. *Harvard Educational Review,* **52,** 133–148.

Martin, T. W., Berry, K. J., & Jacobsen, R. B. (1975). The impact of dual-career marriages on female professional careers: An empirical test of a Parsonian hypothesis. *Journal of Marriage and the Family,* **37,** 734–742.

Marx, M. H. (1963). *Theories in contemporary psychology.* New York: Macmillan.

Masih, L. R. (1967). Career saliency and its relation to certain needs, interests, and job values. *Personnel and Guidance Journal,* **45,** 653–658.

Maslin, A., & Davis, J. L. (1975). Sex-role stereotyping as a factor in mental health standards among counselors-in-training. *Journal of Counseling Psychology,* **22,** 87–91.

Maslow, A. H. (1954). *Motivation and personality.* New York: Harper.

Mason, K. O., Czajka, J. L., & Arber, S. (1976). Change in U.S. women's sex-role attitudes. *American Sociological Review,* **41,** 573–596.

Matthews, E., & Tiedeman, D. V. (1964). Attitudes toward career and marriage and the development of lifestyle in young women. *Journal of Counseling Psychology,* **11,** 374–383.

Maynard, C. E., & Zawacki, R. A. (1979). Mobility and the dual-career couple. *Personnel Journal,* **58,** 468–472.

McCain, N. (1963). Female faculty members and students at Harvard report sexual harassment. *The Chronicle of Higher Education,* **27,** 1, 14.

McClelland, D. C., Atkinson, J. W., Clark, R. A., & Lowell, E. L. (1953). *The achievement motive.* New York: Appleton.

McDaniel, E., Guay, R., Ball, L., & Kolloff, M. (1978). *A spatial experience questionnaire and some preliminary findings.* Paper presented at the annual meeting of the American Psychological Association, Toronto.

McHugh, M., & Frieze, I. H. (1982). *The effects of sex linkage of task, ambiguity of feedback, and competition on the performance expectations of males and females.* Paper presented at the meeting of the American Educational Research Association, New York.

McLure, G. T., & Piel, E. (1978). Career-bound girls and science careers: Perceptions of barriers and facilitating factors. *Journal of Vocational Behavior,* **12,** 172–183.

McMahan, I. D. (1971). *Sex differences in causal attributions following success and failure.* Paper presented at the meeting of the Eastern Psychological Association.

McMahan, I. D. (1972). *Sex differences in expectancy of success as a function of task.* Paper presented at the meeting of the Eastern Psychological Association.

Medvene, A. M., & Collins, A. M. (1976). Occupational prestige and appropriateness: The views of mental health specialists. *Journal of Vocational Behavior,* **9,** 63–71.

Meece, J. L., Eccles-Parsons, J., Kaczala, C. M., Goff, S. B., & Futterman, R. (1982). Sex differences in math achievement: Toward a model of academic choice. *Psychological Bulletin,* **91,** 324–348.

Meek, P. M., & Lynch, A. Q. (1983). Establishing an informal grievance procedure for cases of sexual harassment of students. *Journal of the National Association for Women Deans, Administrators, and Counselors,* **46,** 30–33.

Megargee, E. E. (1969). Influence of sex roles on the manifestation of leadership. *Journal of Applied Psychology,* **53,** 377–382.

Mellor, E. F. (1984). Investigating the differences in weekly earnings of women and men. *Monthly Labor Review,* **107,** 17–28.

Merritt, K. (1976). Women and higher education: Voices from the sexual Siberia. In J. I. Roberts (Ed.), *Beyond intellectual sexism: A new woman, a new reality.* New York: McKay.

Mertens, D. M., & Gardner, J. A. (1981). *Vocational education and the younger adult worker.* Columbus, OH: The National Center for Research in Vocational Education. (ERIC Document Reproduction Service No. ED 215 451).

Merton, R. K. (1957). *Social theory and social structure.* (rev. ed.). Glencoe; IL: Free Press.

Metzler-Brennan, E., Lewis, R. J., & Gerrad, M. (1985). Childhood antecedents of adult women's masculinity, femininity, and career role choices. *Psychology of Women Quarterly, 9,* 371–382.

Mezydlo, L., & Betz, N. E. (1980). Perceptions of ideal sex roles as a function of sex and feminist orientation. *Journal of Counseling Psychology, 27,* 282–285.

Miller, A. G. (1970). Role of physical attractiveness in impression formation. *Psychonomic Science, 9,* 241–243.

Miller v. Bank of America, 418 F. Supp. 233 (N.D. Cal. 1976), revised, 600 F.2d 211 (9th Circuit 1979).

Miner, J. B. (1974). Motivation to manage among women: Studies of business managers and educational administrators. *Journal of Vocational Behavior, 5,* 197–208.

Miner, J. B., & Smith, N. R. (1982). Decline and stabilization of managerial motivation over a 20 year period. *Journal of Applied Psychology, 67,* 297–305.

Mischel, W. (1970). Sex typing and socialization. In P. H. Mussen (Ed.), *Carmichael's manual of child psychology.* New York: Wiley.

Muchinsky, P. M., & Harris, S. L. (1977). The effect of applicant sex and scholastic standing on the evaluation of job applicant resumes in sex-typed occupations. *Journal of Vocational Behavior, 11,* 95–108.

Muldrow, T. W., & Bayton, J. A. (1979). Men and women executives and processes related to decision accuracy. *Journal of Applied Psychology, 64,* 99–106.

Munley, P. H. (1974). Interests of career and homemaking-oriented women. *Journal of Vocational Behavior, 4,* 43–48.

Murray, H. A. (1938). *Explorations in personality.* New York: Oxford University Press.

Murray, S. R., & Mednick, M. T. S. (1977). Black women's achievement orientation: Motivational and cognitive factors. *Psychology of Women Quarterly, 1,* 247–259.

Murray, S. R., & Scott, P. B. (Eds.) (1982). Special issue on black women. *Psychology of Women Quarterly, 6*(3).

Naffziger, K. G. (1972). *A survey of counselor-educators' and other selected professionals' attitudes toward women's roles.* Unpublished doctoral dissertation, University of Michigan.

Nagely, D. (1971). Traditional and pioneer working mothers. *Journal of Vocational Behavior, 1,* 331–341.

Nash, S. C. (1979). Sex role as a mediator of intellectual functioning. In M. A. Witttig & A. L. Petersen (Eds.), *Sex-related differences in cognitive functioning.* New York: Academic Press.

National Academy of Sciences (1968). *Careers of Ph.D's.* Washington, DC: National Academy of Sciences—National Research Council.

National Center for Education Statistics (1979). *Higher education general information survey.* Washington, DC: Author.

National Project on Women in Education (1978). *Taking sexism out of education.* Washington, DC: U.S. Department of Health, Education, and Welfare.

National Science Foundation. (1984). *Women and minorities in science and engineering*. Washington, DC: Author.

Nelson, J. A. (1978). Age and sex differences in the development of children's occupational reasoning. *Journal of Vocational Behavior, 13*, 287–297.

Nevill, D. D. (1984). The meaning of work in women's lives: Role conflict, preparation, and change. *The Counseling Psychologist, 12*, 131–134.

Newcombe, N., Bandura, M. M., & Taylor, D. G. (1983). Sex differences in spatial ability and spatial activities. *Sex Roles, 9*, 377–386.

Newman, D. K., Amidet, N. J., Carter, B. L., Day, D., Kruvant, W. J., & Russell, J. S. (1978). *Protest, politics, and prosperity: Black Americans and white institutions, 1940–1975*. New York: Pantheon.

Nieva, V. F., & Gutek, B. A. (1981). *Women and work: A psychological perspective*. New York: Praeger.

Nilsen, A. P. (1971). Women in children's literature. *College English, 32*, 918–926.

Norton, A. J., & Glick, P. C. (1976). Marital instability: Past, present, and future. *Journal of Social Issues, 32*, 5–19.

Nuttall, E. V., Nuttall, R. L., Polit, D., & Hunter, J. B. (1976). The effects of family size, birth order, sibling separation, and crowding on the academic achievement of boys and girls. *American Educational Research Journal, 13*, 217–223.

Nye, F. I. (1963). The adjustment of adolescent children. In F. I. Nye & L. W. Hoffman (Eds.), *The employed mother in America*. Chicago: Rand McNally.

Nye, F. I. (1974). Emerging and declining family roles. *Journal of Marriage and the Family, 36*, 238–245.

Oakley, A. (1974). *The sociology of housework*. New York: Pantheon.

Oates, M. J., & Williamson, S. (1978). Women's colleges and women achievers. *Signs, 3*, 795–806.

O'Bryant, G. L., & Corder-Bolz, C. R. (1978). The effects of television on children's stereotyping of women's work roles. *Journal of Vocational Behavior, 12*, 233–244.

O'Connell, A. N. (1978). Gender-specific barriers to research in psychology: Report of the Task Force on Women Doing Research—APA Division 35. *Journal Supplements Abstract Service, 1753*, 1–10.

O'Connell, A. N., & Russo, N. F. (1980). Eminent women in psychology: Models of achievement. Special issue of the *Psychology of Women Quarterly, 5*, No 1 (Whole).

O'Connor, K., Mann, D. W., & Bardwick, J. M. (1978). Androgyny and self-esteem in the upper-middle class: A replication of Spence. *Journal of Consulting and Clinical Psychology, 46*, 1168–1169.

O'Donnell, J. A., & Anderson, D. G. (1978). Factors influencing choice of major and career of capable women. *Vocational Guidance Quarterly, 26*, 214–221.

Okun, B. F. (1983). *Working with adults: Individual, family and career development*. Monterey, CA: Brooks/Cole.

O'Leary, V. E. (1974). Some attitudinal barriers to occupational aspirations in women. *Psychological Bulletin, 81*, 809–816.

O'Leary, V. E. (1977). *Toward understanding women*. Monterey, CA: Brooks/Cole.

O'Leary, V. E., & Braun, J. S. (1972). Antecedents and correlates of academic careerism in women. *Proceedings of the 80th Annual Convention of the American Psychological Association, 7*, 277–278 *(Summary)*.

Oliver, L. W. (1974). Achievement and affiliation motivation in career-oriented and homemaking-oriented college women. *Journal of Vocational Behavior, 4*, 275–281.

Oliver, L. W. (1975). The relationship of parental attitudes and parental identification to career and homemaking orientation in college women. *Journal of Vocational Behavior,* 1–12.

O'Neil, J. M., Meeker, C. H., & Borgers, S. B. (1978). A developmental, preventative, and consultative model to reduce sexism in the career planning of women. *JSAS Catalog of Selected Documents in Psychology,* **8,** 39 (Ms. 1684).

Orcutt, M. A., & Walsh, W. B. (1979). Traditionality and congruence of career aspirations for college women. *Journal of Vocational Behavior,* **14,** 1–11.

Orlinsky, D. E., & Howard, K. I. (1976). The effects of sex of therapist on the therapeutic experiences of women. *Psychotherapy: Theory, Research and Practice,* **13,** 82–88.

Orlinsky, D. W., & Howard, K. I. (1980). Gender and psychotherapeutic outcome. In A. M. Brodsky & R. Hare-Mustin (Eds.), *Women in psychotherapy,* New York: Guilford Press.

Orlofsky, J. L., & Stake, J. E. (1981). Psychological masculinity and femininity: Relationship to striving and self-concept in the achievement and interpersonal domains. *Psychology of Women Quarterly,* **6,** 218–233.

Osen, L. M. (1974). *Women in mathematics.* Cambridge, MA: MIT Press.

Osipow, S. H. (Ed.) (1975). *Emerging women: Career analysis and outlooks.* Columbus, OH: Merrill.

Osipow, S. H. (1983). *Theories of career development* (3rd ed.). New York: Prentice-Hall.

Osipow, S. H., & Spokane, A. R. (1983). *A manual for measures of occupational stress, strain, and coping.* Columbus, OH: Marathon Consulting and Press.

Panek, P. E., Rush, M. C., & Greenwalt, J. P. (1977). Current sex stereotypes of 25 occupations. *Psychological Reports,* **40,** 212–214.

Parker, A. W. (1966). Career and marriage orientation in the vocational development of college women. *Journal of Applied Psychology,* **50,** 232–235.

Parsons, F. (1909). *Choosing a vocation.* Boston: Houghton Mifflin.

Parsons, J. E., Frieze, I. H., & Ruble, D. N. (1978). Intrapsychic factors influencing career aspirations in college women. *Sex Roles,* **4,** 337–348.

Parsons, T. (1942). Age and sex in the social structure of the United States. *American Sociology Review,* **7,** 604–616.

Patrick, T. (1973). *Personality and family background characteristics of women who enter male-dominated professions.* Unpublished doctoral dissertation, Columbia University.

Patterson, L. E. (1973). Girl's careers—Expression of identity. *Vocational Guidance Quarterly,* **21,** 268–275.

Patterson, M., & Sells, L. (1973). Women dropouts from higher education. In A. Rossi & A. Calderwood (Eds.), *Academic women on the move.* New York: Russell Sage Foundation.

Pedro, J. D., Wolleat, P., Fennema, E., & Becker, A. D. (1981). Election of high school mathematics by females and males: Attributions and attitudes. *American Educational Research Journal,* **18,** 207–218.

Peng, S. S., & Jaffe, J. (1979). Women who enter male-dominated fields of study in higher education. *American Educational Research Journal,* **16,** 285–293.

Pepin, A. J. (1980). *Fall enrollment in higher education, 1979.* Washington, DC: National Center for Education Statistics.

Pepin, A., Knepper, P., Bales, S. N., Bartell, E., Shulman, C. H., & Williams, M. C. (1982). *Trends and patterns in higher education, 1970–79.* Washington, D.C.: American Council on Education.

Perun, P. J., & DelVento-Bielby, D. (1981). Towards a model of female occupational behavior: A human development approach. *Psychology of Women Quarterly*, **6**, 234–252.

Peters, L. H., Terborg, J. R., & Taynor, J. (1974). Women as Managers Scale (WAMS): A measure of attitudes toward women in management positions. *JSAS Catalog of Selected Documents in Psychology*, (Ms. No. 585).

Pfafflin, S. M. (1984). Women, science, and technology. *American Psychologist*, **39**, 1183–1186.

Phelan, W. T. (1979). Undergraduate orientations toward scientific and scholarly careers. *American Educational Research Journal*, **16**, 411–422.

Pietrofessa, J. J., & Schlossberg, N. K. (1970). *Counselor bias and the female occupational role.* ERIC Document CG006056.

Pingree, S., Butler, M., Paisley, W., & Hawkins, R. (1978). Anti-nepotism's ghost: Attitudes of administrators toward hiring professional couples. *Psychology of Women Quarterly*, **3**, 22–29.

Plake, B. S., & Parker, C. S. (1982). The development and validation of a revised version of the Mathematics Anxiety Rating Scale. *Educational and Psychological Measurement*, **42**, 551–557.

Pleck, J. H. (1977). The work-family role system. *Social Problems*, **24**, 417–427.

Polatnik, M. (1973). Why men don't rear children. *Berkeley Journal of Sociology*, **18**, 45–86.

Poloma, M. M. (1972) Role conflict and the married professional woman. In C. Safilios-Rothschild (Ed.), *Toward a sociology of women.* Lexington, MA: Xerox College Publishing.

Poloma, M. M., & Garland, T. N. (1971). The married professional woman: A study in the tolerance of domestication. *Journal of Marriage and the Family*, **33**, 531–540.

Poole, M. E., & Clooney, G. H. (1985). Careers: Adolescent awareness and exploration of possibilities for self. *Journal of Vocational Behavior*, **26**, 251–263.

Porter, L. W. (1961). A study of perceived need satisfactions in bottom and middle management jobs. *Journal of Applied Psychology*, **45**, 1–10.

Pottker, J., & Fishel, A. (1977). *Sex bias in the schools: The research evidence.* Rutherford, NJ: Farleigh Dickenson University Press.

Powell, G. N., & Butterfield, D. A. (1979). The "good manager": Masculine or androgynous? *Academy of Management Journal*, **22**, 395–403.

Powell, K. S. (1963). Personalities of children and child-rearing attitudes of mothers. In F. I. Nye & L. W. Hoffman (Eds.), *The employed mother in America.* Chicago: Rand McNally.

Prediger, D. J. (1980). The determination of Holland types characterizing occupational groups. *Journal of Vocational Behavior*, **16**, 33–42.

Prediger, D. J., & Hanson, G. R. (1976). Holland's theory of careers applied to men and women: Analysis of implicit assumptions. *Journal of Vocational Behavior*, **8**, 167–184.

Prediger, D. J., Roth, J. D., & Noeth, R. J. (1974). Career development of youth: A nationwide study. *Personnel and Guidance Journal*, **53**, 97–104.

Prediger, D. P., & Cole, N. S. (1975). Sex role socialization and employment realities: Implications for vocational interest measures. *Journal of Vocational Behavior*, **7**, 239–251.

Price, G. E., & Borgers, S. B. (1977). An evaluation of the sex stereotyping effect as related to counselor perceptions of courses appropriate for high school students. *Journal of Counseling Psychology*, **24**, 240–243.

Project on the Status and Education of Women. (1978). *Sexual harassment: A hidden issue.* Washington, DC: Association of American Colleges.

Pryor, R. G. (1983). Sex differences in level of generality of values/preferences related to work. *Journal of Vocational Behavior, 23,* 233–241.

Psathas, G. (1968). Toward a theory of occupational choice for women. *Sociology and Social Research, 52,* 253–268.

Quinn, R. P., Staines, G. L., & McCullough, M. R. (1974). *Job satisfaction: Is there a trend?* Washington, DC: U.S. Department of Labor, Manpower Administration. USGPO.

Rabinowitz, S. (1975). *An examination of the influence of individual difference variables and perceived job stimulation.* Unpublished master's thesis, Michigan State University.

Radloff, L. S. (1975). Sex differences in depression: The effects of occupation and marital status. *Sex Roles, 1,* 249–265.

Ramey, C. T., & Smith, B. J. (1977). Assessing the intellectual consequences of early intervention with high-risk infants. *American Journal of Mental Deficiency, 81,* 318–324.

Rand, L. (1968). Masculinity or femininity: Differentiating career-oriented and home-making-oriented college freshman women. *Journal of Counseling Psychology, 15,* 444–449.

Rand, L. M., & Miller, A. L. (1972). A developmental cross-sectioning of women's career and marriage attitudes and life plans. *Journal of Vocational Behavior, 2,* 317–331.

Randour, M., Strasburg, G., & Lipman-Blumen, J. (1982). Women in higher education: Trends in enrollment and degrees earned. *Harvard Educational Review, 52,* 189–202.

Rapoport, R., & Rapoport, R. (1965). Work and family in modern society. *American Sociological Review, 30,* 381–394.

Rapoport, R., & Rapoport, R. N. (1969). The dual-career family: A variant pattern and social change. *Human Relations, 22,* 3–30.

Rapoport, R., & Rapoport, R. N. (1971). *Dual-career families.* London: Penguin.

Rapaport, R., & Rapoport, R. N. (1972). The dual-career family: A variant pattern and social change. In C. Safilios-Rothschild (Ed.), *Toward a sociology of women.* Lexington, MA: Xerox.

Rapoport, R., & Rapoport, R. N. (1973). Family enabling processes: The facilitating husband in dual-career families. In R. Gosling (Ed.), *Support, innovation and autonomy.* London: Tavistock.

Rapoport, R., & Rapoport, R. N. (1976). *Dual-career families re-examined: New integrations of work and family.* London: Martin Robertson.

Rapoport, R., & Rapoport, R. N. (1980). Three generations of dual-career family research. In F. Pepitone-Rockwell (Ed.), *Dual-career couples.* Beverly Hills: Sage.

Redbook Magazine (1976). **November,** p. 49.

Reilly, T., Carpenter, S., Dull, V., & Bartlett, K. (1982). The factorial survey: An approach to defining sexual harassment on campus. *Journal of Social Issues, 28,* 99–110.

Resnick, H., Viehe, J., & Segal, S. (1982). Is math anxiety a local phenomenon? A study of prevalence and dimensionality. *Journal of Counseling Psychology, 29,* 39–47.

RESOURCE: Careers (1983). *Report of the Dual Career Project.* Cleveland, OH: Author.

Rezler, A. G. (1967). Characteristics of high school girls choosing traditional or pioneer vocations. *Personnel and Guidance Journal, 45*, 659–665.

Ricciuti, H. N. (1974). Fear and the development of social attachments in the first year of life. In M. Lewis & L. A. Rosenblum (Eds.), *The origins of fear.* New York: Wiley.

Rice, D. (1979). *Dual-career marriage: Conflict and treatment.* New York: Free Press.

Rice, J. K. (1977). Perceptions of males and females concerning their graduate education experience in counseling. *Journal of the National Association of Women Deans, Administrators, and Counselors, 41*, 32–37.

Rice, R. W., Bender, L. R., & Villers, A. G. (1980). Leader sex, follower attitudes toward women, and leadership effectiveness: A laboratory experiment. *Organizational Behavior and Human Performance, 25*, 46–78.

Richardson, F. C., & Suinn, R. M. (1972). The mathematics anxiety rating scale: Psychometric data. *Journal of Counseling Psychology, 19*, 551–554.

Richardson, F. C., & Woolfolk, R. L. (1980). Mathematics anxiety. In I. G. Sarason (Ed.), *Test anxiety: Theory, research, and application* (pp. 275–288). Hillsdale, NJ: Erlbaum.

Richardson, J. G. (1979). Wife occupational superiority and marital troubles: An examination of the hypothesis. *Journal of Marriage and the Family, 41*, 63–72.

Richardson, M. S. (1974). The dimensions of career and work orientation in college women. *Journal of Vocational Behavior, 5*, 161–172.

Richardson, M. S. (1981). Occupational and family roles: A neglected intersection. *The Counseling Psychologist, 9*, 13–23.

Richardson, M. S., & Johnson, M. (1984). Counseling women. In S. D. Brown & R. W. Lent (Eds.), *The handbook of counseling psychology.* New York: Wiley.

Ridgeway, C. (1978). Parental identification and patterns of career orientation in college women. *Journal of Vocational Behavior, 12*, 1–11.

Ridgeway, C. L., & Jacobson, C. K. (1979). The development of female role ideology: Impact of personal confidence during adolescence. *Youth and Society, 10*, 297–315.

Ritzer, G. (1972). *Man and his work: Conflict and change.* New York: Prentice-Hall.

Robinson, H. B., & Robinson, N. M. (1971). Longitudinal development of very young children in a comprehensive day care program: The first two years. *Child Development, 42*, 1673–1683.

Roby, P. (1975). Structural and internalized barriers to women in higher education. In J. Freeman (Ed.), *Women: A feminist perspective* (1st ed.). Palo Alto, CA: Mayfield.

Rodenstein, J., Pfleger, L. R., & Colangelo, N. (1977). Career development of gifted women. *Gifted Child Quarterly, 21*, 340–347.

Rogers, C. R. (1951). *Client-centered therapy.* Boston: Houghton Mifflin.

Rogers, L. J. (1983). Hormonal theories for sex differences—Politics disguised as science: A reply to DeBold and Luria. *Sex Roles, 9*, 1109–1113.

Rohfeld, R. W. (1977). High school women's assessment of career planning resources. *Vocational Guidance Quarterly, 26*, 79–84.

Rooney, G. S. (1983). Distinguishing characteristics of the life roles of worker, student, and homemaker for young adults. *Journal of Vocational Behavior, 22*, 324–342.

Rose, G. L., & Andiappan, P. (1978). Sex effects of managerial hiring decisions. *Academy of Management Journal, 21*, 104–112.

Rosen, B., & Jerdee, T. H. (1973). The influence of sex-role stereotypes on evaluations of male and female supervisory behavior. *Journal of Applied Psychology, 57*, 44–48.

Rosen, B., & Jerdee, T. H. (1974). Effects of applicant's sex and difficulty of job on evaluations of candidates for managerial positions. *Journal of Applied Psychology,* **59,** 511–512.

Rosenberg, M. (1965). *Society and the adolescent self image.* Princeton, NJ: Princeton University Press.

Rosenberg, M. (1979). *Conceiving the self.* New York: Basic Books.

Rosenberg, N., & Rosenberg, E. (1978). Shared careers. In S. S. Peterson, J. M. Richardson, & G. V. Kreuter (Eds.), *The two-career family: Issues and alternatives.* Washington, D.C.: University Press of America.

Rosenkrantz, P., Vogel, S., Bee, H., Broverman, I., & Broverman, D. (1968). Sex role stereotypes and self-concepts in college students. *Journal of Consulting and Clinical Psychology,* **32,** 287–295.

Rosenthal, D. A., & Chapman, D. C. (1982). The lady spaceman: Children's perceptions of sex-stereotyped occupations. *Sex Roles,* **8,** 959–966.

Rosow, I., & Rose, K. D. (1972). Divorce among doctors. *Journal of Marriage and the Family,* **34,** 587–598.

Rossi, A. S. (1965). Women in science: Why so few? *Science,* **148,** 1196–1202.

Rossi, A. S. (1970). Discrimination and demography restrict opportunities for academic women. *College and University Business,* **February,** 1–4.

Rossi, A. S., & Calderwood, A. (Eds.). (1973). *Academic women on the move.* New York: Russell Sage.

Rubowitz, P. (1975). Early experience and the achieving orientations of American middle class girls. In M. Maehr & W. Stalling (Eds.), *Culture, child and school.* Monterey, CA: Brooks/Cole.

Rule, S. (1977). Long distance marriages on the rise. *New York Times,* **October 31,** *Section M:31.*

Russo, N. F. (1976). The motherhood mandate. *Journal of Social Issues,* **32,** 143–153.

Russo, N. F. (1979). Overview: Sex roles, fertility and the motherhood mandate. *Psychology of Women Quarterly,* **4,** 7–15.

Russo, N. F., & Denmark, F. L. (1984). Women, psychology and public policy: Selected issues. *American Psychologist,* **39,** 1161–1165.

Russo, N. F., & O'Connell, A. N. (1980). Models from our past: Psychology's foremothers. *Psychology of Women Quarterly,* **5,** 11–53.

Rynes, S., & Rosen, B. (1983). A comparison of male and female reactions to career advancement opportunities. *Journal of Vocational Behavior,* **22,** 105–116.

Rytina, N. F. (1982). Earnings of men and women: A look at specific occupations. *Monthly Labor Review,* **105,** 25–31.

Saario, T. N., Jacklin, C. N., & Tittle, C. K. (1973). Sex role stereotyping in the public schools. *Harvard Educational Review,* **43,** 386–416.

Sadd, S., Lenauer, M., Shaver, P., & Dunivant, N. (1978). Objective measurement of fear of success and fear of failure: A factor analytic approach. *Journal of Consulting and Clinical Psychology,* **46,** 405–416.

Sadker, M. P., & Sadker, D. M. (1980). Sexism in teacher-education texts. *Harvard Educational Review,* **50,** 36–46.

Safilios-Rothschild, C., & Dijkers, M. (1978). Handling unconventional asymmetries. In R. Rapoport & R. Rapoport (Eds.), *Working couples.* New York: Harper.

Saleh, S., & Lalljee, M. (1969). Sex and job orientation. *Personnel Psychology,* **22,** 465–471.

Sandler, B. R. (1981). Sexual harassment: A hidden problem. *Educational Record,* **62,** 52–57.

Saul, L. (1976). Living apart, but together. *New York Times*, **Sept. 26**, Section 11:191.

Sauter, D., Seidl, A., & Karbon, J. (1980). The effects of high school counseling experience and attitudes toward women's roles on traditional or nontraditional career choice. *Vocational Guidance Quarterly*, **28**, 241–249.

Scanzoni, J. H. (1972). *Sexual bargaining: Power politics in the American marriage*. New York: Prentice-Hall.

Scanzoni, J. H. (1978). *Sex roles, women's work, and marital conflict*. Lexington, MA: Heath.

Schachter, S. (1963). Birth order, eminence, and higher education. *American Sociological Review*, **28**, 757–768.

Schaefer, A. T., & Gray, M. W. (1981). Sex and mathematics. *Science*, **211**, 231–232.

Schein, V. E. (1973). The relationship between sex role stereotypes and requisite management characteristics. *Journal of Applied Psychology*, **57**, 95–100.

Schein, V. E. (1975). Relationships between sex role stereotypes and requisite management characteristics among female managers. *Journal of Applied Psychology*, **60**, 340–344.

Schiffler, R. J. (1976). Demographic and social factors in women's work lives. In S. H. Osipow (Ed.), *Emerging woman*. Columbus, Ohio: Charles E. Merrill.

Schlossberg, N. K., & Goodman, J. (1972). A woman's place: Children's sex stereotyping of occupations. *Vocational Guidance Quarterly*, **20**, 266–270.

Schlossberg, N. K., & Pietrofessa, J. L. (1973). Perspectives on counseling bias: Implications for counselor education. *The Counseling Psychologist*, **4**, 44–54.

Schuler, R. S. (1975). Sex, organizational level, and outcome importance: Where the differences are. *Personnel Psychology*, **28**, 365–376.

Schwartz, J. L. (1975). A study of guidance counselor sex biases in the occupational recommendations made for female students of superior intelligence. *Dissertation Abstracts International*, **35**, 2069.

Schwartz, P., & Lever, J. (1973). Women in the male world of higher education. In A. S. Rossi & A. Calderwood (Eds.), *Academic women on the move*. New York: Russell Sage.

Scott, K. P. (1981). Whatever happened to Jane and Dick? Sexism in texts re-examined. *Peabody Journal of Education*, April, 135–140.

Sedney, M. A., & Turner, B. F. (1975). A test of causal sequences in two models for the development of career orientation in women. *Journal of Vocational Behavior*, **6**, 281–291.

Sekaran, U. (1982). An investigation of the career salience of men and women in dual-career families. *Journal of Vocational Behavior*, **20**, 111–119.

Sekaran, U. (1986). *Dual-career families*. San Francisco: Jossey-Bass.

Sells, L. (1973). High school mathematics as the critical filter in the job market. In: Developing opportunities for minorities in graduate education. *Proceedings of the Conference on Minority Graduate Education, University of California, Berkeley*.

Sells, L. W. (1982). Leverage for equal opportunity through mastery of mathematics. In S. M. Humphreys (Ed.), *Women and minorities in science* (pp. 7–26). Boulder, CO: Westview Press.

Senesh, L. (1973). *New paths in social science curriculum design*. Chicago: Science Research Associates.

Sewell, W. H., Haller, A. O., & Ohlendorf, G. (1970). The educational and early occupational attainment process: Replications and revisions. *American Sociological Review*, **35**, 1014–1027.

Sewell, W. H., Haller, A. O., & Portes, A. (1969). The educational and early occupational attainment process. *American Sociological Review*, **34**, 89–92.

Sewell, W. H., Haller, A. O., & Strauss, M. A. (1957). Social status and educational occupational aspiration. *American Sociological Review*, **22**, 67–73.

Sewell, W. H., & Hauser, R. M. (1975). *Education, occupation, and earnings*. New York: Academic Press.

Shaffer, L. F., & Shoben, E. J., Jr. (1956). *The psychology of adjustment* (2nd ed.) Boston: Houghton Mifflin.

Shann, M. H. (1983). Career plans of men and women in gender-dominant professions. *Journal of Vocational Behavior*, **22**, 343–356.

Shavelson, R. J., Hubner, J. J., & Stanton, G. C. (1976). Self-concept: Validation of construct interpretation. *Review of Educational Research*, **46**, 407–441.

Shaw, E. A. (1972). Differential impact of negative stereotyping in employee selection. *Personnel Psychology*, **25**, 333–338.

Shepherd, D. M., & Barraclough, B. M. (1980). Work and suicide: An empirical investigation. *British Journal of Psychiatry*, **136**, 469–478.

Sherman, J. (1967). Problem of sex differences in space perception and aspects of intellectual functioning. *Psychological Review*, **74**, 290–299.

Sherman, J. (1978). *Sex-related cognitive differences*. Springfield, IL: Thomas.

Sherman, J. (1979). Cognitive performance as a function of sex and handedness: An evaluation of the Levy hypothesis. *Psychology of Women Quarterly*, **3**, 378–390.

Sherman, J. (1981). Girls' and boys' enrollments in theoretical math courses: A longitudinal study. *Psychology of Women Quarterly*, **5**, 681–689.

Sherman, J. (1982a). Continuing in mathematics: A longitudinal study of the attitudes of high school girls. *Psychology of Women Quarterly*, **7**, 132–140.

Sherman, J. A. (1982b). Mathematics the critical filter: A look at some residues. *Psychology of Women Quarterly*, **6**, 428–444.

Sherman, J. (1983). Girls talk about mathematics and their futures. *Psychology of Women Quarterly*, **7**, 338–342.

Sherman, J., & Fennema, E. (1977). The study of mathematics by high school girls and boys: Related variables. *American Educational Research Journal*, **14**, 159–168.

Sherman, J., & Fennema, E. (1978). Sex-related differences in mathematics achievement and related factors: A further study. *Journal of Research in Mathematics Education*, **9**, 189–203.

Shinar, E. H. (1975). Sexual stereotypes of occupations. *Journal of Vocational Behavior*, **7**, 99–111.

Shullman, S. L., & Carder, C. E. (1983). Vocational psychology in industrial settings. In W. B. Walsh & S. H. Osipow (Eds.), *Handbook of vocational psychology—Vol II: Applications*. Hillsdale, NJ: Erlbaum.

Shullman, S. L., & Fitzgerald, L. F. (1985). *Capturing a moving target: The objective measurement of sexual harassment in the workplace*. Paper presented to the convention of the American Psychological Association, Los Angeles.

Siegel, A. E., & Haas, M. B. (1963). The working mother: A review of research. *Child Development*, **34**, 513–542.

Siegel, C. L. E. (1973). Sex differences in the occupational choices of second graders. *Journal of Vocational Behavior*, **3**, 15–19.

Simas, K., & McCarrey, M. (1979). Impact of recruiter authoritarianism and applicant sex on evaluation and selection decisions in a recruitment interview analogue study. *Journal of Applied Psychology*, **64**, 483–491.

Simon, J. C., & Feather, N., T. (1973). Causal attributions for success and failure at university examinations. *Journal of Educational Psychology*, **64**, 45–56.

Simpson, R. L., & Simpson, I. H. (1961). Occupational choice among career-oriented college women. *Marriage and Family Living*, **23**, 377–383.

Singer, J. N. (1974). Sex differences-similarities in job preference factors. *Journal of Vocational Behavior*, **5**, 357–365.

Slevin, K. F., & Wingrove, C. R. (1983). Similarities and differences among three generations of women in attitudes toward the female role in contemporary society. *Sex Roles*, **9**, 609–624.

Smith, E. J. (1980). Desiring and expecting to work among high school girls: Some determinants and consequences. *Journal of Vocational Behavior*, **17**, 218–230.

Smith, E. J. (1983). Issues in racial minorities' career behavior. In W. B. Walsh & S. H. Osipow (Eds.), *Handbook of Vocational Psychology* (pp. 161–222). Hillsdale, NJ: Erlbaum.

Smith, E. J. (1981). The working mother: A critique of the research. *Journal of Vocational Behavior*, **19**, 191–211.

Smith, E. J. (1982). The black female adolescent: A review of the educational, career, and psychological literature. *Psychology of Women Quarterly*, **6**, 261–288.

Smith, M. D., & Self, G. D. (1981). Feminists and traditionalists: An attitudinal comparison. *Sex Roles*, **7**, 183–188.

Smith, M. L. (1979). Counselor "discrimination" based on client sex: Reply to Donahue and Costar. *Journal of Counseling Psychology*, **26**, 270–272.

Smith, M. L. (1980). Sex bias in counseling and psychotherapy. *Psychological Bulletin*, **87**, 392–407.

Sobol, M. G. (1963). Commitment to work. In F. I. Nye & L. W. Hoffman (Eds.), *The employed mother in America*. Chicago: Rand-McNally.

Somers, A. (1982). Sexual harassment in academe: Legal issues and definitions. *Journal of Social Issues*, **38**, 23–32.

Sommers, D. (1979). *Empirical evidence on occupational mobility*. Columbus, OH: The National Center for Research in Vocational Education (ERIC Document No. ED 185 347).

Sorenson, J., & Winters, C. J. (1975). Parental influences on women's career development. In S. H. Osipow (Ed.), *Emerging woman*. Columbus, OH: Merrill.

Sorkin, A. L. (1972). Education, occupation, and income of non-white women. *Journal of Negro Education*, **41**, 353–351.

Sostek, A. B. (1963). *The relation of identification and parent-child climate to occupational choice*. Unpublished doctoral dissertation, Boston University.

Spence, J., & Helmreich, R. (1972). The Attitudes toward Women Scale: An objective instrument to measure attitudes toward the rights and roles of women in contemporary society. *Journal Supplements Abstract Service Catalog of Selected Documents in Psychology*, MS No. 153.

Spence, J. T. (Ed.) (1983). *Achievement and achievement motives*. San Francisco: Freeman.

Spence, J. T., & Helmreich, R. L. (1980). Masculine instrumentality and feminine expressiveness: Their relationships with sex role attitudes and behaviors. *Psychology of Women Quarterly*, **5**, 147–153.

Spence, J. T., & Helmreich, R. L. (1981). Androgyny versus gender schema: A comment on Bem's gender schema theory. *Psychological Review*, **88**, 365–368.

Spence, J. T., & Helmreich, R. L. (1983). Achievement-related motives and behaviors. In J. T. Spence (Ed.), *Achievement and achievement motives*. San Francisco: Freeman.

Spence, J. T., Helmreich, R., & Stapp, J. (1974). The Personal Attributes Questionnaire: A measure of sex-role stereotypes and masculinity-femininity. *JSAS Catalog of Selected Documents in Psychology*, **4**, 127.

Spence, J. T., Helmreich, R., & Stapp, J. (1975). Ratings of self and peers on sex role attributes and their relation to self-esteem and conceptions of masculinity and femininity. *Journal of Personality and Social Psychology, 32*, 29–39.

Sperry, R. W., & Levy, J. (1970). *Mental capacities of the disconnected minor hemisphere following commission.* Paper presented at the convention of the American Psychological Association, Miami, FL.

Spitz, R. A. (1945). Hospitalism: An inquiry into the genesis of psychiatric conditions in early childhood. *The psychoanalytic study of the child, 1*, 53–74.

Stafford, I. P. (1984). Relation of attitudes toward women's roles and occupational behavior to women's self-esteem. *Journal of Counseling Psychology, 31*, 332–338.

Stafford, R. E. (1961). Sex differences in spatial visualization as evidence of sex-linked inheritance. *Perceptual and Motor Skills, 13*, 428.

Stake, J. E. (1976). The effect of information regarding group performance norms on goal setting in males and females. *Sex Roles, 2*, 23–28.

Stake, J. E. (1978). Motives for occupational goal setting among male and female college students. *Journal of Applied Psychology, 63*, 617–622.

Stake, J. E. (1979a). The ability/performance dimension of self-esteem: Implications for women's achievement behavior. *Psychology of Women Quarterly, 3*, 365–377.

Stake, J. E. (1979b). Women's self-estimates of competence and the resolution of the career/home conflict. *Journal of Vocational Behavior, 14*, 33–42.

Stake, J. E. (1981). Promoting leadership behaviors in low performance self-esteem women in task-oriented mix-sex dyads. *Journal of Personality, 49*, 401–414.

Stake, J. E., & Levitz, E. (1979). Career goals of college women and perceived achievement-related encouragement. *Psychology of Women Quarterly, 4*, 151–159.

Stake, J. E., & Orlofsky, J. L. (1981). On the use of global and specific measures in assessing the self-esteem of males and females. *Sex Roles, 2*, 653–662.

Standley, K., & Soule, B. (1974). Women in male-dominated professions: Contrasts in their personal and vocational histories. *Journal of Vocational Behavior, 4*, 245–258.

Starr, B. S. (1979). Sex differences among personality correlates of mathematical ability in high school seniors. *Psychology of Women Quarterly. 4*, 212–220.

Steinkamp, M., & Maehr, M. (Eds.). (1983). *Women in science.* Greenwich, Conn: JAI Press.

Steinmann, H., & Fox, D. J. (1966). Male-female perceptions of the female role in the United States. *Journal of Psychology, 64*, 265–276.

Stephan, C. W., & Corder, J. (1985). The effects of dual-career families on adolescents' sex-role attitudes, work and family plans, and choices of important others. *Journal of Marriage and the Family, 47*, 921–929.

Stericker, A. B., & Johnson, J. E. (1977). Sex role identification and self-esteem in college students: Do men and women differ? *Sex Roles, 3*, 19–26.

Stevens, G. E., & DeNisi, A. S., (1980). Women as managers: Attitudes and attributions for performance by men and women. *Academy of Management Journal, 2*, 355–361.

Stewart, A. J. (1980). Personality and situation in the prediction of women's life patterns. *Psychology of Women Quarterly, 5*, 195–206.

St. John-Parsons, D. (1978). Continuous dual-career families: A case study. *Psychology of Women Quarterly, 3*, 30–42.

Stolz, A. (1960). Effects of maternal employment on children: Evidence from research. *Child Development, 31*, 749–782.

Stouffer, S. A., Suchman, E. A., DeVinney, L. C., Starr, S. A., & Williams, R. M. (1949). *The American soldier: Adjustments during army life.* Princeton, NJ: Princeton University Press.

Strauss, A. (1968). Some neglected properties of status passage. In H. D. Becker, B.

Geer, D. Reisma, & R. S. Weiss (Eds.), *Institutions and the person.* Chicago: Aldine.

Stricker, G. (1977). Implications of research for psychotherapeutic treatment of women. *American Psychologist, 32,* 14–22.

Stringer, D. M., & Duncan, E. (1985). Nontraditional occupations: A study of women who have made the choice. *Vocational Guidance Quarterly, 33,* 241–248.

Stringer-Moore, D. M. (1981). Impact of dual-career couples on employers: Problems and solutions. *Public Personnel Management Journal, 10,* 393–401.

Strong, E. K., Jr. (1933). *Vocational Interest Blank for women.* Stanford, CA: Stanford University Press.

Super, D. E. (1951). The criteria of vocational success. *Occupations, 30,* 5–8.

Super, D. E. (1955). The dimensions and measurement of vocational maturity. *Teachers College Record, 57,* 151–163.

Super, D. E. (1957). *The psychology of careers.* New York: Harper.

Super, D. E. (1963). Self-concepts in vocational development. In D. E. Super, R. Starishevsky, N. Martin, & J. P. Jordan (Eds.), *Career development: Self-concept theory.* New York: CEEB Research Monograph No. 4.

Super, D. E. (1973). The Work Values Inventory. In D. G. Zytowski (Ed.), *Contemporary approaches to interest measurement* (pp. 189–205). Minneapolis: University of Minnesota Press.

Sutherland, E., & Veroff, J. (1985). Achievement motivation and sex roles. In V. E. O'Leary, R. K. Unger, & B. S. Wallston (Eds.), *Women, gender, and social psychology* (pp. 101–128). Hillsdale, NJ: Erlbaum.

Swaney, K., & Prediger, D. (1985). The relationship between interest-occupation congruence and job satisfaction. *Journal of Vocational Behavior, 26,* 13–24.

Swatko, M. K. (1981). What's in a title? Personality, job aspirations, and the nontraditional woman. *Journal of Vocational Behavior, 18,* 174–183.

Tangri, S. S. (1972). Determinants of occupational role innovation among college women. *Journal of Social Issues, 28,* 177–199.

Tangri, S. S., Burt, M. R., & Johnson, L. B. (1982). Sexual harassment at work: Three explanatory models. *Journal of Social Issues, 38,* 33–54.

Tanney, M. F., & Birk, J. M. (1976). Women counselors for women clients? A review of the research. *The Counseling Psychologist, 6,* 28–32.

Taveggia, T. C., & Ziemba, T. (1978). Linkages to work: A study of the central life interests and work attachments of male and female workers. *Journal of Vocational Behavior, 12,* 305–320.

Taylor, J. C., & Bowers, D. G. (1972). *Survey of organizations: A machine-scored standardized questionnaire instrument.* Ann Arbor, MI: University of Michigan.

Taylor, M. C., & Hall, J. A. (1982). Psychological androgyny: Theories, methods, and conclusions. *Psychological Bulletin, 92,* 347–366.

Teglasi, H. (1981). Children's choices of and value judgments about sex-typed toys and occupations. *Journal of Vocational Behavior, 18,* 184–195.

Terborg, J. R. (1977). Women in management: A research review. *Journal of Applied Psychology, 62,* 647–664.

Terborg, J. R., & Ilgen, D. R. (1975). A theoretical approach to sex discrimination in traditionally masculine occupations. *Organizational Behavior and Human Performance, 13,* 352–376.

Terman, L. M., & Oden, M. H. (1959). *Genetic studies of genius: V. The gifted group at midlife.* Stanford, CA: Stanford University Press.

Tetenbaun, T. J., Lighter, J., & Travis, A. (1984). The construct validation of an attitude towards working mothers scale. *Psychology of Women Quarterly, 8,* 69–78.

Thomas, A. H., & Stewart, N. R. (1971). Counselor response to female clients with deviate and conforming career goals. *Journal of Counseling Psychology, 18*, 352–357.

Thomas, G. E. (1980). Race and sex group inequity in higher education: Institutional and major field enrollment statuses. *American Educational Research Journal, 17*, 171–181.

Thornton, A., & Camburn, D. (1979). Fertility, sex role attitudes, and labor force participation. *Psychology of Women Quarterly, 4*, 61–80.

Thornton, A., & Freedman, D. (1979). Changes in the sex role attitudes of women: 1962–1977. Evidence from a panel study. *American Sociological Review, 44*, 831–842.

Tickamyer, A. R. (1979). Women's roles and fertility intentions. *Pacific Sociological Review, 22*, 167–184.

Tidball, M. E. (1980). Women's colleges and women achievers revisited. *Signs, 5*, 504–517.

Till, F. (1980). *Sexual harassment: A report on the sexual harassment of students.* Washington, DC: National Advisory Council on Women's Educational Programs.

Tinsley, D. J., & Faunce, P. S. (1978). Vocational interests of career and homemaker oriented women. *Journal of Vocational Behavior, 13*, 327–337.

Tinsley, D. J., & Faunce, P. S. (1980). Enabling, facilitating, and precipitating factors associated with women's career orientation. *Journal of Vocational Behavior, 17*, 183–194.

Tobias, S. (1978). *Overcoming math anxiety.* New York: Norton.

Tomkins v. Public Service Electric & Gas Co., 568 F.2d 1044 (3rd Cir. 1977).

Tremaine, D. J., & Hartmann, H. I. (Eds.) (1981). *Women, work, and wages: Equal pay for jobs of equal value.* Washington, DC: National Academy Press.

Tremaine, L. S., & Schau, C. G. (1979). Sex-role aspects in the development of children's vocational knowledge. *Journal of Vocational Behavior, 14*, 317–328.

Trigg, L. J., & Perlman, D. (1976). Social influences on women's pursuit of a nontraditional career. *Psychology of Women Quarterly, 1*, 138–150.

Turner, B. F., & McCaffrey, J. H. (1974). Socialization and career orientation among black and white college women. *Journal of Vocational Behavior, 5*, 307–319.

Tyler, C. (1977). The encounter with poverty—its effects on vocational psychology. In H. J. Peters & J. C. Hanson (Eds.), *Vocational guidance and career level* (3rd ed). New York: Macmillan.

Tyler, L. E. (1964). The antecedents of two varieties of vocational interests. *Genetic Psychology Monographs, 70*, 177–227.

Tyler, L. E. (1965). *The psychology of human differences.* New York: Appleton.

Tyler, L. E. (1978). *Individuality.* San Francisco: Jossey-Bass.

Umstot, M. E. (1980). Occupational sex-role liberality of third-, fifth-, and seventh-grade females. *Sex Roles, 6*, 611–618.

Underwood, B. J. (1957). *Psychological research.* New York: Appleton.

Unger, R. K. (1979). *Female and male: Psychological perspectives.* New York: Harper.

U.S. Department of Labor, Women's Bureau (1975). *Handbook on women workers.* Washington, DC: U.S. Government Printing Office, Bulletin 297.

U.S. Department of Labor, Bureau of Labor Statistics (1977). *U.S. working women: A data book.* Washington, DC: Bureau of Labor Statistics.

U.S. Department of Labor, Bureau of Labor Statistics (1979). *Employment and Earnings, 26* (January).

U.S. Department of Labor, Women's Bureau (1980). *Job options for women in the 80's.* Washington, DC: U.S. Department of Labor.

U.S. Department of Labor (1984). *Facts on women workers.* Washington, DC: U.S. Department of Labor.

U.S. Merit Systems Protection Board, Office of Merit Systems Review and Studies. (1981). *Sexual harassment in the federal workplace: Is it a problem?* Washington, DC: USGPO.

Van Dusen, R. A., & Sheldon, E. B. (1976). The changing status of American women. *American Psychologist, 31,* 106–116.

Van Maanen, J. (1976). Breaking in: Socialization to work. In R. Dubin (Ed.). *Handbook of work, organization, and society.* Chicago: Rand McNally.

Varca, P. E., Shaffer, G. S., & McCauley, C. D. (1983). Sex differences in job satisfaction revisited. *Academy of Management Journal, 26,* 348–352.

Veroff, J., & Feld, S. (1970). *Marriage and work in America.* Princeton, NJ: Van Nostrand-Reinhold.

Veroff, J., Wilcox, S., & Atkinson, J. W. (1953). The achievement motive in high-school and college age women. *Journal of Abnormal and Social Psychology, 48,* 108–119.

Vetter, B. M. (1980). Working women scientists and engineers. *Science, 207,* 28–34.

Vetter, L. (1973). Career counseling for women. *The Counseling Psychologist, 4,* 54–67.

Vetter, L., & Lewis, E. C. (1964). Some correlates of homemaking versus career preference among college home economics students. *Personnel and Guidance Journal, 42,* 593–598.

Vogel, S. R., Broverman, I., Broverman, D., Clarkson, F., & Rosenkrantz, P. (1970). Maternal employment and perceptions of sex role stereotypes. *Developmental Psychology, 3,* 384–391.

Wagman, M. (1966). Interests and values of career and homemaking-oriented women. *Personnel and Guidance Journal, 44,* 794–801.

Walker, J. E., Tansky, C., & Oliver, D. (1982). Men and women at work: Similarities and differences in work values within occupational groupings. *Journal of Vocational Behavior, 21,* 17–36.

Wallston, B. S. (1981). What are the questions in psychology of women? A feminist approach to research. *Psychology of Women Quarterly, 5,* 597–617.

Wallston, B. S., Foster, M. A., & Berger, M. (1978). I will follow him: Myth, reality, or forced choice—Job seeking experiences of dual career couples. *Psychology of Women Quarterly, 3,* 9–21.

Walsh, M. R. (1977). *"Doctors wanted: No women need apply": Sexual barriers in the medical profession 1835–1975.* New Haven, CT: Yale University Press.

Walsh, M. R. (1979). The rediscovery of the need for a feminist medical education. *Harvard Educational Review, 49,* 447–466.

Walsh, W. B., & Betz, N. E. (1985). *Tests and assessment.* New York: Prentice-Hall.

Walsh, W. B., & Osipow, S. H. (Eds.) (1983a). *Handbook of vocational psychology, Vol. I: Foundations.* Hillsdale, NJ: Erlbaum.

Walsh, W. B., & Osipow, S. H. (Eds.) (1983b). *Handbook of vocational psychology, Vol II: Applications.* Hillsdale, NJ: Erlbaum.

Walum, L. R. (1977). *The dynamics of sex and gender: A sociological perspective.* Chicago: Rand McNally.

Wampler, K. S. (1982). Counseling implications of the housewife role. *Counseling and Values, 26,* 125–132.

Wardle, M. G. (1976). Women's physiological responses to physically demanding work. *Psychology of Women Quarterly, 1,* 151–159.

Ware, M. E. (1980). Antecedents of educational/career preferences and choices. *Journal of Vocational Behavior, 16,* 312–319.

Ware, N. C., Steckler, N., & Leserman, J. (1985). Undergraduate women who choose a science major. *Journal of Higher Education*, **56**, 73–84.

Warr, P., & Parry, G. (1982). Paid employment and women's psychological well-being. *Psychological Bulletin*, **91**, 498–516.

Washburn, S. (1981). *Partners: How to have a loving relationship after liberation*. New York: Atheneum.

Wasserman, M. (1974). *Demystifying schools*. New York: Praeger.

Watley, D. J., & Kaplan, R. (1971). Career or marriage? Aspirations and achievements of able and young college women. *Journal of Vocational Behavior*, **1**, 29–43.

Weeks, M. O., & Gage, B. A. (1984). A comparison of the marriage-role expectations of college women enrolled in a functional marriage course in 1961, 1972, and 1978. *Sex Roles*, **11**, 377–388.

Weiner, B., Frieze, I., Kukla, A., Reed, L., Rest, S., & Rosenbaum, R. M. (1971). *Perceiving the causes of success and failure*. Morristown, NJ: General Learning Press.

Weingarten, K. (1978). The employment pattern of professional couples and their distribution of involvement in the family. *Psychology of Women Quarterly*, **3**, 43–52.

Weishaar, M. E., Green, B. J., & Craighead, L. W. (1981). Primary influences of initial vocational choices for college women. *Journal of Vocational Behavior*, **18**, 67–78.

Weiss, D. J. (1973). The Minnesota Importance Questionnaire. In D. G. Zytowski (Ed.), *Contemporary approaches to interest measurement*. Minneapolis: University of Minnesota Press.

Weiss, D. J., Dawis, R. V., Lofquist, L. V., Gay, E., & Hendel, D. D. (1975). *The Minnesota Importance Questionnaire*. Minneapolis: University of Minnesota, Department of Psychology, Work Adjustment Project.

Weitzman, L. J. (1979). *Sex role socialization*. Palo Alto, CA: Mayfield.

Weitzman, L. J., Eitler, D., Hokada, E., & Ross, C. (1972). Sex role socialization in picture books for preschool children. *American Journal of Sociology*, **72**, 1125–1150.

Weller, L., Shlumi, A., & Zimont, G. (1976). Birth order, sex, and occupational interest. *Journal of Vocational Behavior*, **8**, 45–50.

Weller, R. H. (1968). The employment of wives, dominance, and fertility. *Journal of Marriage and the Family*, **30**, 437–442.

Wells, L. E., & Maxwell, G. (1976). *Self-esteem: Its conceptualization and measurement*. Beverly Hills, CA: Sage.

Wertheim, E. G., Widom, C. S., & Wortzel, L. H. (1978). Multivariate analyses of male and female professional career choice correlates. *Journal of Applied Psychology*, **63**, 234–242.

Werts, C. E. (1965). Social class and career choice of college freshmen. *National Merit Scholarship Corporation Research Reports*, **1** (8).

Werts, C. E. (1966). Career choice patterns: Ability and social class. *National Merit Scholarship Corporation Research Reports*, **2**, (3).

Westervelt, E. M. (1975). *Barriers to women's participation in postsecondary education*. Washington, DC: U.S. Government Printing Office.

White, K. (1967). Social background variables related to career commitment of women teachers. *Personnel and Guidance Journal*, **45**, 648–653.

Whiteley, B. E., Jr. (1979). Sex roles and psychotherapy: A current appraisal. *Psychological Bulletin*, **86**, 1309–1321.

Whitley, B. E., Jr. (1984). Sex role orientation and psychological well-being: Two meta-analyses. *Sex Roles*, **12**, 207–225.

Whitmore, R. L. (1983). *Sexual harassment at UC Davis.* Davis, CA: Women's Resources and Research Center, University of California.

Widom, C. S., & Burke, B. W. (1978). Performance attitudes, and professional socialization of women in academia. *Sex Roles, 4,* 549–562.

Williams, J. (1977). *Psychology of women: Behavior in a biosocial context.* (1st ed.). New York: W. W. Norton.

Williams, J. H. (1983). *Psychology of women: Behavior in a biosocial context* (2nd ed.). New York: Norton.

Williams, S. W., & McCullers, J. C. (1983). Personal factors related to typicalness of career and success in active professional women. *Psychology of Women Quarterly, 7,* 343–357.

Williams, T. (1975). Family resemblance in abilities: The Wechsler Scales. *Behavior Genetics, 5,* 405–409.

Williams, T. (1983). *The relationship between women's occupational self-efficacy and degree of feminist orientation.* Unpublished M.A. thesis, Department of Psychology, Ohio State University.

Williams v. Saxbe. 12 FEP cases 1093 (1981).

Williamson, E. G. (1939). *How to counsel students.* New York: McGraw-Hill.

Wilms, W. W. (1980). *Vocational education and social mobility: A study of public and proprietary school dropouts and graduates.* Report to the U.S. Department of Education, National Institute of Education. Washington, DC: U.S. Government Printing Office.

Wilson, K. R., & Kraus, L. A. (1983). Sexual harassment in the university. *Journal of College Student Personnel, 24,* 219–224.

Wirtenberg, T. J., & Nakamura, C. Y. (1976). Education: Barrier or boon to changing occupational roles of women. *Journal of Social Issues, 32,* 165–180.

Wise, L. L. (1985). Project TALENT: Mathematics course participation in the 1960's and its career consequences. In S. F. Chipman, L. R. Brush, & D. M. Wilson (Eds.), *Women and mathematics* (pp. 25–58). Hillsdale, NJ: Erlbaum.

Wolfe, L. K., & Betz, N. E. (1981). Traditionality of choice and sex-role identification as moderators of the congruence of occupational choice in college women. *Journal of Vocational Behavior, 18,* 43–55.

Wolfson, K. P. (1976). Career development patterns of college women. *Journal of Counseling Psychology, 23,* 119–125.

Wolkon, K. A. (1972). Pioneer versus traditional: Two distinct vocational patterns of college alumnae. *Journal of vocational Behavior, 2,* 275–282.

Women on Words and Images (1972). *Dick and Jane as victims: Sex stereotyping in children's readers.* Princeton, NJ: NOW.

Wong, P. T. P., Kettlewell, G., & Sproule, C. F. (1985). On the importance of being masculine: Sex role, attribution and women's career achievement. *Sex Roles, 12,* 757–768.

Wylie, R. C. (1974). *The self-concept: A review of methodological considerations and measuring instruments.* Lincoln: University of Nebraska Press.

Wylie, R. C. (1979). *The self-concept: Theory and research on selected topics.* Lincoln: University of Nebraska Press.

Yanico, B. J. (1978). Sex-bias in career information: Effects of language on attitudes. *Journal of Vocational Behavior, 13,* 26–34.

Yanico, B. J., Hardin, S. I., & McLaughlin, K. B. (1978). Androgyny and traditional versus non-traditional major choice among college freshmen. *Journal of Vocational Behavior, 12,* 261–269.

Yogev, S. (1982). Happiness in dual-career couples: Changing research, changing values. *Sex Roles*, **8**, 593–606.

Yogev, S. (1983). Judging the professional woman: Changing research, changing values. *Psychology of Women Quarterly*, **7**, 219–234.

Yudkin, S., & Holme, A. (1963). *Working mothers and their children*. London: Michael Joseph.

Yuen, R, K. W., Tinsley, D. J., & Tinsley, H. E. A. (1980). The vocational needs and background characteristics of homemaker-oriented women and career-oriented women. *Vocational Guidance Quarterly*, **28**, 250–256.

Zikmund, W. G., Hitt, M. A., & Pickens, B. A. (1978). Influence of sex and scholastic performance on reactions to job applicant resumes. *Journal of Applied Psychology*, **63**, 252–254.

Zuckerman, D. M. (1980). Self-esteem, personal traits, and college women's life goals. *Journal of Vocational Behavior*, **17**, 310–319.

Zuckerman, D. M. (1981). Family background, sex-role attitudes, and the goals of technical college and university students. *Sex Roles*, **7**, 1109–1126.

Zukerman, D. M., & Sayre, D. H. (1982). Cultural sex role expectations and children's sex role concepts. *Sex Roles*, **8**, 853–862.

Zytowski, D. G. (1969). Toward a theory of career development of women. *Personnel and Guidance Journal*, **47**, 660–664.

INDEX